WESTERN CIVILIZATION

Volume 1

From the Origins Through the Seventeenth Century

WESTERN CIVILIZATION

Volume 1
From the Origins
Through the Seventeenth Century

Robert Edwin Herzstein
University of South Carolina

Geoffrey Bruun, Consultant

HOUGHTON MIFFLIN COMPANY BOSTON
Atlanta Dallas Geneva, Illinois
Hopewell, New Jersey Palo Alto London

To my teacher and friend Dr. Henry Noss

Cover: Ambrogio Lorenzetti
Good Government in the City Palazzo Publico, Siena
Scala, New York/Florence

Printed in the U.S.A.
Library of Congress Catalog Card Number: 74-15596
ISBN: 0-395-19370-2

Contents

THREE
Medieval Civilization: Greatness and Decline

Maps

Foreword

In preparing this concise history of Western civilization, Professor Herzstein has carried through a formidable assignment with noteworthy success. His primary purpose was to abridge the Ferguson and Bruun *Survey of European Civilization* so that a condensed alternate version would be available for courses in which a briefer textbook may be preferred. While compressing or excising existing material, however, Dr. Herzstein undertook a further responsibility: to rewrite and reinterpret the discussion where, in his judgment, such revision might make the presentation more cogent and relevant.

We count ourselves fortunate that the publisher was able to persuade a historian of Professor Herzstein's reputation, eloquent style, and admirable industry to undertake this exacting task. He has earned our gratitude by completing, with skill, insight, and sensitivity, a labor for which we lacked the necessary time and energy. It is a pleasure to record our indebtedness to him and our appreciation of his achievement.

It is also a pleasure to have this opportunity to express once again our lasting thanks to the publisher, with whom we have enjoyed a long and pleasant relationship.

WALLACE K. FERGUSON
GEOFFREY BRUUN

Preface

The interaction of the West and the rest of the world should be of particular interest to college students. That interaction did not begin with Henry Kissinger's policy of détente or with former President Nixon's trip to China or even with the new imperialism of the late nineteenth century. It has been a vital process at least since the "Dark Ages," and in this book I have tried to give it its full due. Occidental civilization does not owe its ancient origins exclusively to Europe. North Africa, the Near East, Persia, and Egypt all are inextricably bound up with any study of the origins of the West. After 1400 Europe expands to the Americas, and Europeans crucially influence Asia and Africa. By 1900 we can see Western influence over most of the globe. Hence, this book is about Western civilization in its global, not merely European context.

Because of changes in the teaching of Western civilization courses, there is now a demand for comprehensive but concise books. History students seem no longer to be governed by the old textbook approach, which involved the reading of a lengthy text that attempted to cover every major detail of Western civilization. Price in this time of economic contraction is one reason for the change. Another is the greater leeway many instructors have to choose supplementary readings and textbooks. The desire to offer a variety of historical writing to the student naturally leads to the search for a brief history of Western civilization, one that is flexible but thorough, up-to-date yet respected. I have tried to produce such a volume. Only readers' reactions will determine whether I have succeeded, but preliminary critiques by faculty at major universities, colleges, and community colleges have been encouraging and helpful.

As a freshman history student in 1957, I tremendously benefited from reading Wallace K. Ferguson and Geoffrey Bruun's *Survey of European Civilization,* and my admiration for it grew over the years, particularly when as a college teacher I used it in my own classes. I have in *Western Civilization* extensively revised the most recent edition of that popular and respected text to create a book suitable for students and instructors of the mid-1970s. Avoiding the detailed political, diplomatic, biographical, and military narrative which dominates most textbooks on Western civilization, I have accentuated social and intellectual development by presenting traditional political and biographical history in a concise form and in the context of the bumpy evolution of Western civilization. To show beginning history students that historians' views are subject to criticism, to change, and to the pressures of their own environment, I have added historiographical material, trying in this way to introduce students to the fascinating dynamics of history and history writing. This material is a good antidote to the magisterial aloofness, the omniscient hindsight, that most texts affect, for it shows historians to be fallible human beings interpreting the past as objectively as they can, given their framework of human subjectivity and an ever changing social environment.

At the end of each chapter is a list of books related to the subject of the chapter. The bibliographies have been compiled through the use of the most recent American Historical Association *Guide to Historical Literature.* They reflect my own research and professional consultation. A list of titles without at least some indication of the nature of the book is not much use to the freshman college student. Hence, in most cases I have provided a brief description of the content of the book. The availability of paperback editions is also indicated.

The maps and photographs in *Western Civilization* are closely related to the text. They elaborate on the material they illustrate and are not simply decorative.

Geoffrey Bruun and Wallace Ferguson gave me total freedom to prepare this text. I am profoundly grateful for that confidence, offered by two scholars whom I have deeply respected since my days as a college history student. If this is a good book, it is because those two men gave me the latitude necessary to produce it. If it is not, it is because I failed to profit from such professional liberty. I learned a great deal about both writing and scholarship in many fields in the course of completing this project.

The wisdom and scholarship of the readers of various drafts of the manuscript have greatly aided me, and I hope the result does not disappoint them. Professor David Hicks of New York University offered useful suggestions about the Renaissance and early modern chapters. Professor Warren Roberts of the State University of New York at Albany made valuable comments about the entire manuscript, and I have profited from his thoughtful advice. Professor John Scarborough of the University of Kentucky offered useful criticism of my interpretation of ancient history. My colleagues Professors Charles Coolidge and Richard Rempel of the University of South Carolina encouraged me by their continuing interest in the project. Professor Geoffrey Bruun wrote several critiques; his sympathy for the difficulties of this undertaking has been a source of encouragement. Professor Donald Michelson of Miami-Dade Community College offered helpful ideas; his enthusiasm for my work has given me great satisfaction. He has also written an outstanding Instructor's Manual to accompany this text. My friend Donald R. Koenig of the Trinity School in New York City helped me prepare several of the nineteenth-century chapters. Kenneth Wilburn, my assistant, kindly aided me with the physical preparation of the final manuscript. Dennis Halac examined the galleys for consistency, and I wish to thank him for his suggestions.

I am grateful to several of my colleagues for their assistance with the bibliographics. Dr. John P. Dolan reviewed the Renaissance and Reformation titles. Dr. Owen S. Connelly assisted me with the French Revolution and Napoleonic eras. Dr. Charles Coolidge helped me in the area of modern British history. My former graduate assistant Patricia Ali helped me complete the bibliographies, and a former student, Salley Wood, typed them. I want to thank them all.

In 1957–1958 I was a freshman at New York University. I was fortunate enough to study Western civilization under Professor Henry Noss, later a dean at the university. His enthusiasm and teaching brilliance were major influences upon my academic career, and his course was a model of how freshman history should be taught. He used Ferguson/Bruun as a textbook, and he spoke of it with great respect. In reading it, I came to mirror that respect and enthusiasm, and it is a great source of pride to me that I am able to dedicate to him this successor to that book.

ROBERT EDWIN HERZSTEIN

Introduction

> Not to know what happened before one was born is always to be a child.
>
> CICERO

Through the centuries, the peoples of the Western world have devoted most of their time and energy to four major problems, and keeping them in mind helps to make the history of any people more understandable. First is the problem of resources. To survive, every living organism must obtain nutriment. At first primitive people, like other animals, hunted or gathered their food. Later they learned to grow crops, domesticate animals, build towns. They also learned to employ the natural forces around them—to make fire, to catch the wind to move their boats and the water to turn their water-wheels. The tribes, the nations, that utilized resources most effectively increased and prospered.

A second problem that all human communities have had to face is social order. If members of a family frequently fought one another, if inhabitants of a village robbed and slew their neighbors, their existence, as the philosopher Thomas Hobbes observed, would be "solitary, poor, nasty, brutish, and short." To advance, to prosper, the members of a community have to work together, share, and cooperate. Some classes—slaves, for instance—might labor through coercion rather than cooperation. But no community can long endure unless a majority of the individuals who compose it respect the welfare and the possessions of their neighbors.

A third problem that has confronted people throughout history is defense. To remain stable and secure, a community has to avoid internal revolt and anarchy and defend itself against external foes. Land-based empires have protected their frontiers with extensive fortifications: the Great Wall of China is one impressive example. Seafaring peoples, who mastered the waters around them, as the inhabitants of Tyre, Carthage, and Athens did, have depended on their fighting ships to keep enemies at bay. Great empires sometimes maintained order over large areas for centuries. But when an empire collapsed and disintegrated, each town, each hamlet, might have had to defend itself. Local leaders would erect walls around their dwellings, dig moats, or build fortified castles on hilltops. Man, whose weapons have enabled him to vanquish other animals, has found that his most dangerous enemy is man.

The fourth problem to which each family, each community, has given close attention is education. As human societies progressed, they developed ever more complex customs, arts, and techniques that had to be taught anew to each generation. Since the remote era when primitive people first kindled a fire, their descendants have treasured fire as an invaluable aid for protection, warmth, and light. Later they learned its importance for cooking, pottery making, metal smelting. No child to this day, however, has been born with the ability to make a fire. No child is born with the ability to speak clear and intelligible words. If a newborn baby were to be reared in isolation by people who could neither speak nor hear, such a child would grow up ignorant of these activities. If all formal education were discontinued for several generations, if no elder had time to teach the young to read and write, to use and operate and repair the instruments of power and precision that civilized man has developed, the human race would revert to a primitive state. Education is the transmission of culture: when it fails, civilization ceases.

In meeting the problem of resources, the Europeans were fortunate. The area they inhabited included an unusually large proportion of naturally fertile and cultivable land. Most of this land received an adequate rainfall, and the climate was temperate but stimulating. Few severe earthquakes, few destructive storms, and no tidal waves afflicted Europe. Broad forests throughout much of the continent provided fuel for heating and timber for buildings and for boats. Boats were important because Europe is surrounded by great bodies of water, from the Atlantic Ocean to the Baltic and Black seas. Ocean fish, preserved by salting, supplemented the European diet from prehistoric times, furnishing extra protein and essential minerals. Europe was fitted by nature to support a large and sturdy population.

The indented coastline and proximity to salt water invited many Europeans to become mariners, and in this advantage also their future was shaped by their geography. At the close of the Middle Ages, when they found themselves hemmed in on the south and east by the "obstructive Turk," they improved their ships and sought ocean routes to the Indies. The resulting Age of Exploration brought Europeans mastery of the oceans and opened a new era, not only in the history of Europe but in the history of the world.

In dealing with the second problem, social order, the West compromised between tradition and pragmatism. The order and prosperity of Roman times was followed by the economic decline and political fragmentation of the early medieval period. The little unity the West preserved was religious rather than political. Even when the Protestant revolt moved half the peoples of Europe to reject papal supremacy, the main tenets and traditions of the Christian faith were retained despite sectarian rivalries. The heritage of Roman law, modified by Christian doctrines and feudal customs, was molded into the legislation of the emerging territorial states. The sanctity of life and property, trade, taxation, bequests, inheritances, was defined and regulated by codes and customs. Despite war, plague, famine, and peasant revolts, the Europeans maintained sufficient social order and organization that by the late Middle Ages they were increasing their food supply and their population.

After the Roman Empire declined, the Western world became vulnerable to attacks from beyond its frontiers. In the centuries that followed, Europeans were constrained to revise and improve their methods of defense. The granting of feudal fiefs to local leaders in return for military service was in part a response to this need. For over a thousand years, while great empires rose and waned on their eastern and southern borders, the disunited peoples of Europe struggled to protect their territories. From Attila the Hun to Genghis Khan, the armies of Asian conquerors invaded eastern Europe. From the seventh to the seventeenth century, Moslem forces confronted Christendom from the Iberian Peninsula to the Balkans. The Crusades, the Moslem conquest and Christian reconquest of Spain, the fall of Constantinople in 1453, the naval Battle of Lepanto in 1571, the

Turkish siege of Vienna in 1529—all were chapters in the long history of European defense. In addition, the Europeans often fought among themselves—from the feudal strife of the Middle Ages to the religious and dynastic wars that followed the Protestant revolt and the rise of centralized territorial states.

It was on the sea rather than on the land that Western peoples first achieved a decisive supremacy in the art of war. By the seventeenth century their initiative and audacity had begun to establish a new balance of world power. The discovery and colonization of the Americas and the domination of seaborne trade with Asia and Africa made Europe the center of a world-embracing maritime empire. Because no people on any other continent could match them at sea, all the coasts and islands of the globe were open to trade or attack by the Europeans. The essential instrument with which they won and held this maritime supremacy was the sailing ship armed with cannon. But they also needed the magnetic compass, improved astronomical tables, more subtle mathematics, and more accurate maps, each of which helped them to impose lines of latitude and longitude on the trackless oceans.

To cope with their fourth problem, education, the Western people also developed an invaluable instrument—the printed book. The revival of learning that came with the Renaissance and the simultaneous spread of printing from movable type exerted an extraordinary influence on European thought and culture. Without print the teaching of Luther and Calvin could not have precipitated a religious revolt: it has been said that the Protestant reformers "substituted an infallible Bible for an infallible pope." Without print the speculations of Copernicus, Galileo, and Newton might never have provoked a revolution in science. European culture became, for five centuries, a book-and-reader culture. Books gave influential writers a special dignity and prestige: they formed an elite group in the Republic of Letters. Books proved the most effective teaching machines yet invented. Even more important, they became repositories for the masterworks of science and literature. Shakespeare did not exaggerate the durability of the printed word when he boasted,

> Not marble, nor the gilded monuments
> Of princes, shall outlive this powerful rime.

Like other Elizabethans, Shakespeare was stirred by the prospects of the "brave new world" that the Age of Discovery had revealed. With a poet's intuition he felt around him "the prophetic soul of the wide world dreaming on things to come." His contemporary Sir Francis Bacon likewise prefigured a future that would be full of marvels. But Bacon did not expect these marvels to come about through intangible or supernatural causes; he foresaw them as the products of man's own genius and labor. "The true and lawful goal of science," he declared, "is that human life be endowed with new powers and inventions," and he noted that printing, gunpowder, and the magnetic compass had already "changed the whole face and state of things." Gazing into the future, in the first quarter of the seventeenth century, Bacon made a prediction that may seem obvious to us but demonstrated astonishing foresight in his own day. Science, he prophesied, and new scientific methods and instruments, would bring about "the enlarging of the bounds of human empire to the effecting of all things possible."

GEOFFREY BRUUN

WESTERN CIVILIZATION

Volume 1

From the Origins Through the Seventeenth Century

From Mankind's Origins to the End of the Classical World

ONE

The Birth of Western Civilization

1

What seest thou else
In the dark backward and abysm of time?
SHAKESPEARE, *THE TEMPEST*, ACT I, SCENE 2

I have given thee the divine office, that thou mayest rule the
Two Lands as king of Upper and Lower Egypt.
INSCRIPTION ON TEMPLE WALL AT ABU SIMBEL:
THE GOD PTAH TO RAMSES II

The Origins of Mankind

The origins of modern man (*Homo sapiens*) are shrouded in mystery. We know that people were living and hunting in fairly sizable groups well over thirty thousand years ago. They made weapons out of flint and other types of stone—hence the designations Old Stone Age and New Stone Age for their periods of development. Caves and rock shelters served as their seasonal abodes; in eastern and central Europe the earliest purposely constructed dwellings date from this time. A variety of animals—bison, cattle, horse, reindeer, mammoth, and woolly rhinoceros—were among the chief objects of their hunt. These people possessed a well-developed aesthetic sense and remarkable artistic skill.

As man's physique evolved, human culture, manifested in technology, economy, art, religion, and social organization, became complex. Tools became more profuse, much finer, and more specialized, and appeared in a greater range of types. Beautifully made blade, bone, and antler tools, as well as ivory objects and implements with handles, came into use. Hunting, in which missile weapons such as the bow and arrow were employed, was conducted on a communal basis. New inventions included needle and thread, skin clothing, specialized hunting and fishing equipment, and stone lamps to light dark caves, where the earliest paintings and engravings are preserved. The location and arrangement of certain settlements reflect the increasing complexity of man's social organization.

The change in way of life which marked mankind's emergence from the Old Stone Age was, however, infinitely more important and comprehensive than the mere production of polished stone axes. This change, known as the Neolithic Revolution or New Stone Age, began in the Middle East around 7000 B.C. Its essential element—the most revolutionary in cultural history—was that people gradually ceased to be food-gatherers or hunters and became food-producers. This change occurred at different times in different regions. People learned how to raise crops and domesticate animals. Having become farmers, they ceased to wander in search of game or the scarce food that nature provided, and they settled down. A settled existence necessitated the development of more complex forms of social organization; people clustered together in village communities and learned to cooperate for defense or to irrigate and work their fields. For the first time it became possible to produce a surplus of food, so that some individuals could devote themselves to specialized crafts and exchange their products for the food grown by others. The result was rapid technological advance. Neolithic men and women not only developed the basic forms of farming and animal husbandry but also invented spinning and weaving, stone hand-mills for grinding grain into flour, and—one of the most important developments of all—the shaping and firing of clay pottery. They also learned to construct houses of mud brick and to build walls around their villages for defense.

From Neolithic village communities in the fertile river valleys of Egypt and Mesopotamia, there gradually developed cities and with them the earliest civilizations. By about 3000 B.C., with the invention of writing, the period of recorded history began.

Mesopotamia: Land of the Two Rivers

The two earliest civilizations that we know of were cradled in fertile river valleys in the Near East, one in the broad and easily accessible basin formed by the Tigris and Euphrates rivers in lower Mesopotamia, the other in the long narrow valley of the Nile in Egypt. Progressive desiccation, which followed the last Ice Age, made the higher lands less habitable and partially dried the swamps of the river valleys. In these watered lowlands, as well as in northern Palestine, village communities first made their appearance, in Mesopotamia probably as early as 7000 B.C., in Egypt possibly two thousand years later. During the following two or three thousand years, these nascent civilizations passed through the transitional stage from Neolithic village culture to a well-developed political organization.

THE ANCIENT NEAR EAST

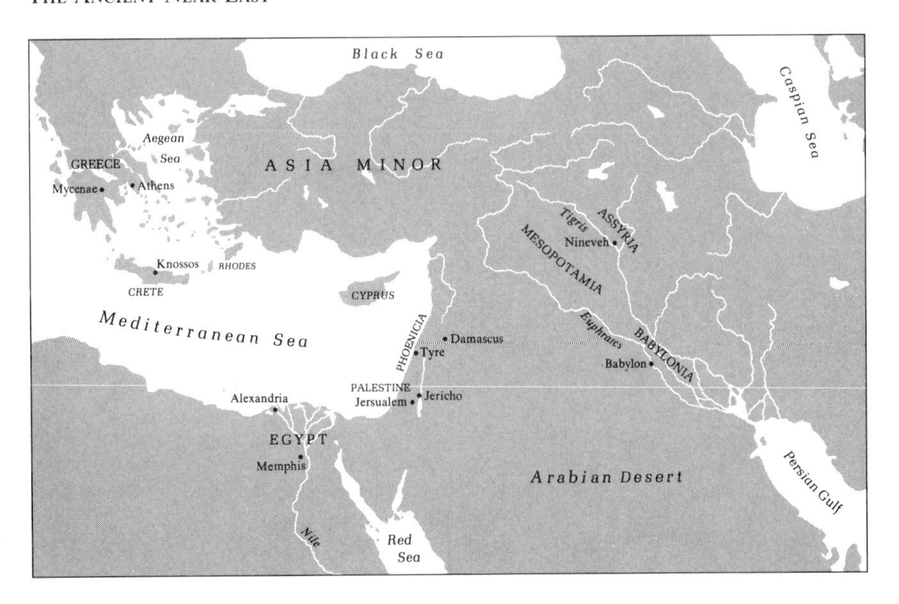

We have no written records from this early period; thus it is known to us through the material remains which archaeologists have discovered. Progress during these millennia was slow, but its cumulative effect was extraordinary. Mesopotamia and Egypt could support a growing population only by the use of intensive irrigation, which demands intensive social organization as well as technological knowledge. When both civilizations emerged into the full light of recorded history, they possessed urban centers, religions, and governmental systems. They had also acquired impressive craft techniques and considerable engineering skill. Both employed some metallurgy in weaponry and handicrafts, with bronze as its hallmark. This period is known as the Bronze Age. Before long other centers of civilization came into existence in neighboring lands—on the islands of the Aegean and in the strip of fertile land that runs up the Mesopotamian valley and westward and southward down the Syrian coast, forming what has been called the Fertile Crescent.

The first people to emerge from the shadows of Mesopotamian prehistory were the Sumerians, who occupied the lower Mesopotamian valley sometime before 3000 B.C. In all probability they were not the first inhabitants of the land but were preceded between about 5000 and 3000 B.C. by several cultures which laid the foundations upon which the Sumerians built. These forerunners, however, remain anonymous, whereas the Sumerians are known through both archaeological remains and written records. The language in which their legacy is preserved can be read with a high degree of accuracy; yet it is mysterious in that it stands alone, having no demonstrable relation to the Semitic, Indo-European, or other language groups.[1]

As the population increased, a number of city-states were formed in the Sumerian land. Meanwhile, the Akkadians, a people to the north, were growing in strength, and about 2350 B.C. they overran the vulnerable Mesopotamian valley. But neither this conquest nor the many subsequent conquests by other peoples materially changed the culture of Mesopotamia, which continued to bear the distinctive stamp of the Sumerians, flourished under the Babylonians and Assyrians, and declined only after the Land of the Two Rivers was absorbed into the Persian Empire in the sixth century B.C.

The Sumerians gave to Mesopotamia the art of writing. The approximate date of this invention was 3000 B.C., and it was then as now the essential medium for the preservation and diffusion of intellectual achievements. Wherever Mesopotamian influence prevailed, written signs came to be composed of wedges—hence the modern name "cuneiform," meaning wedge-shaped—normally formed by impressing the angle of a square-shaped stylus onto a clay tablet. The concept of writing, as distinct from the actual script itself, traveled still farther afield; this is perhaps how writing was introduced to Egypt. The alphabet, which came into being about the second millennium B.C. along the Syro-Palestinian coast, is in effect no more than an extreme simplification of the original idea of writing.

Alphabetical writing made possible the emergence of literature, which took

[1] The terms "Semitic" and "Indo-European" refer to peoples whose language belongs to one of these language groups. The Semitic languages are concentrated in the Middle East. The Indo-European group includes most of the languages of Europe as well as Armenian, Persian, and Sanskrit, the ancient language of India. The languages in each group have a similar grammar and a vocabulary with many common roots. In the nineteenth century these terms became confused with racial delineations. Such usage is incorrect.

the form of Sumerian and Akkadian epics such as the story of the great Sumerian hero Gilgamesh. This literature traveled not only to Persia, Syria, and Palestine, but also to Egypt and to the Hittite centers in Asia Minor. The Greeks may well have borrowed from Mesopotamia the form of the epic, and they certainly imported and translated Mesopotamian animal fables.

Mesopotamia produced a succession of legal codes, of which the celebrated Code of Hammurabi is by no means the oldest. Fragments exist of three collections of laws dating from considerably earlier than that of the great Babylonian legislator, and the existence of still older laws may be assumed. Hundreds of thousands of cuneiform legal texts have been recovered amid archaeological remains.

To Babylonia we also owe the beginnings of algebra, the division of the circle into 360 degrees, the division of the day into hours of sixty minutes, and the twelve signs of the zodiac. The contributions of Mesopotamian culture to the origins of Western civilization include writing, the literary epic, law, politics, agriculture, metallurgy, and astronomy.

Egypt: Land of the Nile

Egyptian civilization, like that of Mesopotamia, was born in a river valley and nourished on the rich alluvial soil washed over the land by annual floods. But, although the geographic factors which gave birth to the two oldest civilizations were in many ways similar, the peculiar character of the Nile Valley gave Egyptian civilization a unique form. The Nile River rises in the mountains of equatorial Africa but reaches Egypt only after it has passed a series of cataracts which prevent navigation. From the last cataract, the Nile cuts its way northward through a desert plateau for some six hundred miles until, about a hundred miles from the Mediterranean coast, it fans out into a triangle or delta of natural waterways. Below the flat and heavily irrigated delta country, the Nile Valley is a narrow trough, ten to twenty miles wide, between limestone cliffs flanked by arid desert. The teeming life of upper Egypt was crowded into the thin ribbon of land in the valley bottom, whose soil was fertilized by silt brought down each year in the Nile floods, and where, despite a rainless climate, intensive agriculture was made possible by irrigation. Although lower Egypt, the delta, is open to the sea and lies close to the western horn of the Fertile Crescent, ancient Egypt was free from the threat of invasion during the greater part of its history. Egyptian civilization was thus able to develop more or less independently, though not untouched by outside influences.

The beginning of the historical era in Egypt, as in Mesopotamia, was preceded by a period of two or three thousand years during which village communities grew into larger states and undertook to harness the Nile and use its water to irrigate the land, a task requiring a high degree of cooperative effort. Satisfactory control of the river on which the life of Egypt depended could not be achieved, however, without a centralized authority over the whole land. This final step was taken about 3000 B.C., when the rulers of the so-called first dynasty, or ruling family, united upper and lower Egypt and welded the whole Nile Valley from the first cataract to the sea into a single political unit.

The unified system of government introduced at this time reached its fullest development in the period from about 2700 to 2200 B.C., which is generally called the Old Kingdom and lasted from the third through the sixth dynasties. Religious beliefs and practical needs combined to give the pharaohs, as the rulers were called, authority unparalleled in any other civilization. The pharaoh was not merely an absolute monarch; he was a living god, the son of Ra, the sun god. The pharaoh was the source of all power, though in practice his supernatural authority was largely delegated to officers of the royal household and to the governors of the *nomes* or provinces into which Egypt was divided. He was also in theory the owner of the entire land, and the surplus wealth of the state was at his disposal. The peasants, who made up the mass of the population, lived strictly regimented lives and were liable at any time for service on the great engineering and monumental projects undertaken by the government. Agriculture was the basis of the Egyptian economy, but there was a middle class of skilled artisans living in cities, a large part of whose labor was required to supply the needs of the pharaoh and his court.

Convinced that their existence in this life and after death depended on supernatural forces, the Egyptians were extremely religious, though in a somewhat materialistic fashion. Much of the wealth of the state was expended to support the temples of the gods, and the priests who served them formed a rich and powerful class. Aside from the pharaohs, the Egyptians worshiped a great variety of gods, with the most important of whom the pharaoh himself was

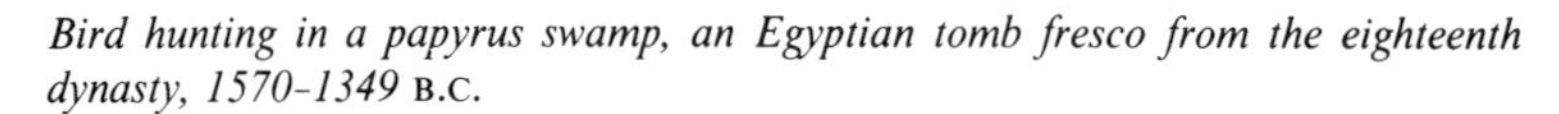

Bird hunting in a papyrus swamp, an Egyptian tomb fresco from the eighteenth dynasty, 1570–1349 B.C.

associated. The most striking characteristic of Egyptian religion, however, was its obsession with immortality, one of the most important factors in shaping the civilization of Egypt for thousands of years. It was believed that the soul would continue to live as long as the body remained intact and was supplied with the necessities of life. A great deal of public and private wealth, therefore, went to the construction of stone tombs to preserve the mummified bodies of kings and nobles. These tombs were furnished with miniature replicas or painted reliefs which represented the food, servants, and furniture necessary to keep the soul comfortable. They are our best source of knowledge about Egyptian life.

Since all Egyptian life revolved around the person of the divine pharaoh, it was natural that special attention should be given to preserving his mortal remains. The construction of tombs drained the resources of the state throughout the entire period of the pharaohs' rule, but none of the later tombs equaled in magnitude the immense pyramids constructed by the pharaohs of the fourth dynasty. Two thousand years later, the Greek historian Herodotus was told that it took a hundred thousand men twenty years to build the pyramid of Khufu (or Cheops, as Herodotus called him), and the estimate seems not improbable. This vast pile, 755 feet square at the base and 481 feet high, contains over 2 million blocks of stone, each weighing about two and a half tons. It is a masterpiece of engineering skill and at the same time a striking testimonial to the administrative efficiency required to feed and supply such a large army of workers.

So complex an administrative system as that of the Old Kingdom would be almost inconceivable without some means of keeping written records, and it is

The colossal statue of Ramses II, part of the façade of the temple at Abu Simbel. Such statues, indicating by their size the superhuman power of the pharaohs, were typical of Egyptian sculpture.

probably no coincidence that the earliest known Egyptian writing dates from the first dynasty. From the beginning, Egyptian writing appears in two forms, the hieroglyphic picture-writing used for monumental inscriptions and the simplified cursive script used by scribes. The basic conception of Egyptian writing was similar to that of the Mesopotamian and was probably borrowed from it. The actual form of Egyptian script, however, was original. It was intended not to be impressed upon clay tablets but to be carved on stone or written with pen and ink on papyrus. From at least as early as the second dynasty, papyrus rolls made from strips of the papyrus reed glued together were in common use as writing paper. Thanks to the dry Egyptian climate, vast numbers of these rolls have survived, and they have been deciphered since the early nineteenth century of our own era.

Crete and Mycenae

During the third and second millennia B.C., while Mesopotamia and Egypt were experiencing the zenith of their civilizations, another rich and vigorous civilization arose on the island of Crete. Completely unknown until the present century, this flourishing civilization is generally called Minoan for Minos, the great Cretan king of Greek legend. Archaeologists have uncovered the remains of a people who were every bit as advanced and sophisticated as those of Mesopotamia and Egypt, yet whose culture was totally different. At Knossos, their capital, Cretan kings lived in an enormous palace so sprawling and complicated that it gave rise, among later generations of Greeks, to the myths of the labyrinth and Minotaur. No walls surrounded it—or, for that matter, palaces in any of the other towns of Minoan Crete. Perhaps the Minoans, possessing a strong navy, felt secure in their island isolation. Recent excavations at Mallia and Hagia Triada, however, suggest that the Minoan culture was less isolated and self-sufficient than was once thought. Discoveries at these excavations point to ties with Egyptian and Anatolian cultures.

The palace at Knossos, as reconstructed by Sir Arthur Evans after 1900, knew such comforts as baths with piped-in water. An abundance of underground storerooms served to preserve the royal taxes (paid in produce and precious or useful artifacts) and keep the larders well stocked. Chamber walls were decorated with paintings utterly unlike those found in Egypt or Mesopotamia, paintings characterized above all by movement and a love for living things, particularly sea creatures. The same qualities appear in sculptures and reliefs. The Minoans had their own form of writing, and archaeologists have brought to light hundreds of

An inlaid bronze dagger, found in Mycenae, vividly portraying figures in motion.

clay tablets inscribed with their distinctive script. In 1952 the scholar Michael Ventris showed Linear B, as the Minoan script is known, to be a form of Greek, though he was unable to decode it. This impressive Cretan civilization seems to have begun its growth about 3000 B.C. and to have reached its height between 2000 and 1500 B.C.

A day's sail northward from Crete lies the Greek peninsula. Around 2300 or 2200 B.C. the peninsula was invaded by the first of that group of Indo-Europeans who were destined to make so great an impression on the history of the world: the Greeks. Historians, however, are careful to distinguish these Bronze Age Greeks from those who appear later in Greek history by referring to them as "Mycenaeans" (so called for Mycenae, the first of their towns to be excavated) or, as Homer called them, "Achaeans." They built fortress-citadels protected by massive walls. Primitive at the outset, they elevated their culture by borrowing heavily from their sophisticated Minoan neighbors to the south. In time the Mycenaeans grew so strong that by about 1400 B.C. they dominated the Aegean and even exercised a kind of overlordship of Minoan Crete.

The Mycenaeans were Greek-speaking but borrowed the art of writing from the Minoans. A great seafaring people, the Mycenaeans conducted a flourishing maritime commerce that extended westward to Italy and eastward to the shores of the Levant and Egypt. Around 1200 B.C. they may have launched an attack on the prosperous city of Troy in western Asia Minor, an "event" immortalized in Homer's epic poem.

About 1200 B.C. the prosperous civilizations of the Near East suffered a rude and in some places disastrous shock. A new wave of Indo-European invaders moved down from the lands north of Greece, through the Greek peninsula and through Asia Minor into Syria. From Asia Minor the invaders drove south to the borders of Egypt. They were checked by the heroic resistance of the Egyptians, but thereafter Egypt remained confined within its own frontiers and ceased to be a power in Near Eastern affairs. The movement eventually played itself out, leaving pockets of the invaders settled here and there. Among the best known of these were the Philistines, who, after being turned back from their attempted invasion of Egypt, settled in Palestine. In Greece itself the invaders, traditionally called Dorians, swept across the peninsula and the islands of the Aegean, destroying the Mycenaean citadels and much of Mycenaean civilization. Much less civilized than their Mycenaean predecessors, the new Greeks ushered in an age during which Greece remained isolated from the outside world and lost the art of writing.

Phoenicians and Hebrews

The Phoenicians, as the Greeks called them, were a Semitic people, mostly of Canaanite origin, settled along what is today the Lebanese coast. They took to the sea and founded a commercial empire based in Tyre, Sidon, and other coastal towns. Although they had highly skilled industries, the Phoenicians were primarily merchants. Like the Greeks during the same period, they had sailed to every part of the Mediterranean world. By 700 B.C., they had established trading colonies, some of which grew to be powerful cities, as far west as Carthage and Cadiz. Their culture was largely borrowed from the Egyptians and Mesopotamians, but their contribution as disseminators of civilization throughout the Mediterranean was extremely important. Through them the alphabet was introduced into Europe and spread throughout the Near East, replacing the cumbersome cuneiform and hieroglyphic scripts. The Phoenicians did not invent the idea of an alphabet. Experimental alphabets can be dated several centuries earlier. But the Phoenician alphabet of only twenty-two signs, each representing a consonantal sound, was so simple and easily learned that it was widely adopted. The Greeks based their own alphabet upon it, and it has directly or indirectly fathered most of the alphabets of Western civilization.

Of still greater importance for their influence on Western civilization were the Hebrews, who lived to the south of the Phoenicians in Palestine. Their history is told in the Old Testament and is therefore more familiar than that of any other ancient people. The earliest part of their story is traditional and largely unverifiable, but from about the end of the second millennium it becomes more clearly historical and can be checked and supplemented from other sources. The Hebrews were a Semitic people, originally nomadic, who had emigrated from Mesopotamia about the twentieth century B.C. Later some of the Hebrews migrated to Egypt, where they were oppressed by the pharaohs until their release from captivity by Moses, probably in the thirteenth century B.C. In Palestine the Hebrew tribes fought among themselves and with their warlike neighbors, especially the Philistines, until they were united under Saul and his successor, King David (c. 1010–970 B.C.), who conquered the Philistines and other surrounding peoples and ruled a strong kingdom from his capital at Jerusalem. Under David's son Solomon (c. 970–930 B.C.), the Hebrew state reached the peak of its wealth and power, but it was soon weakened by civil strife and became divided into two kingdoms. During the eighth century before Christ, the northern kingdom, Israel, was conquered by the Assyrians. Many of its inhabitants were forced to emigrate, thus disappearing from the biblical story. A second disaster occurred in 586 B.C. when the Babylonian king Nebuchadnezzar captured Jerusalem, the capital of the southern kingdom of Judah, and took its people into captivity in Babylon, where they remained for fifty years until they were freed by the Persian king Cyrus and permitted to return to Palestine.

It is not, however, the story of the wanderings, triumphs, and tribulations of the Hebrew people that makes the Old Testament one of the most significant collections of writings produced by the ancient world. Its contents include, besides the historical books, the moral and religious teaching of the prophets, the glorious collection of hymns and prayers known as the Psalms, some of the finest poetry and stories in world literature, and the accumulated wisdom of a thoughtful and highly ethical people. The unique contribution of Hebrew thought was an exclusive monotheism, a profound faith in the existence of one all-powerful and benevolent God, Yahweh, or Jehovah, as he is called in the King James English translation. He watched over the fortunes of his chosen people but demanded of them, on pain of severe punishment, exclusive devotion and a high standard of moral and ethical conduct. Nowhere else in the ancient world was religion so closely bound to morality and to an ethical system based on principles of justice and mercy. Founded upon the Ten Commandments, which Moses is said to have received from Yahweh on Mount Sinai during the exodus from Egypt, and upon the laws and ceremonial regulations laid down in the first books of the Old Testament, the Hebrew religion was rigid and formal in its earliest manifestations. However, it grew in breadth and depth through centuries of adversity, as generations of prophets contemplated the problems of man's relation to God and his fellow men and spoke in tones of inspired authority to the conscience of the Hebrew people. Out of the religious and moral thought of this small and frequently afflicted people eventually grew Christianity, along with Islam one of the two great monotheistic religions of the medieval world.

Suggestions for Further Reading

Here and in the suggestions for further reading in subsequent chapters, the letters AHA followed by a page number indicate that the annotation is from the American Historical Association's *Guide to Historical Literature,* edited by George F. Howe and others (New York, 1963). When only part of the *Guide*'s descriptive phraseology is used, the fact of omission has been indicated.

J. H. Breasted, *A History of Egypt from the Earliest Times to the Persian Conquest* (1909). A classic account of Egyptian history. Still well worth reading, although many new developments have appeared since the 1909 version [AHA, 98, in part].

H. Frankfort, *The Art and Architecture of the Ancient Orient** (1971). Frankfort was one of the great scholars in this area: he related his knowledge of the ancient past to theology, philosophy, mythology, and the arts.

O. R. Gurney, *The Hittites** (1954). History of the Hittites described on the basis of the excavated remains and Hittite written documents. Provides excellent reconstructions of the Hittite state, its social and political organization, laws, and economy. There are also sections on language and race, religion, literature, and art [AHA, 83].

W. C. Hayes, *The Scepter of Egypt: A Background for the Study of the Egyptian Antiquities in the Metropolitan Museum of Art* (1953). Accurate, well-written description of a collection with a background equivalent to the whole history of each period. Well-illustrated, superior bibliography [AHA, 98].

P. K. Hitti, *History of Syria* (1951). Hitti has long been one of the outstanding students of Middle Eastern history. His scholarship is solid, his style felicitous.

S. N. Kramer, *The Sumerians: Their History, Culture and Character** (1963). A comprehensive treatment of Sumerian civilization, emphasizing the originality of this people and its contributions to Western civilization.

A. T. Olmstead, *History of Assyria* (1923). Covers the whole subject, and based on original sources known and understood at the time [AHA, 98].

A. T. Olmstead, *History of the Persian Empire** (1948). A detailed political history, still most valuable.

J. B. Pritchard, ed., *Ancient Near Eastern Texts Relating to the Old Testament* (1955). A major series of translated epics and documents, drawn from many pre-Hebrew sources.

G. Steindorff and K. C. Seele, *When Egypt Ruled the East** (1957). Concise and readable account of Egyptian culture and history which concentrates on the New Kingdom [AHA, 98, in part].

J. A. Wilson, *The Culture of Ancient Egypt** (1956). Stimulating and authoritative treatment of Egyptian history, written from a somewhat controversial viewpoint, but offering an abundance of fact and sound observation [AHA, 98, in part].

*Available in a paperback edition.

The Hellenic World

2

> Ours is a constitution which does not imitate those of our neighbors, but is rather a pattern to others. Because power rests with the majority and not with the few, it is called a democracy.
>
> PERICLES OF ATHENS

> Would that the people of India may believe me to be a god. For wars depend upon reputation, and often even what has been falsely believed has gained the place of truth.
>
> ALEXANDER THE GREAT

The Formation of Greece, c. 1200-500 B.C.

With the single exception of the Hebrews, no ancient people seems closely akin to us until we come to that group of tribes who by the year 1000 B.C. had settled Greece, the islands of the Aegean, and the coastline of Asia Minor, and who called themselves Hellenes. Even their earliest surviving literature, probably dating from the eighth century B.C., speaks directly to us. And by the fifth century there existed in the Greek city-states a civilization in which we can feel ourselves at home. The Greeks are more to us than dim figures reflected in the poetic imagery of an epic story. Their human forms are preserved in imperishable marble, and their ways of thinking in equally imperishable poetry and prose. Here we find poetry, drama, art, philosophy, scientific speculation, and political institutions that we can comprehend because they are the forerunners of our own. We are bound to these Greeks by a cultural tradition that has never been broken. When we trace many branches of our secular culture back to their roots, these roots will often be found embedded in the rocky soil of Hellas.

Historic Greece was founded by the second (or Dorian) wave of invaders, who entered the peninsula about 1200 B.C., wiped out or subjugated their Mycenaean predecessors, and introduced a dark age in Greek history which lasted for several centuries. Formed by the fusion of successive groups of invaders with the indigenous peoples of the peninsula, the historical Greeks were at no time a united or homogeneous nation, although when Greek met Greek they recognized in one another certain common cultural traits. The topography of the lands they settled was partly responsible for this lack of unity. The Greek peninsula is mountainous, with a deeply indented coastline, and beyond it are the innumerable islands of the Aegean archipelago and the long coast of Asia Minor.

For centuries the Greeks' small communities were largely agricultural. But the cultivators, instead of living on their farm plots, clustered their homes about strong points or fortresses and so created small cities which eventually grew into city-states, thus forming political institutions markedly different from those in the kingdoms of the East.

Our first literary evidence about the life of the early Greeks comes from the two great epic poems ascribed to Homer, the *Iliad* and the *Odyssey,* composed probably in the eighth century B.C. Scholars have long debated whether these epics are the work of one poet or an amalgam of poems composed over many centuries. According to a recent theory, many poems composed by bards to be sung at banquets and festive occasions were passed orally from one generation of bards to the next, until finally one poetic genius, drawing upon the whole oral tradition as raw material, created the two epics in more or less the form in which we have them now. The length and carefully formed structure of the poems suggest that they were written down when this "Homer" composed them, and that by the eighth century the Greeks had adapted the Phoenician alphabet to their use, adding the necessary vowel sounds and so creating the form of writing they were to use thereafter. In any case, the *Iliad,* the story of the siege of Troy by Agamemnon, king of Mycenae, and the Achaean princes, refers to "events" which may have taken place some four hundred fifty years before the recording of the poems. Both the *Iliad* and the *Odyssey,* which tells of the wanderings of Odysseus (Ulysses), refer to an earlier, post-Mycenaean society, but they also tell us much about conditions in the poet's own time. The framework of the society Homer depicts is the tribe, and within the tribe the patriarchal family. It was a decidedly aristocratic society. The king or *basileus* was the most powerful chieftain and claimed descent from a god—usually Zeus, "father of gods and heroes." He was the commander in war, the chief judge, and the high priest who performed sacrifices to appease the gods. But he was not an absolute ruler. Surrounding him were lesser kings, tribal chiefs, and heads of great families, whom he consulted on affairs of state and especially on military matters, for these small kingdoms were often at war with one another. Those of the people who had a tribal and a family status also had a voice in decisions affecting the whole community; on such occasions the king would call an assembly and the nobles would debate the problem before the people. No vote was taken and rarely did the commoners speak, but they could express their opinions by ominous silence or shouts of acclamation.

Athenian Democracy

The political structure of the Greek communities began to assume its distinctive form during the seventh and sixth centuries B.C. Each of the small, independent states was composed of a city and its surrounding territory. The city-state, or *polis,* was the framework within which the political, religious, and cultural life of the Greek people flourished, as well as the sole focal point of their patriotism and loyalty. Even the Greek colonies, once founded, became city-states almost entirely independent of the mother city. To this unique form of state the modern world owes many of its traditions of government, citizenship, and justice. Most city-states were small enough for the citizens from the surrounding countryside to easily gather in the city. Here were the market place, the shops of the craftsmen, the temples, and the seat of government.

With the growth of great estates, the wealthy land-owning aristocrats gained increasing control over government in the city-states. The kings of the

Homeric age disappeared or were deprived of all but their religious functions. The extent to which power was concentrated in the hands of a few varied from city to city but, in general, the right to vote was confined to citizens possessing a certain amount of landed property, and the right to hold office was limited to members of a few families or at most to the wealthiest citizens. Monarchy was thus often followed by aristocracy or by oligarchy, i.e., the rule of a few.

In many cities of Greece, especially those near the coast, the oligarchies were threatened by the growing demand of the rest of the citizens for a voice in the government. The small landholders resented the rule of their creditors; the citizens whose wealth, derived from commerce and industry, was in money rather than in land demanded the revision of property qualifications. Leaders arose who offered to redress these grievances in return for popular support in deposing ruling families. Having seized power, the popular leader ruled illegally as a dictator or "tyrant." Thus, oligarchy was in many instances succeeded by tyranny, which, in turn, paved the way for democracy, for to maintain power the tyrants had to make concessions to the people.

Unlike most Greek cities, the evolution of Athens' political institutions had been accomplished with little bloodshed. From the middle of the seventh century B.C. the power of its king had been severely curtailed. Indeed, kingship became an elective office with purely formal duties, held for only a year. The customary law of the land was committed to writing. To Solon, elected chief magistrate in 594–593 B.C., is attributed a series of fundamental reforms, including the division of the population into classes based on property, each with its political privileges and obligations, the grant of citizenship to the poorest classes, and the prohibition of slavery for indebtedness. Under the tyrant Pisistratus, land was taken from the old noble families and given to the poor, and tenant farmers were given ownership of their land. At the end of the sixth century came Cleisthenes, whose reforms laid the firm foundation of Athenian democracy and determined the form which the political institutions of Athens retained during the period of its greatest power.

As a means of checking factional feuds and breaking the power of the old aristocratic families, Cleisthenes redivided the population into territorial groups which cut across the old units. Ten new tribes were created, with equal representation in a Council of Five Hundred. The council was broadly representative of the free male citizenry. To insure that it was a fair sample of the citizen body, a requisite number of members were chosen by lot, and men who had held the office twice were ineligible. The council did not make the final decision on legislation, but it prepared the bills to be brought before the Popular Assembly, issued decrees to facilitate the execution of decisions made by the assembly, and negotiated with the representatives of foreign powers.

In the case of Athens we may see the outlines of a pattern common to some of the ancient Greek city-states during this period: a transition from tribal aristocracy through dictatorship to institutionalized democracy. This democracy, however, was checked in its effect by the growing complexities of the Athenian economy and by the domestic and foreign political challenges which confronted the Athenian state. These developments made political specialization a necessity, and at times opened the way to the political predominance of a single individual or clique.

The council collaborated with magistrates in the work of administration. Cleisthenes allowed the old magistracies to remain, but a large part of their political power passed to a new board of ten *strategoi,* or generals, who were elected annually. Originally created to command the army, the strategoi soon became the chief executive officers of the state; they could be re-elected year after year. Pericles, for example, held the office for many years.

Broad as the base of Athenian democracy seems to have been in comparison with other ancient political systems, it was actually restricted to that part of the population of the state whose ancestors had been Athenian citizens. Although in the sixth century some aliens long resident in the city and others who were only partly Athenian were enfranchised, citizenship became increasingly exclusive. In the middle of the fifth century, when Athens was at the peak of its power and the leader of a federal empire, citizenship was limited to those whose parents were both citizens. This jealous guarding of the privileges of citizenship, characteristic of other Greek states as well, was one of the major weaknesses of the city-state system. It prevented Athens from strengthening its citizen body by taking in the numerous and prosperous *metics,* or resident aliens, who carried on a large part of Athenian commerce and industry. And it prevented any city-state from expanding except by conquest and by treating the conquered peoples as subjects rather than citizens. In short, Greek democracy was for citizens only. It was not founded on a doctrine of the equality of all men, and was not incompatible with the oppression of subject peoples and the institution of slavery.

Slavery was perhaps the most typical economic institution of the ancient and classical worlds. We do not know what percentage of the population of Athens in the fifth century B.C. were slaves. Perhaps one-third of the individuals resident within Athenian territory around 450 B.C. fell within that category. Few poets or philosophers in Greece questioned the naturalness of this institution. Indeed, slavery was essential to classical institutions from Athenian democracy to the Roman agrarian and domestic economy. Slave labor provided the leisure and wealth necessary for the accomplishments of Greek culture.

The Persian and Peloponnesian Wars

Until the beginning of the fifth century B.C., the Greek city-states were left free to develop their political institutions and to war incessantly among themselves without serious interference from any foreign power. The rise of the Persian Empire in the sixth century, however, presented an increasingly grave threat to Greek independence. From the land to the east of Mesopotamia, the Persians had rapidly expanded their domain, driving eastward to the borders of India and westward to the Mediterranean. The Persian Empire was the most centralized and efficiently governed ancient empire of the first millennium B.C. The king's satraps, or governors, could depend on their own unquestioned authority and on the facilities of an unrivaled road and postal network. Before the end of the sixth century B.C. the Persians had added Egypt to their empire and had subjugated the Ionian Greek cities on the coast of Asia Minor. To prevent rebellion or challenge to his authority the Persian king, Darius, determined to conquer the independent cities of the Aegean islands and the Greek mainland. The stage was thus set for a life-and-death struggle between the small Greek city-states and the great "barbarian" empire of the Persians.

The Persian War was chronicled by Herodotus, the first Greek historian whose works are known to us. His vivid narrative has kept alive the memory of the Athenian victories at Marathon and Salamis and the heroic stand of the

Spartans at Thermopylae. Between 490 and 479 B.C., the Greeks repulsed three Persian invasions and effectively ended the Persian threat.

The Greco-Persian confrontation was an important event in the history of Western civilization, for, had the Persians been successful, the brilliant culture of Greece might have been crushed just as its Golden Age was dawning. Persia and Greece represented two distinct types of culture, and the threat to Greek culture was all the greater because the Persian attack was directed primarily at Athens, the center of Greek civilization in the fifth century.

After the victory over Persia, Athens rose to a position of leadership among the Greek cities. It had now become one of the most prosperous cities in Greece. Its port, Piraeus, connected by long, fortified walls with the city itself, was a thriving commercial center; the work of Athenian craftsmen was famous; and by the end of the sixth century Athens had outstripped Corinth, its chief economic rival in Greece, in industry and trade.

Greek cities in Asia Minor had originally been more economically advanced than those in Greece proper; but their prosperity had been undermined by the Persian domination, and in the fifth century Greek trade with the western Mediterranean was growing. The result was to shift commercial leadership from Asia Minor to the cities of the Greek mainland. The fleet which the Athenians had built to meet the Persian invasion put them in a position to take advantage of this shift. To wrest from the Persian king Xerxes the Greek cities still under his

THE GREEK WORLD IN THE FIFTH CENTURY B.C.

domination, to prevent Persia from regaining power in the Aegean, and to insure mutual defense, the cities of Asia Minor and the islands agreed, in 478 B.C., to form a maritime confederacy with Athens at its head. Headquarters were established at Delos, an island centrally located in the middle of the Aegean, and a constitution was drawn up giving each member representation on the council and demanding from each ships or money in proportion to its wealth. Athens, strongest and wealthiest of the cities, dominated the confederacy and gradually transformed it into an empire. In 454 the treasury of the confederacy was moved from Delos to Athens and its contents were thereafter handled by the Athenian government. The allies who resented Athenian domination and attempted to withdraw from the confederacy were brought back into line by force. Athens interfered in the internal affairs of these cities, favoring the democratic parties and encouraging the election of magistrates who would be subservient to its will.

During the half-century following the Persian War, Athens was not only the most powerful city but also the intellectual and artistic center of Greece. Under the brilliant administration of the great Pericles, who was elected *strategos* year after year from 461 to 430 B.C., Athenian culture reached the peak of its development. But the very success of Athens and the arrogance it bred in Athenian citizens made powerful enemies. The subject cities were restless; Corinth resented Athens' intrusion into the trade between Greece and the western Mediterranean; and Sparta, at the head of a league of Peloponnesian cities which included Corinth, watched the growth of the Athenian Empire with sullen jealousy. Sooner or later a war between Athens and Sparta and their respective allies seemed bound to occur, if only because of the mutual antipathy of two powerful, arrogant, and fundamentally different peoples. This was the interpretation of Thucydides, our major source for the history of the war.

The great Peloponnesian War which grew out of that mounting antagonism lasted from 431 to 404 B.C., and involved nearly all the Greek states on one side or the other. It was a disaster from which Greece never fully recovered. The grim struggle finally came to an end with the surrender of Athens. The conditions of peace imposed by Sparta included the breakup of the Athenian Empire, the destruction of the long walls between Athens and Piraeus, the surrender of the Athenian fleet, and the establishment of an oligarchy in Athens in the hands of thirty men approved by Sparta.

Economic Bases of Hellenic Society

The economic system of Homeric Greece was one in which each family produced the necessities of life on its own estate, and even the nobles took part in working the fields. There was little industry or commerce, since commerce was largely in the hands of the Phoenicians. At about the end of the ninth century B.C., however, economic change began. More land was brought under cultivation and the wealthier families enlarged their holdings. No significant improvements were made in farming methods, but there was more extensive cultivation of vineyards and olive groves. The Greeks were also turning more and more to the sea, first as pirates and later as traders, thus regaining the hold they had had on maritime commerce in the Mycenaean age. Active commerce began earlier and progressed more rapidly in the Greek cities of Asia Minor than on the Greek mainland. These cities were advantageously situated for trade and had the additional advantage of closer contact with the economically advanced countries of the Middle East. Taking the products of these eastern countries as models, they also began to develop industries. Wool from the flocks which grazed the plateaus provided material for textiles; clay offered an opportunity for the further development of ceramics; wood and leather lent themselves to the growing skill of craftsmen. As early as the eighth century coined money was introduced, greatly facilitating exchange and giving impetus to commerce.

Although commerce and industry became increasingly important features of Greek life from the eighth century on, the great majority of Greeks still derived their living from the land. The growth of population, the relatively poor soil, and the encroachments of great estates seriously threatened the livelihoods of the small holders who made up the greater part of this majority. The large landholders had enough income to invest in improvements and in lucrative vineyards and olive groves, but the peasants were often without means to tide them over a bad season. When disaster ruined his crops, or when some improvement was necessary, the small holder might borrow from the owner of a large estate, but as security he had to pledge not only his land but himself and his family. Failure to repay the loan meant slavery. Peasant holdings became smaller, the number of those in bondage increased, and the ranks of the landless grew. It was, in large part, to alleviate these conditions and to diminish the danger of revolt that colonies were founded.

From the eighth century to about the end of the sixth, groups of colonizers went forth from the older communities, first from those of Asia Minor and later from Greece, to form new and independent city-states along the shores of Thrace and the Black Sea and westward to southern Italy and Sicily. In the history of Greece these colonies played no small part: they were involved in political struggles, contributed to the cultural achievements of Greece, and contributed mightily to the development of trade and industry, at first as the recipients of Greek manufactured goods for which they exchanged food and raw materials. Later some of them developed their own industries, and others became centers of trade. Some, indeed, were founded as trading posts. Foremost in colonization was the Ionian city, Miletus, from which bands of settlers went to the Black Sea region. Chalcis and Eretria rivaled each other in establishing colonies in Thrace. Corinth looked farther westward; its most famous offspring was Syracuse, on the island of Sicily.

Agriculture furnished a broad base for Greek prosperity, although it supported few large fortunes. In the democratic states in particular, where legislation discouraged the accumulation of large estates, farms were usually small and were owned and worked by citizens. Resident aliens, or metics, who controlled some of the largest commercial enterprises, were forbidden to buy land, and in general there seems to have been little tendency to invest commercial capital in large landed estates. The soil of Greece is poor, but it lends itself to the production of olive oil and wine; thus small farmers could produce crops for which there was a profitable commercial market.

Industry, too, furnished a living for a large number of workers, rather than large fortunes for a few capitalists. Although industrial enterprises multiplied during the fifth and fourth centuries B.C., industry never became large-scale. The typical shop was composed of a master craftsman, a few slaves and hired assistants, and perhaps an apprentice. The outstanding exception was mining; mines belonged to the state. Citizens, and occasionally metics, were granted concessions to extract the metal in return for rent and royalties.

With the rise of urban centers devoted to commerce and industry, the demand for foodstuffs increased. It has been estimated that by the fourth century B.C. Athens had to import 75 per cent of the grain it consumed. Grain and livestock came to Athens from Thrace and the Black Sea region. Corinth imported these necessities from the West, and when Athens attempted to tap this source Corinth took steps to exclude it. The problem of the food supply was of such importance that states passed laws to limit re-exportation of grain brought to the ports and to insure distribution at low prices, especially in times of distress. In addition to grain, Athens imported fish, salted meats, fruit, and wine. Raw materials were another large item in Athenian imports: metals, wood and pitch, wool, and flax were needed by craftsmen. From the East came luxury goods. Slaves, too, were brought from the East as well as from Thrace and the Black Sea region. In exchange Athens exported olive oil, silver, marble, lead, manufactured products, and works of art. Trade, except in grain, was largely free. The state levied only small export and import taxes. By far the greater part of commerce was carried on by sea, since roads were generally poor and the cost of inland transportation was prohibitive.

One of the most important developments in Greek economy was the use of commercial loans. A merchant might borrow funds to purchase a cargo; but because the risks were great, interest rates were high. Not all investments, however, were in trading ventures. Men with surplus funds could invest in industrial enterprises, buy houses in Athens and lease them, or purchase slaves for hire. By the end of the fifth century another field for investment was opened to citizens and metics alike—banking. The banks of the fourth century B.C. did not employ credit instruments to the extent that modern banks do, but they effected the exchange of money without the actual transfer of coin. They also received deposits and acted as agents in investing other people's money.

The Hellenic Golden Age

The Golden Age of Greek culture has been identified as the period in the middle of the fifth century B.C. when Pericles led the Athenian democracy, but in a broader sense it covered the greater part of the fifth and fourth centuries, beginning before the Persian War. In these years Athens and the other Greek cities produced the finest works of classical art, which, characterized above all by simplicity, clarity, and proportion, have remained for all time the norm of classical beauty.

In mythology Greek art of the classical period found inexhaustible inspiration. The worship of the gods involved no dogma or systematized theology. The ritual accompanying worship was not the special office of a priestly caste; in some city-states priests were elected like other magistrates. Each city claimed a god or goddess as patron, and the worship of this deity was fraught with keen patriotism. The adventures of the gods formed a rich mythology; their spiritual attributes were identified with moral laws; but as an outlet for religious feeling the mystery cults were more satisfactory. The worship of Dionysus, "the beautiful, weeping creature, vexed by the wind, suffering, torn to pieces, and rejuvenescent again at last," and the Eleusinian mysteries dedicated to Demeter and Kore were of great antiquity. Both cults sprang from a deep awareness of the mystery of the seasons, the death of the earth in winter and its rebirth in spring. To the initiate both promised personal immortality and purification from sin.

Wars and the ravages of time have destroyed most of the temples and public buildings erected by the Greeks. Those which still stand are in ruins. But from these ruins we can reconstruct the harmonious lines and excellent proportions of the original edifices; in the fragments of sculpture that remain we can glimpse the strength and beauty of the figures that adorned the temples. In contrast to their temples and public buildings, the private homes of the Greeks were insignificant. Simply designed, these dwellings lined narrow, crooked streets. Occasionally a wealthy citizen would build a more imposing house in the country, or even in the city, but these were relatively scarce.

Drama was born and flourished in Athens. Its beginnings are shrouded in mystery. All that we know for sure is that it arose in connection with the worship of Dionysus. In its earliest form the plot seems to have been unfolded by a single narrator, together with a chorus which sang and performed solemn dances. When, early in the fifth century, Aeschylus (525–456 B.C.) introduced a second actor and told his story through dialogue, the dramatic form emerged. Sophocles (496–406 B.C.), the most popular dramatist of his day, was Aeschylus' younger contemporary and rival. He increased the number of actors and relegated the chorus to the less important role of commenting on the action of the plot and expressing the emotions of the spectators. In the plays of Sophocles the characters are more sharply delineated; the structure of the plot is more complex and is concentrated more exclusively on one tragic issue. In the greatest of his plays, *Oedipus the King,* character and fate cooperate to bring about the inevitable tragedy. Oedipus is enmeshed in a web of circumstance which leads him to fulfill

Detail of the frieze of the Parthenon, a temple to Athena, patron goddess of Athens. Sculpted in relief in the middle of the fifth century B.C., *the frieze shows a procession in honor of Athena.*

his prophesied destiny by unwittingly killing his father and marrying his mother. In the tragedies of Euripides (c. 480–406 B.C.) the characters are more human, and passion pervades the plot.

The interest in humanity evident in Greek art, and pre-eminently in Greek drama, is manifested also in the writing of history. Prose chronicles, of which only fragments have survived, were written in the sixth century, but history in the modern sense of the word dates from the generation of the first Greek dramatists. Herodotus (484–425 B.C.) has been called, with good reason, "the father of history" and "the first great European prose writer." The central theme of his *History* is the story of the Persian War, but he wandered from it repeatedly to give discursive accounts of the geography, social customs, religion, and ethnic character of almost all the peoples of the ancient world from Egypt to the Black Sea. He had traveled widely and wherever he went he had observed and listened. He had an insatiable curiosity and an inexhaustible interest in his fellow men. And he could make a good story out of everything he saw or heard.

The second great Greek historian, Thucydides (c. 460–400 B.C.), wrote history of a very different kind, much closer to the scholarly or "scientific" history of modern times. His account of the Peloponnesian War was written with a passion for accuracy and objectivity and in the conviction that, since human nature is everywhere much the same, analysis of the motives and actions of the leaders on both sides of the conflict would prove a useful guide to future statesmen and generals. The care with which his work has been studied throughout the

The Acropolis, a commanding hill in the center of Athens atop which the Athenians built their finest temples and public buildings. The prominent columned building is the Parthenon.

centuries supports his conviction. If he lacked the storytelling art and leisurely charm of Herodotus, he set a standard for thoughtful, accurate, and impartial historical scholarship that has seldom been surpassed.

One of the strongest traits in ancient Greek thought was a desire to find rational explanations for things. Having few instruments of precise measurement, and thus few accurately ascertained facts, the Greeks were forced to rely on pure speculation, with generally erroneous results. Yet their attempt to find rational explanations was itself a superb achievement and an inspiration to future generations. The science of medicine attracted some of the best minds of the fifth century B.C., and though here, too, they were hampered by lack of reliable knowledge, their approach to the problem of healing was scientific. Hippocrates (c. 460-370 B.C.), the most famous physician of this period, rejected supernatural explanations and cures, and observed and recorded symptoms carefully. His theory that the liquid parts of the body are composed of four "humors"—blood, phlegm, bile, and black bile—and that disease is caused by a disturbance of the equilibrium between them, was commonly accepted until the beginning of the modern age. Though his physiological theory was erroneous, his prescriptions for careful nursing were sound enough, and his devotion to the welfare of his patients is still echoed in the Hippocratic Oath taken by every American medical student on graduation.

Greek science was limited in immediate technological accomplishments for one major reason: the existence of slave power made the demand for labor-saving devices feeble. Hence, Greek medicine is more impressive than Greek machinery. The greatest triumphs of the Greek mind in this period were in philosophy rather than science, although a good deal of natural science was included in philosophy. The Greek philosophers of the fifth and fourth centuries B.C., however, were interested not only in explaining the nature of the universe, but also in ethical and moral problems, and the means of achieving the most perfect form of life for the individual and society.

The pioneer in a new direction taken by Greek philosophy in the fifth century was Socrates (469-399 B.C.). Since he himself wrote nothing, we know his teaching and personality only through the works of Plato and other disciples. He was a stonemason by trade, an ugly little man who by sheer charm, character, and intelligence attracted about him a group of the most brilliant young aristocrats in Athens. Socrates was primarily interested in the ethical and moral problems that are common to all people. His method was not to lecture but to ask questions, demonstrate the logical fallacies in the answers, and then ask more questions, thus forcing his disciples to clarify their own ideas and define what they meant by such concepts as temperance, courage, or justice. The technique was peculiarly suited to the discussion of ethics, for data could be drawn from every individual's personal experience. Few philosophers have examined human motives more closely or set a higher standard of ethical conduct than Socrates. However, his association with the aristocratic faction in Athens, and his disintegrative habit of questioning accepted opinions, aroused suspicion and he was condemned to death on a charge of impiety and corrupting the youth of the city.

Plato (427-347 B.C.), one of the young aristocrats who fell under the influence of Socrates, both altered and added to his master's teaching. His philosophical writings took the form of dialogues, like those conducted by Socrates, and in many of them Socrates is represented as the chief interlocutor. The early dialogues are Socratic inquiries into the essential characteristics of the good life, but thereafter Plato went on to construct a new theory of knowledge. What Plato sought to discover by rational thought were eternally valid universal "forms" or, as he called them, "ideas," of which individual actions and things are imperfect and transitory manifestations. These ideas—for example, the ideas of man and horse as distinct from individual men and horses—he thought to exist and to be the only perfect realities. Through knowledge of these universal ideas man could discover the rational order which Plato believed to exist throughout the cosmos. Plato's faith in reason as the necessary guide to the highest form of life also led him to propose a theory of the ideal state as one in which the ruling class would be composed of philosophers. This concept, discussed in his famous dialogue *The Republic,* has always held a strong appeal for those who distrust democracy and would prefer government by an aristocratic elite.

The third of the great Greek philosophers, Aristotle (384-322 B.C.), adapted the ideas of his predecessors and applied them to a far wider range of subjects. His interests were very different from theirs; more than Socrates and Plato he was concerned with the natural sciences and with factual knowledge of the workings of the material universe. Though he did not abandon them, Aristotle rejected the belief that universal ideas have a real existence apart from the individual objects they represent. His study of the biological sciences, too, made him aware of the constant process of change in nature, not acknowledged by Plato's unchanging ideas. Finally, he abandoned Plato's poetic use of myth and dialogue as a means of conveying truth, in favor of sober scientific prose. In the form in which they have come down to us, at least, Aristotle's writings have none of the superb literary style that distinguished Plato's dialogues.

The range of Aristotle's work was encyclopedic, covering the fields of physics, astronomy, biology, psychology, metaphysics (i.e., the study of first principles and basic ideas about nature), formal logic, ethics, politics, and the theory of rhetoric and poetry. Aristotle's logic was a system of deductive reasoning, still regarded as basic to any study of formal logic, but in his scientific work he recognized the value of observation, experiment, and inductive thinking. Much of his science, indeed, seems based on little more than commonsense explanations of phenomena he had observed. For two thousand years many of his theories were accepted because they appealed to men's common sense, even when they were based on erroneous premises. In his own time Aristotle's reputation rested not least on his status as tutor to a young man later to be known as Alexander the Great.

Alexander of Macedon and the Hellenistic Age

Macedonia, in the north of Greece, was a relatively backward country still no more than semi-civilized in the fourth century B.C. Although kin to the Greeks, the Macedonians had not been greatly influenced by Greek culture. They had never developed city life or the city-state system, and still retained much of their tribal organization under a landholding aristocracy. Although the monarchy was growing stronger during the first half of the fourth century, not until the accession of Philip II in 359 B.C. was Macedonia welded into a strong state. Philip had spent three years of his youth as a hostage in Greece, where he had learned something of Greek culture and military organization and had also had an opportunity to observe the lack of unity among the Greek city-states. Two years after his accession Philip invaded Thrace and seized the gold mines of Mount Pangaeus. With the wealth extracted from these mines he organized an army, recruiting foot soldiers from the free peasants and shepherds of the Macedonian hills and cavalry from the landed aristocracy. The foot soldiers he trained to fight in the tactical formation known as the *phalanx,* a massed body of pikemen eight to sixteen ranks deep. Rigidly disciplined and in constant training, the Macedonian troops were to be the most effective standing army the Western world had yet encountered.

During the first twenty years of his reign Philip advanced slowly toward the conquest of Greece. Playing one city off against another, gaining adherents through bribery and threats, he moved steadily southward. At last in 338 B.C. he was ready for the final stroke. For years the great Athenian orator and statesman, Demosthenes, had warned his fellow Greeks of the approaching menace. His warnings went largely unheeded, and at the last moment only Athens and Thebes and a handful of smaller states rallied to meet the invader. They were decisively defeated by the Macedonian army at Chaeronea, and Philip became master of Greece. Before the year was over, Philip called a council at Corinth which Sparta alone refused to attend. There a Hellenic League was organized with Philip at its head. Greek history had reached a dramatic turning-point, but before he could carry out any further plans, Philip was assassinated. His son Alexander, only twenty years old, succeeded to the throne.

Athens, taking advantage of the temporary confusion caused by the death of Philip, planned revolt, and Thebes actually revolted. Alexander retaliated by destroying the city of Thebes, and then turned to Persia. Most of the Greek cities of Asia Minor accepted him without a struggle. To undermine the effectiveness of the Persian fleet, Alexander determined to take its bases. This he accomplished by defeating the Persian army at Issus and, after a seven months' siege, capturing Tyre. These victories gave him possession of the coasts of Asia Minor, Syria, and Phoenicia. Egypt next proved an easy conquest, for the Egyptians, long since fallen into abject servitude to foreign powers, sullenly resented Persian rule, and Egypt was far from the center of Persian power. Returning to Asia, Alexander inflicted a crushing defeat on the Persian forces in Babylonia in 331 B.C. But still he was not satisfied. In a triumphant march eastward, he led his army into India, halting only when his weary soldiers refused to advance deeper into an area of intolerable climate and deadly fevers.

Alexander's conquests were more than a series of military victories, brilliant though these were; they were also the medium through which Greek culture was to be disseminated throughout the ancient world. Alexander himself had a deep-seated admiration for the cultural achievements of the Greeks: not for nothing had Aristotle been his tutor. Following each successful campaign he founded cities in the newly conquered territory, cities which served a military purpose, but which also attracted emigrants from Greece and became centers for the dissemination of Greek culture.

When Alexander returned from India, the great problem confronting him was that of administration. How was he to govern his vast domains? The question can never be adequately answered, for Alexander died before he could effect a permanent solution. But from his temporary measures we can infer something of his intent. As he proceeded from conquest to conquest, Alexander left the recently acquired territory in the hands of Macedonian generals, who were to exercise a general authority, but he apparently made no effort to alter the existing forms of local government. There is, indeed, reason to believe that Alexander had in mind the fusion of Greek and Persian elements throughout his realm. He adopted Persian dress and manners, married a Persian princess, and encouraged his followers to marry Persians. He also introduced Persians into the administration and the army. But this policy was too ecumenical to be readily accepted by his Macedonian followers, and it did not outlast his lifetime. What did last was the diffusion of Greek culture throughout the Middle East, which resulted from the founding of cities colonized by Greeks and the creation of a Greek-speaking upper class.

When Alexander died in 323 B.C. at the age of thirty-three, there was no one who could fill his place. His Macedonian generals carved up the newly conquered empire among themselves, and for more than forty years they and their successors fought over the division of the spoils. With the exception of Macedonia, these Hellenistic or Greco-Oriental kingdoms were in reality oriental despotisms ruled by Macedonian dynasties. They depended upon the support of a Greek or Greek-speaking upper class.

Alexander's successors maintained his policy of founding new cities and attracting Greeks to settle in them. Great numbers of enterprising Greeks flocked to Syria, Egypt, and other Hellenistic kingdoms to engage in trade or to acquire positions in the royal bureaucracy, and everywhere they formed a ruling class. Their culture was the nucleus of Hellenistic civilization. But the line between Greeks and non-Greeks was not sharply drawn. Descendants of those whom the

ALEXANDER'S EMPIRE AND THE HELLENISTIC WORLD

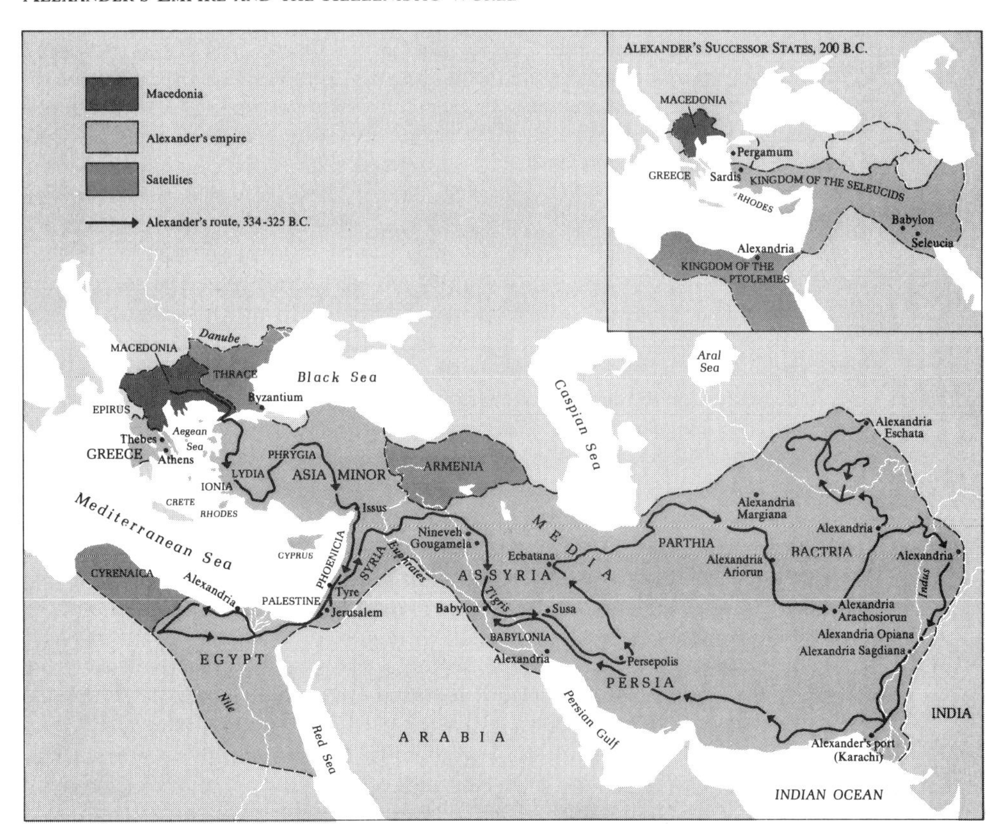

Greeks had once called barbarians, educated in Greek schools and speaking Greek, now took their places in the ranks of the true Greeks to form a Greco-Oriental upper class. There remained, however, a cleavage between the Hellenized upper classes and the predominantly peasant natives, who retained their traditional speech and customs.

Hellenistic absolutism found its most complete expression in Egypt. There autocracy extended to economic as well as to political life. Ptolemy, one of Alexander's generals, became ruler of Egypt, and his successors (Ptolemy I–XIII) reigned there from 305 B.C. to 44 B.C. The Greek Ptolemies took advantage of the traditional prerogatives of the pharaohs to bring agriculture, commerce, and industry under their control. Vast royal estates, scattered throughout the country, were worked by tenant farmers for the benefit of the king. Since the cultivation of most of the land was directly or indirectly under governmental supervision, the inefficient traditional agriculture could be replaced by the latest, most scientific methods, ensuring a maximum output. This enabled Egypt, particularly in the third century B.C., to become the greatest single supplier of grain in the eastern Mediterranean. Egypt's wealth, however, did not depend solely on this commodity. The Ptolemies saw to it that industries were developed as well. Under a royal monopoly, workshops turned out fine linens, glass, cosmetics, and above all, papyrus. From this period until the end of the ancient world, Egypt was practically the sole supplier of cheap writing paper.

The civilization of the Hellenistic Age marks a transitional stage from the city-state culture of classical Greece to the universal and composite culture of the Roman Empire. Rome could not so easily have absorbed the ancient civilizations clustered about the eastern end of the Mediterranean had they not already been fused into a common cosmopolitan civilization by the Hellenizing influence of Alexander and his successors. Cosmopolitanism was accompanied by a rootless individualism very different from the spirit of the small, exclusive, and tightly organized city-states of the Golden Age of Greece. Greek culture dominated the new and larger world: the Greek tongue became the language of all educated men; with some modification Greek art forms persisted; Greek economic developments were the bases of Hellenistic organization. But the milieu in which the Greeks had fashioned this culture was gone. The place of the city-state, with its laws and mores and the demands it made upon the loyalty of its citizens, was taken by vast and impersonal kingdoms. And, lacking the close identification with the community characteristic of the old city-states, people sought the reason and the source and the end of their being within themselves. Escapism and resignation, along with universalism, became typical of Hellenistic philosophy.

In the arts the individualism and restless vitality of the Hellenistic Age were expressed most vividly in sculpture, at least as far as we can determine, since almost all Hellenistic painting has disappeared. Hellenistic sculptors produced thousands of statues for royal and other wealthy patrons, and many of these have survived in the original or in later Roman copies. They represent an amazing range of subject matter, from gods and goddesses through various human types to realistic portraits. The restraint and serenity characteristic of the classical age gave way to a new feeling. Hellenistic sculpture was more naturalistic, more highly individualized, more intensely emotional. The Dying Gaul was a brilliant embodiment of human suffering executed in realistic detail. The Laocoön Group, from the first century B.C., is an example of the later art of the period, when naturalism gave way to exaggerated realism and emotion to theatricality.

While this rich but tormented Hellenistic culture dominated the eastern

Above: The Dying Gaul, a gladiator slumping over his broken sword. A Roman copy in marble of a bronze original of c. 230–220 B.C., *this is an effective example of Hellenistic naturalism. Below: The Laocoön Group. Laocoön, a priest of Apollo, warned the Trojans against accepting the wooden horse. As punishment the gods sent sea serpents to devour him and his sons. This Hellenistic original, partially restored, was found in 1506.*

Mediterranean and the Near East, a small city-state along the Tiber River in Italy was engaged in a fateful struggle for existence and expansion. This was Rome; we now turn to a study of the origins and early development of the Roman people.

Suggestions for Further Reading

A. Andrewes, *The Greek Tyrants** (1956). A short but good and balanced account [AHA, 127, in part].

E. Barker, *Greek Political Theory** (1951). History of Greek political theory from its origins through Plato, with emphasis on Platonic theory [AHA, 134, in part].

J. B. Bury, *History of Greece to the Death of Alexander* (1951). A standard history of Greece to the time of Alexander, brought up-to-date by its careful revision [AHA, 126, in part].

M. Cary, *A History of the Greek World from 323 to 146 B.C.* (1951). Compact and well-organized general history [AHA, 128].

M. I. Finley, *The World of Odysseus** (1954). Short and "popular" account of Homeric society [AHA, 127, in part].

H. D. F. Kitto, *The Greeks** (1951). The best introduction to ancient Greece's people, society, and culture. Informal in style, impeccable in scholarship.

H. D. F. Kitto, *Greek Tragedy: A Literary Study** (1969). A detailed analysis by a witty and urbane British scholar.

M. L. W. Laistner, *A History of the Greek World from 479 to 323 B.C.** (1957). Good general account of the history of Greece in the classical period [AHA, 128].

M. P. Nilsson, *The Mycenaean Origin of Greek Mythology** (1972). A brilliant foray into the difficult area where myth, religion, and legend meet archaeology and history.

C. A. Robinson, *Alexander the Great* (1947). A somewhat idealistic and romantic account of Alexander [AHA, 138].

M. I. Rostovtzeff, *The Social and Economic History of the Hellenistic World,* 3 vols. (1941). Indispensable for the study of Hellenistic history. A very comprehensive interpretation with full discussion [AHA, 128, in part].

T. A. Sinclair, *A History of Greek Political Thought* (1952). A succinct and clearly written sketch of the development of Greek political thought [AHA, 134].

W. W. Tarn, *Alexander the Great,** 2 vols. (1948). Volume 1 is a short narrative of Alexander's career; Volume 2, a discussion of the sources and various problems. The most generally useful account of Alexander for the serious student [AHA, 138].

A. E. Taylor, *Plato: The Man and His Work** (1966). A good introductory exposition by a sophisticated student of metaphysics.

A. E. Taylor, *Socrates: The Man and His Thought** (1959). A clear account by a famous classicist.

A. Zimmern, *The Greek Commonwealth** (1931). Long considered the classic account; an attempt to portray the essence of ancient Greek society, especially in its "golden age." Gracefully written.

*Available in a paperback edition.

Rome: From Res Publica to Imperium

3

> I found Rome brick and I leave it marble.
>
> AUGUSTUS CAESAR

Social Conflict and Territorial Expansion

The Latin peoples who settled the fertile plain of Latium on Italy's western coast south of the Tiber were already well established when the neighboring district of Tuscany to the north of the Tiber was conquered by the Etruscans some time prior to 800 B.C. The Etruscans were a seafaring people of mysterious but probably Eastern origin, more civilized than the Italians among whom they settled. Their language, which is not Indo-European, still baffles scholars, although their alphabet is adapted from the Greek and their culture shows strong evidence of Greek influence. With them came the first elements of the highly developed civilization of the eastern Mediterranean, including the political form of the city-state. Their industrial and artistic products, brought to light by the excavation of thousands of Etruscan tombs, adhere to Greek models too closely to reveal much originality, but show a high degree of technical skill; the remains of their roads, bridges, and tunnels give evidence of remarkable engineering ability. In the seventh century they began to spread their territorial domination southward among the poorly organized tribes of Latium. Throughout most of the sixth century Etruscan kings ruled Rome and the neighboring Latin cities, contributing in no small degree to the development of Roman culture and institutions. Meanwhile, during the seventh and sixth centuries, Italy was brought into still closer contact with the civilization of the East as Greek colonies were founded in Sicily and on the southern coast of the peninsula.

The sixth century was drawing to a close when the Romans rose in rebellion against the Etruscan kings and established an independent republic. The traditional date, 509 B.C., is probably fairly accurate. The constitution of the new republic was conservative and aristocratic. The existing social distinction between the wealthy patrician families and the plebeian mass of the people was given legal sanction and formed the basis of a political caste system. Intermarriage between the two classes was forbidden, while all offices, as well as membership in the Senate, were reserved for patricians. The executive and legislative branches were carefully balanced so as to prevent radical action. Full executive authority, including command of the army and, in the early period, broad judicial powers, were shared by two consuls elected for a year. The consuls were advised by the Senate, a body of three hundred elder statesmen appointed for life, at first by the consuls, later by the censors. The constitutional powers of the Senate were rather vague, but its practical influence was great.

As the Republic expanded in later centuries, new offices were created to take over parts of the consuls' duties. It became the custom to appoint all who had held offices to the Senate, which thus became a body of experienced administrators whose advice the short-term magistrates could scarcely reject. Legislative power and final sovereignty theoretically rested not with the Senate but with the citizens, who, through a number of legislative bodies, expressed their will and elected magistrates. The voting procedures of these bodies, however, were such that only during certain limited periods did their political decisions reflect the views of the people at large. Most of the time government remained safely in the hands of the landed aristocracy. More and more, small farms were bought up to be incorporated into large estates, while the discontented plebeians organized their political strength in the hope of securing relief from debt or allotments of public land from conquered territory.

The struggle between the classes, which was the underlying motif of Roman politics for centuries, began early in the history of the Republic. The plebeians used threats of secession from the state and the promise of bloodshed in order to realize their goals. They kept up a steady political pressure, and during the course of little more than a century and a half succeeded in bringing about a revolution. Early in the fifth century B.C. they gained the right to elect tribunes to protect their interests. A plebeian assembly was then created, and its authority steadily increased until, by 287 B.C., it was recognized as a law-making body with full powers, subject only to the formal assent of the Senate. Even this check was abolished before long. Meanwhile the plebeians had secured the right of intermarriage with the patricians and eligibility for nearly all state offices. They had also secured some economic relief through a modification of the laws regarding debt and through small allotments of public land. In part the plebeian victory was a hollow one, for the plebs dominating the Comitia Tributa, or Council of the Plebs, were often clients of the rich who did their bidding.

These were dangerous years, during which Rome was forced to lead the group of Latin communities which formed the Latin League in a series of defensive wars against belligerent neighbors until the nearest and most threatening had been defeated. It was to the indispensable part they played in the army during these wars that the plebeians owed much of their political success. When Rome entered on a period of more rapid expansion in the latter part of the fourth century B.C., the plebs had thus secured an active share in government and the power to control legislation when they chose to do so. For a long time they remained content with that. Inevitably, however, it was the more wealthy among the plebeians who had the means and leisure to undertake public office. In the course of time these individuals tended to become almost indistinguishable from the patricians in both political point of view and social standing, thus reopening the gap between the ruling class and the mass of the people.

From about the middle of the fourth century B.C., Rome was drawn into one war after another, each of which brought about further territorial expansion. By 290 B.C., Rome dominated all of Italy south of the Po Valley, with the exception of the Greek cities scattered about the southern tip of the peninsula. These were conquered within the next two decades.

Exercising rare political wisdom, the Romans refrained from reducing the conquered Italians to complete subjection, as was the habit of ancient conquerors. Rome allowed the defeated cities and tribes almost complete local autonomy, contenting itself with control of their military forces and foreign policy. Separate treaties with each welded the Italian peoples into a firm federation under Roman leadership. The terms of the treaties varied with varying conditions, making possible more satisfactory relations than could have been established under any single consistent scheme. In addition, Roman and Latin colonies with full or partial Roman citizenship were founded at strategic points throughout Italy. This accomplished the dual purpose of accelerating the Romanization of the peninsula and supplying the poorer Roman and Latin citizens with much-needed land. These colonies also had the important economic effect of turning the surplus Roman population back to the land rather than into industry or commerce. The Romans remained a nation of farmers and landowners.

Rome was soon to have need of its allies, and its wise treatment of them was amply justified by their loyalty during the long struggle with Carthage, which began scarcely more than a decade after the last wars in Italy. Carthage, perhaps founded by Phoenician traders as early as 800 B.C., had long been a wealthy state. It had a powerful navy, and its wealth enabled it to hire large armies of well-trained mercenaries. Although the Carthaginians owned rich landed estates on the fertile African coast and worked with slave labor, their wealth was derived mostly from commerce and depended on their control of western Mediterranean trade. Hitherto Rome and Carthage had been friendly enough, for Rome was a land power interested chiefly in agriculture, and there was not sufficient contact to arouse enmity. The Roman conquest of the commercial Greek cities in southern Italy altered this situation, making the two powers dangerously close neighbors. The first Punic War (so called for the Latin name for the Phoenician people of Carthage) began in 264 B.C. Its causes are still obscure, but in 242 B.C., after more than two decades of incessant fighting, Rome won a decisive naval victory and took command of the seas. Carthage had no alternative but to abandon Sicily, and the following year to sue for peace.

The war left Rome exhausted, but able to recoup part of its losses by exacting a large indemnity from Carthage and levying an immense tribute of grain from the newly acquired territory in Sicily. The conquest of Sicily marked the beginning of a new policy for Rome, the first step toward empire. A few friendly cities were treated as liberally as the Italians had been, but the greater part of the island was ultimately made a Roman province governed by a Roman official and obliged to pay a tithe of its produce to the Roman people. This system of government had been employed by the Syracusan kings in eastern Sicily. A few years later Rome acquired still more territory by taking Sardinia from Carthage.

The peace that followed the first Punic War was no more than a truce of exhaustion. The military party in Carthage, led by Hamilcar Barca, was determined on revenge and the recovery of Sicily and Sardinia. Meanwhile, Hamilcar attempted to compensate for these losses by founding commercial colonies in Spain. After his death his brilliant son, Hannibal, continued his work until he had an army in Spain which he believed to be strong enough to invade Italy. Entering northern Italy through the Alps in 218 B.C., Hannibal was able neither to rally Rome's Italian allies nor to win a final victory over the Roman army.

Though he remained in Italy for years and laid waste large sections of the peninsula, the city of Rome and the Roman state remained intact. The loss to Rome in men and material wealth due to Hannibal's long presence in Italy was tremendous. Yet Rome was still capable of taking the offensive. In 204 B.C. an expeditionary force under Scipio Africanus was sent to Africa, and Hannibal was forced to return to defend Carthage. The war ended with his decisive defeat at Zama in 202 B.C. By the terms of peace, Spain became a Roman province and Carthage was forced to pay a huge indemnity, surrender its fleet, and accept Roman dictation of its foreign policy. There could not longer be any doubt about Rome's complete domination of the western Mediterranean.

The Crisis of the Roman Republic

Expansion, whether imperialistic or accidental, created a sizable overseas empire. This situation inevitably affected the social and economic life of the Roman people. Wealth flowed to Rome from the plunder and tribute of the provinces, greatly increasing both public and private capital. Very little of this new capital, however, was invested in industry or commerce, so that the character of Roman economy changed less than might have been expected. Though industrial production was increasing in volume with the growing demands of a wealthy class of consumers, it was still limited largely to manufacture by small artisans of goods for daily use, with little or no surplus for export.

The most significant change was the introduction of large quantities of slaves (c. 202–90 B.C.), prisoners taken during the decades of continuous warfare. This phenomenon naturally tended to drive free labor out of competition and had the undesirable effect of adding to the number of poverty-stricken and discontented urban plebeians. Commerce, too, was growing in volume, but, except for army and state contracts let out to citizens, the greater part of this

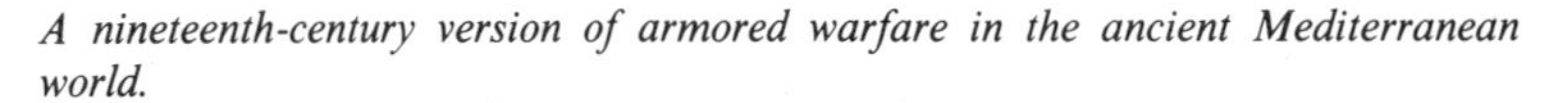
A nineteenth-century version of armored warfare in the ancient Mediterranean world.

activity was left to the more commercially experienced Eastern merchants who had been drawn into Rome's expanding orbit.

Among the Romans themselves, financial affairs were now largely in the hands of the increasingly important class of knights or *equites,* so called because in earlier times they had been distinguished from the poorer plebeians by their ability to afford the expense of a horse and to serve in the cavalry. By the second century B.C., however, they had ceased to be a military class and had become businessmen with a special interest in banking and finance. In general they found safer and more substantial profits from investment in contracts for public works or army supplies or for the exploitation of state mines and forests than in competition with the skilled merchants of the East. The knights, too, enjoyed a privileged position in the provinces as bankers and contractors for the collection of the provincial taxes. By the end of the second century many of them were very wealthy and becoming powerful in politics.

The greater part of Roman capital was still invested in land. The second Punic War had greatly accelerated the growth of large estates. Whole sections of Italy had been deserted following their devastation by Hannibal's armies, and after the war these lands were taken over by the government to be leased to anyone who could invest the necessary capital to restore them to use. Roman senators, who as a class were barred by tradition and law from engaging in trade, took advantage of this situation to acquire large estates from the public land. Later the capital obtained from exploitation of the provinces enabled many senators to expand their estates still further. The possession of capital also permitted the owners of large estates to combine scientific methods of cultivation with slave labor to produce cash crops such as wine, olive oil, and wool.

Such estates were operated with the sole aim of making a profit for their owners, who, more often than not, were absentee landlords who lived in Rome and devoted themselves to maintaining their political and social status. It required considerable capital to plant a vineyard or olive orchard or to stock a sheep ranch, and there was a long delay before vines and orchards began to bear fruit. The initial cost of the large number of slaves required to work the estate was also considerable. But once established, the large estate produced a steady and handsome income. Small farmers could not compete with these new methods, and, as more and more of them were forced to give up their land, social discontent rose to a dangerous pitch.

It was the hope of re-establishing the class of small landowning citizens, who had been the military and political backbone of the Republic during the first period of expansion, that inspired the reforms proposed by Tiberius Gracchus. As one of the tribunes for the year 133 B.C., he proposed to the Popular Assembly a law for the redistribution of all public lands held in excess of the legal limit for individuals specified by laws which had been ignored for many years. Gracchus had supporters among the upper classes, but the Senate soon came to fear a loss of power and violently opposed the law, not only because most of its members were large landowners, but also because Gracchus had secured its passage by the Popular Assembly, which had taken no reform initiative in politics for nearly a century. This was a revolutionary move and posed an immediate threat to senatorial authority. When the idealistic reformer stood for election again the following year, riots broke out in which Gracchus himself was killed. The redistribution of public land was continued for some years after his death, and then came to a standstill until, ten years later, his unfinished task was taken up by his younger

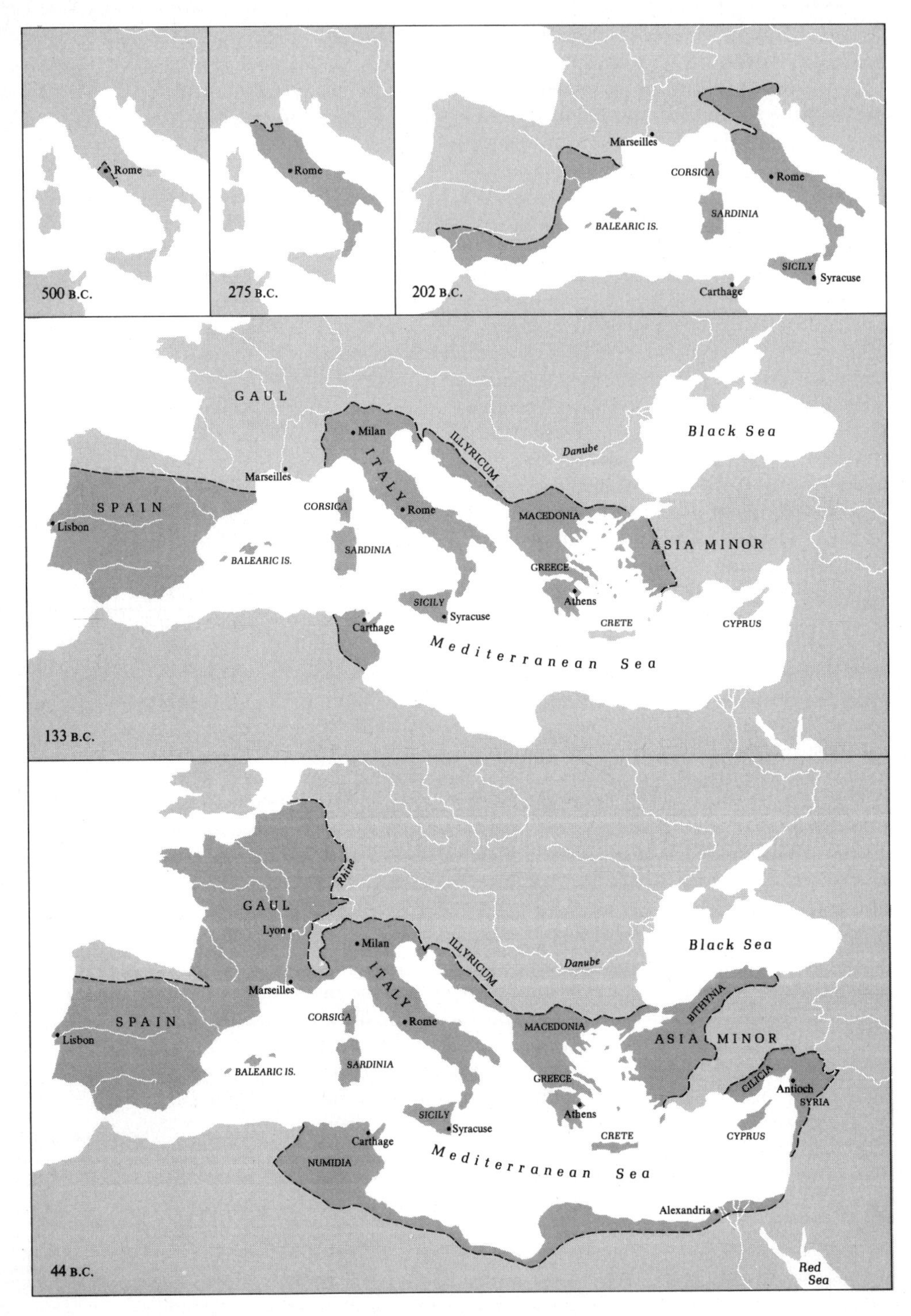

THE EXPANSION OF ROMAN TERRITORY, 500 B.C.–44 B.C.

brother, Gaius Gracchus. The reform program of the younger Gracchus was much more extensive, and given time he might have accomplished much good. Like his brother, however, he was defeated and killed while his reforms were still in their initial stage.

A new spirit of violence characterized the political conflicts of the rest of the century and spread eventually to the Italian allies, who, despite their loyalty in time of desperate danger, had never been admitted as a body to Roman citizenship. In 91 B.C. they rebelled and were pacified by the long-desired gift of citizenship only after three years of destructive warfare (91-88 B.C.). Under other circumstances this act might have furnished the Republic with a broader and more stable political base, but the new citizens, like the old, were not allowed to vote unless present in person in Rome. They merely increased the number of discontented citizens who might follow a revolutionary leader.

To this unstable political situation, the army added a new element of danger. During an otherwise unimportant war in Africa against the Numidian king Jugurtha, the army had been reorganized by Marius, the consul for 107 B.C., who had the backing of the Popular Assembly. Instead of drafting the property-owning citizens, as was the ancient custom, he recruited a volunteer army composed mostly of landless men, who served as professional soldiers for pay. The new army represented discontented elements in Roman society and thus might prove a dangerous weapon in the hands of an unscrupulous general.

The disintegration of republican government in the first century B.C. was closely connected with economic and social developments in Italy, but in a more fundamental way was the result of Rome's expansion and the exploitation of the conquered provinces. Irresponsible senatorial governors and the financiers who held contracts for the collection of provincial taxes cooperated to fleece the helpless provincials. Both the upper classes, senators and equites, were rapidly adopting a policy of barefaced imperialism, motivated by no more altruistic aim than to rob the conquered peoples of the East.

In 63 B.C. the brilliant Roman general, Pompey, opened up new fields for plunder by adding the rich provinces of Bithynia, Cilicia, and Syria to Rome's growing empire. Rome had now become a parasitical state, draining the provinces of their wealth with disastrous results for itself as well as for the unfortunate provincials. The great fortunes amassed by conquering generals, senatorial governors, and tax-collecting equites went to increase the size and number of large estates in Italy. This in turn swelled the number of small farmers who, having lost their land, were forced to join the degraded city populace living on the dole from the provincial revenues. The final result of imperialism seemed to be the ruin of the provinces and the demoralization of Roman citizens of every class. The republican government of a small city-state was proving totally inadequate to the administration of an empire. The only solution seemed to be the dictatorship of an individual strong enough to suppress party strife by force and to restore honest and efficient government. The necessary force could be provided by the great professional armies created as a result of the military reforms of Marius.

Half a century of civil wars between rival leaders elapsed, however, before a permanent dictatorship was established. For a time Julius Caesar seemed destined to accomplish it. He was the most able politician of his generation and won a great reputation and the loyalty of his army in a long series of wars which ended with the conquest of Gaul and the invasion of Britain. Returning in 49 B.C., he entered into a civil war with his old ally, Pompey, who had ruled Rome in his absence. The defeat of Pompey left Caesar master of the state. His power was that of an armed dictator, though he exercised his authority through the old republican offices and institutions. He instituted a number of admirable reforms and, given time, might have reconstructed the state on a permanent basis and won the loyalty of the Roman people. But Caesar was ambitious. The belief that he intended to establish himself as a king of the Hellenistic type aroused intense opposition among the old senatorial aristocracy, and on the Ides (the fifteenth) of March, 44 B.C., he was assassinated.

The murder of Caesar did not restore free republican government. His place was taken by a triumvirate composed of Mark Antony, Lepidus, and Caesar's grandnephew and heir, Octavian, and there followed a civil war with the senatorial party led by Brutus and Cassius. The triumvirs were victorious, but the selfish bond that held them together could not withstand the strain imposed by the necessity of sharing power. While Octavian earned the confidence of the Romans for just government in Italy, and rid himself of one rival by forcing Lepidus to retire to private life, Antony followed his own designs in the East, where he married Cleopatra, the queen of Egypt. Octavian marched eastward, defeated Antony in 31 B.C., and annexed Egypt.

Octavian was now master of the state, as his great-uncle had been before him. Though he asserted his intention of restoring the republic and retained the Senate, the consuls, and the old machinery of government, he kept control of the government in his own hands during a long lifetime and passed his power to the emperors who succeeded him. In 27 B.C. the Senate conferred upon him the name of Augustus, and it was under that name that he proceeded to organize the Roman Empire and establish the great period of Augustan peace.

The Political Organization of the Roman Empire

For two centuries, from 31 B.C. to A.D. 180, the Mediterranean world often enjoyed peace and prosperity such as it had never known. Not a large area by today's standards, but it comprised all the lands that had attained any degree of civilization, save for those countries in western Asia and the Far East known to the Roman citizen through the luxuries imported from India by Alexandrian merchants. Various types of culture—Middle Eastern, Greek, and Latin—existed within this great empire, their roots striking deep into the past. Now, with no political barriers to keep them apart, and with easy intercourse guaranteed by the protection of the Roman government, they met and, though each retained aspects of its own identity, gradually fused to form a new composite which, for lack of a better name, we call Roman civilization. It was not, however, Roman in the narrow national sense in which the culture of the Republic was Roman, i.e., the product of the Roman or Italian people; all the more civilized peoples within its borders contributed to the civilization of the Roman Empire, the provincials no less than those who could claim descent from the citizens of the old Republic. Neither the "Roman peace" nor Roman civilization was destined to last. When the former ended, the latter declined. But what was left of Roman culture was to form a major part of the legacy of Western civilization.

The greater part of the lands included in the Roman Empire had been conquered by the Roman Republic. But, though the republican government succeeded in conquering the Mediterranean world, it proved unable to rule it.

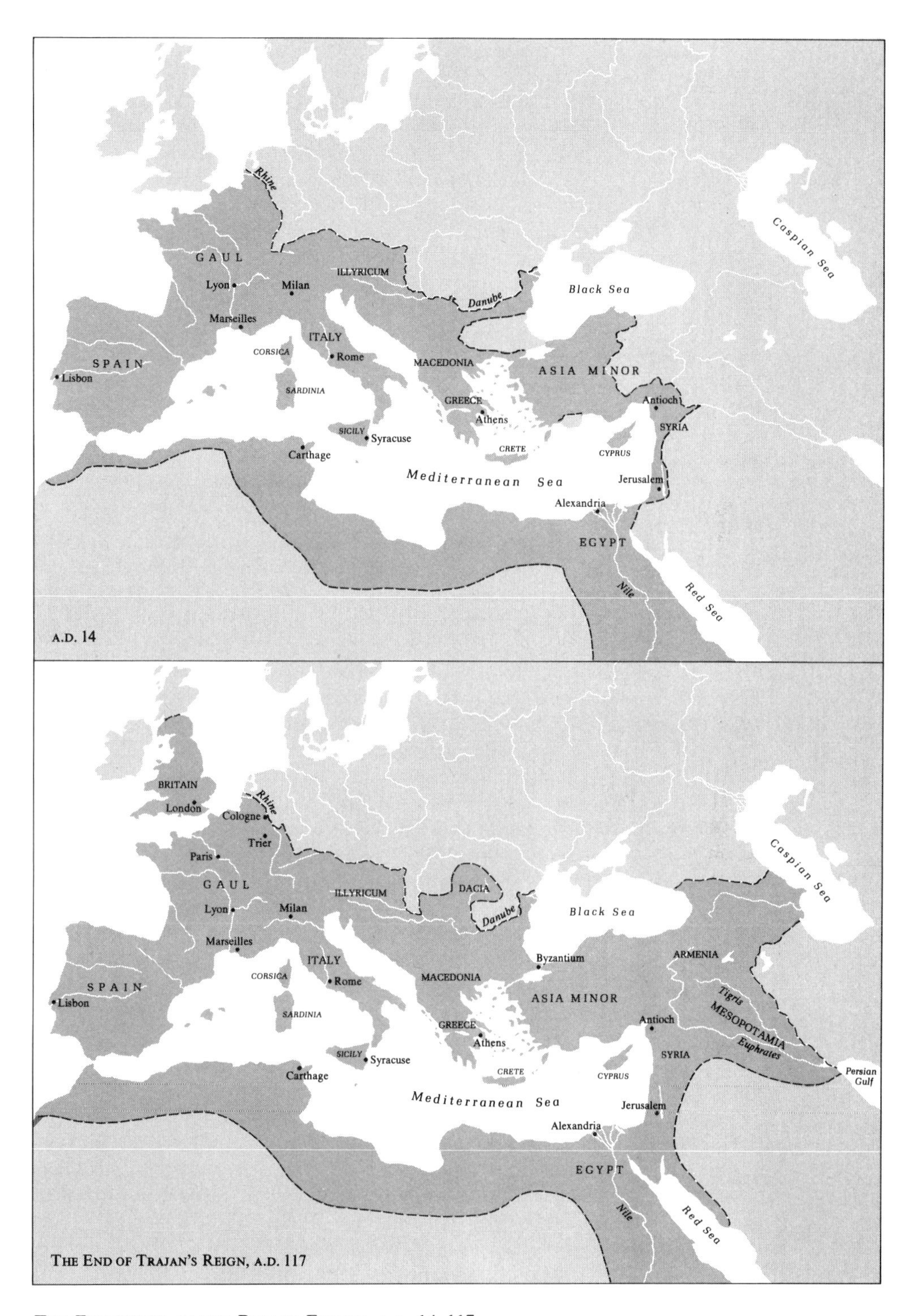

THE EXPANSION OF THE ROMAN EMPIRE, A.D. 14–117

When, therefore, Augustus seized control of the Empire in 31 B.C. backed by a victorious army, the majority of the people, Roman and provincial alike, were prepared to accept him as the savior of the state. And Augustus made it as easy as possible for the Romans to accept his authority. He avoided all unnecessary offense to their republican sentiments. Claiming for himself only the military title of *imperator* and the civil title of *princeps,* or first citizen, he exercised his authority through the offices and institutions of the Republic.

On the death of an emperor the Senate became the governing body of the state and had, theoretically, the right to choose his successor, although, as events were to prove, the deciding vote was likely to be that of the army. Augustus himself secured a peaceful succession by designating his stepson Tiberius as his heir. The three subsequent emperors—Caligula, Claudius, and Nero—also had family ties with Augustus and owed their position largely to the loyalty of the army to the family of the great founder of the Empire. The fact that any member of the senatorial aristocracy could, in theory, aspire to the principate, however, bred suspicion in the minds of these emperors and led to wholesale prosecutions which thinned the ranks of the old senatorial families.

After the death of Nero in A.D. 68, the army revolted and created four emperors in one year; the last of these, Vespasian (69-79), was able to restore order and re-establish a constitutional principate. He was, indeed, the first of a series of strong rulers who gave the Empire more than a century of good government. Under their rule the Senate came to represent the whole Empire rather than the exclusively Roman aristocracy and was brought firmly under the emperor's domination. During most of this period the emperors happened to be childless, and so solved the problem of succession, as Augustus had done, by adopting the ablest man available and naming him heir. Unfortunately the last of the "good emperors," the philosopher Marcus Aurelius (121-180), did have a son, Commodus, whose vicious, depraved reign opened the way to the military anarchy that was to plague the Empire for another hundred years.

The powers of imperial officials stopped short of interference in local government. In this sphere, which most closely affected the lives of the people, the emperors wisely allowed almost complete freedom. For administrative purposes, Italy and the provinces were divided into *civitates* or municipalities. In the eastern part of the Empire, these represented survivals of the ancient city-states, with their traditions of self-government and civic patriotism. In the newer barbarian West, tribes or cantons were organized into municipalities with a city as the capital. The citizens (as a rule not including the poorest classes) elected their own officers and their own *curia* or council, chosen from a local aristocracy of wealth corresponding to the senatorial class at Rome. In each municipality the old republican government of Rome was reflected in miniature, with variations depending on the ethnic origins and traditions of the individual city.

Free municipal citizenship did much to keep the provincials contented. But the Empire could never become a truly united world-state so long as the invidious distinction between Roman citizens and all others remained in effect. Roman citizenship conferred important legal privileges which were not shared by the new provincial subjects of Rome, even though they might be citizens of their own municipalities. These privileges included the right to appeal the sentence of a local court to the emperor, and exemption from degrading punishments such as scourging.

Rome, unlike the Greek city-states, became relatively liberal in granting citizenship to conquered peoples, and the emperors realized early the advantages to be gained from extending citizenship to provincials. This policy would level all classes under their authority, broaden the foundations of their power, increase the loyalty of the provincials, and weld all parts of the state more closely together. Hence, despite the opposition of the Italians, who were unwilling to share their special privileges as Roman citizens, they gradually extended citizenship to the most influential classes in the provinces, until by the Constitutio Antoniana of 212 all freeborn citizens of the municipalities throughout the Empire were made Roman citizens.

Authority and Law in the Roman Empire

The army played an important part in the dissemination of Roman citizenship. The legions, which formed the bulk of the standing army, were recruited by voluntary enlistment from the body of Roman citizens. When these proved insufficient, provincials were admitted and by virtue of their military service granted citizenship. The number thus honored was greatly increased by the military reforms of Vespasian (69–79), who barred Italians from service in the legions. The aristocratic youth of Italy might still serve as praetorian cohorts, the select imperial bodyguard, and after training there might be transferred as officers to the legions or auxiliary troops. But the rank and file of the legionaires were now mostly provincial. The army, some four hundred thousand strong, was usually stationed at strategic points along the frontiers, where there was the greatest danger of invasion. The term of service was from twenty to twenty-five years, after which the retired soldier was often granted land near his old camp. Many of the legions' camps became permanent centers of Roman influence and

Members of the Praetorian guard, an elite military corps stationed in Rome.

formed the nucleus of new provincial towns. Some of these towns, formed around the *castra* or camp of the legions, still exist, as is illustrated by such English names as Chester, Lancaster, Manchester.

In order to establish common ties between the peoples of the Empire, imperial patriotism had to replace, or be imposed upon, local civic patriotism. This was accomplished in part through the institution of emperor-worship. Many characteristics of the old Roman religion prepared the way for acceptance of emperor-worship in the West, and, as Eastern influence grew with the further unification of the state, it became firmly established. Domitian (81-96) was the first emperor to claim the title *dominus et deus* in Rome during his own lifetime. Under his successors, emperor-worship became a recognized state religion, in which all citizens participated, whatever their other religious traditions. There was little protest, since few of the ancient religious cults were exclusive or barred their followers from the worship of other gods.

Even more important than emperor-worship for the unification of the state was the formulation of Roman law into a universal civil code. As the Roman Empire assumed far-flung Mediterranean proportions, and commerce between the provinces increased, a body of law with common jurisdiction over subjects as well as citizens in all parts of the Empire was urgently needed.

As early as the second century before Christ, such a body of law had evolved from the praetors' edicts and the decisions and comments of jurists on cases tried in the Roman courts. This collection of praetors' law and of the precedents established by judges' decisions was strongly influenced by the best local laws and current practices of businessmen throughout the Empire. In time it came to form a common code applicable to free men everywhere. Based on jurisprudence rather than legislation, the Roman code was constantly reinterpreted to keep it in harmony with the changing needs of the age. The great value of this reinterpretation by edict and precedent lay in the general recognition by Roman jurists of the fundamental principles that equity is more important than strict legality and that all free men are equal before the law. About the beginning of the second century A.D., the emperors' rescripts and decrees—or "constitutions," as they were called—began to replace the praetors' edicts, thus continuing the construction and reinterpretation of the code. The tradition of jurisprudence also continued unbroken. Even during the troubled third century a series of distinguished jurists made invaluable contributions to the elucidation and systematization of law.

Social and Economic Life

During the prosperous years of the first two centuries, the urban upper classes possessed great wealth, and spent it freely in adding to the beauty and dignity of their native cities. Rome was proverbial for the splendor of its temples, theaters, circuses, forums, public baths, and palaces, while in the provincial cities the same magnificent buildings were to be found in proportionately lesser degree. Even the smaller towns of Gaul and Britain were well planned, well kept, and sanitary. The streets were wide, straight, fully paved, and clean. Great aqueducts carried water to the cities in plentiful supply. There were statues and monuments everywhere. Private houses, too, were built with every facility needed to make life pleasant and agreeable. They had shaded central courts in which fountains played to cool the midday heat, running water, and, in some cases, central heating. The ruins of Pompeii, preserved intact by their mantle of volcanic ash, reveal a degree of comfort and convenience in public and private life not to be experienced again until relatively modern times. And Pompeii was little more than a third-rate town.

Many of the buildings and public works were constructed by the emperors or municipal governments. The majority, however, owed their existence to the civic pride and generosity of wealthy citizens. Markets, bridges, roads, and aqueducts, as well as all kinds of public buildings, were donated to the city by men who had been honored with public office in the local government, by those who hoped to be so honored, or by others motivated simply by that passionate love of their native city which was so strong in the ancient municipality. The circuses, banquets, and other public amusements of that sociable age were also due in many cases to private liberality. Social standing and civic honors were alike the monopoly of wealth; but wealth carried with it heavy duties of service and generosity, rigidly enforced by public opinion.

The municipal aristocracy was made up of citizens who had sufficient property to qualify for offices in the local government or membership in the curia. The list of *curiales,* as those eligible for membership in the curia were called, was revised every five years. From this group men of servile birth were usually excluded. Yet former slaves, freedmen, often rose to positions of wealth and power. Many a highly educated Greek slave, or Syrian who possessed commercial genius, was able to acquire sufficient money to buy his freedom and afterward to make a fortune in trade. The mass of the citizens—shopkeepers, artisans, and so forth—and the poorer proletariat, who were sometimes excluded from citizenship, led obscure lives of little or no social or political importance, as did the peasants who lived outside the cities. There were, however, frequent public amusements, gladiatorial shows, chariot races, games, and pantomimes to alleviate the tedium of their lives, and most of them belonged to clubs which organized banquets and social gatherings and afforded them the comforting sense of belonging to an exclusive society. The slaves were the lowest social class. They were the property of their masters, without social or civil rights, though a

The Pont du Gard, a triumph of Roman engineering skill, located in southeastern France. The structure combines a bridge on the lower level with an aqueduct on the upper level.

growing humanitarian spirit was mitigating the brutality with which many were treated in the early days of Rome's conquests. They also became less numerous because of the frequency of manumission and because the Empire now fought only defensive wars and no longer took great numbers of prisoners.

Superimposed upon the municipal aristocracy, and recruited from it, was an imperial or Roman aristocracy made up of two classes, the senators and the equites. By the second century these classes had lost their purely Roman character and included provincials who had risen in the imperial service. The equites were mostly men of moderate wealth, who had held offices in the imperial administration or the army. The senatorial aristocracy, as its numbers dwindled, was recruited by the emperor from the equites who had won his gratitude by faithful service. Both the imperial and municipal aristocracies were clearly defined castes, based partly on heredity and partly on wealth. Class distinctions were sharply drawn but not permanent. The birth rate in aristocratic families was low, and the families soon died out. Their places were taken by people from the lower classes.

When Augustus ushered in the two centuries of Roman peace, he also introduced an era of unprecedented prosperity to Italy and the provinces. The wars which had devastated the Empire were ended. The civilized Western world had been united in a single state, under a government strong enough to guarantee peace and security. Merchants might carry their wares freely from the Black Sea to Spain, from the Nile to the Thames, without crossing a frontier. And wherever they went they found the same laws, the same coinage, the same privileges, and the protection of the same government. During the first two centuries the emperors allowed full freedom to commerce, except for slight interprovincial duties, and abstained from governmental interference in industry. New and safe markets were established in the barbarian provinces. New cities were founded everywhere, providing at once the supply and the demand for a new economic life.

A major share of the amazing revival of commerce must be credited to the ease and security of communications within the Empire. The Mediterranean Sea, though stormy and treacherous, was a broad highway through the center of the Roman world, and the imperial fleet kept it free of pirates. In each province the emperors repaired or constructed a skillfully planned network of roads, connecting all the important cities. These roads, stone-paved and permanent, were built originally for the legions, but served the merchants equally well. Over them messengers of the imperial service, equipped with relays of horses, could average fifty miles a day. Ordinary travelers could maintain an average speed of five miles an hour in districts where five hundred years later roads were almost impassable or nonexistent. Communications in Europe and the Middle East were never again so rapid or so safe until the advent of the railroad.

Though great fortunes were made from commerce, much of the prosperity of the Roman world resulted directly from manufacturing. Industry was mostly in the hands of small independent artisans, and contributed to the livelihood of the masses rather than to the fortunes of the few capitalists. When the goods manufactured were intended for the local market, as was usually the case, artisans were merchants as well as manufacturers, selling their wares to the consumer in their own little shops. Only in the case of goods intended for a distant market was there any attempt at mass production. Wealthy men sometimes employed large numbers of slaves or free workers in their shops. However, this process differed from our own factory system in that each article was manufactured by a single worker, from beginning to end, and little use was made of any but the simplest machinery. But even goods intended for export were often produced by independent workers.

Roman Culture

During the second century B.C., as the eastward trend of foreign policy brought the Republic into ever-closer relations with the Greek world, a knowledge of Greek became a necessary part of a Roman gentleman's education; by the following century, it had become a second mother tongue to the Roman literati. Greek slaves and freedmen swarmed into Rome, bringing the artistic techniques of the Hellenistic East and, in many instances, serving as tutors to the sons of wealthy families.

While the Golden Age of Latin poetry was yet to come, the prose writers of the late republican era created a Latin style that has never been surpassed. Latin oratory flourished in these years under conditions similar to those which had given rise to the rhetorical style of republican Athens, partly under the influence of Greek models. The hectic political life of the dying Republic placed a premium on oratory, and every young Roman aristocrat studied rhetoric as the essential preparation for a career in public office, the Senate, or the law courts. Cicero (106–43 B.C.), the unrivaled master of Latin prose, had a long and distinguished career in public office and was one of the most intransigent leaders of the conservative senatorial party in opposition to the dictatorial ambitions of Caesar and the triumvirate. His rhetorical style was developed in the heat of political controversy. In the philosophical treastises *On Friendship, On Duty, On Old Age,* and others, he demonstrated the capacity of the Latin language to express the finest shades of meaning, at the same time transmitting to the Latin world the best moral teaching of the Greek philosophers. Julius Caesar, too, was a master of prose style, although of a more simple and direct sort. His *Commentaries on the Gallic Wars* is a masterpiece of historical literature.

The Golden Age of Latin literature began amidst the political tumult, wars of conquest, and civil strife of the dying Republic; but it reached its full development in the tranquillity of the Augustan Age. By that time the Latin writers had learned what Greece could teach them, and the classical Latin style had been formed by such masters as Cicero and Catullus. When Octavian seized control in 31 B.C., a brilliant group of poets and prose writers were ready to begin their mature work under the favorable conditions his rule was to provide. The dictator himself was eager to promote a Latin literature that would serve to reawaken Roman patriotism and reflect glory upon the Augustan state; at his court liberal patrons, like the wealthy Maecenas, gave encouragement and material support to writers ready to carry out the emperor's program.

Roman patriotism, pride in the past and hope for the future, is the constant theme which runs through the poetry of Virgil (70–19 B.C.), the greatest of all Latin poets, who has been called "the voice of Rome incarnate." In the *Aeneid,* the magnificent epic which connects the origins of Rome with Homeric Troy, the theme of Roman virtue and Roman glory swells into a great celebration. The *Aeneid* is modeled on the Homeric epics, to which it is related as a kind of sequel, but it is never slavishly imitative. Its spirit is Roman.

So much of the important literature of this period was written in Latin that we are apt to forget that it was not the only language of the Empire. It was, indeed, rapidly becoming the only literary language of the western half of the Empire, spreading with Roman civilization to the provinces of Africa, Spain, Gaul, and Britain, where no old established culture existed to resist it. The number of writers who were born in the provinces, especially in Spain, is proof that mastery of Latin was no longer an Italian monopoly. The eastern half of the Empire, however, remained predominantly Greek-speaking, as it had been throughout the Hellenistic period. Plutarch (c. A.D. 46-120) is almost the only Greek man of letters from this period whose name is widely known today; his great series of biographies of Greek and Roman personalities arranged in pairs, the *Parallel Lives,* are an enduring part of the world's literature.

The grandeur of Rome found expression in the magnificent buildings erected during the first two centuries of the Empire, not only in Rome but also in many provincial cities. Greek influence is evident in the use of columns, though they are seldom purely Greek in form, but the limited spatial range of the low rectilinear Greek temple could not satisfy the Roman demand for grandeur of design. The most characteristic Roman contributions, which continued to influence western European architecture for centuries, were the arch, the vault, and the dome. These forms enabled the Romans to erect on a grand scale buildings which expressed the spirit of the Roman Empire just as the perfect proportions of the Greek temple had expressed that of Greece.

The crisis of the Roman Empire involved all aspects of Roman life, including cultural change and economic decline. The grandeur of Rome's buildings could not conceal the weaknesses inherent in the Empire's social and political structure.

Suggestions for Further Reading

R. H. Barrow, *The Romans** (1951). The best brief introduction to Roman civilization. A classic of concise, urbane historical writing.

A. E. R. Boak and W. G. Sinnigen, *A History of Rome to 565 A.D.* (1965). A clear and concise survey, based on excellent knowledge of sources and modern discussions [AHA, 145, in part].

J. Carcopino, *Daily Life in Ancient Rome** (1946). Excellent treatise, especially good on the city of Rome and conditions of the lower classes [AHA, 161, in part].

M. P. Charlesworth, *The Roman Empire* (1951). Excellent brief account of the Roman Empire from Augustus to Constantine, less devoted to narrative than to cogent comment on its more significant aspects [AHA, 151].

R. G. Collingwood and J. N. L. Myres, *Roman Britain and the English Settlements* (1936). The fullest account of the development and institutions of the province [AHA, 152, in part].

D. Dudley, *The Civilization of Rome** (1960). A pleasant survey of Roman culture and society.

*Available in a paperback edition.

J. W. Duff, *Literary History of Rome from the Origins to the Close of the Golden Age** (1953). Introductory history [AHA, 162, in part].

J. W. Duff, *Literary History of Rome in the Silver Age from Tiberius to Hadrian** (1953).

A. S. L. Farquharson, *Marcus Aurelius: His Life and His World* (1951). A study of Roman imperial society at its height, before its first plunge into major crises. Marcus Aurelius (A.D. 161-180) was the philosopher-emperor who believed in the stoic world-view.

I. A. Richmond, *Roman Britain* (1955). Brief but outstanding synthesis by a leading British archaeologist [AHA, 152].

E. T. Salmon, *A History of the Roman World from 130 B.C. to A.D. 138* (1957). A well-informed and critical survey of the period on the traditional plan [AHA, 151].

H. H. Scullard, *A History of the Roman World from 753 to 146 B.C.** (1951). A judicious, sober, and readable history [AHA, 148, in part].

C. G. Starr, *Civilization and the Caesars** (1954). Attributes the decline of classical civilization to the absolutism inherent in the Augustan system. Valuable for range and information, despite an uncertain thesis [AHA, 161].

R. Syme, *The Roman Revolution** (1960). A brilliant interpretive and narrative work; the best treatment of Rome's transition to empire and the attendant social and political upheavals.

L. R. Taylor, *Party Politics in the Age of Caesar** (1949). Penetrating and lively analysis of the practical working of the Roman political system in the late republic, with descriptions of the manipulations by individuals and groups of the assemblies, the voting, religious restrictions, and the courts [AHA, 149, in part].

The Decline of the Roman Empire

4

Life is warfare and the sojourn of a stranger in a strange land, and after fame is oblivion.

EMPEROR MARCUS AURELIUS

Beginning of the Decline: The Third Century

Symptoms of a general decline in the vitality of the Roman Empire were already apparent in the third century. Among the most significant were economic changes that were undermining the prosperity of the Empire and producing a social situation which was both materially and spiritually unhealthy. It is difficult to isolate the causes of the economic regression, since they were intimately related, as we shall see, to the effects of civil war and the burden of taxation which, in the next two centuries, became ever more crushing as the defense of the Empire made increasing demands on its wealth and manpower. There is, however, positive evidence that agricultural production, on which so much of the Empire's economy depended, was declining, and thus decreasing the food supply of the cities and the buying power of the land-owning classes. In parts of Italy and North Africa, and possibly in other areas as well, deforestation had resulted in soil erosion, and overcropping of marginal land had led to soil exhaustion. A more important factor, however, was the widespread decline of scientific farming on the great estates which had largely replaced small independent farms throughout the Empire. By the third century, slave labor was becoming scarce, and owners of large estates were abandoning the attempt to make a profit by supplying produce to the city markets. Instead they rented the land to small tenants, who lacked the capital, equipment, and skill to farm in the most productive way. Moreover, as we shall see, a combination of economic factors and imperial laws bound these tenants to the land so that they lost their freedom and much of their incentive to vigorous enterprise. The great estates, like the later medieval manors, were beginning to produce largely for their own consumption, and so the mutually profitable economic exchange between country and city gradually died out.

Equally significant is the fact that Roman commerce and industry apparently experienced a declining rate of growth after the second century. The annexation of the half-barbaric and economically undeveloped provinces of the West had at first opened up a great field for commercial and industrial exploitation on the part of the more highly developed East. Furthermore, the advance of these western provinces from semi-barbarism to a standard of living comparable to that of the rest of the Empire helped to maintain a steady rate of expansion in the economy of the Empire as a whole. By the second century, however, the West was fully developed and the last economic frontier had vanished. Thereafter further expansion would have to occur largely within the existing limits of a stable society.

New methods of cheaper mass production might have maintained growth by lowering the price of goods and increasing the quantity that could be sold. A more equable distribution of wealth and higher wages might have had a similar effect by increasing the buying power of the population. But neither of these things happened. The Romans made no significant inventions of machinery to speed production, and an increasingly large proportion of the wealth of the state was being concentrated in a relatively small aristocratic class, who invested it in large landed estates rather than in commerce or industry. As a result, the economy of the ancient world lost the stimulus of expansion, and a capitalist economy that ceases to grow is in imminent danger of decline.

While it is clear that many of the causes of the Empire's decline were inherent in the economic structure and could not have been avoided, it is also true that some of the most serious economic and social evils can be traced to the failure of the imperial government in the third century and the policies of the later despotic emperors. Bad government began with the reign of Commodus (A.D. 180–192) the son of the philosophical Marcus Aurelius, and did not end with his assassination at the hands of mutinous soldiers.

There followed a century of chaos and anarchy, during which the army took government into its own hands. Imperial power had always depended essentially on the support of the legions, but hitherto the emperors had been able to control them. Now the army assumed control of the emperors, creating and destroying them at will. Recruited largely from the least civilized parts of the Empire and stationed permanently on the frontiers, many of the legions had lost all sense of responsible citizenship and were ready to follow any commander who chose to bid for the imperial title. Between the years 192 and 284, there were thirty-three emperors, most of whom died by violence.

The Reforms of Diocletian

The reign of Diocletian (284–305) marks a turning-point in the history of the Empire almost as significant as the transition from Republic to Empire under Augustus. Like Augustus, Diocletian was faced with the task of preventing the disintegration of the state, and strove to solve the problem in the arbitrary fashion that came most naturally to a half-civilized soldier who had fought his way up from the ranks by sheer force of will. His first step was to assume all power and to free himself from constitutional checks. The emperors had been gaining steadily in power since the days of Augustus; but hitherto the old forms of senatorial government had been preserved. Diocletian, however, became a divine ruler, surrounded by all the pomp and ceremony of an Eastern despot, demanding servile obedience from his subjects. This was a far cry from the days when Augustus had posed as the first citizen of Rome, to whom the body of citizens had delegated imperial authority. The very idea of Roman citizenship now disappeared. There remained only subjects, but subjects who were still proud to call themselves Roman.

The second step was to rationalize imperial administration so as to bring the whole system of government more directly under the emperor's control. Diocletian realized that the task of personally governing so vast a state was beyond the power of one man, and recognized that the Greek East and the Latin West were drifting apart. He therefore chose a colleague in the year 286, a trusted general named Maximian, who was to share with him the title of Augustus or emperor and to govern the Western half of the Empire. Further, to avoid interference by the army in the succession to the throne, each of the two Augusti adopted a younger man, who took the title of Caesar. The Caesar was to assist in the task of governing and to succeed to the title of Augustus on the death or abdication of his superior. To systematize the civil administration, Diocletian then divided the Empire into four great prefectures, each governed by a prefect directly responsible to the emperor of his half of the Empire. The prefectures in turn were divided into a varying number of dioceses (seventeen in all), each administered by a vicar responsible to the prefect. The dioceses in turn were divided into provinces, much smaller than the old provinces (there were one hundred and one in the whole Empire), each under a governor responsible to his vicar. Instructions could thus be passed down from the emperor, and cases could be referred back to him, through a regular chain of command. Each of these officers was assisted by a host of civil servants and special agents. There were also scores of officials attached to the imperial courts to assist in the central administration. This highly organized system took over all the duties of local as well as imperial government. The municipalities lost their free self-government and the municipal curiales, or councilors, became mere unpaid servants of the state, who carried out the dictates of the imperial officers.

The third step in reform was to reorganize the army so as to make it more efficient, more dependent on the emperor, and entirely separate from the civil administration. Senators and citizens were gradually excluded from the army, as

THE ROMAN EMPIRE IN THE FIFTH CENTURY

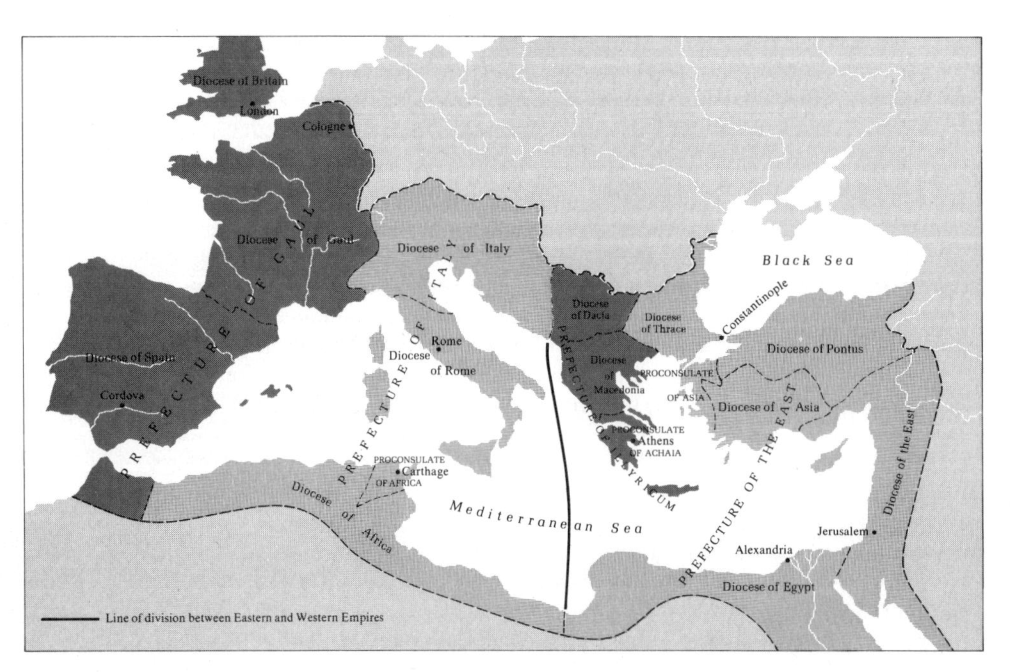

they had other services to perform for the state, and soon lost all military spirit and ability. The old legions were posted along the frontiers as hereditary guards, while a new and more mobile force was recruited from German barbarians and the most uncivilized subjects of the Empire. This barbarous army served only for pay and had no interest in the welfare of the state. Its officers rose from the ranks by a regular system of promotion, the highest office being that of *magister militum* or master of the soldiers. In the late fourth and fifth centuries this office was usually held by a German of barbarian origin, Romanized though he might be.

These changes immediately strengthened the imperial authority. But the elaborate imperial courts, numerous administrative officials, and large mercenary army were very expensive. The emperors needed money and still more money, while the waning economic prosperity of the Empire made the collection of taxes more difficult. To secure a sufficient income, Diocletian instituted a new system of taxation, which was simple, uniform, and efficient from the government's point of view, but deadly in its effect upon the people. It was to be responsible for many of the economic and social ills of the later Empire. Merchants and artisans paid a special and very heavy tax.

Each year the emperors calculated the amount of taxes needed. This sum was divided and subdivided among the various administrative divisions of the Empire until a definite sum was assigned to each municipality. The municipal curia was held responsible for the collection of that sum. The system sounds reasonable enough, but it allowed too many opportunities for graft and oppression on the part of the administrative officials.

Diocletian's system was somewhat modified by his successors, but by and large it remained in force until the middle of the fifth century. The practical working-out of many details was left to Constantine the Great (313-37), who in 324, after several years of civil war between rival Augusti and Caesars, reunited the Empire under his exclusive rule. Diocletian's plan for decentralizing the administration of the Empire and controlling the succession had not worked very well, but the actual division between East and West was growing too strong to be ignored. Constantine himself demonstrated this by founding a new capital at Constantinople in the East. After his death the Empire was again divided, and there were nearly always two emperors thereafter, though it must not be forgotten that the division was solely for administrative purposes. In theory the Empire remained one and united, under two rulers of equal power.

The success of Diocletian's reform of the administration and the army depended on the collection of sufficient taxes to pay for their upkeep. The most important taxes were those on land and on agricultural workers. This tax weighed most heavily on the small landholders and tenant farmers, who either paid the tax directly or had it passed on to them by their landlords in the form of rent. Many of these people, unable to make a living after paying the taxes or heightened rents, were forced to abandon their land; they either drifted to the cities to join the host of unemployed living on the dole, or sought the protection of great landlords who needed workers. As a result a good deal of marginal land was deserted and went out of cultivation, reducing the amount of taxable property. To check this development, which would soon prove disastrous to the imperial income, Constantine issued laws binding the agricultural worker, and his children after him, to the land he worked. The tax on the land and that on the worker were now united and became an hereditary obligation. No matter who owned the land, the workers remained as hereditary tenants, still legally free but unable to leave their land. They were called *coloni.* Slaves could no longer be sold off the land, and as their value as salable property was nullified they were given the partial freedom of the coloni. All farm workers, then, were leveled to the same condition of partial servitude. A series of severe laws punished the *colonus* who left his land as rigorously as though he were a runaway slave. Great numbers of the population were thus forced to give up all hope of changing their economic or social status.

Merchants and artisans in the cities met the same fate. They had to pay a special tax, heavy enough to be ruinous in a time of constant economic depression. Certain necessary trades were being deserted since there was no longer any profit in them. The autocratic emperors could think of no way to improve conditions except to issue new laws forcing the merchant or artisan to continue in his occupation. The workers in each trade formed an hereditary caste. A baker must remain a baker, and all his sons must become bakers. There was no legal escape, even though it might thus become impossible to make a living, and though there might be better opportunities in other occupations.

But of all the people of the Empire, the once well-to-do upper and middle classes of the municipalities, the curiales, suffered most, being reduced to universal and perpetual bankruptcy by the disastrous system of taxation. The curiales had been the mainstay of the flourishing municipal life of the early Empire. Membership in the curia had been an honor eagerly sought. Now it became a ruinous burden, for the curia was made responsible for the collection of all taxes in the municipality. If it could not collect the full amount assigned to it, the members had to make up the deficit—and there usually was a deficit—from their own pockets. To keep the curia filled, the emperors issued strict laws forcing all men possessing sufficient property to enroll in the curial class, and forcing all curiales to take their turn in office. In 336 Constantine made the curial position hereditary. By the beginning of the fifth century men of curial descent were barred from the army, the administration, and the priesthood. They could not leave their cities, even on short trips, without permission; they could not reside in the country; and they could not sell or dispose of their property by will without the permission of the governor of the province. Many were reduced to such despair that they forfeited their property and sought to disguise themselves as coloni on senatorial estates.

The crisis of the Roman Empire leads us to the consideration of one of the great historical issues: what caused the decline and fall of Rome?

Some Views on the Decline of the Roman Empire

Modern historians have often felt themselves to be living and working in a civilization which is in a state of crisis. This has been the case particularly since 1914. Thus, it is not surprising that the crisis of the Roman Empire should prove intriguing to so many modern historical minds. Nor is it surprising that many modern historians have allowed their allegiances and world-views to affect the ways in which they interpret the problems of the fourth and fifth centuries.

The impressive advance of the physical and natural sciences in the middle of the nineteenth century led certain students of the later Roman Empire to apply "scientific" theories to the solution of the problem. For example, it has been suggested that the most important single factor in the crisis of the later Empire was the exhaustion of the once fertile soil of the Western Empire. Another scholar, Ellsworth Huntington, argues that climatic changes in the Far East indirectly caused the collapse of the Western Empire. According to his theory, a drastic decrease in the annual rate of rainfall in northern China led nomadic peoples such as the Huns to move westward. They, in turn, put pressure upon various Germanic nations, and several of these peoples converged upon the already weakened Roman Empire, ultimately destroying it. An argument against the soil theory is that important fifth-century sources give no indication of soil exhaustion (as opposed to erosion and deforestation, which were undoubtedly factors) in Gaul, a key region of the Western Empire. Agricultural problems did, to a great extent, account for the crisis of the Roman Empire, but they may be attributable to absentee landlordism and fiscal abuses. As for Huntington's rainfall theory, an examination of the annual growth rate of trees whose origin dates back to the early Christian era tends to repudiate it. Ancient trees, which should reveal a negative fluctuation in their growth rate during the later Roman period, do not provide such evidence.

Repulsive misuse of the lore of modern science characterizes certain attempts to solve the riddle of the decline of the Roman Empire. The racialist or anthropological interpretation misused biological concepts in order to prove that the crisis of Rome resulted from "racial intermixture" and demographic pollution. Such false conclusions would not be significant except that they have appealed to the prejudices and sensibilities of many scholars and laymen in Germany, England, and America since the turn of the twentieth century. One of the vital aspects of the Roman Empire was its "universalism," the cultural richness which was a product of the contributions of many peoples. The stolid Roman virtues of the early Republic may have indeed have disappeared during the imperial period, but it is more likely that they did so because they had originated in a small city-state. Such virtues were not suited to the burdens of the universal Empire. This interpretation, however, is a far cry from racialism.

"Darwinian" theories have not always been applied in such a vulgar form. The nineteenth-century German historian Otto Seeck believed that the disturbances of the later Empire—civil wars, predatory taxation, overwhelming centralization—caused the destruction of the best elements of the society. Thus, the reversal of the famous prescription, "the survival of the fittest," occurred. Seeck saw in the later Roman Empire the "destruction of the fittest." But Seeck's interpretation was informed by a conservative viewpoint that resulted in part from a hostility toward popular demand for social change in the Germany of Bismarck and William II. Thus, Seeck spoke repeatedly in disparaging terms of the parasitical mobs of the city of Rome and believed the universal citizenship edict of 212 (the Constitutio Antoniana) to be an example of the furtherance of mediocrity through its encouragement by a corrupt, centralized despotism.

Twentieth-century historians have refocused on the agrarian problem as a major factor in the economic and intellectual decline of later Roman civilization. Their work shows that the free peasantry was stronger in the eastern part of the Empire than it was in the western. The free peasantry in Italy had passed through a period of crisis and decline as early as the third and second centuries B.C. This decline presaged a decrease in the absolute numbers of the agrarian population. The decline of the free peasantry affected the agrarian and urban economies of the Roman Empire, particularly in Gaul and Italy. Depopulation of drastic proportions weakened Rome in the west. Scholars also emphasize the more advantageous military position of the Eastern Empire in the face of the barbarian invasions after the third century. There were other reasons why the East did not fall. It had a greater population, and a tradition of large urban trading centers. The administrative division of the Roman Empire late in the third century tended to deprive the West of resources drawn from the eastern provinces of the Empire, resources upon which it had always been dependent. Because of the agrarian crisis and the growing isolation of the overwhelmingly agricultural West, the entire Roman economy was thrown out of focus. The crises confronting the state increased the need for centralization, which in turn increased the demand for taxes. This fact has led some modern historians to conclude that the heavy weight of taxation was a root cause of the economic weakening of the Roman Empire.

In the eighteenth century, Montesquieu had pointed to environmental factors in explaining the decline of Rome, while Edward Gibbon argued that the decline of the Empire was the result of a weakening of ancient Roman virtue, the rise of the Christian religion, and the triumph of barbarian and luxury-oriented mores. Moreover, ever since Fustel de Coulanges began his work on the origins of medieval France a century ago, historians have had to consider the possibility of continuity as well as change when treating the later Roman problem. Fustel argued that "History does not indicate that the Germans replaced Roman mores with new concepts of behavior. They did not display hostility to the cities, to landed estates, nor to the Roman luxury of repast and bath." He showed that the Germanic tribes of the fifth century were not like those mentioned by Tacitus at the end of the first century. They had been greatly decimated by internecine wars but, though they were culturally backward from a Roman point of view, centuries of contact had caused them to look with favor upon the amenities of Roman civilization. Hence, Fustel does not see the collapse of the Roman Empire in the West as an overwhelming cataclysm, but as a political change that strengthened the tendencies toward cultural amalgamation which had existed for centuries. In this process of acculturation, the Roman factor, representing an advanced civilization, was the most important.

A generation later the Austrian historian Alfons Dopsch supported the general conclusions of Fustel, but added to them both a wealth of social and economic data and a more advanced grasp of modern historical methodology. Fustel and Dopsch may both have overemphasized the elements of social, intellectual, and economic continuity between the later Roman and early medieval periods, but their work has proved a fruitful antidote to the older tendency of historians to assume a sharp break between the two eras.

Rome was indeed the educator of barbarian peoples, and it performed its task well, as we shall see in examining the barbarian invasions.

Suggestions for Further Reading

M. Chambers, ed., *The Fall of Rome: Can It Be Explained?** (1957). Selections from the writings of various historians who have advanced differing views on the reasons for the fall of Rome.

E. Gibbon, *The History of the Decline and Fall of the Roman Empire** (originally 1776–1788; best edition, J. B. Bury, ed., 7 vols., 1896–1900). The great eighteenth-century classic, still worth reading for its style and viewpoint.

*Available in a paperback edition.

Gibbon felt that Christianity was a major causal factor in the decline of Rome.

A. H. M. Jones, *The Decline of the Ancient World* (1966). A thorough, factual survey of the later Roman empire by a leading scholar in the field.

A. H. M. Jones, *The Later Roman Empire,* 2 vols. (1964). An immensely detailed study. Jones' book just cited is to some extent a condensation of this major work.

M. Rostovtzeff, *The Social and Economic History of the Roman Empire* (1957). A masterful work by a great historian. Rostovtzeff, a refugee from Russia, tended to see analogies with twentieth-century social classes and problems in his studies of the ancient world.

The Germanic Peoples Enter European History

5

We cannot impose religion, because no one can be compelled to believe against his will.

THEODORIC THE OSTROGOTH

The Early Germans

Beyond the frontiers of the Empire lay the barbarian world, alien and sometimes a menace to Roman civilization. Roman statesmen could never forget for long the danger threatening from the north, where restless and warlike German tribes milled along the Rhine-Danube border. Time and again, since before the days of Julius Caesar, the legions had been called upon to expel barbarian invaders. Until the fourth century they were always successful, but the task became increasingly difficult, for the Empire was rapidly weakening as a result of the general decline. Meanwhile, great numbers of Germans had entered the Empire peacefully, in small groups, to serve in the army or work on the large estates. Having settled within the Empire, these barbarian immigrants were, in the course of time, more or less Romanized, though as their numbers increased they undoubtedly helped to lower the general level of Roman civilization. But if the Roman melting pot could assimilate a slow barbarian infiltration, it could not absorb whole nations, once the barbarians succeeded in making an armed invasion. Invasions began in 376, when the Visigoths crossed the Danube frontier, setting an example for other tribes all along the northern border. In wave after wave, they broke across the shattered frontier; within a century the Western Empire was shattered. This added to Roman culture a second ingredient of medieval civilization: the influence of the Germanic peoples, who from this time on were a dominant force in western Europe.

The original home of the Germans or Teutons was, in all probability, the northern part of modern Germany near the Baltic coast and the southern portion of the Scandinavian peninsula. In Caesar's time they occupied the entirety of land he knew beyond the Rhine. Closer contact with Roman commerce now brought them better tools and weapons, making it easier to maintain life, and the population thereafter increased more rapidly.

Our knowledge of the early Germans before they impinged upon the Roman Republic, and thus made their first tumultuous entrance onto the stage of history, is necessarily vague and uncertain. It is derived from the field of archaeology rather than history. Yet from the implements and weapons excavated at tombs and village sites we can learn something of their daily life and trace the general trend of their civilization. For actual historical information we are indebted chiefly to a brief account in Caesar's *De Bello Gallico* and a fuller and more circumstantial account of their manners and customs in the *Germania,* written by the Roman historian Tacitus in A.D. 98. The reliability of the *Germania* has been the subject of endless debate. But even if we accept it as reliable, it must not be forgotten that nearly three centuries of contact with Roman civilization and development of social and political customs passed between the date of Tacitus' work and the first successful invasions of the Empire. Further information may be gleaned from the German laws, written down later but based on ancient custom. The mass of Anglo-Saxon, German, and Scandinavian folk literature, too, in its earliest origins dates back to the period of the invasions and supplies us with valuable material with which to reconstruct the characteristics of the Germans of that period.

The family, as in most societies, was the most important social unit of the tribe, but there also existed a larger kinship group, the sib or clan, composed of families originally related by blood ties. Members of the clan felt a mutual responsibility for the welfare of their fellows, avenged the death of their kinsmen, and supported them in lawsuits and in battle. This clannish loyalty was necessary for the protection of the individual at a time when central government was loosely and ineffectively organized. Distinct from these family and kinship groups was the *comitatus,* a band of warriors who voluntarily bound themselves to a chief renowned for his courage and skill in war. These "comrades" were attached to their chief by a strong bond of personal loyalty; they fought at his bidding and considered it a disgrace to survive him if he was killed in battle. And in return he supplied them with arms, clothing, food, and opportunities for plunder.

During the period of migration, many of the tribes united to form larger groups. The dangers which attended the mass migration of a whole people

A mounted German warrior dating from about 700. This relief is a good example of early medieval Germanic art.

demanded a more highly centralized government than had been needed in the early days. Before the age of the invasions nearly all the Germanic peoples were ruled by kings, with the aid of an advisory council of chieftains. The development of kingship was by no means uniform among the tribes, and the powers of the king were probably not clearly defined, depending instead on the character of the individual king and on circumstances of stress or danger.

The social and political ideas of the early Germans were largely personal, involving family relationships and personal loyalties to a chief or king. The concept of a territorial state as a political entity had not arisen among them. This personal orientation is reflected in their laws, which dealt mostly with injuries or obligations between individuals. These laws, moreover, were not the product of legislation and precedents established by the decisions of judges, like those of the Romans, but were made up of immemorial customs of the tribe handed down from generation to generation, though not put into written form until after the invasions. A crime was considered not an offense against the state, but an injury to an individual, for which the law gave him a means of procuring satisfaction. A trial or lawsuit, then, was a contest between two individuals, with the court merely acting as arbiter and imposing the customary sentence. Its principal function, indeed, was to serve as a substitute for private vengeance, which might initiate an endless blood feud. No attempt was made to sift evidence, as in the Roman courts, in arriving at a decision. Instead, the court appealed to the gods—or, after the Germans were converted to Christianity, to God—to decide the issue. Normally the defendant was allowed to clear himself by taking a solemn oath of innocence, frequently supplemented by the oaths of friends. If he or any of his oath-helpers or compurgators, as they were called, hesitated or made the slightest slip in reciting the exact words of the oath, he was declared guilty on the assumption that God would not permit a guilty man to perjure himself successfully. When the oath was judged insufficient to prove innocence, the accused man had usually to clear himself by undergoing an ordeal.

The penalty imposed on the guilty was usually a fine paid as compensation to the injured party or, if he had been killed, to his family. The amount to be paid for killing a man, the *wergeld* or man-money, or for any of a great variety of injuries, was fixed by custom and varied widely with the rank of the injured man. Those collections of law which have survived are consequently valuable evidence regarding the relative status of different social classes. Crude as this judicial procedure was, it had the virtue of simplicity, and in the general barbarization of the Empire that followed the invasions it gradually replaced the more rational and sophisticated practice of the Roman courts and continued to administer such justice as there was in western Europe for centuries.

The Migrations Before 376

The wandering of the peoples, or *Völkerwanderung* as German scholars call the great migrations into the Empire after 376, had in reality begun long before that date. For centuries the increase in population had driven German tribes to seek more fertile or less thickly populated lands, while the pressure of expansion from the interior of Germany piled up the southern tribes against the barrier of the Roman frontier.

As we have said, the press of population outside the frontiers of the Empire caused great numbers of Germans to drift across the border to seek employment in the Roman army or settle peacefully in the rich and protected provinces. By the time of Constantine, the barbarian element in the army had begun to predominate over the Roman, and during the subsequent two centuries, in the West at least, the imperial soldiers and officers, including those of the highest rank, were mostly German. Of those who entered the Empire as farmers, some were given land in deserted regions by the state, while others became tenants on large private estates. In either case they swelled the class of half-servile agricultural workers. Certain entire tribes were allowed to enter as *foederati*, or allies, and were given grants of land within the frontier on condition that they aid in repelling further invasions. This gradual infiltration of barbarian elements into the Empire helped to ease the shock of the great invasions, for the Roman provincials were already acquainted with German customs and the invaders found many people of their own type, partly Romanized, already settled in the provinces.

By the middle of the third century, the Goths had completed their long migration from the Baltic shores and had divided into two separate units, the Visigoths or West Goths and the Ostrogoths or East Goths. The river Dniester formed the boundary between them. The Visigoths were brought into closest touch with the Empire, which lay just across the Danube from them. During the first three-quarters of the fourth century, except for a brief period, 367–369, the Visigoths were on peaceful terms with the Romans, and a considerable trade sprang up between them.

It was during this quiet interlude that Christianity was first introduced among the Goths, gaining great numbers of converts. Credit for this belongs in large measure to Bishop Ulfilas, who began forty years of active missionary work among the Visigoths in 341. He was not himself of pure Gothic origin, being descended from a Christian family of Cappadocia taken prisoner by the Goths in the preceding century, but was a Goth at heart. As part of his missionary activity, he translated the Bible into the Gothic tongue, inventing for the purpose an alphabet modeled on the Greek and thereby laying the foundation for a written Germanic literature. Hitherto the Germans had had no script except crude runic letters, suitable only for carving brief inscriptions on tools and weapons. The translation of as large a work as the Bible into a language which had no tradition of writing must have involved immense labor. The gentle bishop quietly omitted the more bellicose tales from the Book of Kings as an unnecessary stimulant to a people already too prone to war. Modern philologists owe a great debt to Ulfilas for this specimen of one of the Germanic dialects three centuries older than any other that has survived. From the Visigoths Christianity spread before the end of the fourth century to the Ostrogoths, Vandals, and other Germanic nations. The Christianity they adopted was heretical. Almost all the barbarian invaders of the Empire were either pagans or heretics, which further strained their relations with the orthodox Romans among whom they settled.

The final invasion of the Empire by the Visigoths was not undertaken of their own volition or with the aim of conquest, but was forced upon them by fear of the Huns, a horde of Asiatic barbarians new to Europe. For centuries these

Mongolian nomads had driven their herds in yearly migrations from the northern to the southern steppes of central Asia, following the seasonal changes in pasture. Forced at last by some disturbance among the peoples of the interior of Asia to seek new lands, they moved westward into Europe, falling upon the flank and rear of the Ostrogothic kingdom about 371. Short, broad-shouldered, and bow-legged from riding, with yellow skin and hideous, beardless faces marked by deep scars inflicted in childhood, unspeakably dirty—thus did the Gothic historian Jordanes later describe these fierce and untamed savages, who seemed more barbarous to the Goth than did the Germanic barbarian to the civilized Roman. The Huns lived, fought, ate, and even slept on horseback. They were far more mobile than the German tribes, and their ability to cover great distances in an incredibly short time led the Goths to exaggerate their numbers. By 375 they had conquered the Ostrogoths. The following year the Visigoths, after a vain attempt to check them at the Dniester, turned in panic to seek protection within the Roman frontier.

The Great Invasions

In 376, when the Visigoths petitioned for permission to cross the Danube and settle within the Empire, the imperial government had been seriously weakened

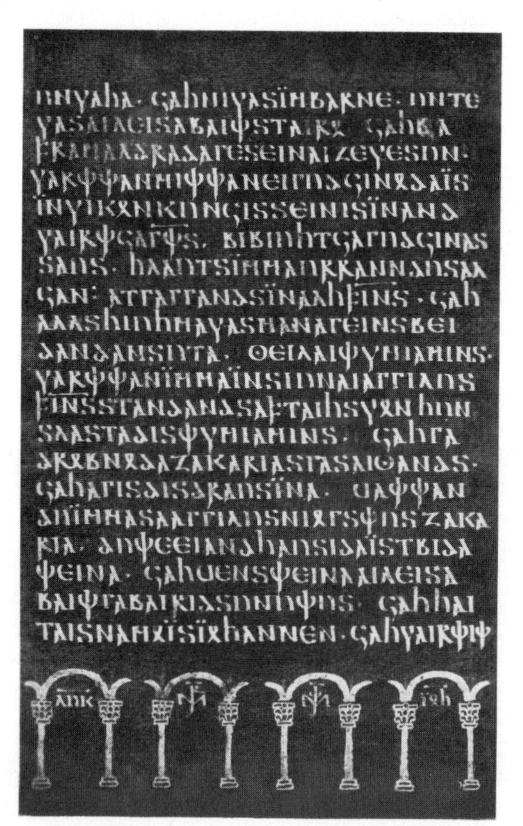

A page from the New Testament in Gothic translated by Ulfilas. The lettering of this manuscript is in silver.

by the recent death of Valentinian I, the able and energetic emperor of the West and the dominating spirit in the imperial partnership. His younger brother Valens, the Eastern emperor, was thus left to confront the crisis alone, for he would not accept the guidance of his nephew, the youthful but brilliant Gratian, who had succeeded his father in the West. The dilemma presented by the Goths might well have troubled a stronger man than the cautious and vacillating Valens. To refuse their petition was to risk a serious war; to grant it was to admit a potential enemy to the heart of the Empire. After a long, and to the Goths maddening, delay he decided to admit them on condition that they surrender their arms, give hostages, and settle as foederati. All might have been well had these terms, humiliating though they were to a warlike people, been strictly enforced. But the corrupt and avaricious officials who supervised the transportation of the barbarians across the Danube neglected to secure their arms, while at the same time plundering them and taking many of their young men and women as slaves. Moreover, no provision was made for feeding the newcomers. Within a year the Visigoths, enraged by this treatment and made desperate by famine, broke their oath of allegiance and set out to plunder Thrace.

The clash of arms culminated in the Battle of Adrianople (378), in which the emperor Valens was killed and his army cut to pieces. The Romans lost, largely because of the lack of military coordination with the West. Even more decisive was the triumph of Gothic cavalry over Roman infantry at Adrianople, which established cavalry as the dominant force in European warfare for a thousand years.

The ill omens of the day were not only political and military. The Romans saw mystical and religious signs of the end of the world. The last oracle of the Delphic god prophesied about Rome to the emperor Julian the Apostate (killed in 363) that "the water springs that spoke are quenched and dead." The ancient Olympic Games were celebrated for the last time in 393. Contemporaries report that the reign of Honorius, which began in 395, was noteworthy for the number of ominous eclipses and comets that appeared in the sky. The day of the twelfth and last vulture, symbolizing the end of Roman power, was seen by those who followed omens on earth and in heaven.

Contact between Romans and barbarians in the fifth century was not always hostile or ominous. The Germanic peoples, at least in the beginning, generally wished to be regarded and employed as Roman foederati. Later, in times of triumph, they tried to achieve the status of "protectors" of Roman public, and sometimes private, land. This type of settlement, when formally offered by the imperial government, was known as *hospitalitas.* The Germanic people sometimes received one-third of the public land and in some cases two-thirds. This did not necessarily mean the displacement of residual Roman landholders, though in areas where there had been intensive and destructive military action for a long period of time, it is conceivable that most, if not all, of these landholders had fled. Their land would thereupon be seized by the conquering Germanic "ally." It is indeed remarkable how rapidly some of the Germanic peoples adopted the amenities of Roman civilization, even while staying aloof from the native Roman or Romanized population.

Certain barbarian peoples were more ferocious and formidable than others. The Vandals and the Huns come to mind in particular. The seizure of Rome by the Vandals in 455, for example, was marked by greater devastation than that done by the Goths in 410. The Huns' major raid into Gaul in the year 451, culminating in the Battle of Châlons, terrified the Romanized residents of that area. At other times, social conditions, particularly in agriculture, may have been so bad that the Romanized coloni welcomed the barbarian intruder.

By the middle of the fifth century, the Franks were threatening parts of northeastern Gaul, and Burgundians and Visigoths had settled in the south of that land. The Visigoths had conquered Spain; the Vandals sacked Rome in 455. Various barbaric chieftains fought for supremacy in Italy. Roman forces evacuated Britain early in the fifth century, leaving the Romanized Celtic population of that land prey to increasingly forceful raids by northern European peoples such as the Angles, Saxons, and Jutes.

Emperors still ruled in the West, in name if not in fact, until 476 or 480. In 475 the last Western Roman emperor recognized by Constantinople, Julius Nepos, was deposed by his barbarian *magister militum,* Orestes. Nepos was replaced by the son of Orestes, satirically named Romulus Augustulus, a diminutive combined version of the name of the founder of Rome and the name of the founder of the Roman Empire. He was never recognized as legitimate emperor by Constantinople. In 476 another barbarian military chieftain, Odoacer, displaced Romulus Augustulus, and at some point adopted the title *rex* (king). The East continued to recognize the authority of Julius Nepos, who had fled to

BARBARIAN KINGDOMS AT THE END OF THE FIFTH CENTURY

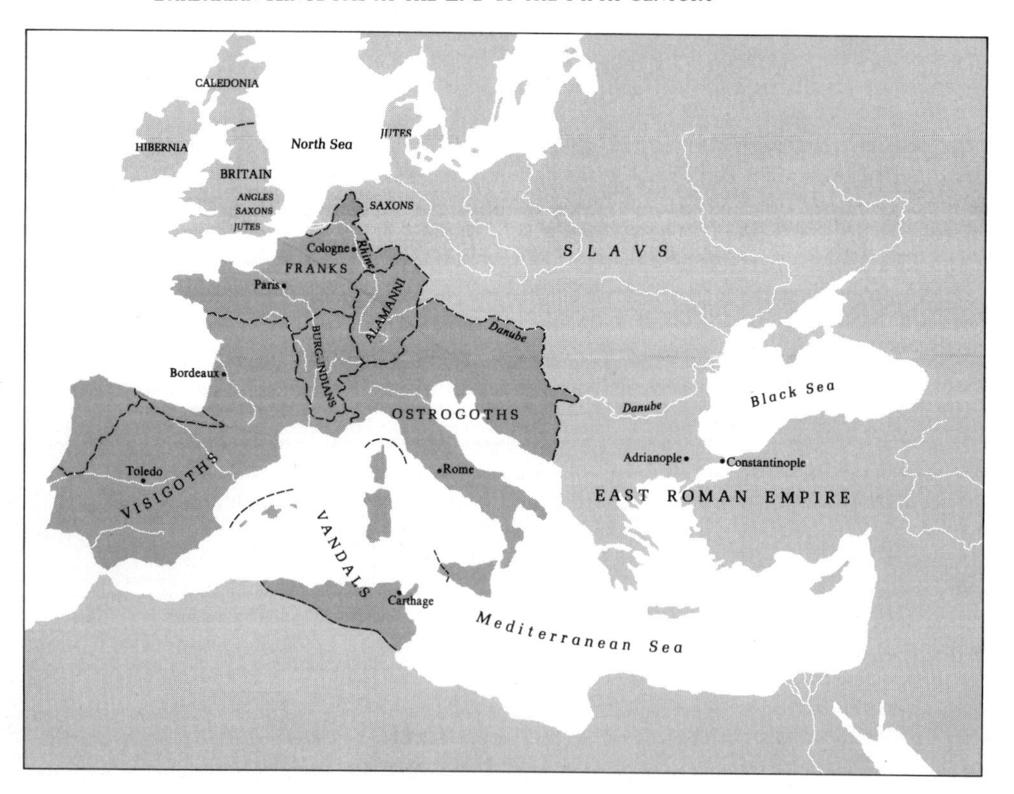

Dalmatia, but in 480 Odoacer tracked him down and killed him. The political authority of the Roman Empire in the West, a fiction for some years, thus ceased to exist even in name.

The last century of Roman rule in western Europe was marked by the rise and fall of titanic figures: Stilicho, Aëtius, Attila the Hun, and Odoacer. In the nineteenth century, this period—characterized by migrations and the founding of kingdoms which, in however vague and distant a sense, were to be the predecessors of the medieval European polities—inspired many poets, historians, and composers of operas. Of greatest concern to us, however, is the manner in which Roman civilization reacted to the new barbarian domination. Let us take as a case study the Ostrogothic kingdom in Italy in the early sixth century.

The Ostrogoth Kingdom in Italy

After thirteen years of undisputed rule in Italy, Odoacer, like so many of the emperors whose place he had taken, found his position threatened by a new barbarian invasion. The Ostrogoths had freed themselves from the overlordship of the Huns after the death of Attila and had migrated into the Balkan provinces of the Eastern Empire, where they alternately ravaged the country and fought for the emperor as foederati. Under the vigorous leadership of their king, Theodoric, they became a serious menace to the Empire, almost equally dangerous as friends and as enemies. Theodoric had passed most of his youth in Constantinople as a hostage. He had gained a thorough knowledge of Roman institutions, which revealed to him the weakness of the Empire, though at the same time it aroused in him a great respect for Roman traditions and civilization. Oddly enough, he seems never to have learned to write; he traced his name with the aid of a gold plate in which the letters had been cut. In 488, the Emperor Zeno sought to rid himself of a dangerous ally by commissioning Theodoric to invade Italy and suppress Odoacer. After some delay, the Ostrogoths reached Italy in 489. Odoacer was defeated in battle and took refuge in the impregnable city of Ravenna. For nearly three years the Goths besieged the city in vain. At last Theodoric resorted to treachery. Having tricked Odoacer into negotiating a peace treaty, he assassinated him. This typical act completed the conquest of Italy.

For thirty-three years Italy enjoyed the advantages of a just and moderate government under the Ostrogothic king. Despite occasional reversions to barbaric cruelty and treachery, Theodoric (493–526) proved a worthy successor to the best of the Roman emperors. We may discount the effusions of court poets, but the estimate of Procopius, the historian of the Eastern Empire, may be taken at face value: "His manner of ruling over his subjects was worthy of a great emperor; for he maintained justice, made good laws, protected his country from invasion, and gave proof of extraordinary prudence and valor." He gave proof, too, of unusual wisdom and tact in handling a delicate situation, for although he was to all intents and purposes the independent ruler of Italy, his constitutional position was rather ambiguous. He was the legitimate king of his Ostrogothic people, but as far as the Italians were concerned his position was that of a nominal agent of the emperor, who had conferred upon him the title of Patrician. Realizing that to do so strengthened the legitimacy of his government without curtailing his real power, Theodoric continued to recognize the formal superiority of the Eastern emperor.

The dual character of Theodoric's government arose from the fact that he ruled two distinct peoples without making any attempt to encourage fusion. The Goths had appropriated about one-third of the land (of the public land, according to some scholars) and had settled quietly among the resident Romans. Each people retained its own legal and judicial system, though cases involving both Romans and Goths were apparently tried in the Gothic courts. The status of the two peoples was strongly influenced by the fact that the army was purely Gothic. The Goths remained the military caste; their courts were military courts; and their land was granted to them according to late Roman custom as federate soldiers who were serving the state.

The civil government was just as purely Roman. Theodoric made no change in Roman administration or laws insofar as they affected Roman citizens, and all civil offices were filled by native Italians. The old imperial officers, the consuls, and the Senate persisted with remarkably little change and were among the most loyal supporters of the Gothic king. Even the difference in religion between the heretical Goth and the orthodox Roman, though it caused some friction, seems not to have placed any serious strain upon their relations. Theodoric made no attempt to force his own religion on his subjects; instead, he maintained a policy of absolute toleration. "We cannot," he wrote through his secretary Cassiodorus, "impose religion, because no one can be compelled to believe against his will."

Perhaps the greatest change made by the Gothic king was the introduction of peace, security, and revived prosperity in Italy during his long reign. Agriculture and commerce flourished as they had not for a century. Justice was administered with greater firmness and integrity. Long-neglected harbors, aqueducts, and public buildings were restored and new ones were erected. Italy was still far removed from the good old days of Roman prosperity, but was better off than it had been or was to be again for centuries to come. Unfortunately, Theodoric's work died with him. Factional strife broke out soon after his death, and by 555 the Ostrogothic kingdom in Italy had been crushed by the armies of the Eastern emperor, Justinian.

Suggestions for Further Reading

W. C. Bark, *Origins of the Medieval World** (1958). A challenging series of essays [AHA, 172, in part].

E. S. Duckett, *The Gateway to the Middle Ages** (1938). A highly readable introduction to the early Middle Ages, using the biographical method in a pleasant way.

A. R. Lewis, *Emerging Medieval Europe: A.D. 400-1000** (1967). A fine synthesis, reflecting the author's interest in trade and commerce.

F. Lot, *The End of the Ancient World and the Beginnings of the Middle Ages**

*Available in a paperback edition.

(1931). Analysis of Mediterranean and Germanic civilizations from the third to the sixth century [AHA, 152, in part].

J. M. Wallace-Hadrill, *The Barbarian West** (1961). A concise, beautifully written study of early medieval Europe, one which captures the turbulence and drama of the centuries between Alaric and Charlemagne.

The Rise of the Christian West

TWO

The Christian Church

6

> The brethren ought to be occupied at specified times in manual labor, and at other fixed hours in holy reading.
>
> SAINT BENEDICT OF NURSIA

The Spiritual Crisis of Roman Culture

The gradual loss of hope and confidence that characterized late classical pagan life and culture in the third and fourth centuries was accompanied by the decay of the old official religions. These religions emphasized the duties of the citizen to the state. They proved vulnerable to the spread of mystery religions originating in the Near East, which offered spiritual comfort in this world and the hope of a happier life after death. Before the end of the Republic, the old pagan religion of Rome was losing its hold upon the educated classes. The emperors from Augustus to Marcus Aurelius strove to revive the official cults, but with little real success, and thereafter they became increasingly empty formalities. Even before the disastrous third century, when public and private calamities caused people to search more eagerly than ever for supernatural comfort, the twilight had begun to settle over Olympus. It was soon to darken into night, though the old gods long maintained a shadowy existence in official practice and literary tradition.

For the majority of the people of the Empire, the vacuum left by the decay of classical paganism was filled by mystery religions, which had spread through the Hellenistic East during the three centuries before Christ and which began to penetrate the West in the last years of the Roman Republic. Thereafter, aided by the unification of the Mediterranean world under the Empire, they spread rapidly through the western provinces, following the lines of trade and the march of the legions. By the third century, they were the dominant religious force in the West as well as the East. The most important of the mystery religions were those of the Great Mother (Magna Mater) from Asia Minor, Isis from Egypt, and Mithra from Persia.

Despite a great variety of ceremony and belief, the mystery religions had many characteristics in common, and all satisfied much the same human needs. Each cult centered upon a divine savior, but all recognized the existence of a supreme divine force, which might be worshipped through the medium of other deities as well. Their primary appeal was that they satisfied the universal desire for individual salvation. They offered purification from sin and freedom from the sense of guilt, and promised immortality to those who had been initiated into the mystery. Through participation in their sacred rites, the initiate was brought into mystic union with the divine being and thereby transcended the miseries of mortal life. The ceremonies themselves, performed by a professional priesthood, had a strong appeal for men and women wearied by a drab and hopeless existence. Since they placed major emphasis on immortality rather than on life in this world, they did little to encourage the vigorous performance of worldly tasks, though in this respect Mithraism—popular in the army—was a partial exception. Some historians have regarded the spread of the mystery religions as one of the causes of the decay of the ancient civilization. It would be more accurate to say that people turned to these religions because they had lost confidence in the Roman system.

The Origin and Spread of Christianity

As the old pagan Roman Empire decayed, there grew in its midst a new spiritual empire, which in the course of time was to replace it in the West and to carry on in western Europe the Roman tradition of unity in administration, law, language, and culture through the long chaotic centuries of the Middle Ages. Christianity was the one vital force and the Church the one living organism in the Roman world during the last two centuries of the Western Empire.

The Roman Empire was no more than two generations old when the foundations of the Christian religion were laid by the teaching of Jesus of Nazareth, whom his followers hailed as Christ, the son of the living God. Christ and his earliest disciples were Jews, and Christianity inherited from Judaism the exclusive, monotheistic belief in one God and the preoccupation with moral and ethical problems that were the unique characteristics of the ancient Hebrew religion. But, although rooted in Judaism, Christianity as a statement or synthesis was original, not only in the belief that Christ was the long-awaited Messiah, the savior of mankind through whose redeeming sacrifice the faithful might obtain eternal salvation, but also in the quality of its ethical teaching, a quality perhaps best represented by Christ's Sermon on the Mount (Matthew, chapters 5-7).

Mithra, god of the sun, killing a bull. The ceremonial slaughtering of a bull was part of the cult of Mithra, whose worship was widespread among the Roman legions.

As the new religion spread to the Jews beyond Palestine and to the other peoples of the Empire, its development was influenced by Greek philosophy and by some of the concepts and practices of the mystery cults. Saint Paul, who was well-educated and trained in Greek philosophy, was the most influential figure in the first period of expansion, both for the contributions he made to the growth of Christian theology and for the incentive he gave to missionary work among the Gentiles. It was he, more than any of the other apostles, who freed Christianity from Jewish national exclusiveness and made it a world religion.

Christianity inherited the Hebrew Scriptures as a repository of divinely revealed truth, and to these, during the century or so after the death of Christ (about A.D. 33), were added a number of new and distinctively Christian works, which came to be regarded as the New Testament. It is characteristic of the increasing cosmopolitanism of Christianity that these Christian Scriptures were written in Greek, the international language of the Hellenistic world. To the first four books of the New Testament, the Gospels ascribed to Matthew, Mark, Luke, and John, we owe most of what we know about the life and teaching of Christ. Although probably written between the years 60 and 110, they were evidently founded upon a well-established oral tradition. The remainder of the New Testament, except for the final book, the visionary Book of Revelation, is composed of pastoral letters. Nearly half of these are from Paul and were written between the years 50 and 62. These twenty-one epistles, which discuss problems of doctrine, ethics, and church organization, contributed profoundly to the development of a systematic theology and to the conception of a universal Christian Church.

For three centuries, Christianity spread slowly; it was apparently only one, and by no means the most popular, of a number of cults of eastern origin. But slow as its progress was at first, it gained ground steadily, and by the middle of the third century there were well-organized Christian communities in every city of the Empire. The fact that the new religion was long regarded by outsiders as no more than a fanatical Jewish sect undoubtedly hindered its growth. The exclusive monotheism of the Jews, as well as their persistently rebellious attitude toward the imperial government, had made them unpopular.

The Jews had had a stormy history for a thousand years. In recent centuries, they had been dominated first by a Hellenized Eastern despotism; then, in the middle of the first century B.C., their former territory was conquered by the Roman general Pompey the Great. There were many splits within the Jewish community and hierarchy. Hellenic culture, and even religious influence, had been strong among the Jews since the fourth century B.C., and the revolt of the Jewish Maccabees in the second century B.C. had been a protest against such alien influences. Most Jewish people were united in a common hatred of foreign oppression. When occupied by foreign powers, religion was the focal point of their social and national existence. Thus, Jews revolted in great numbers against Roman domination twice during the duration of the Empire: once in the period A.D. 66–70 and again three generations later. When Jesus was a young boy in Galilee, rumors were rife in Judaea of expected messiahs who would lead the Jewish people in a final revolt against "Babylon"—that is, against Rome—throwing off the foreign yoke and bringing about the promised land for the Jews in this world. Rome was suspicious of such ideas insofar as they endangered the security of the Roman position in Syria and Palestine.

The Christians, while breaking with the national exclusiveness of the Jews, were also rigidly monotheistic. Their refusal to participate in the official cults or to recognize the validity of other religions antagonized both government officials and devotees of the mystery cults. Moreover, Christianity spread most rapidly at first among the underprivileged classes, including slaves, and was regarded as socially disreputable. The fact that Christians held their meetings in secrecy also aroused the suspicion of government officials and enabled their enemies to circulate wild stories ascribing to them horrible orgiastic rites.

Yet, despite all the disadvantages under which it labored, there were elements in Christianity which made it irresistible. The figure of Christ loomed large in the early Church. His followers had as the central fact of their religion a personal savior, who supplied that connecting link between man and God for which the philosophers and the devotees of the pagan cults were blindly groping. This faith in a personal savior, whom his first disciples had known in the flesh and whose words they reported, made possible a conviction of the reality of salvation, the expiation of sin, and the immortality of the soul (all questions that obsessed the mind of the ancient world) far greater than was possible for adherents of the mythological pagan or mystery cults. At the same time, Christianity gave people hope for the future, not only for themselves as individuals but also for the world. Where the pagan looked back with nostalgic longing to a mythical golden age, the Christian, especially in these first centuries, looked forward with confident expectation to a future golden age when the second coming of Christ would herald the establishment of the Kingdom of God on earth. The closely knit organization of the Church, too, which bound together Christians from all parts of the Empire in bonds of brotherhood, gave it an advantage over the mystery religions, which never attempted more than local organization. Finally, Christian ethics and morals, difficult though they were for the pagan to accept, bore fruit that could not be ignored in the admirable lives led by the early Christians. Nor could the pagans fail to see that they had peace of mind, hope, and certainty, strong enough to carry them through the fires of persecution, when for the rest of the world there was no peace, hope was dying, and certainty unattainable.

Persecution and Triumph

Christianity as a religion and the Church as an association were banned by the imperial government as soon as they became strong enough to attract the attention of the emperors. About the year 111, Emperor Trajan issued a rescript to provincial governors instructing them to prosecute those openly charged with adherence to the new religion, but neither to seek them out nor to continue prosecution if they were willing to take part in the ceremonies of the official cult. This rescript may be taken as an adequate definition of the imperial policy for the following century and a half. Christianity was not a legal religion and its members might be punished even by death, but there was no general or systematic attempt to suppress them. The initiative was left to the provincial governors, who enforced the law with more or less severity as they chose. By the middle of the third century, however, conditions had changed and reforming emperors took stronger action.

One may well ask why the imperial government, usually so tolerant of all religions, should have maintained so hostile an attitude toward Christianity over a period of two centuries. Yet there was reason enough, and from their own point of view the emperors were amply justified. Christianity was at odds with the whole spirit of Roman civilization and imperial government. The most serious specific charges brought against the Christians were that they were stubborn and consistent law-breakers, that they refused to discharge the duties of citizens toward the state, and that they were organized in illegal, seditious societies. These charges were well founded. Christians, strict monotheists as they were, were forbidden to take part in the emperor-worship which was the patriotic duty of all citizens. A Christian could not accept public office or serve in the army without violating his principles, as both demanded participation in certain official and, to the Christian, idolatrous ceremonies. The attitude of Christian men and women toward the whole governmental system, so closely bound up with paganism, was one of suspicion if not actual hatred, and in any case they felt that they owed their first loyalty to a higher fatherland than the worldly Empire.

Such an attitude in individuals was sufficiently dangerous, but it was made more objectionable by the compact and efficient organization of the Church. In nearly every community the Christians had a strong corporate organization under recognized bishops. They were in constant communication with other churches throughout the Empire. Christianity was becoming a state within and opposed to the Empire which no autocratic ruler could afford to ignore. As their numbers increased, especially after the beginning of the third century when they were joined by many members of the upper classes, the Christians became an ever greater menace to the state.

During the third century, the Christians were alternately persecuted and tolerated, according to the policy of the various emperors. From each persecution they emerged with numbers greatly diminished but their organization still intact, and at the first sign of toleration, the apostates—as deserters were called—returned and with them came new converts, won over by the example of the martyrs. Despite persecution, Christianity was growing stronger and more popular. It was also becoming more inimical to the government and hence more dangerous. The last and most thorough attempt to stamp it out was begun in 303 by Diocletian, the great reformer and reorganizer of the Empire, and was continued by his successors until 311. They succeeded only in proving that the Christians could not be crushed.

Diocletian's abdication in 305 was followed by years of bitter civil strife. By 312 there were four rival emperors, of whom one was Constantine the Great. Supported only by the legions of Gaul and Britain, he was the least powerful of the four. His rival in the West was Maxentius, who held Italy, Spain, and Africa, while Licinius and Maximianus divided the East between them. His position was very uncertain, but he was able to form an alliance with Licinius to defeat their respective opponents in the West and East. Like Constantine, Licinius had taken a neutral stand during the most recent persecution, while Maxentius and Maximianus had actively oppressed the Christians. Gathering his legions, Constantine marched swiftly into Italy, staking his whole career on the chance of victory against greatly superior forces. It was probably during that daring march that he decided to seek the support of the Christians. At any rate, to that period belongs the story, so variously interpreted, of his vision of a fiery cross in the sky and the words *Hoc vince* ("By this conquer"), which he took as his standard. At Saxa Rubra, a few miles from Rome, he met the army of Maxentius, destroyed it completely, and became sole emperor of the West.

The following year Constantine met his colleague Licinius, who had also been successful, at Milan, and there issued an edict of general and complete toleration of all religions including Christianity. Licinius was unwilling to go farther than that, but in 323 Constantine defeated him and united the whole Empire under his rule. From that time on Constantine's attitude toward the Christians became steadily more favorable, until he was finally baptized into the faith a few days before his death in 337. He took no action against paganism, but his patronage of the Church set Christianity well on its way to becoming the state religion.

Christianity was but one of the significant new religious currents prevalent in the last centuries of the Western Roman Empire, and its eventual triumph could not have been foreseen in the third century except by very far-sighted individuals. We do know of a marked and common tendency toward monotheistic belief in the minds of the Roman elite from the third century onward. The fate of traditional Roman religion, even in its Hellenized form, was closely linked with the fate of the Empire. As the Empire entered a period of troubles in the third century, official religion seems to have declined, at least insofar as it held the religious allegiance of great masses of people. There was also during this time a marked tendency toward syncretism—that is, a search for a comforting, all-encompassing world-view that by its very eclectic nature drew upon not one religion but several. Late in the third century, emperors such as Aurelian (270-275) began to invoke *sol invictus,* the unconquered sun, a symbol of the oneness and totality of the universe, in their prayers and on their coins. That too was a manifestation of the hunger for monotheism in a time of crisis for a polytheistic Empire. It is against the background of this crisis of belief and confidence that Constantine's religious policy and conversion should be studied.

That Constantine's policy was inspired to any significant degree by religious motives seems most unlikely. He was no doubt drawn toward the idea of monotheism, as were so many intelligent pagans, and in his later years he came to consider Christianity its truest expression. But his action was that of a keen and far-sighted statesman rather than a convert. The Christians were still a minority in 312 (probably not more than one-tenth of the population of the Empire), but they were a very determined and well-organized minority, settled for the most part in the cities and wielding far more influence than their numbers would indicate. Constantine had seen the failure of Diocletian's attempt to crush them. Where Diocletian had failed, he himself could have little hope of success; and if the Christians could not be crushed, it would be better to have them as allies than as enemies. In 312 Constantine had needed the support of the Christians against Maxentius, and after 323, when he became emperor of both East and West, he needed the aid of any organized force that would help to hold the Empire together. The compact organization of the Christian Church appealed strongly to Constantine's political sense. It had shown its power in the days of persecution, when it had threatened to disrupt the state. Now it might be equally effective in helping to unify and preserve the Empire.

Church and State: The Struggle Against Heresy and Paganism

The fourth century was a period of astounding growth in the Christian Church. The century opened with the persecution of the Christians, still a small minority of the population, by a pagan emperor. At its close, Christianity was the sole official religion of the Empire, claiming at least the formal adherence of the great majority of the population, and protected by a Christian emperor who issued laws persecuting pagans and all who departed in any way from the accepted doctrines of the state church.

But this rapid growth did not represent pure gain to the Church. The influx of great numbers of the indifferent and self-seeking inevitably lowered the general level of morality and religious zeal in the Church, and at the same time introduced non-Christian elements into its doctrine and practice. Before the Edict of Milan, the Christians had been a select group of earnest believers prepared to sacrifice a good deal, though not all were prepared to face death, for their faith. Now it was to the advantage of all to join the triumphant religion. The easy conversion of those who were merely pursuing the line of least resistance or of personal advantage signified no very vital change in their style of life or thought. The cults of saints and martyrs sprang up to take the place of the many local gods of pagan mythology.

The West, less accustomed to the Greek language and philosophical tradition, was long to pride itself on its orthodoxy. As early as the sixth century, the Western Church took pride in the fact that "it had never erred." While there occurred an occasional lapse, error was usually due to alien political influence, sometimes stemming from pressure by an Eastern emperor like Justinian (527–565). The Latin language was not as gifted in its potential for philosophical and religious discourse as was Greek, and the more advanced urban civilization of the East did not have to wrestle as often with the crises of deprivation, famine, and isolation as did the more militarily threatened West. Urban leisure and philosophical tradition encouraged theological speculation in the East, with results that were sometimes heretical. Political, cultural, and linguistic divisions between the Latin West and the Greek East contributed to, and were exacerbated by, these religious differences during the later Roman and early medieval centuries. The Arian heresy proves this point.

Like most early heresies, Arianism arose from the dilemmas presented by the doctrines of the Trinity and the Incarnation, which obsessed the minds of Greek Christians. Was Christ, the Son of God, fully divine, of the same nature as God? Were the Father and the Son, the first two persons of the Trinity, one, or were they distinct? Was the latter a creature, created in time and hence of a lower order than the former? Had Christ become fully human? If not, how could his suffering save and redeem mankind? Stripped of all its involved subtleties and distinctions, the doctrine propounded by Arius, a priest of Alexandria, about the year 318 was a denial of both the absolute divinity and the complete humanity of Christ. His argument was logical in a literal-minded way, but would have robbed Christianity of its essential meaning. Both his supporters and his opponents, feeling the question to be of vital importance, took firm stands in the controversy.

When Constantine took over the government of the East after his defeat of Licinius in 323, he found the Church divided into apparently irreconcilable parties. The emperor never did understand just what the argument was about, but he was quite certain that it must be ended. He had favored Christianity and was prepared to support it still further in the hope that the well-organized Church would help to unify the Empire. It would have just the opposite effect, however, if the Church were split into two antagonistic parties. The unity of the Church was a vital political issue. To preserve that unity, one side of the argument or the other (Constantine did not greatly care which) must be established as orthodox, and those who would not accept it of their own free will must be forced to do so by the state. As a means of reaching an authoritative decision, the emperor called the first general or ecumenical council of the Church to meet at Nicaea in 325. All the bishops were invited to attend, but only seven delegates came from the West. The majority of the bishops were opposed to Arius, and the emperor used all his influence to make the decision unanimous. The council condemned the Arians and drew up the Nicene Creed, which asserted both the full divinity and the humanity of Christ.

After the Council of Nicaea, Arius and his followers were banished from the Empire by imperial decree. But Arianism was by no means dead. It continued to spread from the East to the Germanic tribes north of the frontier, and most of the later invaders of the Empire were Arians. Because Arianism was mostly an Eastern problem, it was up to the Eastern emperor Theodosius to crush it. In 380 he issued an edict threatening all heretics with legal punishment, and the following year he convened at Constantinople the second ecumenical council of the Church, which confirmed the Nicene Creed and condemned Arianism. Further imperial edicts restored all orthodox bishops and forbade the Arians to hold services or build churches. Arianism was suppressed by the power of the state. It persisted strongly among the barbarians, but within the Empire its cause was lost. Meanwhile, Gratian was taking steps to stamp out paganism, and in 391 and 392 Theodosius issued stringent laws against idolatry. Sacrifice to pagan gods, whether in public or private, was to be regarded as treason, and paganism gradually died out during the following century. The legal triumph of the Church over heresy and paganism and its evolution from a persecuted sect to a persecuting state church were complete.

The Growth of Monasticism

The single most important phenomenon to a historian studying the medieval Church is monasticism, a form of religious life in which people withdraw from society in order to pray and contemplate and try to achieve the salvation of their individual souls. Christian monasticism involved countless thousands of men and women in both parts of the Empire after the third century. In the aspirations which at its best it embodied it represented the highest ideals of the Christian Church. Western monasticism was simultaneously a social movement and the undertaking of individuals seeking the path to salvation. It reflected as many extremes—psychological, social, and religious—as existed in later Roman and early medieval society. Attempts to reform important monastic orders often represent turning-points for the historian studying the Middle Ages. The importance of monasticism even antedates the political rise of the Roman Papacy.

Monasticism sometimes had profound revolutionary implications. Medieval Christians, gathered together in monastic orders, attempted to create the human approximation of a divine order to facilitate the salvation of their individual souls. The impact of this effort spread beyond the walls of monasteries. The impulse to reform the Church most often originated in the efforts of great medieval monastic leaders. Yet in another sense monasticism was profoundly conservative. It often embodied a continuing respect for ancient learning, sometimes the only manifestation of such respect in a ravaged backward society, and its very existence implied a constant restatement of the fundamental themes of Christian hope and belief.

Monasticism began in the East. The first monk of whom we have definite knowledge was Saint Anthony, an Egyptian, who in the last years of the third century fled to the Thebaid desert. He lived as a hermit in constant prayer, fasting, and self-inflicted suffering. The tales of his holiness, his visions, and the miracles attributed to him spread through Egypt and attracted others in great numbers to follow his example. The natural human instinct to live in some kind of organized society soon asserted itself, even among hermits who had fled from society, and before 325 the monk Pachomius founded the first monastic community with a definite rule of government. As monasticism spread from Egypt throughout the East, thousands embraced it, the majority preferring the orderly communal life with provisions for daily labor prescribed by the rule of Pachomius. There were still many who preferred solitude, however, and among them asceticism was often carried to the most eccentric extremes. The classic example is that of Saint Simeon Stylites, who in the fifth century spent thirty-six years on top of a pillar, exposed to the weather and without sufficient space even to lie down. But for the most part, the communal life triumphed over the solitary, and

Detail from The Temptation of Saint Anthony *by the fifteenth-century Flemish painter Hieronymus Bosch. Saint Anthony was one of the earliest desert monastics.*

life triumphed over the solitary, and an improved rule written by Saint Basil before his death in 374 was adopted by most monks in the Greek Church.

Western monasticism was originally imported from the East, though it soon became acclimatized and developed along characteristically Latin lines. Introduced at Rome, apparently by Saint Athanasius in 339, it soon attracted numbers of both men and women. At first there was some opposition to what seemed an antisocial movement, and Saint Jerome, the most vigorous and influential champion of the monastic ideal in the West, aroused a good deal of antagonism by encouraging a number of noble Roman ladies to desert the world. But, once introduced, monasticism could not be checked. It became increasingly popular, spreading from Italy to all the provinces, and attracted adherents for a variety of reasons. The ascetic impulse was still, of course, the strongest motive, but there were many who embraced monasticism as a means of escape from intolerable social or family obligations. Monasticism was now a substitute for martyrdom, which was no longer available. The movement passed through the same course of development from the solitary to the communal life as it had in the East, but Western monasticism was always more practical and orderly, laying greater stress on the necessity of discipline and labor.

To trace the full development of monasticism in the West, we must transcend the chronological limits of this chapter and look to the sixth century and the epoch-making work of Saint Benedict of Nursia. Born about 480 of a wealthy and noble Italian family, Benedict fled at an early age from the temptations and distractions of the world and, like so many of his generation, sought salvation in a hermit's cell. For three years he lived a life of rigid asceticism and complete solitude, his home an almost inaccessible cave in a precipitous rock. But his very efforts to escape from the fellowship of men brought men to him. The fame of his holiness attracted to his vicinity numbers of monks, who begged him to be their leader. About the year 520 Benedict founded the famous monastery of Monte Cassino, and some time later wrote for the guidance of his monks the rule which was to regulate monastic life for centuries. Wherever the rule was adopted, it checked the restless wandering and dangerously irregular asceticism of the monks. It provided that the monk, after a probationary period of a year during which he had time to determine whether he was suited to the monastic life, should take the three fundamental vows of perpetual poverty, chastity, and obedience; thereafter he was bound to remain in the same monastery for life, to obey his superior with humility in all things, to give up all private property, and to cut himself off from all relations with people, including his own family, outside the monastery. Each monastery was a separate institution, ruled by an abbot elected by the other monks for life. His powers were limited only by the provisions of the rule and the supervision of the bishop of the diocese.

Each Benedictine monastery was a small self-contained community. Its members all lived under the same roof and shared the same food at a common table. Saint Benedict had had personal experience of the dangers and temptations that accompanied too much solitude, idleness, and unbridled asceticism. He therefore provided for a full schedule of daily activity and forbade all unusual ascetic practices. Part of each day—to our minds a large part—was devoted to prayer, meditation, and religious services at prescribed hours, while six or seven hours were to be spent in manual labor in the fields or about the house, or in reading and copying manuscripts. The monks were to produce their own food and other necessities and so be free from dependence on the outside world. Food, though not of a luxurious sort, was to be provided in sufficient quantities to maintain health. There were also special rules for the care of the sick or aged. It was an austere, hard life, but not an impossible one.

The sanity, moderation, and orderly government of the Benedictine rule appealed strongly to the western mind, and in subsequent centuries it was adopted by all monasteries in the West. It was also applied to the nunneries. As a result of the provisions for labor in the fields and copying manuscripts, the monasteries became centers of civilization and play an important part in cultivating waste land, improving agricultural methods, and preserving literature and learning.

The Latin Church and the Rise of the Papacy

The center of interest in religious history shifts during the fifth century to the West. The church in the East had conquered its most dangerous heretical opponent, though other heresies arose in profusion, springing for the most part from the attempt to define further the exact nature of the union of perfect God and perfect man in Christ. Political rivalry between the patriarchs of Alexandria, Antioch, and Constantinople, who were all fighting for supremacy in the Eastern Church, added bitterness to these controversies. But in the long run peace was restored, the primacy of the Patriarch of Constantinople—the imperial capital—was recognized, and through the patriarchs who were their creatures the emperors maintained control of the Church, which gradually sank into a stagnant and somewhat servile quietude. In the West, on the other hand, where the imperial power was being weakened and finally destroyed under the shock of successive barbarian invasions, the Latin Church was growing rapidly in organization, independence, and authority. With a theology peculiarly its own, it came under the leadership of the bishops of Rome, who fell heir to the universal authority abdicated by the emperors.

The Church in the West was predominantly Greek during the first two centuries after its foundation, Christianity having spread first among the Greek-speaking commercial classes. As it was adopted by all classes, however, it necessarily drew its adherents from the Latin-speaking majority of the population. Before the end of the persecutions, the Western Church was almost entirely Latin. There arose, in the last years of the fourth century and in the fifth, a school of Latin theology and church policy, quite different from the Greek, destined to shape the thought of Western Christendom for more than a thousand years.

The leaders of this movement were three men, Ambrose, Jerome, and Augustine, who, together with Pope Gregory the Great, have been accorded the title Fathers of the Church in Latin Christendom. Though differing widely in character and in the nature of their contributions, all three were stoutly orthodox, doughty champions of the unity and authority of the Catholic Church.

Ambrose (c. 340–397) was a practical administrator. From his father, the prefect of Gaul, he inherited the tradition of Roman government. In 374 he was elected Bishop of Milan, where the emperor was then residing, and soon became the most influential official in the Western Church. In all his relations with the government he insisted on the maxim that the emperor is *in* the church, not *over* it, and he had the courage and character to force even the great Theodosius to submission, refusing to administer the sacraments to him until he had done full penance for massacres he had caused at Thessalonica. Ambrose is also credited with introducing the singing of hymns into the Western Church; he himself wrote several. He has, indeed, been called the founder of Latin hymnody. In his writings and his example, he left to the Western Church a priceless tradition of discipline and independence.

His contemporary, Jerome (c. 340–419) was the most learned of the three, a masterly scholar and linguist. Aside from his numerous works against heresy and his active promotion of monasticism at Rome, his great service was the translation of the Bible from the original Hebrew and Greek into forceful and eloquent Latin. This arduous task, which occupied twenty years, was completed in 405. The Vulgate, as this version of the Bible is called, was soon accepted as the authoritative text by the Latin Church and had an incalculable influence on ecclesiastical literature during the following centuries.

Augustine (354–430) was the real founder of Latin theology and the most powerful mind in the history of the Western Church. Born in the Roman province of Africa, he was trained in philosophy and classical literature and was much influenced by Neoplatonism before he fell under the influence of Bishop Ambrose and was converted to Christianity. In 395 he was made Bishop of Hippo in Africa and spent the rest of his life in active pastoral work and writing. His *Confessions,* written about the year 400, ranks high among the world's great autobiographies and among the finest works of religious inspiration. His longest work, *The City of God,* was undertaken after the sack of Rome in 410 to demonstrate that the calamities which had overtaken the Empire were not due to its desertion of the ancient gods but were merely signs that the old worldly empire was passing, to be replaced by a new spiritual empire, the Christian Church.

Augustine wrote numerous works in which he constructed a dogmatic system, in opposition to such heretics as the Pelagians, who held that human nature is not essentially evil and that men are able to seek the good of their own free will, and the Donatists, who believed that the validity of the sacraments depended on the moral character of the priest. Typically Latin, Augustine was not vitally interested in the metaphysical speculations that so attracted the Greeks. On the contrary, his thought revolved about the more human problem of how the individual Christian obtains salvation. This problem he resolved into a logical and almost Roman legal system of divine justice. Augustine pictured all human beings as damned by the original sin inherited from the fall of Adam, were it not that some have been predestined or chosen from the beginning for salvation through Christ's sacrifice. Such salvation comes to them not by virtue of any action of their own will, for the human will is powerless, but through the working of divine grace upon those who are chosen. This was the orthodox belief, though in spirit the Church never completely accepted the extreme statement of Augustinianism.

The period which marked the growth of Latin theology also witnessed the completion of a centralized system of government in the Western Church. The building of a clerical hierarchy of ascending offices was a matter of slow growth, in which the Church followed the lines of imperial administration. Within each Roman municipality since the second century, the bishop had been recognized as the head of the local church, with authority over the priests and deacons. The next step was to create a higher authority that could impose uniformity in belief and practice and enforce discipline over these isolated communities. In the third century, councils of all the bishops in a given province of the Empire were common. By the end of the fourth century the bishop of the provincial capital, who presided at these councils, had been recognized as the superior of the bishops in his province and given the title of Metropolitan or Archbishop. However, the Latin genius for government, and the need for a centralized administration in a time of frequent heresies and barbarian invasions, demanded some still higher authority over the whole Church. This led during the fifth century to the elevation of the Bishop of Rome to a position of supremacy in the Latin Church, comparable to that of the emperor in the civil government. The administrative complexity and hierarchical order of this organization reflected the great changes that had taken place in the Church since its beginnings in the first century.

As head of the Christian community in the ancient capital of the Empire, the bishop of Rome occupied a position of great political influence at home and prestige abroad. As early as the fourth century, the pagan Ammianus Marcellinus had noted, with a mixture of admiration and contempt, the wealth, pomp, and power of the Roman bishops. Their importance was greatly increased after 402, when the emperor deserted the capital to establish his court in the hitherto impregnable city of Ravenna, sheltered by its impassable marshes. Thereafter the bishops became the most powerful officials in the city. After the sack of Rome by the Visigoths in 410, Bishop Innocent I (402–417) took the lead in directing and aiding reconstruction. It was Innocent, too, who first emphatically asserted his right to supremacy in the Western Church. From the beginning of his reign, he claimed that all the churches of the West owed obedience to the Roman bishop and that in all matters of discipline and usage they should accept his decisions and follow the custom of the Roman Church.

Bishops were assuming greater powers in all the provinces because of the collapse of the imperial administration under the shock of successive invasions. In many cities they took over the duties of the imperial officers, acting as judges and governors and using their influence to protect the citizens from their barbarian conquerors. These new responsibilities caused them to feel more keenly the need for moral support from some higher authority and to look eagerly to the Roman bishop for guidance. Thus by the middle of the century, Leo the Great (440–461) was able to exercise full authority over the Church. As pope (we may now use that term for the bishop of Rome) he felt entitled to that authority. The papal status was granted imperial sanction by a law of Valentinian III, which conferred upon the pope jurisdiction over all the bishops in the Western Empire.

Leo I was in many ways the most impressive figure of his generation, a man of remarkable energy, courage, and statesmanlike vision. When Rome was threatened by the Huns in 451 and sacked by the Vandals in 455, it was Leo who carried out the negotiations, successful in the former case, on behalf of the defenseless city. With inflexible purpose he forced the bishops of the farthest provinces to obedience, and in the heretical controversies of his time he boldly asserted his right to settle the questions at issue as the final authority in matters of faith.

From the first, the Roman bishop occupied a unique position in the church, as heir in a sense to the authority of both Augustus, the founder of the Roman Empire, and of Saint Peter, the traditional founder of the Church in Rome. Rome's dominant position in the Empire, as the capital and center of imperial administration, gave to the head of the Christian community there a prestige which no other bishop could equal, and made it natural that he should become the head also of the ecclesiastical administration. Moreover, according to the tradition generally accepted in the Church, the apostle Peter had been the first bishop of Rome, and to him, as the Bible tells, Christ had given the care of his flock and the keys of heaven and hell, saying, "On this rock will I build my church." As successors to Peter, the bishops of Rome claimed the full powers given to him by Christ. The Roman bishopric was generally known as the See of Peter or the Apostolic See. Finally, this rise to supremacy was aided by the reputation for orthodoxy built up by a long line of Roman bishops, who, with the Latin instinct for law and order, adhered steadfastly to the letter of the orthodox creeds.

Suggestions for Further Reading

R. H. Bainton, *Early and Medieval Christianity* (1962). Roland Bainton, an authority on the history of Christianity from its origins through the Reformation, introduces the main themes of the subject.

M. Burrows, *The Dead Sea Scrolls* (1955). An authority on the nature and significance of the Dead Sea Scrolls, Burrows shows how the Scrolls throw light on the history of early Christianity and its links with Jewish communal sects.

C. Dawson, *The Making of Europe** (1956). A brilliant synthesis and interpretation of early medieval Europe, with an emphasis upon the Church and its role in molding the early Middle Ages.

T. R. Glover, *The Conflict of Religions in the Early Roman Empire* (1960). A fascinating study of competing religions in the Roman Empire: this is useful background material for understanding the growing appeal of Manichaeanism, Christianity, and Neoplatonism in the later Empire.

A. H. M. Jones, *Constantine and the Conversion of Europe* (1948). Brief but excellent account of the economic, social, and religious problems of the reign and times of Constantine [AHA, 152].

M. L. W. Laistner, *Christianity and Pagan Culture in the Later Roman Empire** (1951). Excellent, brief introduction to the role of classical culture in the Christian Roman Empire.

K. Latourette, *History of Christianity** (1953). A useful survey by one of the great authorities on the subject.

H. B. Workman, *The Evolution of the Monastic Ideal** (1913). An excellent, readable study of Saint Benedict and the rise of early medieval monasticism, putting them in the context of those turbulent centuries.

*Available in a paperback edition.

Justinian and Mohammed

7

When we had arranged . . . the hitherto confused mass of imperial constitutions, we then extended our care to the vast volumes of ancient law.

PREFACE TO *THE INSTITUTES OF JUSTINIAN*

Whosoever fighteth for the religion of God, whether he be slain or be victorious, we will surely give him a great reward.

THE KORAN

The Age of Justinian

The history of Europe since the days of the ancient Greeks has been the story of the interaction between Western civilization and other cultures. It would be difficult to understand Athens in the fifth century without examining the Greek struggle with the Persians. The history of Rome is the story of the development of a small city-state into an empire which included and was profoundly influenced by many non-Roman peoples. The history of medieval Europe cannot be understood without recognition of this interaction between Latin Christendom and its borderlands. Although the Eastern Roman, or Byzantine, Empire in the East was part of the Christian world, its language and culture differed profoundly from those of the Latin West. Byzantium—the Byzantine Empire and culture—was rich and highly urbanized. Constantinople, the Empire's major city, was almost a mythical place to the West, at least until the Crusaders sacked it in 1204-1205. To write the history of the Latin West without studying Byzantium and its relations with the West would be impossible.

Islam was a more alien phenomenon from the Latin Western viewpoint, but it is impossible to understand the Latin West without knowing something of Moslem religion and culture. We hear much of the Crusades, of the military conflicts between the Latin West and Islam. Perhaps more typical of the relation between the two cultures, however, was the commercial and intellectual interaction of these civilizations. At times Islam was a profound threat to both the Latin West and the Byzantine East. It represented a dangerous peripheral or borderland area, beyond the range of vision of the average early medieval European. Until the late eleventh century the military and political dynamics of the situation favored Islam; then, at least for awhile, the tide turned. At all times, however, peaceful interaction was an important factor in the history of both cultures.

For more than a century after the death of the great Theodosius in 395, the Empire in the East was not distinguished by strong government. Its rulers were able to do little more than preserve their state from the assaults of barbarian enemies, making little attempt to save the West from destruction or to reform conditions in their own Empire. A new and more glorious era in the imperial annals opened with the proclamation of the Emperor Justin in 518. An Illyrian peasant, Justin had neither education nor experience in government beyond that supplied by his training in the army. But he had a nephew named Justinian, who soon became the power behind the throne and directed his uncle's government until the death of Justin in 527, when Justinian succeeded him as emperor.

Thanks to his uncle's generosity, Justinian had been given all the advantages of education and training that the older man lacked. Moreover, he had intelligence of a high order and an amazing capacity for work. His tireless attention to the details of administration caused one of his courtiers to describe him as "the emperor who never sleeps." In moments of stress, however, Justinian sometimes showed a sad lack of firmness and decision. This weakness was fortunately counterbalanced by the iron nerve of his wife Theodora, who more than once—such as during the Nika riots in Constantinople in 532—bolstered his failing courage and saved him and the Empire from disaster. Theodora knew the people as Justinian never could. She was the daughter of a bear-keeper in the

THE EXPANSION OF THE BYZANTINE EMPIRE, 527-565

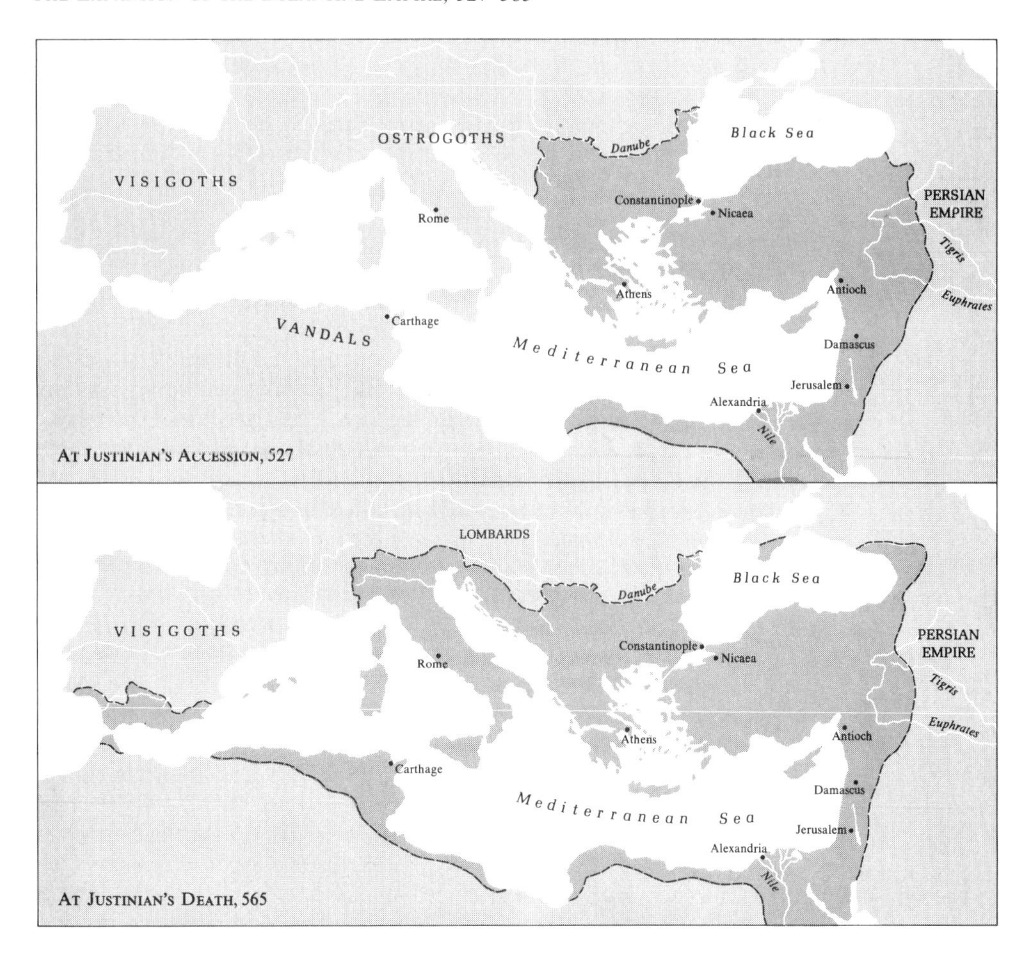

hippodrome and had herself been a popular actress there. All contemporary writers agree on her charm and beauty, her keen intelligence, and her influence over Justinian, whom she had married before he was elevated to the throne. As empress her power was greater than that of any of her predecessors.

The Byzantine Empire was Hellenistic in language and culture by the time of Justinian. This does not, however, mean that the universalism inherent in the Roman idea of empire had died out. Justinian, though Greek speaking, saw himself as a Roman emperor and taxed the full resources of his provinces in order to restore the sacred unity of the entire Roman Empire. Thus, he paid the Persians to secure his eastern frontiers and inflicted the ravages of the sword on Italy for twenty years in an ultimately "successful" effort to destroy Ostrogothic rule in that impoverished land. Justinian annihilated the Vandal power in North Africa and reconquered part of southern Spain from the Visigoths. While this was going on, he had to build extensive fortifications in the Balkans in order to defend the Empire against Slavic tribes, and later fight numerous wars with the restored and sophisticated Persian Empire. These efforts depleted the treasury and military energy of the Greek Empire. Within a few years of the death of Justinian, a new east Germanic people, the Lombards, poured into Italy and undid most of Justinian's work in that suffering land. Within three generations of his death, Islam overran his richest Asian and African possessions.

After Justinian's time, Byzantine diplomacy, basically defensive in nature, was perhaps more successful than Byzantine arms. Byzantine diplomacy pitted one barbarian tribe against another in an attempt to divide the enemy and protect the crucial heartland of the Greek Empire: Anatolia (Asia Minor), the lower Balkans, and Constantinople. Marriage was a factor in Byzantine diplomacy, and Byzantine emperors married Greek princesses to German kings and Russian princes.

Byzantium was remarkably successful, existing into the middle of the fifteenth century and surviving storm after storm. In its clever diplomacy Byzantium made full use of the splendors of the imperial capital, Constantinople. The grandeur of its buildings, the magnificence of its court, and the impressive pomp of the imperial ceremonies impressed many ambassadors from western nations and barbarian tribes. The Greeks viewed the West as barbarian, but throughout the Middle Ages Byzantine cultural and commercial contacts with the West, particularly Italy, were frequent and vital.

Justinian was sincerely anxious to be a good as well as a great ruler, but his constant need of money forced him to tolerate the methods of his hated minister, John of Cappadocia, who fleeced the people unmercifully. The Nika riots (so named because crowds running through the streets yelled "Nika, nika!"—"Destroy, destroy!") were a protest against his administration and were suppressed only after Belisarius had massacred some thirty thousand rioters. After this affair, Justinian undertook to reform the administration so as to protect the taxpayer from illegal exactions and at the same time to increase the income of the government by checking corruption and making the civil service more efficient. The result was an administrative machine which preserved the Empire through many a crisis in the following centuries.

Justinian was a theologian at heart. He asserted the right of the emperor to decide disputed points of dogma and to force acceptance of his opinions by the Church and the people. He thus became the effective head of the Church in matters of faith as well as of government, while the Church episcopate became a department of the state. The Greek Church was unable to free itself altogether from this subservience to the emperors. On the other hand, Byzantium slowly but steadily lost control of the Roman Papacy. By 750 the popes were looking to the Catholic Franks rather than to the distant, weakened Orthodox Greek emperors for protection against the Lombards.

One further task undertaken by Justinian, the most important in its permanent and far-reaching effects on later European civilization, remains to be mentioned. This was his codification of Roman law, the work with which his name is most commonly associated. Two kinds of law were recognized by the Roman courts. First, there was the direct imperial legislation, laws called "constitutions" issued by the emperors themselves. Then there was a great body of jurisprudence, composed of decisions handed down by authorized judges and lawyers. Through the centuries a huge mass of law had accumulated, eventually becoming unwieldy and confusing. An attempt to straighten out this legal tangle had been made by Theodosius II, who in 438 had issued the Theodosian Code composed of the imperial constitutions since Constantine. However, much still remained to be done if Roman law was to be preserved.

Justinian set himself to the task in the first year of his reign, appointing a committee of ten jurists to compile a new code. The *Codex Justinianus,* or Justinian Code, was completed the following year and given final form in 534. It included all previous imperial legislation in condensed and simplified form, excluding everything obsolete, contradictory, or repetitious, and arranged in logical order. The still more difficult task of a similar condensation and simplification of jurisprudence was begun in 530 and completed in three years. It is known as the *Digest* or *Pandects.* To this was added a brief official handbook or

Justinian attended by both secular and ecclesiastical dignitaries. This sixth-century mosaic in the Church of San Vitale in Ravenna symbolizes the emperor's political and spiritual authority.

text for the use of students, called the *Institutes.* These three works, together with the *Novels,* a collection of the laws issued by Justinian himself, are collectively known as the *Corpus Juris Civilis,* the body of civil law. It preserved all that was most valuable in Roman law in a clear and accessible form and is the basis of civil law in most European countries today.

Society and Culture in Byzantium

Through all its changes of fortune the Byzantine Empire enjoyed an economic strength that enabled it to recover from the most serious reverses. The geographic position of the Empire, and especially of the capital, gave it unequaled opportunities for trade. Straddling the narrow Sea of Marmora, between Europe and Asia, the Black Sea and the Mediterranean, the Empire was the meeting-place of trade routes running east and west, north and south. The commerce of the world was transshipped in the harbors of Constantinople, bought and sold in its markets. For centuries it was one of the richest cities of the world, "the city of the world's desire." Stimulated by trade, the capital and other imperial cities became centers of thriving industry. Constantinople was especially famous for the manufacture of articles of luxury. The city was nearly impregnable. Wave after wave of invasion, which might have destroyed the Empire, broke against the city walls. Only twice since the days of Constantine has it been taken by siege, once by the Crusaders in 1204 and again by the Turks in 1453.

Much has been written about the vices and weakness of this cultivated, luxurious, and pleasure-loving society, always excitable, capricious, and easily aroused to factional passion. No doubt these characteristics have been overemphasized; as one historian remarks, "It may be doubted whether any empire can live by vice alone." There must have been counterbalancing qualities of thrift, industry, and tenacious courage. Yet it cannot be denied that the society of the later Empire was politically unstable. Disputes over points of theological dogma, economic or political grievances, the ambitions of a popular leader, or the unpopularity of a minister could stir feelings to fever pitch.

The hippodrome, center of Byzantine social life, was the scene of popular riots which sometimes assumed dangerous proportions. Two rival parties, the Greens and the Blues, sponsored the chariot races which were the chief attraction of the hippodrome, and the victory of one or the other was a matter of statewide importance. These parties included in their ranks almost the entire population, from the imperial family to the poorest laborer. They were in reality political parties and furnished a ready-made organization for popular leaders. Justinian, however, broke the power of these factions.

The Byzantine people were intensely religious and always keenly interested in theological questions. The most exacting differences in the statement of dogma could arouse fanatical passions which were often used by political leaders to gain the support of the populace for their own ends. The monks and the clergy could become dangerous enemies of the government. A great struggle between monks and the imperial government, the iconoclastic dispute, occurred in the eighth century and recurred sporadically even in the ninth. Fanatical monks, imbued with the sense of the purity of the Christian religion, rejected the pictorial or iconographic aspects of the Byzantine ritual, objecting to the use of pictures for religious purposes. Because they were the smashers of icons, they were known as iconoclasts. Monasticism was an important force in the Byzantine Empire, and the government and elements of the Byzantine urban elite were frightened by the sight of thousands of monks up in arms over a politically volatile issue such as iconoclasm. The iconodules, or worshippers of icons, gained the upper hand in 787 at the Second Council of Nicaea.

For the most part the emperors were able to maintain their absolute control of the Church, sternly suppressing all heresies or movements for independence, and they found in it a useful instrument for preserving the unity of the Empire. The Eastern Church had become thoroughly Greek in spirit and tradition. Differences of language, culture, and interest had divided it since the fourth century from the Latin Church of the West. For years at a time all communion between the two was broken off, until between 1054 and 1204 the schism or split became explicit and permanent. Thereafter the Greek Orthodox Church, to which the Byzantine and Slavic peoples adhered, was separated by a barrier of theological belief and religious practice from the Roman Catholic world of the West.

The importance of religious interest can be clearly seen in its effect on Byzantine education and literature. The Bible and the works of the Fathers of the Greek Church occupied a prominent place in the curriculum of the schools, while theology was the subject of at least half of the literature produced under the Empire. A second influence, equally strong, was Greek antiquity. Byzantine culture was essentially Greek, though it had absorbed much from the Middle East—from Syria, Persia, Egypt, and later from the Arabs. The people of the

A Byzantine icon showing the Virgin enthroned and surrounded by angels and saints. Such religious pictures retained this traditional style for centuries.

Empire were proud of their inheritance from ancient Greece, and the Greek classics formed the basis of Byzantine education. Century after century the writers of Byzantium imitated the classics, wrote learned commentaries upon them, and strove to preserve the ancient Greek style. This led to a growing differentiation between the written language and spoken Greek. In the cultured society of Byzantium, laymen of the upper classes continued to be well educated during centuries when in the West only some of the clergy was literate.

Byzantine architects adapted earlier Roman forms of construction for their churches, making considerable use of arches, vaults, and domes, although their lavish use of color in interior decoration seems more characteristic of the Middle East than of Rome. The most magnificent of all the Byzantine churches was Sancta Sophia (Holy Wisdom), built by Justinian to grace his capital; still standing, it has been little touched by time though somewhat marred by the hand of man. Sancta Sophia is at once the supreme expression of Byzantine religious aspiration, the most perfect example of Byzantine art, and a daring triumph of engineering skill exemplified in the use of the arched pendentive, which vaulted the entire structure. The architects used space, light, and color with unrivaled effect. The nave is 100 feet wide, and above it the great dome soars to a height of 179 feet. Light flows in from forty windows about the base of the dome. Before the Moslem Turks covered the Christian decorations with whitewash, the interior glowed and sparkled as the varicolored marbles and mosaics caught and reflected the light. Procopius, who saw it when it was new, wrote: "It is flooded with sunlight, both direct and reflected. You would imagine that it was not merely illuminated from without by the sun, but that radiance springs from within it, such a superabundance of light pours into this holy temple."

The colorful effect of Byzantine church interiors was enhanced by the liberal use of mosaics as pictorial decoration. Although Byzantine artists practiced both fresco and panel painting, mosaics were the most characteristic form of Byzantine pictorial art. These were large mural pictures, made up of countless tiny bits of colored glass or stone set in cement. In many mosaics the background was composed of gold leaf set between pieces of glass. The mosaics are remarkably effective as mural decoration, for they lie flat against the wall rather than suggesting a three-dimensional space set into the wall. The polished surface of glass and stone, moreover, lends them a glowing vitality that no paint can equal.

The lack of three-dimensionality in Byzantine mosaics and murals was not accidental, nor was it a product of technical backwardness. Rather, the "flat" figures suggest the overpowering majesty of the religious or imperial figures they portray. Three dimensions suggest time and space; the two dimensions of the great Byzantine mosaics suggest eternity and infinity.

Byzantine civilization spread far beyond the narrow confines of the Empire. It had a permanent influence on the Slavic countries of eastern Europe, as great as that of Rome on the Germanic nations of the West. The Slavs who had settled in the Balkans, and the various Slavic peoples who later combined to form Russia, looked to Byzantium for religious and cultural leadership. The church of most Slavs was Greek Orthodox; their writing was based on the Greek alphabet and their literature on Byzantine models; their art and architecture were strongly Byzantine in character; and their foreign trade was mostly with the Empire.

Throughout the Middle Ages Byzantium defended the Christian West against barbarian and Islamic threats. Its cultural and economic ties with the West were constant and profound.

Sancta Sophia, Justinian's great church in Constantinople, a monument to Byzantine artistic and engineering skill. The minarets were added by Moslem conquerors. The windows at the base of the dome let brilliant light into the interior.

Mohammed and the Founding of Islam

A few years after the death of Justinian, a man was born in an Arabian town near the Red Sea who was to have a far greater influence on the history of the world than that of the great Byzantine emperor. In the century following Justinian's attempt to restore the old Roman Empire, Mohammed founded a religion which has since been the most powerful rival of Christianity, and at the same time laid the foundations for an empire that spread until it included the former Roman provinces in Syria, northern Africa, and Spain and extended eastward to the borders of India. In this empire, composed of varied peoples bound together by a common religion, there developed in subsequent centuries a civilization higher and in many ways more enlightened than that of early medieval Europe, and one from which the peoples of the West learned much, despite religious antagonism. That empire has long since fallen to pieces, but millions of people still follow the teaching of Mohammed and pray with their faces turned to the town in which he was born.

The life of the seventh-century Arabs was not unlike that of the early Children of Israel as pictured in the Old Testament. The family or tribe was the social and political unit, under the authority of the head of the family. Their religion, however, was still a crude and superstitious paganism in which idolatry played an important part, though Jewish tribes and Christian merchants had spread some knowledge of their religions in Arabia before Mohammed, and the idea of monotheism at least was apparently not unknown. Some vague unity was given to Arab religion by the common veneration of certain sanctuaries, of which the most important was a small temple, square in shape, called the Kaaba (Cube) and situated in Mecca, a commercial town some fifty miles inland from the middle of the Red Sea coast. To Mecca Arabs came from all parts of the country on annual pilgrimages during the sacred months when tribal warfare was forbidden. The city of Mecca was, then, to some degree the center of Arab religion before the days of Mohammed.

It was in Mecca that Mohammed was born about the year 570. Later tradition tells us a good deal about his early life, appearance, and character, but very little of it is trustworthy historical information. Though pious legend ascribed to him important family connections, he was the son of a merchant and a member of the important tribe of the Koreish. Mohammed was left an orphan at an early age and lived in poverty until he was about twenty-four years old, when he entered the service of a wealthy widow named Khadija. While working for her, he led at least one caravan on a trading trip to Syria. About the year 595, he married his employer and for the next fifteen years Mohammed lived the comfortable, if uneventful, life of the ordinary well-to-do Meccan merchant. He was described as a kindly man, gifted with a winning personality. His later career shows him to have had a strong will and ruthless determination, combined with sound practical sense and great ability in judging men.

The beginning of Mohammed's prophetic mission is dated from his fortieth year, though there is good reason to believe that he had given much thought to religious matters before that time. Tradition tells us that he spent one month of every year in solitary meditation on a mountain near Mecca. Here occurred the first revelation. The revelations on which his teaching was based resulted from some kind of trance, which, later at least, the prophet could induce at will. The first converts were members of Mohammed's own family and close friends.

Among them, his cousin Ali and his friends Abu Bakr and Omar later played important roles. Mohammed called his religion *Islam,* meaning "submission"—i.e., to the will of God—and his followers *Moslems,* those who had surrendered themselves. At first the Moslems formed a secret society. When at last they made their faith public, they met with opposition and persecution from the pagan Meccans, who feared that Mohammed's insistence on one God, Allah, would destroy the people's faith in idols and hence the profitable trade with the pilgrims who came annually to the Kaaba.

As Islam slowly gained ground at Mecca, persecution became more severe. Finally, Mohammed decided to flee from the city and to seek a safer place of refuge for his followers. He found it in Medina, a city to the north of Mecca, where Jewish and Arab tribes had for some time been engaged in civil strife. The way was prepared by missionaries, and in 622 a delegation of some seventy converts from Medina invited Mohammed to their city. The flight of the prophet and his followers to Medina, known as the Hegira, marks the beginning of the Moslem calendar. Taking advantage of the feuds which divided the people of Medina, Mohammed soon became its ruler and made it the capital of a rapidly growing state.

A thirteenth-century Persian painting showing a caravan on the way to Mecca.

In the years following the Hegira, the character of Islam changed materially. It became a fighting religion and the prophet a political leader. Forced to provide for the refugees in his care, Mohammed began to prey upon the caravans that passed near Medina on the way to Mecca. This practice led to a war with Mecca which dragged on for years. The Moslems continued to raid caravans and nearby villages and to plunder the Jewish tribes. As a victorious religion promising plunder and profit in this world and the blessings of paradise after death, Islam attracted converts from many of the Bedouin tribes. By 630, Mohammed was strong enough to conquer Mecca almost without opposition. Henceforth Mecca was to be the religious center of Islam, toward which all Moslems turned to pray, and the Kaaba its most sacred *mosque* or temple, though Medina remained for some time the political capital. By taking over the pilgrimages, the sacred city, and the sanctuary from Arab paganism, Mohammed made it easier for converts to join the new religion. Before his death at Medina in 632, he had succeeded in gaining at least the formal adherence of the greater part of Arabia.

From the beginning of his mission until his death, Mohammed published a series of divine revelations, containing all his teaching on moral and theological questions, as well as his legislation on purely political matters and his comments on current events. Together they make up the Koran, collected and put in order soon after the prophet's death and since handed down with little or no change. The revelations were originally dictated by Mohammed to his friends or secretaries (it is very doubtful that he himself could write), and preserved as separate fragments with no attempt at chronological order. In the final edition of the Koran, they were arranged according to length, the longest chapters first, then the shorter, in diminishing order. Because Mohammed's ideas developed with experience or changed with the needs of the moment, the lack of dates makes it a very confusing book. Often later revelations modify or cancel earlier ones. The contradictions, however, seem to have aroused no skepticism. Despite difficulties of interpretation, the Koran has always been accepted by Moslems as the final authority on all matters of faith and morals.

The theological doctrines of the Koran are simple enough. There is but one God and Mohammed is his prophet. There have been other prophets in the past—Noah, Abraham, Moses, Jesus—to each of whom a part of the truth was revealed; but the final revelation was made only to Mohammed. After death there will be a bodily resurrection and a future life—for the faithful in a paradise of sensuous pleasures, for the infidel in a hell (gehennem) of perpetual fire. There are also many moral regulations. The prophet commands his followers to practice the virtues of charity, humility, and patience, and to forgive their enemies. He condemns avarice, lying, and malice, and prohibits drinking and gambling. Polygamy is permitted, the prophet setting the example by marrying several times after the death of Khadija. The practices and ceremonies of Islam are described in detail, including prayers at stated intervals during the day, pilgrimages to Mecca, and fasts from sunrise to sunset during the sacred month of Ramadan. The remainder of the Koran is occupied chiefly with legislation for the government of the Moslem state. Mohammed drew freely upon Christianity, Judaism, and Arab paganism, though his knowledge of the first two was uncertain and inaccurate, picked up apparently from casual conversations rather than from reading. Yet the result of this mixture of ideas was a doctrine, original when taken as a whole, and designed to appeal to the simple Arab of the prophet's day, though simultaneously capable of holding the faith of more literate people.

The Rise of the Moslem Empire

The death of Mohammed in 632 was a shock and surprise to his followers. It precipitated a spiritual and political crisis which threatened to destroy the young Islamic state. Quarrels over the mantle of Mohammed involved both familial and geographical claims, the Medinese being jealous of the Meccan companions of the Prophet. Eventually, Abu Bakr was chosen caliph—a title which implied the religious and political domination of all Islam. Its geographical base, subject to historical change, was first Mecca or Medina, then Damascus, and later Baghdad. Later in the history of Islam there were further caliphates; for example, the Fatimite caliphate in Cairo, the Umayyad caliphate in Spain, and the Ottoman caliphate in Constantinople. Different but contemporary caliphates implied the ultimate fragmentation of the Islamic empire, for the differences between them were not so much dogmatic and theological as political and familial, the argument over kindred relationship to Mohammed and his near relations being eternally significant in Islam.

No sooner had the Arabs been united under the rule of the caliph than they launched upon that amazing series of conquests which in time was to extend their empire from the Indus to Spain. It has often been said that the motive which drove them to conquest was religious fanaticism, the determination to force Islam upon the infidel. Mohammed's teaching did, in fact, furnish a bond to hold the Arab tribes together, and his promise of paradise to those who died fighting the infidel gave them a strong fighting spirit. Actually, however, the Arabs made little or no attempt to force their religion upon conquered peoples, and the motives which inspired the raids into foreign countries were really economic and political. Arabia had for some time been suffering from an economic decline, and its tribes were restless and discontented. The naturally rich lands of Syria, Persia, and Egypt attracted them as the fertile provinces of the Roman Empire had attracted the Germanic barbarians. Only their previous lack of unity had prevented them from making the attempt earlier. At the same time, the caliph realized that to hold the wild Bedouin tribes in subjection and to check their intertribal feuds, some outlet must be provided for their warlike energy. The conquest of the rich neighboring countries offered such an outlet, combined with the promise of plunder beyond the dreams of the average Arab. Moreover, the Byzantine Empire and Persia had just completed a long and devastating war which had left both exhausted. The time was ripe for the venture. The Syrian provincials, crushed by imperial taxation, seem rather to have welcomed than resisted the conquerors. A similar apathy, indeed, favored the conquerors in most parts of the Byzantine Empire and Persia they invaded. To the people, conquest often merely meant a less oppressive government.

The conquest of North Africa was a long, slow process, due more to the resistance of the Berber tribes than to that of the Byzantine government. By about 708, however, the Berbers were thoroughly conquered and they soon adopted Islam. The next step in the westward march of the Arabs was the conquest of Spain from the Visigoths, begun in 711 and completed with the aid of Berber allies within two years. From there they pushed on across the Pyrenees into southern Gaul in search of plunder. Meanwhile the Moslem Empire had reached its farthest extent in the East, stretching as far as the river Indus in India and to the borders of China in central Asia.

During the century of Umayyad rule in the East, a considerable transformation took place within the Moslem Empire. The caliphs made little attempt to convert the conquered peoples, for so long as there were infidels to tax, the

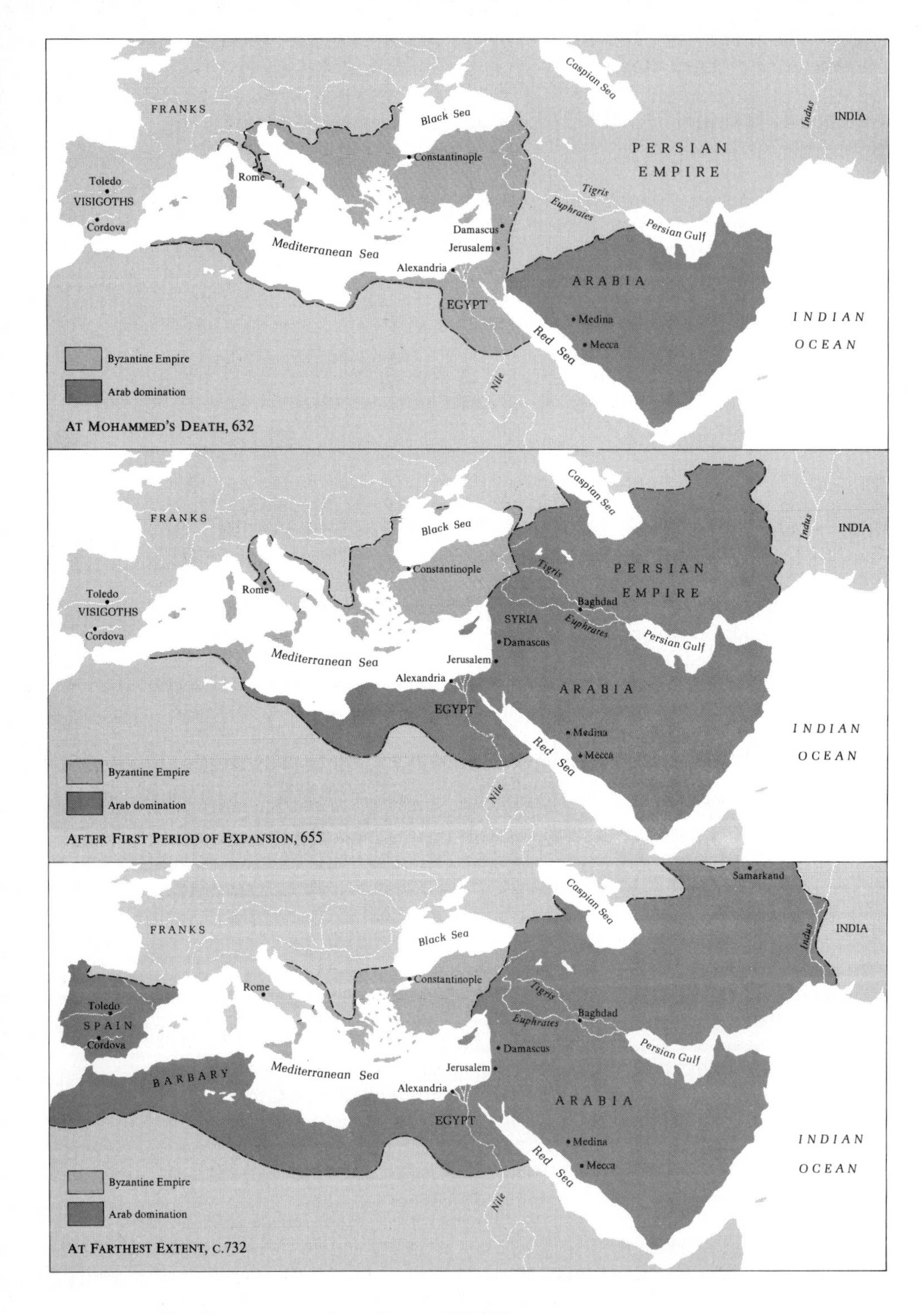

THE EXPANSION OF ARAB POWER, 632–732

faithful could be relieved of financial burdens. But the taxes in themselves encouraged conversion, as did the desire of the conquered peoples to share in the political and other privileges reserved for the faithful; by the end of the seventh century great numbers of the conquered had adopted Islam. The Arabs, meanwhile, though still the ruling class, had become scattered and were mingling with the other peoples of the Empire. Thus, as the majority of the subject peoples became Moslem, the distinction between the conqueror and the conquered, the Arab and the non-Arab, was partially effaced by the growth of common religious interests. Islam, then, rather than Arab nationalism, was becoming the important factor in Moslem patriotism. And the Umayyads, though acting as both religious and political rulers, had always represented Arabian rather than the broader Moslem interests.

Discontented with Umayyad rule, the more devout Moslems, especially in Persia, turned to the Abbasid family for leadership. Descended from Abbas, the uncle of Mohammed, the Abbasids could rely on their relation to the prophet's family to attract the loyalty of devout Moslems of all races. After some years of political disturbance, the Umayyad dynasty was finally overthrown in 750 and the Abbasid dynasty took its place, though an Umayyad emir continued to rule in Spain, separating it from the rest of the Empire. Persia now took the place of Syria as the center of the Empire, and the capital was moved from Damascus to Baghdad on the Tigris. The Abbasids continued to stress their claims to Moslem rather than purely Arab loyalty, and the Arab aristocracy was succeeded by a mixed official aristocracy drawn from all the Moslem peoples. The caliphs took on the character of oriental despots, with all the pomp and ceremony of the old Persian kings. And in this new Abbasid Empire there developed a composite Moslem civilization that was partly Arab, partly Persian, and partly Greek, the whole welded into a new synthesis by the doctrines of Islam and the common use of the Arabic tongue.

Moslem Civilization Under the Caliphates

For about seventy-five years after the fall of the Umayyads, the Abbasid caliphs enjoyed an era of absolute power and great prosperity. The reign of Haroun al Rashid (786–809), whose name is familiar to all who have read the *Arabian Nights,* marks the point of greatest power in the history of the caliphate. Baghdad was one of the richest cities in the world, the center of an empire stretching from central Asia to the Atlantic, for though Spain was now politically independent it still recognized the religious authority of the successors of the prophet. But that empire was too large and composed of too many varied peoples to be held together for long under the despotic rule of one man, unless he was a statesman of unusual strength and genius. Shortly after Haroun's reign, the powers of the caliph declined and the Empire began to disintegrate. The tenth century saw a further disintegration. The Umayyad emir in Spain took the title Caliph of Cordova, and in Egypt a member of the Fatimite family, descended from Mohammed's daughter Fatima, founded the caliphate of Cairo, which later came to include Syria. From 945 to 1055 the caliphs of Baghdad were completely dominated by a Persian dynasty of emirs. They were "liberated" by the Seljuk Turks, who had come originally from central Asia and had adopted Islam with fanatical zeal. For two centuries, Turkish emirs and sultans ruled in the name of the puppet Abbasid caliphs, reviving for a time the political strength of the Empire and recovering Syria. It was with them that the Christian crusaders had to deal. At last, in the middle of the thirteenth century, they, too, were overcome by a fresh invasion from Asia, that of the Mongol hordes, and with them the Abbasid caliphate finally disappeared.

Despite political divisions, the Moslem world retained throughout this period a strong economic, religious, and cultural unity. The converts, who introduced their inherited cultures into Islam, undoubtedly contributed more to its civilization than did the Arabs, who had little cultural tradition of their own; but, because it was expressed in the Arabs' tongue, the resulting synthesis of cultures has often been referred to as Arabic. Under the favorable conditions created by a common religion, a common language, and an economic revival that concentrated great wealth in the cities throughout the Islamic Empire, Moslem learning, literature, science, art, and technology far surpassed anything to be found in Western Christendom during the early Middle Ages.

This flourishing society rested on a solid foundation of commercial and industrial prosperity, and its spread throughout the whole Moslem world was due in large measure to the freedom of commercial intercourse of the Moslem Empire. Even after the political disintegration of the caliphate, commerce circulated wherever Islam was recognized, with a freedom reminiscent of the old Roman Empire. There was also a great foreign trade, especially to the East. Moslem captains navigated the Tigris from Baghdad or put out from Aden and other Red Sea ports to trade with all the lands bordering on the Indian Ocean. Here they met and exchanged goods with merchants from as far east as China. At the same time camel caravans struck out overland, eastward through central Asia to China and India, north into Russia, and south and west into Africa.

Thus, the spread of the Islamic faith brought about a great expansion of African and Asian trade, as well as significant intercultural contacts and influences. The West in the early Middle Ages had nothing comparable to offer in terms of high culture. The greatest empire of early medieval Europe was that of Charlemagne in the late eighth and early ninth centuries. Yet even this empire revealed in its institutions and personality that it had arisen out of a haphazard union of "barbaric" German and collapsing Roman elements.

Suggestions for Further Reading

N. H. Baynes and H. Moss, eds., *Byzantium: An Introduction to East Roman Civilization** (1948). Essays on many facets of Byzantium, judiciously edited by two outstanding British byzantinists.

C. Diehl, *Byzantium: Greatness and Decline** (1957). Includes bibliography containing many references to works dealing with interrelations of Easterners, Westerners, and Muslims [AHA, 172, in part].

D. J. Geanakoplos, *Byzantine East and Latin West: Two Worlds of Christendom in Middle Ages and Renaissance* (1966). Essays on the cultural and religious split between East and West before the thirteenth century. The author

*Available in a paperback edition.

shows a particular feeling for theological disputes and cultural differences, and his viewpoint demonstrates great empathy for Byzantine civilization.

H. A. H. Gibb, *Mohammedanism: An Historical Survey* (1953). Brief, accurate introduction to the subject.

P. K. Hitti, *History of the Arabs** (1956). The most popular general narrative of events in the Arab world [AHA, 222].

J. M. Hussey, *The Byzantine World** (1961). Brief introduction to the subject by an outstanding contemporary authority.

B. Lewis, *The Arabs in History** (1958). Brief and general survey, especially concerned with the early development and full efflorescence of Muslim civilization [AHA, 222].

G. Ostrogorski, *History of the Byzantine State,* trans. by J. Hussey (1969). The classic German study of the Byzantine state, in a fine translation. Quite detailed.

S. Runciman, *Byzantine Civilization** (1933). Highly readable survey of the subject, touching upon all major themes.

P. N. Ure, *Justinian and His Age* (1951). Masterful recreation of the world of sixth-century Byzantium.

A. A. Vasiliev, *History of the Byzantine Empire** (1952). A detailed political and dynastic history of the Empire.

W. M. Watt, *Muhammad at Mecca* (1953). Embodies an analysis of the social and moral background of Mohammed's teaching and its relevance to the contemporary situation [AHA, 230].

W. M. Watt, *Muhammad at Medina* (1956). Particularly worthy of note are those parts dealing with the tribal system in north and central Arabia and the social reforms instituted by Mohammed [AHA, 230, in part].

The Franks from Clovis to the Viking Invasions

8

They stand firm as a wall, as a circuit of solid ice, and slaughter the Arabs with the sword.

CONTEMPORARY DESCRIPTION OF CHARLES MARTEL'S ARMY AT POITIERS

He affirmed he would not have entered the church that day, even though it was so high a Church festival, if he had known what the pope intended to do.

EINHARD, *VITA CAROLI,* ON THE CORONATION OF CHARLEMAGNE

The Franks in the Merovingian Age

In the three centuries which followed the deposition of the last Roman emperor in the West in 476, the foundations of medieval civilization were laid; the blending of Roman, Germanic, and Christian elements was to make up the composite culture of the Middle Ages. Frankish Gaul between 450 and 900 witnessed the emergence of an early medieval culture resulting from the fusion of these three elements. In that period the Eastern Roman Empire became Byzantine. Justinian in the sixth century sought to make it once more a world empire, but in the next century the rising power of Islam stripped Byzantium of all but a fraction of its provinces. In the same period the early Germanic kingdoms, Ostrogothic, Vandal, and Visigothic, were destroyed. Meanwhile, two new powers, which were to be of supreme importance in shaping the Middle Ages, were rising to dominate the West in close alliance with each other. They were the Franks, the only Germanic nation—with the exception of the Anglo-Saxons—to found a permanent kingdom, and the Roman popes, rulers of the Catholic Church and heirs to the tradition of the Roman Empire. In between, exercising a strong influence on the destinies of both, were the Lombards, last of the Germanic invaders.

In the year 481 a fifteen-year-old prince named Clovis, grandson of that Merowech after whom the royal Merovingian family was named, became king of one of the Frankish tribes. He was a thorough barbarian, ruthless, treacherous, and avaricious, but endowed with great ability. He was not long contented with his little kingdom. Gaul, divided and weakened by war, was his for the taking. In 486, he conquered territory south to the Loire. Ten years later, he crushed the Alamanni and added their lands to his growing kingdom. Meanwhile, he had married a niece of the Burgundian king, named Clotilda, who unlike most of the

Burgundians was a Catholic. When the battle with the Alamanni was going badly and his heathen gods seemed unable to help him, he prayed—so legend tells us—to the God of Clotilda and promised allegiance in return for victory.

The conversion of Clovis and his followers to Christianity was in itself an important event, but it was his adoption of the orthodox Catholic form of Christianity that was most significant and destined to have far-reaching results. The story of the conversion is based on legend, and none too trustworthy. In all probability Clovis was motivated chiefly by political considerations. Certainly the baptism of the king with three thousand of his soldiers caused no real change of heart. All the other Germanic peoples who had settled within the Empire were Arian Christians, that is, heretics in the eyes of the more Romanized Catholic provincials. By embracing Catholicism, Clovis became the champion of orthodoxy and gained the support of the Gallo-Romans, who still made up the majority of the inhabitants, and especially of the powerful Catholic clergy. Bishop Gregory of Tours, whose *History of the Franks* (575-594) is almost our only source for early Frankish history, stresses the fact that Clovis made his attack on the Arian kingdoms of Gaul a holy war. We quote his report of Clovis's address to his soldiers on the eve of his campaign against the Visigoths in 507. "It grieves me that these Arians should hold part of Gaul. Let us march, with the help of God, and reduce them to subjection." They marched and, with the help of the Catholic population at least, conquered the Visigothic kingdom as far south as the Pyrenees. In the remaining years of his life, Clovis consolidated the Frankish tribes. By a series of brutal and treacherous murders, he eliminated all the rival Frankish kings, leaving a united kingdom to his sons in 511.

The successors of Clovis continued his career of conquest for half a century. The kingdom was divided among his four sons, according to the German custom, as though it were a private estate. The theoretical unity of the kingdom

THE GROWTH OF FRANKISH POWER, 481-561

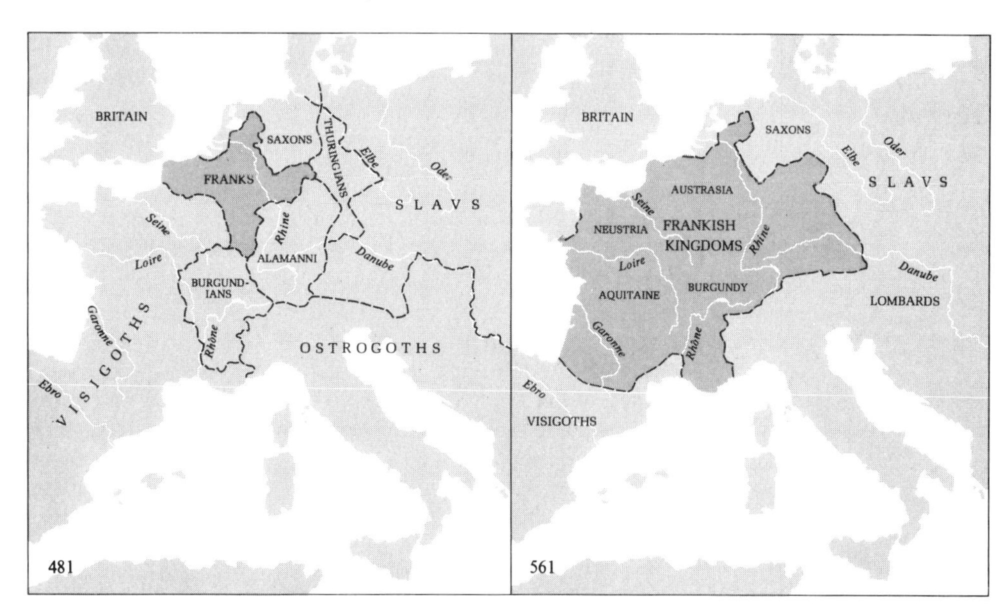

was preserved, however, and, though the kings quarreled and murdered among themselves, they cooperated in extending its boundaries. Burgundy was conquered in 534, and Provence was taken from the Ostrogoths two years later. The Frankish kings now ruled all Gaul except a narrow strip of Visigothic territory on the Mediterranean. They also pushed across the Rhine and subjugated the Bavarians, Thuringians, and Franconians in central and southern Germany.

From 613 to 639, Chlotar II and Dagobert, the last of the actively ruling Merovingian kings, in turn reigned over the reunited Frankish kingdom, but already the royal power was weakening. A century of absolute power and unrestrained debauchery had fatally weakened the health and character of the Merovingian stock. After Dagobert, the Merovingian kings became mere puppets in the hands of their chief ministers, the mayors of the palace, who now ruled the country in the king's name. For more than a century these pathetic "do-nothing kings" dragged out a useless existence, shut up in a villa in the country and brought out once a year, riding in an oxcart, to be seen by the people and to read an address prepared by the all-powerful mayor. Weak in mind and body, they made no attempt to assert their authority. Most of them died in their twenties.

For a generation or more after the death of Dagobert, the civil wars between Neustria, Austrasia, and Burgundy were revived and carried on by the mayors of the palace of the three kingdoms. At last, however, the mayor of Austrasia, Pepin of Heristal, decisively defeated the Neustrians at Tertry in 687 and reunited the whole Frankish realm under his rule. During his long reign of twenty-seven years (687–714), Pepin held the Frankish kingdom together, repressing rebellious nobles and subjecting the frontier duchies, which had become almost independent. He has been called the "second founder of the Frankish kingdom." Pepin was also the first of a long line of able and statesmanlike rulers of the family known as Carolingians for the most famous of their number, Charles the Great.

Society and Institutions in the Merovingian Age

The gradual blending of the Roman and Germanic elements of medieval civilization occurred for the most part under Frankish rule. Other barbarian peoples who settled in the Roman provinces were in time absorbed by the Roman population. Still others, like the Saxons in Britain, destroyed Roman civilization and remained staunchly Teutonic. The unique contribution of the Franks is that in their kingdom, which came to include almost all Christian western Europe, they held the balance between the two great sources of European civilization, making possible a fairly equal blending of the two. Three factors favored this development. First, their conquest of Gaul was an expansion of their original holdings, rather than a migration. They did not leave their ancient base along and beyond the Rhine to travel among an alien people, but extended their conquests while retaining their original homeland. Second, their conquests spread in both directions, to the south and west into Romanized Gaul and to the east and north into Germany, so that the Roman and German elements remained balanced. Third, the adoption of Catholic Christianity by the Franks, and the conversion of the Arian Germans whom they conquered, placed the Germans and Romans on the same religious plane and facilitated the fusion of their institutions.

The Franks were always a minority in Roman Gaul, except in the north-eastern corner which had been their home. To the south of the Loire they confiscated none of the land belonging to the Gallo-Romans, except in rare instances. They had conquered the Visigoths with the aid of the provincials, whom they therefore dared not alienate. The Franks contented themselves, therefore, with taking the land of those Visigoths who retired to Spain, especially of the Visigothic leaders. In Burgundy, too, they seem to have left private property untouched and taken only the lands of the Burgundian king, which were extensive enough. The population of Gaul, then, was not radically changed by the Frankish conquest. In western Gaul, which became the kingdom of Neustria, and above all in the area south of the Loire known as Aquitaine, the Roman population and culture predominated. Here the language remained essentially Latin in origin, developing in time into the French tongue. In Austrasia, the German element predominated, especially beyond the Rhine where it was almost unaffected by borrowings from Latin. In Burgundy, which the Burgundians had already made half-German before the Frankish conquest, the two elements were most evenly mixed. Throughout the Frankish realm the extent of Roman and German cultural influence varied like the colors in a spectrum, from the almost pure Roman of Aquitaine in the southwest to the almost pure German of the northeast end of Austrasia, passing through all the intermediate stages between. But because it was all under Frankish government, all parts were affected by the blending of Roman and Germanic institutions.

In some respects the Merovingian monarchy borrowed from Roman precedent, while in others it retained German traditions, but the blend produced a new institution. The Merovingian king had the absolute authority of a late Roman emperor over all his subjects, but that authority was exercised purely by right of heredity, through his descent from the Merovingian line. The Franks never developed the concept of a state composed of citizens who delegate supreme authority to their ruler, which was the original theory of the Roman Empire. On the contrary, the Frankish king regarded his kingdom as a private domain, which he had inherited and would divide among his sons according to the Germanic custom for the inheritance of private property. Yet even when divided, the kingdom remained theoretically united, ruled by members of the Merovingian family each of whom assumed the title king of the Franks. The only limits to the king's authority were those imposed by the growing strength of the aristocracy, who might disregard his commands, revolt, or assassinate him. While he remained in power, however, he was the sole legislator, supreme judge, chief executive, commander-in-chief of the army, and practical head of the Church. These powers, it is true, were gradually assumed by the mayor of the palace, but the theory remained unchanged, with the mayor exercising absolute authority in the name of the king.

The administrative system of the Merovingians, if it can be called a system, developed haphazardly to meet the needs of the moment in the most convenient way. The Roman system of taxation and of administration by a hierarchy of officers was too complicated for the German mind, and indeed had broken down in some places before the Franks arrived in Gaul. The expenses of government were small. The army and the local government were self-supporting, and fines covered the expenses of justice. The expenses of the royal court were met for the most part from the income of the king's own extensive estates. No distinction was made between the king's private purse and the state treasury. Thus, the king's personal servants, who had charge of the king's estates and income, naturally took over the financial administration of the state as well. A corps of officials administered the business of the palace, and since the king had no ready-made administrative system, it was easiest for him to extend their powers from the palace to the whole state. Thus the marshal, who had charge of the royal stables, became commander of the cavalry; the count of the palace, the king's legal adviser, became the head of the royal courts of justice; the referendary or royal secretary took charge of all documents of state. But of all these palace officials, the chief was the mayor of the palace, who had authority over all the others. It was he who became the king's chief minister and finally his master.

For local administration, the kingdom was divided into units, which in Gaul usually corresponded to the Roman *civitates* or municipalities with their surrounding territory, and in Germany to the land occupied by a tribe. Over each of these divisions the king appointed a count, who had full jurisdiction as administrator and judge. After 614, the counts were chosen from the noble families in the county and the title tended to become hereditary. In some parts of the kingdom, especially along the frontiers, a number of counties were gathered together under the command of a duke whose duties were chiefly military. The counts and dukes were paid no salaries, but supported themselves by the income from land granted to them by the king as remuneration for their services, by judicial fines and fees of various kinds, and by exploitation of the people. They were often half-independent of the king and many of them oppressed the people cruelly. Throughout the whole of Frankish history they were a menace to king and people alike.

The Church played a tremendously important part in Merovingian life, barbarous though the age was in general. The bishops, who governed the church, were among the most important administrative officials of the state. The bishop's diocese was usually coextensive with the territory ruled by a count, and his political power within that territory was often as great as that of the count. This was particularly true in the cathedral city where the bishop had his residence. The Franks at first cared little for town life and left the Gallo-Roman institutions of town government untouched. With the continuous decline of urban economy, however, the towns shrank in size; the old institutions withered away; and the bishop gradually took over the effective government. He had at his disposal great wealth, drawn from the numerous estates bequeathed to the Church, and immense moral and religious prestige. He acted as judge in many cases, supervised education, gave relief to the poor, kept up roads and public works, and protected the people from the exactions of king or count. Most of the bishops were of noble family, many of them Gallo-Romans. Unfortunately, the king often interfered in episcopal elections to nominate men of his own choosing, some of whom had little savor of sanctity about them. It was perhaps too much to expect of the king that he leave such wealthy and powerful officials free from his control, and, indeed, it was important that the Church work in close alliance with the monarchy. The effect, however, was to make the Church more worldly and to lower the general level of morality among the clergy. Still, the bishops were usually far superior in character to the counts and were in many ways the strongest moral force in the kingdom.

The laws of the Frankish kingdom provide us with some of the clearest evidence of the way in which Roman and German traditions existed side by side and eventually mingled. The Franks, like all early Germans, believed that every man had the right to be judged according to the traditional laws of his own people. Except for royal edicts dealing with specific problems, there was no uniformity of law. The Gallo-Roman retained Roman law, while the Frank, Burgundian, and Bavarian each had an ancestral customary code. However, the German codes did not cover many cases arising from the new conditions in Gaul and so laws were borrowed from the Roman code. Indeed, our knowledge of Germanic law stems from codes drawn up in Latin translation. This is another example of the influence of Roman civilization upon the Franks and other Germanic peoples. As the population became more mixed, the distinction between Roman and German gradually died out, and with it the distinction between legal systems. The result was a residue of laws in which the Roman and German elements were preserved to the degree that they suited the needs of the people and the age.

The Lombards and the Papacy

It was due to the Lombard threat to the Papacy that the Franks ultimately became involved in a Roman imperial adventure that molded the history of France, Germany, and Europe during the Middle Ages. It was while Clovis was establishing the Frankish kingdom in Gaul that Theodoric, the Ostrogothic king, carved out for his people a kingdom in Italy; and while the sons of Clovis were conquering the remainder of Gaul, Justinian was making Italy once more a province under imperial rule. Within three years after the death of Justinian, another great change took place. A new nation of barbarian invaders, the Lombards, swept down into Italy and opened a new chapter in its history.

The Lombards were one of the East German peoples. They migrated south and east to the Danube, where they were converted to the Arian form of Christianity, and in 568 they followed the track of earlier Germanic invaders from the Balkans down into northern Italy. About 575, marauding bands of Lombards began to push farther south, and within a decade had occupied the center of Italy almost to the southern end of the peninsula. By 605 the Lombards had conquered all of Italy except the territories around Ravenna, Rome, Naples, and the extreme south. These areas were still ruled by representatives of the emperor, nominally under the exarch of Ravenna, though Rome and the other imperial possessions were so cut off from the exarchate as to be practically independent. The unity of Italy was completely destroyed. The Lombard kingdom itself was not strongly united. The Lombard dukes were always half-independent and often rebellious, especially in the two large duchies of Spoleto and Benevento in the center and south, which were never firmly attached to the kingdom.

Out of the chaos of this last barbarian invasion, one Italian power, the Roman Papacy, emerged with greater authority than ever before. The popes had lost much of their prestige since the days of Leo the Great, though they had gained considerable wealth from estates bequeathed to them in all parts of Italy. The restoration of imperial rule in Italy had been a serious blow to their authority, for Justinian had introduced the domination of the Church by the state which had long been recognized in the Eastern Empire but had never been enforced in the West. Moreover, the pope's authority outside of Italy had suffered. The bishops of Gaul were controlled by the Frankish kings, and Spain under the

Visigoths was Arian almost to the end of the sixth century. But the Lombard conquests broke the power of the emperor over the pope, and in 590 the Roman Church found in Pope Gregory the Great a leader who was to set the Papacy back on the road to independence and spiritual dominion in the West.

Gregory was a thorough Roman, born to a noble and wealthy Roman family. In early life he held some of the most important administrative posts in the city, but gave up his political career to retire to a monastery. He was called forth to serve the Church, and finally, in 590, to become pope. In that difficult position he proved himself an able administrator, a diplomatic statesman, and a staunch defender of papal supremacy. Gregory had an indomitable will, untiring energy, and the self-confidence of the born autocrat, all qualities needed by the man who occupied the chair of Saint Peter in those troubled times. Rome was constantly in danger from the Lombards who surrounded the Roman territory. The imperial governor, cut off from his superior at Ravenna, was powerless. It was the pope who undertook the defense of the city, negotiated with the Lombards, and used his resources to maintain public works and relieve the poor. Though still recognizing the overlordship of the emperor, Gregory made himself the practical ruler of Rome and the land around it. At the same time he pressed his claims to universal authority over the Catholic Church with the greatest vigor. He was not always successful. The Frankish bishops were polite rather than obedient, but they learned to look more often to Rome for guidance.

Gregory also increased the influence of the Papacy by extending the boundaries of the Catholic Church. The Anglo-Saxons in England were still heathen, though missionaries from the Celtic Church in Ireland, which had been isolated from the Roman Catholic Church since the Saxon conquest of Britain,

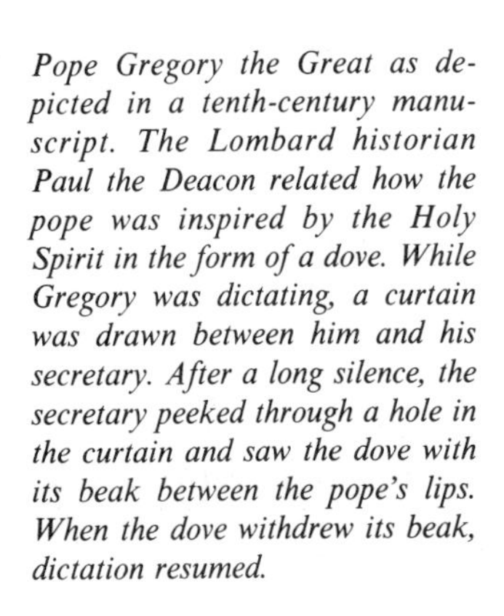

Pope Gregory the Great as depicted in a tenth-century manuscript. The Lombard historian Paul the Deacon related how the pope was inspired by the Holy Spirit in the form of a dove. While Gregory was dictating, a curtain was drawn between him and his secretary. After a long silence, the secretary peeked through a hole in the curtain and saw the dove with its beak between the pope's lips. When the dove withdrew its beak, dictation resumed.

had begun to work in the north. Gregory believed that the Saxons were ripe for conversion, and was proven correct. The mission headed by Saint Augustine of Canterbury, which Gregory sent to England in 596, met with extraordinary success. During the following century the whole of England was brought into the Roman Church, but not until a long struggle with the Irish Church had been won.

In the midst of a busy life, Gregory found time to write, besides numerous letters, a long commentary on the Book of Job called the *Moralia,* and a book of instructions to the clergy entitled *Pastoral Care.* These works, widely read during the Middle Ages, earned him the title of Father of the Church. Yet in style, erudition, philosophical background, and intellectual breadth, he cannot be compared to the earlier Fathers, Ambrose, Jerome, and Augustine. He knew no Greek; his Latin style, though simple and forceful, was far from classical; and his thought was encumbered with superstitions. Nothing shows more clearly the cultural decline that had taken place in Italy in the previous two centuries than the intellectual gap which separates Gregory from Augustine. Gregory's influence, nevertheless, was very great, all the greater perhaps because he was not too far above the intellectual level of subsequent centuries. Throughout the Middle Ages a persistent tradition ascribed to him the authorship of the Gregorian chant, the magnificent plainsong melodies that in the generations after his death became the universally accepted setting for the Roman Catholic liturgy. Modern scholars no longer accept his authorship, but there is evidence that he did contribute in some way to the codification of the music of the Roman liturgy. Certainly its adoption throughout the Church was in accord with his strong feeling for the unity of the Catholic Church under the primacy of the Roman Papacy.

The seventh century witnessed little change in the relative positions of the three powers in Italy: the Papacy, the Lombards, and the imperial government. The gradual conversion of the Lombards to Catholicism was the most important event of the period. The emperors, absorbed in the struggle with Persia and later with the rising Moslem Empire, made no serious attempt to recover the land lost to the Lombards or to re-establish control of the Papacy. Early in the eighth century an imperial decree forbidding the presence of icons in churches caused a break between the pope and the emperor. The decisive schism between the Roman Catholic and Greek Orthodox Churches did not occur until 1054, but after the iconoclastic controversy in 725 the popes could no longer look to the emperors for protection. When the Lombards threatened to capture Rome and deprive the pope of his independence, he was forced to turn to the only other power strong enough to aid him, the ruler of the Frankish state.

The Frankish Kingdom and the Church

Charles Martel, illegitimate son of Pepin of Heristal, was by 720 recognized as mayor of the palace in all parts of the Frankish kingdom. Charles was above all a warrior, at a time when a fighting prince was needed. His reign was filled with campaigns, for the most part successful, against rebellious counts and dukes, the heathen Germans to the north, and the Moslems to the south. Bands of Arabs had invaded Gaul as far as the Loire when Martel met them at Poitiers in 732.

In that famous battle the Franks struck a blow that checked an advance of Islam to the west. At the end of his reign Charles left the kingdom greatly strengthened and his family firmly established as the real rulers of the Franks.

One of the most difficult tasks Charles had to undertake was the subjection of the German tribes beyond the Rhine who were nominally under Frankish rule. The problem was made all the more difficult by the fact that many of them were still heathen. Charles realized that they could never be brought fully under Frankish rule until they had adopted the religion of the Franks. He therefore gave enthusiastic support and armed protection to missionaries working for their conversion. Of these by far the most important was an English monk, Winfrith, better known by his Latin name, Boniface. Wherever his work took him, this great missionary founded Benedictine monasteries as outposts of Christianity and organized the new Church as part of the Roman hierarchy.

On the death of Charles Martel in 741, the Frankish kingdom was again divided between his two sons, Pepin (misnamed "the short") and Carloman. After six years, however, Carloman renounced the world and retired to a monastery in Italy, leaving the whole kingdom in Pepin's capable hands. The latter proved himself a true member of his illustrious family, ruling with wisdom and firmness, defending his kingdom, and protecting the Church. He crushed rebellions in the German duchies, defeated the "wild Saxons," and in the last years of his reign completely subjugated Aquitaine, which had made a strong bid for independence. For three generations now the Carolingian mayors had ruled as sovereigns in everything but name.

By 751, Pepin felt that he was firmly enough established to risk deposing the puppet Merovingian and assume the title of king. But he needed some sanction other than force to offset the traditional loyalty of the people to the ancient Merovingian house, and turned naturally to the Church, the greatest moral force of the age, appealing to the pope for advice. The appeal reached Rome at a crucial moment. Ravenna had just fallen to the Lombards and Rome was threatened. Glad of the opportunity to win favor with the powerful ruler of the Franks, the pope replied that "it was better that he should be called king who had the power, rather than he who had none." Pepin, thus fortified, called an assembly of the nobles and clergy of the kingdom at Soissons in November 751, and there proclaimed himself king of the Franks. The saintly Boniface, as representative of the Papacy, consecrated him with holy oil. The consecration was a new departure and a significant one. It invested the king with a special character and supplied a divine sanction to royal authority which served it well for centuries. It also represented a recognition of papal supremacy over the Catholic Church, bound Church and state closer together, and placed Pepin in the pope's debt. He was soon called upon to discharge that debt in full.

Meanwhile, the pope's position was growing more desperate. The Lombards were threatening to take from him his independent government of the land about Rome. In the winter of 753-754, Pope Stephen III journeyed to the Frankish court to make a personal appeal to Pepin for aid. There he reconsecrated Pepin, giving the Carolingian house the full sanction of the Roman Church. In return, Pepin made expeditions against the Lombards in 754 and 756, both successful. After the second expedition, he forced the Lombard king to give up to the pope not only the Roman lands but also the land of the late exarchate. The gift of this land, stretching from Rome to Ravenna clear across central Italy, is known as the Donation of Pepin. The keys to the cities included in it were laid upon the tomb of Saint Peter, together with a deed giving them in perpetuity "to the Roman Church, to Saint Peter, and his successors the popes." Thus was founded an independent principality in Italy under the rule of the pope and known as the Papal States, or the States of the Church.

Carolingian Society and Administration

Few names occupy so prominent a place on the pages of history and legend and in the minds of men as that of Charles, eldest son of King Pepin. Historians by common consent have called him Charles the Great, or Carolus Magnus, as the Latin chroniclers wrote it, and medieval legend has popularized the name in the Romance form, Charlemagne. When his father died in 768, Charles was not yet thirty. For three years he shared the kingdom with a younger brother, Carloman, but the unity of the kingdom was preserved by the death of the latter, as it had been in the preceding generation by the retirement of the elder Carloman. Thereafter Charles ruled alone until his death in 814.

We are fortunate in possessing a description of Charles which rescues him from the obscuring mists of medieval legend and romance. In his *Vita Caroli* (*Life of Charles*), the royal secretary Einhard has left us a vivid portrait of the genial giant who was his friend as well as his king. Here we see Charles as a tall, vigorous man, so well proportioned that his stoutness was not a noticeable defect. He was fond of hunting and swimming, temperate in his use of food and drink, though in his last years stubborn in his preference for roast meats against the advice of his physicians. He was an eager student, having acquired a fair knowledge of Latin and some Greek, but his studies had begun too late in life for him ever to have learned to write. Above all he was a tireless worker, with an inexhaustible interest in all the varied details of government. For the rest, Einhard pictures him as a kindly yet masterful man, a good companion, and a fond father, whose only defect was the unrestrained interest in women which gave rise to more than one scandal at court.

The force of Charlemagne's personality and his reputation for greatness gave to the Frankish Empire a more stable and civilized image than reality justified. Charlemagne's government depended on the great landholders and large abbeys of Austrasia, east of the Rhine. Carolingian society was administratively decentralized to an extent that is almost impossible for us to picture today. It was overwhelmingly rural, communications were poor, and literacy was rare. The king's reputation, his personal visits, and the activities of agents whom he could trust held the vast Carolingian realm together. Despite the Carolingian use of Latin terminology for administrative and fiscal purposes, there is no similarity between the centralized Roman administration of the second century and the essentially barbarian kingdom ruled by Charles the Great in 800.

The counts were in charge of local administration, though closely associated with the bishops, who had become recognized administrative officers of the state as well as the Church. Much of Charles' success in maintaining his authority throughout the realm depended on the close personal scrutiny he maintained over these local officers. This was accomplished through the institution of the *missi dominici* ("those sent by the king"). The missi had been known in earlier times as representatives of the king on special missions. Charles now regularized their duties, sending them out each year in pairs to visit all parts of a given territory. The two missi traveling together were usually a layman and an ecclesiastic: a count and a bishop or abbot. It was their duty to examine the administration of both Church and state in their territory, to see that the king's orders were carried out, to preserve close relations between the central and local administrations, and to prevent injustice and oppression. This system checked the independence of the counts during Charles' reign, but it had no permanent value, for it was merely an extension of personal rule whose success in the long run depended entirely on the character and strength of the ruler.

As long as the Lombard kingdom prevailed, the pope would never be secure in his government of the Papal States in central Italy. After Pepin's death, the Lombard king, Desiderius, had retaken the cities of the exarchate which had been ceded to the pope, and in 773 Pope Adrian called upon Charles to rescue the Papacy as the king's father had done before him. Charles marched into Italy with a large army, defeated and deposed Desiderius, and, in 774, declared himself king of the Lombards. He celebrated Easter that year in Rome and there renewed the Donation of Pepin.

Another of Charles' important conquests was the heathen Saxon land, which extended from the Frankish frontier on the Rhine north to the borders of Denmark and east to the river Elbe. The "wild Saxons" had long been dangerous and lawless neighbors. They clung stubbornly to their pagan religion and their freedom, realizing, as did Charles, that the two were inseparable. Whether the desire to protect and extend his frontiers or to convert the heathen weighed more strongly with the Frankish king cannot be determined. Certainly conquest and conversion went hand in hand, and the invaders came armed with both sword and cross. Charles led his first campaign against the Saxons in 772, but thirty-two years passed before the conquest was completed. During that time Charles directed eighteen campaigns into the Saxon land, pillaging, laying waste the country, and sometimes massacring or deporting part of the population.

Meanwhile, other wars occupied a great deal of Charles' time and energy. He put down revolts in Aquitaine and Lombardy, conquered Bavaria, and also waged war with neighboring nations. In 778 he invaded Moslem Spain, taking advantage of a rebellion there to strike a blow against the powerful Umayyad emir, who threatened again to become a menace to Frankish security as in the days of Charles Martel. This campaign was a failure, though Charles later secured a strip of territory to the south of the Pyrenees known as the Spanish March. While returning through the Pyrenees, the rear guard of the Frankish army, led by a noble named Hruodland (Roland), was cut off and destroyed by Basque mountaineers in the pass of Roncesvalles. This event, of little historical importance in itself, is famous because it gave rise to the greatest of medieval epics, the *Song of Roland.* Against the Mongolian Avars, who had established a kingdom in Hungary and threatened his eastern frontiers, Charles had more success. In 791 he marched through their kingdom, bringing back immense booty. Later they were forced to recognize him as overlord. The protection of the newly conquered Saxon land also forced Charles into wars with the Danes to the north and the Slavs to the east across the Elbe.

As the eighth century drew to its close, the figure of Charlemagne dominated the West. He was the acknowledged ruler of all Catholic Christendom except the British Isles, feared and respected by his heathen and infidel neighbors. Only the Moslem caliph at Baghdad and the Greek Orthodox emperor at Constantinople could rival him in power or prestige, and the latter had fallen upon evil times. Scholars at Charlemagne's court who had studied classical literature began to compare him to the ancient Roman emperors. More than three centuries had passed since there had been an emperor in the West, but the ideal of a universal Roman Empire still cast its spell over people's imaginations. Its memory had been kept alive by the Roman Catholic Church, a universal spiritual empire ruled by the pope at Rome, employing Latin as its official speech, and characterized by a hierarchical government modeled on the imperial administration. The Church gave unity to Catholic Christendom, but many medieval thinkers believed that the divine scheme called for a secular counterpart, a political empire and temporal ruler who would hold secular authority over all Christians (i.e., Catholic Christians) comparable to the pope's spiritual authority. In reality, the king of the Franks held that position; yet to the medieval mind it was inconceivable that such a ruler should not be the Roman emperor. The obvious solution was to make the Frankish king emperor of a revived Roman Empire. Some such reasoning, influenced by Charles' personal ambitions and the pope's need for protection against seditious riots in Rome, must account for the amazing and epoch-making scene which occurred in Rome on Christmas Day of the year 800. As Charles knelt before the altar of St. Peter's Church after the Christmas Mass, Pope Leo III placed an imperial crown on his head and hailed him emperor amidst the shouts of the people. Charles later denied any foreknowledge of the event. Perhaps he had not wished to receive the crown from the pope. If so, he was justified by the troubles which arose from that act in future centuries. But it was accomplished. An empire had been created, Roman in name but more German in fact, and inseparably linked to the Catholic Church.

The whole conception of this Carolingian government was Germanic and paternal. As father of his people, Charles felt responsible for their welfare and issued innumerable decrees or *capitularies* dealing with the most varied aspects of public and private life, religious and moral as well as material; Church and state were so closely bound that it was impossible to make any clear distinction between their respective jurisdictions. Those capitularies that have survived are of great value in helping the historian form a picture of the age. Some are detailed instructions for the management of the royal estates; others regulate the discipline and organization of the Church; still others are general decrees applicable to the whole realm and published everywhere by the counts and bishops. Taken together, they justify the description of Charles as one of the great legislators of the Middle Ages.

Many of Charles' capitularies deal with economic problems. By far the majority of the people were engaged in farming or drew their income from the land. The most interesting of the capitularies are those dealing with the management of the royal estates. These give evidence of a considerable improvement in agricultural methods, which were copied on the great villas or estates of the nobles and the Church. The consolidation of large estates proceeded steadily through this period, as small landowners lost their land and freedom under the stress of compulsory military service, which often proved too great an economic strain on the small farmer. This situation, of course, added to the power of the nobles and the great churchmen, a fact that was to have important results in the next century. Industry was limited almost entirely to the production on the estate of the tools, weapons, clothing, and other goods needed by the inhabitants of the villa. Commerce of a long-distance type had declined greatly since the fifth century. In fact, during the eighth century trade was limited more and more to the meeting of local needs, and barter (exchange of goods) was replacing a "money economy" (the buying and selling of goods for cash).

The Carolingian Renaissance

Despite his multifarious activities, Charles found time to take a keen interest in the education of his people and especially of the clergy. As protector of the Church—and in reality its master, whatever the theoretical relation of Church and state—he felt responsible for the purity of its teaching. The religion of the people was steeped in superstition left over from pagan days, and the majority of the clergy were too ignorant to instruct them. Charles realized that the improved education of the clergy was a matter of supreme importance. Wherever possible, he encouraged bishops and abbots to found schools for the training of priests and he himself founded a school at the palace to which he brought scholars from all parts of Europe. Paul the Deacon (Paulus Diaconus), the author of the famous *History of the Lombards,* came from Italy. Theodulphus, whom Charles made bishop of Orléans, was a Spanish Goth. Einhard was one of the few Frankish scholars. But most important of all the teachers at the palace school was Alcuin, a Saxon monk from northern England who had received his education in the school founded by the Venerable Bede. These men devoted themselves to the study of Latin antiquity, both classical and Christian. They also promoted the copying of ancient manuscripts and introduced a more legible style of handwriting, which set a standard followed for centuries. Their work has given to the age the somewhat exaggerated name of the Carolingian Renaissance, or rebirth of culture. Actually they learned little more than the rudiments of the ancient culture, finding more that they could understand in the works of the scholars of the intermediate period, like Gregory the Great, than in the masterpieces of the golden age or the works of the great fourth-century Fathers of the Church.

Nearly illegible pre-Carolingian handwriting. This eighth-century script from the History of the Franks *of Gregory of Tours was executed at the Burgundian monastery of Luxeuil.*

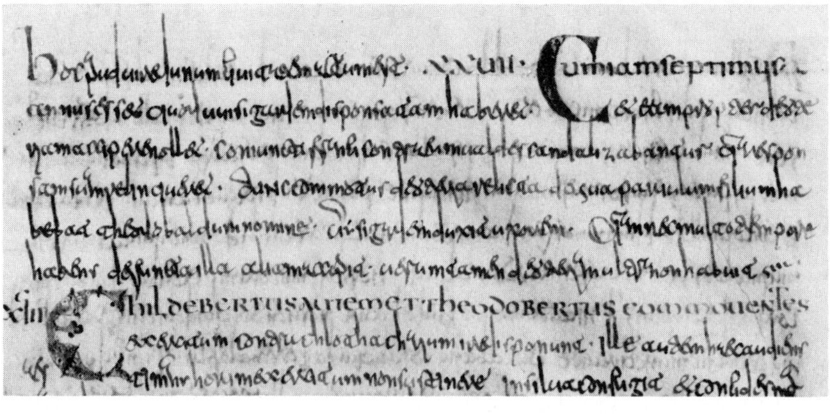

Moreover, education in this age was limited exclusively to the clergy, and, only a small minority of these were more than barely literate. Laymen no longer knew Latin and were unable to read even their own language. The Carolingian revival is important nonetheless, for it marks the beginning of the long process by which the German people assimilated the ancient classical and Christian learning and made it their own.

In speaking of this Carolingian revival of learning, we should not overlook the fact that Charlemagne viewed himself above all else as a Frankish king. He was interested in the ancient Germanic epics and songs of his people and ordered them to be assembled and recopied. However, his son and successor Louis the Pious, influenced by the clerical belief that such pagan Germanic songs were deleterious to the Christian commonwealth over which he reigned, had them destroyed. This act has proven to be a great loss for scholars of early Germanic literature and language.

The Crisis of the Carolingian Empire

Charlemagne died in 814. His reign was followed by a period of disaster, darkness, and chaos. These developments had been delayed but not halted by the great Carolingians, and under the successors of Charlemagne they became stronger than the monarchy. The civil wars arising from the Frankish custom of dividing the realm among all the late ruler's heirs were also a seriously disruptive factor throughout the ninth century. Finally, as though its internal difficulties were not enough, the weakened and divided empire was subjected to a long series of devastating raids and invasions by hordes of Magyar horsemen from the east, by Moslems from the south, and from the north and west by those fierce Scandinavian pirates, the Northmen.

Charles the Great was survived by only one son, Louis (814–840), called "the Pious" because of his devotion to the Church. The year before his death,

Carolingian minuscule. The first three and a half lines after the title read: "Novum opus me sacere cogis ex vetere ut post examplaria scripturarum toto urbe dispersa quasi quidam arbiter sedeam et quia inter se variant quae sint illa quae cum greca consentiant veritate decernam."

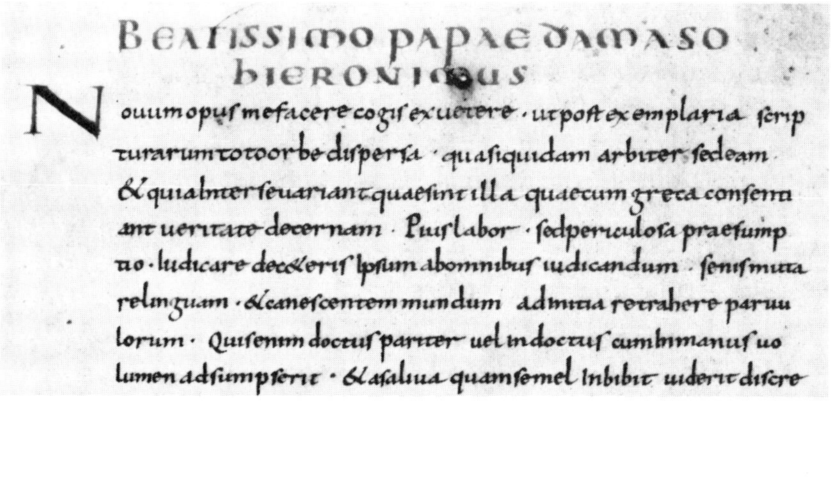
BEATISSIMO PAPAE DAMASO
HIERONIMUS
Nouum opus me facere cogis ex uetere · ut post exemplaria scrip
turarum toto orbe dispersa · quasi quidam arbiter sedeam ·
& quia inter se uariant quae sint illa quae cum greca consenti
ant ueritate decernam · Pius labor · sed periculosa praesump
tio · iudicare de ceteris ipsum ab omnibus iudicandum · senis mutare
linguam · & canescentem mundum ad initia retrahere paruu
lorum · Quis enim doctus pariter uel indoctus cum in manus uo
lumen adsumpserit · & a saliua quam semel inbibit uiderit discre

Charles had bestowed the imperial crown upon Louis, apparently in the hope of breaking the tradition of papal coronation. This precaution was nullified, however, for Louis permitted the pope to crown him in 816. Thus far the unity of the Empire had been saved, as in preceding generations, by the survival of only one heir. But almost at once the fatal principle of division began to cause trouble. In 817, Louis announced his plans for the division of the Empire among his three sons after his death. Six years later these plans had to be revised to include a fourth son, Charles, born to Louis' second wife Judith. This strong-minded woman seems to have completely dominated her amiable husband and was determined to gain a fair share, or more, of the heritage for her son. The remainder of Louis' reign was filled with intrigues, rebellions, and civil wars as each of his sons strove to hold or extend his portion while the country was ravaged, the government neglected, and the imperial authority weakened.

When Louis the Pious died in 840, the question of division was still unsettled. One of his sons had died, but each of the remaining three was dissatisfied with his share. Lothair, the eldest, who had inherited the imperial title, hoped to extend his authority over the whole empire. The two younger brothers, Charles the Bald and Louis the German, as they were called, therefore united against him. In 841 they met in the deadly battle of Fontenoy. Great numbers of the Franks were slain, but neither side won a clear victory. Charles and Louis separated for a time, but were soon forced to reunite. They met at Strassburg in the following year and there took an oath of perpetual loyalty to each other. The text of the oath has survived and gives interesting evidence of the development of separate languages within the Frankish Empire. Louis read the oath in the Romance tongue, the ancestor of modern French, so as to be understood by his brother's troops, most of whom came from western Gaul. Charles, on the other hand, took the oath in the German dialect, which alone would be understood by the men who had followed Louis from the east.

THE CAROLINGIAN EMPIRE, 814–843

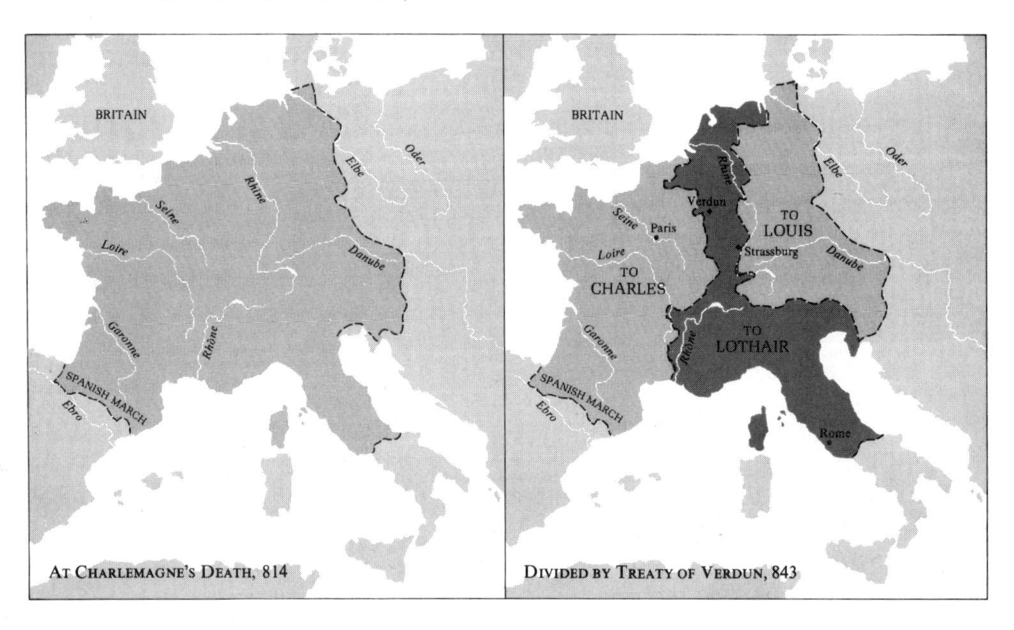

The alliance proved too strong for Lothair, and in 843 peace was concluded by a treaty arranged at Verdun. Lothair was given the imperial title and a strip of territory about a thousand miles long and rather more than a hundred miles wide, running from north to south through the center of the Empire from the North Sea to Rome. It included most of the valleys of the Rhine and the Rhône and more than half of Italy. The portions assigned to the two younger brothers, who assumed the title of kings, had greater geographical and cultural unity. Charles received the Romance-speaking western part (the West Frankish kingdom), while Louis took the German lands to the east (the East Frankish kingdom). The Treaty of Verdun did not create new nations, but did demarcate the territories which were to become the countries of France and Germany and the "middle kingdom," the debatable land over which the French and German nations fought until 1945.

The Coming of the Northmen

The Carolingian Empire decayed largely because of internal weakness, but the process of dissolution was accelerated by the impact of barbarian invaders from the north. The Northmen, who in the ninth century fell upon the entire exposed coastline of western Europe, with fire and sword, destroyed much of the civilization they found, as had their Germanic predecessors, but in the end added new elements to the formation of medieval civilization.

The first Viking raids were directed at the British Isles; the *Anglo-Saxon Chronicle* mentions one as early as 787. But it was not until the beginning of the ninth century that such raids became frequent and assumed serious proportions. In the last years of Charlemagne's reign the Vikings first beached their long boats on the Frankish coast. Thereafter their raids continued, each year bringing more and larger boats manned by more numerous, more experienced, and hence more dangerous crews. It is impossible to distinguish with precision between the Vikings of the various Scandinavian countries. In general, however, those who sailed westward around the north of Scotland to prey upon the coasts of Scotland, Ireland, and the smaller islands were Norwegians. Later they sailed farther west to Iceland, Greenland, and the coast of North America. Both Norwegians and Danes harried the coast of western Europe, while the Danes seem to have been chiefly responsible for the invasion of England. The Swedes took the eastern route by river through Russia to the Black Sea and eventually to Constantinople, where they met other Vikings who had sailed eastward through the Mediterranean from the Straits of Gibraltar. No part of Europe that could be reached by water was safe from these far-wandering men.

The seacoast towns were naturally the first objects of their raids. Masters of the sea, they struck where they chose and enjoyed all the advantages of a surprise attack. Their long open boats appeared unheralded out of the morning mist, and before a force could be collected to ward them off they had sacked the town and carried their plunder off to the safety of the sea. As they grew bolder, the Vikings struck inland, rowing their boats up the navigable rivers on which the most important towns were situated. For centuries these rivers had been the principal highways of trade; they now served the northern pirates equally well. Everywhere the Northmen sought out monasteries and churches, less out of malice toward the Christian clergy than because they had learned that rich plunder was to be found under the sign of the cross and that the monks and clergy had become too accustomed to the protection offered them by religious veneration to have taken the necessary precautions for defense. Great numbers of the monasteries were completely destroyed—a serious blow to learning, since they were the chief centers of education. The fear these rapacious pirates inspired is echoed eloquently in the prayer introduced into the litany, "From the fury of the Northmen, good Lord, deliver us!"

About the middle of the ninth century, the activities of the Northmen entered a new phase. No longer were they content to make annual expeditions in search of movable plunder. Instead they began to settle at strategic points along the coast and to carry on their depredations at closer range. The Frankish Empire had been sadly weakened by the civil war between the sons of Louis the Pious and by the resulting division of the empire. The Danish host took advantage of the weakness of the central government to found permanent camps at the mouths of the great rivers which empty on the western coast. Toward the end of the century, however, their raids were checked as the towns improved their fortifications and the nobles began to build strong castles for defense. In 891, the German king, Arnulf, defeated a large Danish army on the lower Rhine and drove them out of that district. Thereafter the settlements of the Northmen were confined to the lower reaches of the Seine, and the raids on other areas soon ceased. In 911 or 912, the land about the lower Seine, known thereafter as Normandy, was ceded to the Northmen by the Carolingian king, Charles the Simple. Their leader, Duke Rollo, became a vassal of the French king, though a very independent one, and was converted to Christianity. Further immigration continued for some time, and Normandy occupied a rather anomalous position as simultaneously a Scandinavian colony and a French duchy. But by the end of the tenth century, the Normans had adopted the religion, speech, and culture of the French people among whom they lived. By that time Normandy had become definitely French, though it was always more than half-independent of the French king.

In England much the same development had taken place about the middle of the ninth century. In 866, the Danes began a concerted invasion which threatened to overwhelm all England. The invasions of England resembled a mass migration in many places. Mounting themselves on horses stolen from the coast shires, the Danes rode inland sweeping all opposition before them. Anglo-Saxon England was at this time divided into four separate kingdoms which failed to unite against the foreign foe. Within five years the Northmen conquered the kingdoms of Northumbria, Mercia, and East Anglia. In 871, they invaded the southern kingdom of Wessex, the last Saxon stronghold.

There they were finally checked by the skillful and courageous leadership of the young Alfred (871-900), who succeeded his elder brother as king of Wessex in the midst of the invasion. Like Charlemagne, to whom he has often been compared, Alfred was vitally interested in religion and education, though unlike the great Frankish ruler he was himself one of the finest scholars of his day. The heathen "army" had destroyed the greater part of monastic culture in northern England, including the school at York where a century earlier Alcuin had received the education which made him the foremost scholar at Charlemagne's court. Even in Wessex learning had declined. Both people and clergy were ignorant and were reverting to pagan superstition. Realizing the importance of educating the clergy, Alfred gave personal attention to the founding of schools, while he himself undertook the translation from Latin to Anglo-Saxon of such works as the *Pastoral Care* of Gregory the Great, the *Consolation of Philosophy* of Boëthius, and Bede's *Ecclesiastical History*. It was he, too, who was responsible for the institution of the *Anglo-Saxon Chronicle*, our best source for the history of his age. As the founder of the English kingdom and of English literature, Alfred fully deserved his title, "the Great."

Meanwhile, the Danes were settling everywhere north of the Thames, farming and building fortified "boroughs" as military centers; they were also gradually adopting the Christian religion. They failed, however, to develop any strong political organization. In the two generations following Alfred the Great, his son and grandsons were able to complete his work by reconquering the Danelaw—the large area where Danish arms and laws prevailed for a time—and establishing a united kingdom in England. For a time the Danes retained their own laws; but because their language and customs were not radically unlike those of the Saxons, they gradually merged with them into one nation.

Of the Vikings from Sweden who struck out to the east and south by way of the rivers through Russia, we know less. We do know, however, that these Vikings, whom the Slavs called "Russ," occupied Novgorod and Kiev about the middle of the ninth century and under a leader named Rurik carved out some kind of kingdom for themselves—the first Russian state. They traded from the Baltic to the Black Sea and kept up commercial relations with Constantinople and Baghdad. In the course of time, like the Northmen who had gone to England and Normandy, they adopted the speech, religion, and customs of the people among whom they lived and so vanished as a people. The sons of the early Vikings, who had appeared as predators and destroyers, settled down and made major contributions to medieval civilization in Normandy, Russia, England, and southern Italy.

Suggestions for Further Reading

H. Arbman, *The Vikings* (1961).

E. S. Duckett, *Alcuin: Friend of Charlemagne* (1951). Duckett's works are readable introductions, sustained by good scholarship.

E. S. Duckett, *Alfred the Great** (1962).

S. C. Easton and H. Wieruszowski, *The Era of Charlemagne* (1961). An excellent, brief introductory essay, followed by a valuable selection of documents from the Carolingian era.

H. Fichtenau, *The Carolingian Empire: The Age of Charlemagne** (1957). A forthright attempt to examine the disappointing aspects of Charlemagne's work, while also recognizing his positive contributions [AHA, 180].

H. Fichtenau, *The Carolingian Empire,** trans. by P. Munz (1963). A brief, readable survey, covering all phases of the Carolingian Empire and reflecting current research.

M. L. W. Laistner, *Thought and Letters in Western Europe. A.D. 500-900** (1957). A useful survey of European intellectual history, concentrating on key figures such as Isidore of Seville, Gregory the Great, Alcuin, and John Scotus Erigena.

*Available in a paperback edition.

R. Latouche, *The Birth of Western Economy** (1961). A crucial book by an outstanding French scholar. This work treats the much discussed transition from late Roman to "barbarian" early medieval society. Highly readable.

P. Munz, *Life in the Age of Charlemagne* (1969). A good survey of Carolingian society by a noted scholar.

H. Pirenne, *Mohammed and Charlemagne** (1939). Attributes the collapse of Western civilization to the spread of Islam—a bold attempt to apply a questionable theory in a historical setting [AHA, 173, in part].

P. H. Sawyer, *The Age of the Vikings* (1961).

W. Ullmann, *The Growth of Papal Government in the Middle Ages* (1955). Ullmann is the greatest authority on this subject; his books are essential to a study of the medieval Papacy.

The Agrarian Economy of Medieval Europe

9

Master: And which do you think among secular crafts holds the first place?
Councillor: Agriculture, because the plowman feeds us all.
COLLOQUY OF AELFRIC THE GRAMMARIAN (C. 955–1010)

All that the peasant amasses in a year by stubborn work, the knight, the noble, devours in an hour.
SERMON BY JACQUES DE VITRY (C. 1180–1240)

The Manor and Its Technology

Early medieval Europe, devastated by invasions that the debilitated Carolingian Empire could not prevent, was overwhelmingly rural and agrarian. By the end of the ninth century, the manorial system of landholding and cultivation had become common. It served as the economic, social, and judicial framework within which the peasants lived and worked. With a few exceptions, chiefly in mountainous country and in regions given over to sheep- and cattle-grazing, the land was divided into estates, called villas in France and manors in England, of which the owner was a lord or seigneur and the workers were peasant tenants dependent on him. Through the organization of the manor the peasant laborers had their only contact with the military ruling class, which formed the upper ranks of feudal society. The lord of the manor was a member of the fighting aristocracy. He might have a single manor, or as many as hundreds. In any case, the individual manor was often an almost independent unit.

No two manors were exactly alike; there were infinite variations in custom and practice. Yet the general characteristics of the manorial system were sufficiently uniform in all parts of western Europe to justify describing a typical manor, on the understanding, of course, that the details would vary widely from case to case. At the center of the manor, on the highest point of land, stood the manor house, fortified to give protection to the lord and peasants in case of attack. If the manor was the home of a powerful baron, it was a fortified castle, otherwise it was no more than a strongly built house. If the lord was absent or lived on another manor, the manor house was occupied by the bailiff, who acted as his agent and managed the estate. Near the manor house clustered the huts of the peasants, each with a little land, forming the village, an indispensable part of any manor. In the village there was also a mill, a blacksmith's shop, a small church, and a house for the parish priest. Surrounding the village were the cultivated fields and the meadows, wastelands, and woods. Perhaps a third of the cultivated land was set aside for the sole use of the lord; this was called the demesne. It might be all in one piece or scattered in small pieces throughout the manor. The remainder of the cultivated land was parceled out among the peasants of the village. The meadows, wastelands, and woods were not formally divided but were considered common land, shared proportionately by lord and peasants.

On all sides of the village stretched great open fields under cultivation, each containing hundreds of acres. While the crops needed protection, the shepherds, cowherds, and swineherds kept their charges out of the fields by day and enclosed them at night, or the fields may have been protected by temporary fences during the growing season. After the harvest the livestock of the lord and the villagers was turned loose to graze on the stubble. This method of farming is called the open-field system. For purposes of cultivation the land was usually divided into three fields to allow for rotation of the crops. One field was reserved for spring planting of oats or barley; the second for the fall planting of wheat or rye, to be harvested the following summer; the third lay fallow—that is, it was allowed to rest without crop—though it was plowed twice during the year, and the young grass which sprang up served as pasture for the cattle. Each year the fields were rotated, so that each field lay fallow once in three years. This system, possibly a

A medieval manor. In northern Europe, many manors may have been organized along these lines.

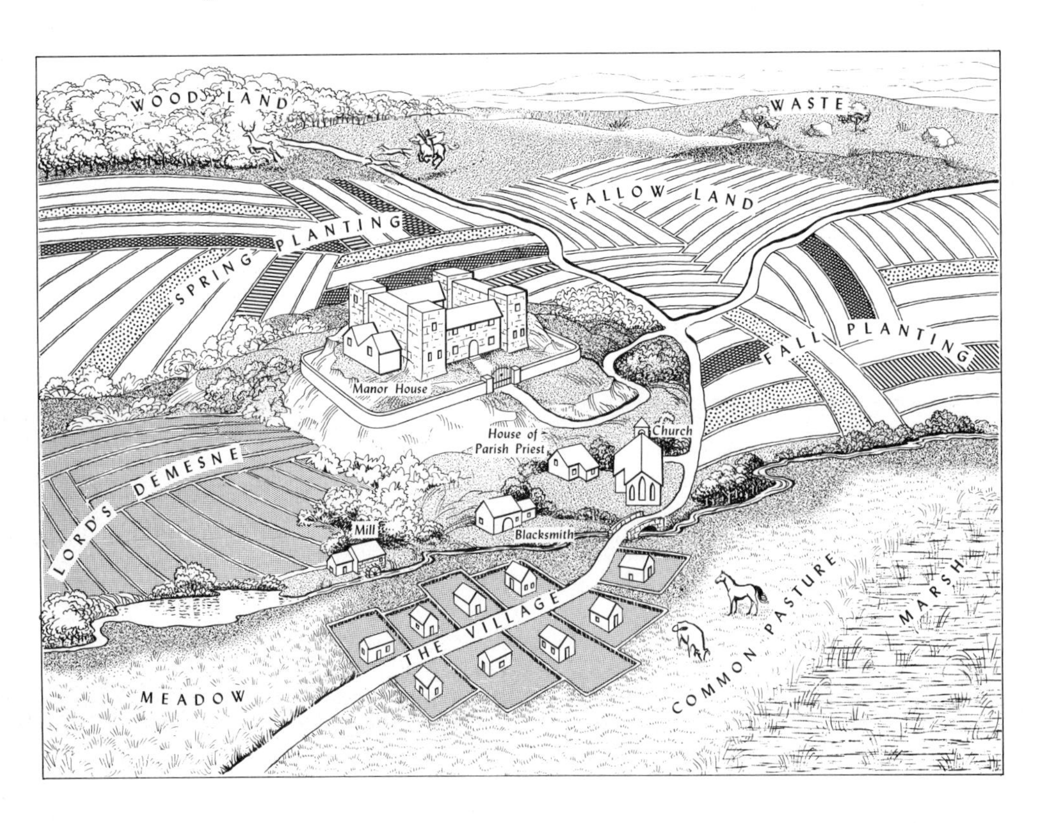

Germanic contribution to Western civilization, was necessary at a time when methods of fertilizing were crude and unscientific. The land would soon have become exhausted if it had not been allowed to recover or if the same crop had been planted on it year after year. On very poor land even one fallow year in three was not enough, and in Italy and parts of southern France where hot summers made spring planting impractical, a two-year rotation was generally employed.

Scattered through the open fields and outside the demesne or the lord's farm were the small holdings of the peasants. Each field was subdivided into long narrow strips separated by thin ridges of grass. The shape of these strips was fixed by the plow. They were usually as long as the lay of the land permitted, so that the heavy plow, drawn by a team of four or eight oxen, did not have to turn too often. Every peasant household held a number of these strips, scattered at random through each of the three fields. Sometimes the lord reserved some of them as demesne (or domain) land, and some strips were assigned to the parish church as glebe land. The latter was land from which the priest received the produce. The amount of land held by a peasant varied, depending on the number of strips he had inherited. This system of so-called intermixed tenure may have originated as a method of giving each of the peasants land of equal value, allowing to none the advantage of an entire plot in especially fertile soil or near the village.

Whatever its origin, the system continued because it was compatible with the method of working the land employed on the manor; though each peasant took the crop from his own strips, the whole village pooled its labor in the communal cultivation of the fields. Because very few peasants were rich enough to own a plow and a complete team of oxen—or the still more costly horses that, after the tenth century, began to replace oxen in some parts of northern Europe—it was necessary for the villagers to combine their resources. The simplest method under the circumstances was for each team to work straight across the field, plowing each strip in turn. Thus the intermixture of the strips guaranteed the same treatment for all.

Medieval agrarian economy is too often treated as an undifferentiated whole. As a matter of fact, there were major differences between the agrarian technologies of northern and southern Europe throughout the Middle Ages. The colder climate and harder soil of northern Europe beyond the Alps challenged the ingenuity of the medieval peasant. In addition, agrarian technology in the

Plowing with an ox team, from a miniature in a fourteenth-century psalter.

north benefited from the innovations of the Germanic peoples. Agrarian traditions there were less fixed than was the case in Italy. This proved to be a boon. Technological innovations occurred in the ninth and tenth centuries which were extremely important for the future of medieval agriculture. An example is the introduction of the choke collar, which enabled peasants in northern Europe to make use of horses rather than oxen in tilling the land. This innovation was significant because it allowed horses to breathe more easily and do more work. They could turn at a sharper angle than oxen. This in turn altered the pattern of cultivation. The iron horseshoe was another crucial technological device. The widespread introduction of iron-tipped plows made it easier to till the hard soil of northern Europe, opening up hitherto undeveloped areas to agriculture. The extensive use of water-wheels and windmills made the production of food more efficient by the eleventh and twelfth centuries, thus providing one of the bases for the great economic and demographic expansion of western Europe during that period. Without such expansion, the subsequent massive growth of trade and urban centers could not have occurred.

In Italy, parts of southern France, and Spain the hamlet was the typical unit of rural life. It allowed for a greater degree of individual ownership than did the village and communal land organization or northern European agriculture. This difference reflected in part the more ancient tradition of southern European agriculture and the difference between Germanic institutions of agrarian cooperation and the Roman tradition of individual ownership of land. Further, the harder, colder land of the north required heavier, more expensive equipment for tillage, which often tended to encourage the pooling of agrarian resources by means of a village land organization. Such differences, however, were not absolute.

A windmill, from a miniature in the margin of a fourteenth-century manuscript. In the medieval period, wind, water for water-wheels, and animal and human muscle-power were the chief sources of energy.

Lord and Peasant

The inhabitants of the village who worked the fields were members of the peasant class. They were all tenants, receiving their land from the lord of the manor, under his jurisdiction and more or less dependent upon him. Yet within this class there were innumerable gradations and shades of social status and degrees of wealth and freedom—or perhaps it would be more accurate to say degrees of poverty and servitude. It is impossible to distinguish clearly between the various grades of peasants; there was little uniformity throughout Europe, and even the names used to describe them are often confusing. The unfree tenants were generally called villeins or serfs. As a rule, they were bound to the land on which they were born and could not leave it without the lord's consent and the payment of a fine. The free tenants were not thus bound, but were nevertheless under the lord's jurisdiction as long as they remained on the manor. The origin of these differences in status is probably to be found in the manner in which the peasants' ancestors first came under the jurisdiction of the lord and in the terms of the original bargain between them; the contract between lord and tenant was hereditary, passed on with little change from generation to generation.

Slavery also existed. Although the Church had combated this institution since early times, it was still widespread in the Middle Ages, particularly in southern Europe. While the serf could claim some vestiges of civil freedom, the slave could boast no such rights. Slavery had been vital to Roman agriculture, and this tradition, as well as the continued activities of slave traders along the Mediterranean slave routes, prolonged its existence well into the medieval period. The relation between the peasant and the lord of the manor is best described as based on an unwritten contract to which custom had given legal sanction. It was not a one-sided bargain. The lord gave the peasant protection, established a court where he could appeal for justice, built a mill, and provided a church for the village. Above all, he furnished the land. All the land of the manor belonged legally to the lord; but custom forbade him from taking the peasant's strips of land, provided the latter had fulfilled all his obligations. Nor could the lord prevent the peasant from taking his customary share of hay from the meadows or pasturing his allotted share of cattle, swine, or geese on the common land. Thus the peasants, though in most cases not free to leave their land, enjoyed the security which came from the hereditary right to its possession.

In return for these privileges, the peasants owed certain payments and services to the lord. All but the freest peasants were obliged to work for the lord a certain number of days each week. This "week work" was devoted to the cultivation of the demesne land and to incidental tasks such as carrying the lord's produce to market or to another of his manors. At certain times of year when the pressure of work was greatest, such as harvest time, all the peasants on the manor were forced to work on the lord's demesne. These special services were called boon works. Labor services were an essential part of the manorial system. Indeed, the whole system may be regarded as a method of securing labor for the lord's land without the payment of money wages. All the tenants also owed the lord payments as rent for their land. Usually made in kind—that is, in produce—these payments might in exceptional cases be made in money. The amount of the payments was fixed by custom, though in some places the lord had the legal right to exact as much as he chose from his serfs. The villagers had also to pay for the use of the lord's mill and the great oven where all baked their bread. There were other occasional dues. On the death of a tenant his heirs had to make a special payment, called heriot, as recognition of the lord's possession of the land and for the renewal of the hereditary contract. The unfree peasant also had to make a payment, called merchet, if his daughter married outside the manor and thus deprived the lord of one of his serfs.

Few of these manors were completely self-sufficient, but this does not mean that they were dependent in the early Middle Ages upon long-range trade or upon the limited urban economy of western Europe. Indeed, the opposite was true. Though distant manors belonging to the same or to different lords might exchange goods to their mutual benefit, they had to be self-sufficient for long periods of time, particularly during periods of military conflict. To the lord of the manor, however, the concept of self-sufficiency would have had little meaning, for the weapons, clothes, and luxury products he desired often had to be brought in by merchants who traveled long distances over poor roads. For the peasant, the manor was largely a self-enclosed entity, whose horizon encompassed his life and death. True, in Italy after 1100, lords often had castles in the towns but northern Europe, at least until about 1200, was overwhelmingly rural. Even after that time the average wealthy town merchant invested much of his capital in land. There was never an absolute division between town and country.

Rural Life and Attitudes

The life of the average person in the Middle Ages was short and uncertain. He was a constant prey to disease, to the malign forces of nature, and above all to the avarice and brutality of his fellow men. Robbers and brigands infested the roads and made travel dangerous for all but large and well-armed parties. Avaricious nobles too rode down from their hilltop castles to rob or hold for ransom the merchants, pilgrims, and priests who passed upon the highway. Not content with that, they often fell upon villages of defenseless peasants or outlying monasteries, where there was always an opportunity for plunder. In time of peace, the nobles were often little better than brigands. In time of war, they were usually worse.

The chief aims of the fighting noble were to weaken and impoverish his enemy by destroying the productivity of his land and to acquire plunder. Consequently, he ravaged his enemy's fields, destroyed crops, burned villages after carrying off the cattle and anything else of value, and massacred or held for ransom the peasants, who were themselves valuable property and the chief source of his enemy's income. Saint Peter Damian summed up the situation when he wrote that, whenever two nobles quarrel, "the poor man's thatch goes up in flame." The following description of feudal warfare from the *Chanson des Lorrains* is abundantly confirmed by less poetic documents:

> They start to march. The scouts and the incendiaries lead; after them come the foragers who are to gather the spoils and carry them in the great baggage train. The tumult begins. The peasants, having just come out of the fields, turn back, uttering loud cries; the shepherds gather their flocks and drive them towards the neighboring woods in the hope of saving them. The incendiaries set the villages on fire, and the foragers visit and sack them; the distracted inhabitants are burnt or led apart with their hands tied to be held for ransom. Everywhere alarm bells ring, fear spreads from side to side and becomes general. On all sides one sees helmets shining, pennons floating and horsemen

> covering the plain. Here hands are laid on money; there cattle, donkeys and flocks are seized. The smoke spreads, the flames rise, the peasants and the shepherds in consternation flee in all directions.

After the campaign, "windmills no longer turn, chimneys no longer smoke, the cocks have ceased their crowing and the dogs their barking, . . . briars and thorns grow where villages stood of old." This is what war meant to the peasants, and in many parts of Europe, war was almost the normal state of society.

Nor was war the only hazard to life in the Middle Ages. Medieval people were far more at the mercy of the elements than we are today. Floods often did terrible damage, sometimes wiping out whole towns or villages. Even today, there are occasional disastrous floods; but in that age they were far more numerous and deadly, for there were no means of controlling them or bringing relief to the victims. More terrible than the floods were the famines that usually followed them or resulted from other adverse weather conditions. Too much or too little rain, unseasonable heat or cold, an unusual number of insect pests, or any of the other natural hazards of farming, which today can be combated by scientific means, might destroy the peasant's whole crop. The French chronicles record forty-eight famine years in the eleventh century. Although by the end of the twelfth century methods of agriculture had improved, there were eleven famines in France during the reign of Philip Augustus. There were also countless local famines, for roads were so bad that it was difficult to transport food even a short distance to places where local weather conditions, floods, or the depredations of a campaign had destroyed the crops. Famine did not mean mere shortage of food for the peasant and poor townsman; it frequently meant death by starvation. The year 1197 saw terrible famines in France. A chronicler of Liège wrote that even the rich suffered great privation, and "as for the poor, they died of hunger."

Epidemics were rife throughout the Middle Ages. Plagues of various sorts wiped out entire communities. The most famous was the bubonic plague, the Black Death of mid-fourteenth-century Europe, which had profound effects upon social and political history. In some areas it wiped out two-thirds of the population. To the medieval man or woman an epidemic of such proportions could only be grasped through the understanding, comfort, or dismay offered by popular superstition and established religion. The churches were filled to overflowing during such epidemics. Groups of flagellants, whipping themselves in penance as they paraded through villages uttering or singing supplications to their God and saints, were common sights in medieval Europe. What medieval people could not grasp as a natural disorder appeared to be the work of a devil or the scourge of a just God visiting catastrophe upon His immoral children.

When his fields suffered insect plagues, the helpless peasant turned for aid to the Church. If he were in good standing with the local clergy, he received its full cooperation, for the priest, though somewhat better educated, was as superstitious as he. A solemn anathema issued by the Bishop of Troyes against the "locusts and caterpillars and other such animals that have laid waste the vineyards" of his diocese shows the Church giving spiritual aid to the peasants on a large scale. Indeed, the excommunication of caterpillars was not uncommon.

The prevailing theory of society, propounded by generations of theologians, recognized three great classes, each of which had a definite function to perform for the good of the whole social body. These were, first, the clergy, whose duty was to pray and to care for the salvation of their fellow men; second, the nobles, whose duty was to fight in defense of the helpless and to keep order; and finally, the peasants and artisans, whose function was to work and to provide the necessities of life for the whole of society, as well as luxuries for the upper classes. These functions were not always faithfully performed, except perhaps by the workers, who had little choice in the matter, but the distinction between the classes was not merely a theory.

The duty of the peasant, then, was clear to all. He was to work and to make no rebellion against his lot. A pious statement from a contemporary chronicle expresses the opinion of noble and cleric alike: "God forbid that the peasants, whose proper lot is daily toil, should abandon themselves to sloth and indolently spend their time in laughter and idle merriment." And toil carried with it the stigma of social inferiority, for in the early feudal ages almost all the workers on the land were to some extent unfree, and even after they obtained personal freedom, their class bore the stamp of servile origin.

The freeborn, fighting nobles, therefore, had nothing but contempt for the servile, laboring peasants. They were necessary to the comfort and prosperity of their masters, but as individuals they scarcely existed. They were regarded as distinctly inferior beings. The romantic literature of the period, composed for a noble audience, reflects this attitude. When individual peasants are mentioned, which is not often, they are described as physically grotesque, stupid, and horribly unclean—as, indeed, they probably were.

It is not surprising to find that the nobles exploited the peasants. There were, of course, good lords who felt responsible for the security of their peasants and acted justly according to their lights, as well as bad lords who squeezed every possible penny from them. But even the best of lords demanded full payment of the heavy manorial dues from their own peasants and were utterly merciless to the peasants belonging to their enemies. "All that the peasant amasses in a year by stubborn work, the knight, the noble, devours in an hour." So wrote Jacques de Vitry, with no more than the customary exaggeration of the moralist. The greatest of medieval popes, Innocent III, gave similar testimony in his *De Contemptu Mundi:*

> The serf serves; he is terrified with threats, wearied with *corvées* [forced labor], afflicted with blows, despoiled of his possessions; for, if he possess nought, he is compelled to earn; and if he possess anything, he is compelled to have it not; the lord's fault is the serf's punishment; the serf's fault is the lord's excuse for preying on him.

The peasants often suffered, too, from the rapacity and dishonesty of the lord's officers. Under a careless lord, the bailiff who acted as his agent, the forester whose duty was to see that the peasants did not cut more than their share of wood or poach the lord's game, and the other petty officials of the manor had a good deal of power, which they frequently abused to extort money from the peasants. These manorial officials themselves sprang from the peasant class, but opportunities for advancement were so few that the desire to take full advantage of those that did arise usually outweighed any fellow-feeling they might have retained for their old neighbors.

The clergy were no less severe than the nobles in exploiting the peasants. The Church held a great deal of land, and ecclesiastical lords were in general no more lenient with their peasants than were the lay nobles. Indeed, modern research has shown that customary dues were retained with less amelioration and that serfdom lasted longer on monastic estates than elsewhere.

The peasant's house was merely a rough wooden hut with a thatched roof. It was a squalid and filthy dwelling. In it we would find what one modern historian has characterized as "poverty unadorned." There was no chimney. Cooking was done out-of-doors in the summer. In the winter, when a fire had to be lighted in the house, the smoke escaped, if at all, by the door, and must have nearly suffocated the inhabitants. Few peasants had ovens. They sent their bread to the manor house to be baked in the great oven there. Even those who had ovens of their own had to pay the customary fee for the use of the lord's oven. Sometimes the hut contained a rough bed, where the entire family slept. More often there was merely a pile of straw, alive with vermin, in one corner. Geese and hens wandered freely about the house, and the oxen were usually stabled in a lean-to beside it. In summer, the peasants were probably comfortable enough, for their standards were not high, but the winters must have been terrible. We know all too little about what clothing they wore, save that it was mostly handmade by the women of the family.

What evidence we have as to the ordinary food of the peasants illustrates better than anything else the extent of their poverty. The medieval farmer ate poorly even in good years, and starved in years of famine. Meat of any kind was apparently a rare luxury. A fifteenth-century writer described the food of the peasants thus: "They feed on brown bread, oatmeal porridge or boiled peas; they drink water or whey." In some places the thirteenth-century peasant was probably better off, but all the evidence shows that the same foods—porridge and black bread made of rye or oatmeal, simple vegetables, cheese and whey, with perhaps an occasional egg—were the staples of diet. Beer was available at times, but by no means universally. Of course, on feast days peasants were sometimes admitted to the lower hall of the manor house, where they would gorge themselves on richer food at the lord's expense.

The peasant's toilsome life was not entirely unrelieved by color or diversion, though there was little enough. On the great religious holidays, when he was forbidden to work, he might have a share in the excitement that attended the celebrations of his betters. In her book *Medieval People,* Eileen Power describes one such festival, attended by the peasant Bodo. Bodo might be admitted to the feast at the castle or be allowed to watch the knights disporting themselves at the tournament. If he were fortunate enough to be sent with produce to a nearby town during a fair, he might watch the jugglers and tumblers, listen to a wandering minstrel, or have his pocket picked while he gaped open-mouthed at the antics of a performing bear. On Sundays and holidays he might join in the dance on the village green or engage in a rough—often very rough—game of football.

According to contemporary writers, the peasant's material destitution was matched by his spiritual poverty. He was totally uneducated; his morals were often little better than animal; his religion was grossly material and more than half superstition. Ecclesiastical writers railed against the peasant for his indifference to religion: he neglected the saints' days; he sometimes worked on Sundays; he showed small respect for the parish priest; and he was unwilling to pay the tithe. They described him as avaricious, quarrelsome, dishonest, suspicious, and sullen. Considering his life of grinding poverty, toil, oppression, and terror, it would have been surprising if he were otherwise. The early medieval centuries afforded the peasant only the most precarious security of life or property. He worked, lived, and died at the lowest rung on the ladder known as the feudal order.

Suggestions for Further Reading

H. S. Bennett, *Life on the English Manor* (1937).

M. Bloch, *Feudal Society** (1961). A work of major importance—broadly conceived and executed with the originality, skill, and remarkable learning found in all that Bloch wrote [AHA, 184, in part].

M. Bloch, *Land and Work in Medieval Europe** (1967).

G. G. Coulton, *Medieval Panorama** (1938). Lively, anecdotal portrait of medieval society (mainly English), with many good quotations from original source materials. Coulton was strongly hostile to organized religion.

J. Evans, *Life in Medieval France,* rev. ed. (1957). Interesting, well-illustrated panorama of courtly life in medieval France, with some presentation of the life of other secular and ecclesiastical groups. Gives one a good feel for "Gothic" France.

U. T. Holmes, *Daily Life in the Twelfth Century. Based on Observations of Alexander Neckham in London and Paris** (1952). By following his medieval source carefully, the author manages to bring to the modern reader some of the excitement, wonder, and reality of daily living in the twelfth century [AHA, 197, in part].

G. C. Homans, *English Villagers in the Thirteenth Century* (1940). An interesting, successful attempt of a sociologist to describe medieval conditions [AHA, 197].

E. A. Kosminsky, *Studies in the Agrarian History of England in the Thirteenth Century* (1956). Marxist in point of view [AHA, 191].

M. W. Labarge, *A Baronial Household of the Thirteenth Century* (1966).

L. White, *Medieval Technology and Social Change** (1962). Fascinating, at times controversial essays on a broad range of subjects. Scholarly, readable, provocative.

*Available in a paperback edition.

The Feudal Order

10

No land without a lord.

MEDIEVAL PROVERB

The Origins of Feudal Institutions

The term "feudalism" refers to a decentralized, predominantly agrarian society in which military force and a hierarchical social structure were the main characteristics of justice, administration, and economic life. Broadly speaking, the eighth and ninth centuries may be described as the age in which feudalism originated; the tenth and first half of the eleventh centuries as the period in which it took definite shape; and the next two hundred years as the time of its fullest development, followed by centuries of slow decay as new forms arose to take its place. Feudalism arose because it was the only system that could satisfy the needs of the age. It resulted from a vast number of bargains and arrangements between private individuals and between individuals and the monarch—bargains in which both parties made the best terms they could according to their needs and ambitions. The fundamental cause of feudalism, then, is to be found in the conditions of the eighth and ninth centuries. Of these conditions the most important was the weakness and eventual failure of the central government, which, in turn, was very largely the result of the economic conditions prevailing throughout western Europe. Lacking the stimulus of external trade, the long-range commerce of Western Christendom diminished in volume and city life of the classical or late Roman variety generally disappeared with it. What remained was a largely agricultural economy based on barter and exchange of services, with very little money in circulation. Moorish, Arabic, and Byzantine coins were highly prized in this backward, early medieval society.

Land became almost the sole source of wealth, and without markets there was no adequate means of turning its products into cash. Under such circumstances, taxes were difficult if not impossible to collect on any significant scale. As a result, the government, deprived of financial support, was forced either to pay for services with grants of land, which always tended to become hereditary, or to delegate its duties and privileges to those landholders who could exert effective authority over the people on their land. In addition, the Frankish government had always suffered from the weaknesses inherent in a primitive system of personal rule. Even in their best days, the Carolingian rulers had never provided an adequate government.

Feudalism made slow progress until the ninth century, when under Louis the Pious and his warring sons the central government gradually collapsed. Weakened by civil wars and rebellions, the later Carolingians were unable to protect their people from the raids of the Northmen and the violence of the nobles, and were forced to leave them, as well as many of the privileges of government, in the hands of the fighting aristocracy, whom they could no longer control and to whom the people were forced to turn for the protection the king could no longer offer.

During the summer months when his land needed the most attention, the freeman was often forced to go on campaigns at his own expense and without pay. For this and other reasons, great numbers of small farmers sank hopelessly into debt, and in order to cancel their debts or to escape military service they gave up their lands to some large landholder. Thereafter they worked the land as dependent tenants under his protection. Freemen who had no land or had lost it, and hence had no way of making a living, also "commended" themselves to a neighboring lord. Henceforth they were his men and were usually given some land to work. In either case they became dependent on the lord and lost their freedom.

During the turbulent ninth century this process was greatly accelerated. The necessity of securing protection forced the remaining small freemen to put themselves and their land under the protection of the local lord, even though it meant the loss of ownership and liberty; in that lawless age security was more important than freedom. At the same time, many great landowners took advantage of their power and the lack of governmental control to force their poorer neighbors into this dependent position. Whatever the steps by which this process was completed—and they are none too clear—by the end of the ninth century almost all the workers on the land had become unfree tenants on large estates. In certain parts of the old empire of the Franks, such as Saxony, revolts by the dying class of free farmers were common through the eleventh century.

While the poorer citizens were sinking on the social scale, the wealthier or more fortunate were forming a military aristocracy. Since the early years of the eighth century, when Charles Martel had placed part of the Frankish army on horseback in order to meet the Moslem cavalry on equal terms, military service had become more expensive. In the course of time practically the whole fighting force came to be made up of mounted men. As a result, only a man with sufficient wealth to provide himself with a horse, as well as with armor and weapons, could afford to fight. The resulting flight from military service so reduced the imperial army that Charlemagne issued edicts forcing the lords to equip and bring into the army, under their own leadership, at least some of the men dependent on them. Thus there developed a class of military dependents, who, unlike the laborers, did not lose their status as freemen, because fighting was considered an honorable occupation.

In the chaos of the ninth century, fighting men were at a premium. They were needed by the king and by the lords, and hence were able to secure more favorable terms for themselves than were the laborers. The warrior who commended himself to a lord was not paid wages for his services, since lack of sufficient money in circulation made regular wages impractical; instead, he normally received from the lord the use of enough land, together with the peasants to work it, to provide him with sufficient income for horse and armor and the leisure for fighting. The freeman who had land enough to maintain himself as a warrior, but who needed the protection of some great lord, gave up his land to the lord and was allowed to retain the income from it in return for military service. By the end of the ninth century, this reciprocal system of landholding and military service had become the general rule. There were some exceptions. Instead of granting land as payment for service, a lord might simply take a warrior into his household and provide him with food, clothing, weapons, and armor. Also, in the unplanned development of the feudal system, some lands, called allods, remained independently owned and not held from any lord. This was particularly true in southern France. The number of these exceptional cases, however, decreased rapidly after the ninth century, and it became a recognized axiom in most parts of Europe that there should be no land and no man without a lord. Like the laborer, the fighter held his land from the lord whose man he was, but his position in the social scale was infinitely higher and tended to become hereditary, thus laying the foundation for a military aristocracy.

In an age of general anarchy like the ninth century, he ruled who had the power to rule, regardless of legal right. The counts and dukes of the Carolingian Empire, whose offices had become practically hereditary, were the natural leaders of their administrative districts. It was easy for them to establish themselves as rulers in their own right, rather than as officers of the crown, though they still recognized the king as their superior. Similarly, lesser lords took over the actual government of their own districts, because they were strong enough to do so.

Military Feudalism: The Fief and the Nobility

Feudal society must be viewed in the context of the economic and technological bases upon which it rested. Let us look first at military technology. The armor of an early medieval knight was expensive and became more elaborate, and hence more expensive, as the centuries passed. On the average, a good suit of armor cost 100 sous in the eleventh century. At the same time, oxen, the most widely used draught animals in French agriculture, sold for 6 or 10 sous; a good *destrier,* or tough cavalry horse, sold for between 25 and 50 sous. The price of the suit of armor alone was equivalent in monetary value to the typical holding of a middle-level peasant in northern France during that period. Such estimates graphically demonstrate that the pastime and justification of early medieval knights—fighting—was based upon the cheap agrarian labor of the downtrodden serf.

There was a popular historical belief in the late nineteenth century, still prevalent in some quarters, that the emergence of feudal cavalry was attributable to the incursion of Moorish warriors into Gaul early in the eighth century. Moorish pressure supposedly led Frankish leaders such as Charles Martel to conclude that it was necessary to organize an effective cavalry as a countermeasure against the swift and devastating mounted Arab raiders. An alternative view of the emergence of cavalry in the eighth century is that Frankish leaders grasped the tremendous technological advantage which the stirrup gave to mounted knights. This interpretation views the threat to Western Christendom presented by the Spanish Arabs as of limited importance. The Moorish threat alone did not provide adequate motivation for the institutional changes wrought in Frankish society by Charles Martel's use of the military benefice. The traditional interpretation held that Charles Martel, needing mounted warriors to fight the Moors, invested Frankish warriors with benefices of land to enable them to outfit themselves with the expensive paraphernalia of mounted warfare. More contemporary views, such as that of Lynn White, suggest a technological explanation.

War was the justification of the ruling class. We have already seen how this class arose through the combination of landholding and military service. Whatever the nature of the original bargain between the fighter and his lord, the amount of land involved was necessarily greater than that granted the laborer by the lord of the manor; and the fighting man's relation to his lord carried no suggestion of servility, but was a free and honorable bargain between two members of the same military aristocracy.

There were many variations in rank and wealth within the military class, extending from the poorest knight, whose land barely furnished him with equipment, to the great count or duke, whose wide lands supported hundreds of knights who rode to battle at his command. But certain characteristics were common to them all. All were warriors, set apart from the base-born; almost all were lords, with a greater or lesser number of dependents, for even the poorest knight was usually lord of a small manor; and each held a fief from some greater lord to whom he owed military service. The fief was the basic land unit of military feudalism. It varied in size with the wealth and importance of the holder—that of a poor knight being a single manor, that of a count or duke a great territory including hundreds of manors. In any case, the holder of the fief was the vassal of the lord from whom he received it; this lord might be a baron, count, duke, king, or any other lord with land enough to grant part of it to a vassal in return for military service. The vassal did not own the fief, just as the peasant tenant did not own the land he worked, but he had an hereditary right to the use of it and could not legally be deprived of it so long as he fulfilled his obligations.

The relations between the vassal and his lord were based on a commonly understood contract, passed on with little change from generation to generation. This contract was formally renewed in a solemn ceremony whenever the death of either party introduced his heir into the relationship. The vassal's part in this ceremony was called homage. He knelt before his lord, bareheaded and unarmed, placed his hands between the hands of his lord, declared himself the lord's man (*homme*), and took an oath to be faithful to him. The lord then responded with the ceremony of investiture, presenting to the vassal a spear, flag, or some other symbol representing the fief. The symbolic ceremony of homage and investiture constituted a binding agreement, defined by custom and enforced by public opinion. It could not be legally broken by one party unless the other failed to live up to the terms of the contract.

The feudal contract imposed a number of mutual obligations. On the vassal's part, the chief of these was to fight for his lord. Originally, no doubt, the vassal was expected to fight whenever and as long as the lord needed him. However, as society became more settled and the need for military aid less constant, the amount of military service owed was usually fixed at a certain number of days (customarily forty) a year. The number of knights required to fulfill the vassal's obligation varied, of course, with the size of the fief. The holder of a single manor, rated at one knight's service, was responsible only for his own service, whereas a baron whose fief was larger was bound to answer his lord's call to arms accompanied by other knights, who in turn were bound to follow him because they held fiefs from him and were his vassals. Closely allied to this military obligation was the court duty. The vassal was obliged to attend the court of justice held by his lord on stated occasions, and also to do his lord honor by his presence at festive celebrations, where the number of vassals in his retinue was an indication of the lord's social importance.

The vassal also owed his lord certain contributions in money or produce.

These payments were made only on special occasions. The heaviest payment in most cases was the relief, sometimes amounting to as much as a year's income from the fief, paid whenever a vassal died and was succeeded by his heir. Like the heriot paid by the peasant tenant under similar circumstances, it was apparently an acknowledgment of the lord's possession of the land and a fee for the renewal of the contract, which was considered to be temporarily broken by the death of one of the contracting parties. In addition to the relief, there were three generally recognized aids. All vassals were obliged to contribute to making up the lord's ransom if he were captured, to defraying the expenses of the ceremony of knighting his eldest son, and to providing a dowry when his eldest daughter married. The vassal was also expected to house and entertain the lord and his retinue whenever he chose to visit the vassal's fief.

The obligations of the lord were not as onerous as those of the vassal. This was natural enough, since, in theory, it was he who provided the land. The lord's most important duty was to protect his vassal from all enemies. He was also obliged to maintain a court where his vassals could appeal for justice, to act as guardian for a vassal's minor heirs, and to secure a suitable husband for the unmarried heiress of any of his vassals. These latter duties, however, were also privileges and often very remunerative. The fines imposed in his court added considerably to the lord's income. His right of wardship over minor heirs was a still more valuable prerogative, since he was entitled to the full income from the fief, which he managed until the heir was old enough to assume the responsibility. The choice of a husband for an unmarried heiress was also a jealously guarded right. It was important to find her a husband as soon as possible, since

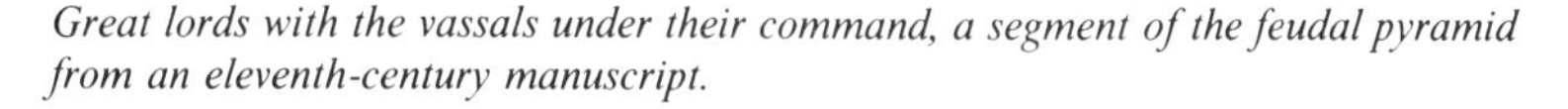
Great lords with the vassals under their command, a segment of the feudal pyramid from an eleventh-century manuscript.

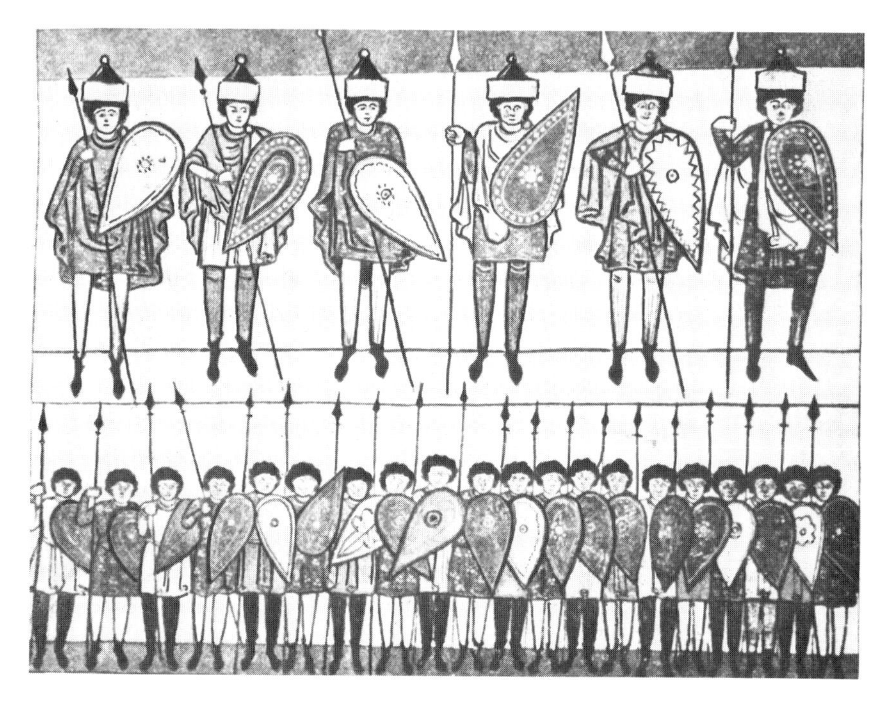

a woman could not perform a vassal's duties, and it was even more important to choose as her husband a man who would fulfill those duties adequately and faithfully. In case there were no heirs, the fief reverted or escheated to the lord, who could then retain it or grant it to another vassal at will.

The personal tie between lord and vassal was the cement that held feudal society together—though very imperfectly. The great nobles, who held fiefs directly from the king as his vassals-in-chief, split the greater part of their land into smaller fiefs, granted to vassals who thus became the subvassals of the king. These subvassals in turn might grant part of their land to vassals of their own, who would become subvassals of the king's vassal, and so on down to the fief so small that it could support only a single knight. This process is known as subinfeudation. Had it worked out according to theory, aristocratic feudal society would have had the form of a symmetrical pyramid, of which the knights formed the base, the great nobles the higher ranks, and the king the apex. But feudalism had not developed according to any preconceived theory. From the beginning, the steps in the feudal hierarchy had been uneven, and with the passage of time natural shifts in family fortunes introduced new complications with every passing generation, until the whole system was reduced to utter chaos.

At the same time, western Europe was gradually becoming more civilized and settled, so that the mutual need for military service and protection was less vital and the personal tie of dependence and loyalty was weakened. In proportion as this occurred, landholding became the most important part of the feudal bargain. Thus it happened that by marriage, conquest, purchase, or inheritance through the mother's family, nobles frequently acquired fiefs from several lords at once, and owed each vassal's service. Furthermore, part of such a vassal's fief might pass into the hands of a much more powerful lord, who would nevertheless become his vassal for that land. The duties of a vassal might thus become extremely complicated. Many were forced to introduce reservations into the oath of loyalty, "saving the rights of his other lords." No matter how complex the system of subinfeudation, every vassal had a liege lord to whom he owed primary allegiance. He could not support a more powerful lord against his liege lord, even if he held more land from, and owed more service to, the greater lord. Theoretically, all vassals holding lands from the king had to recognize the monarch as their liege lord. In practice, of course, such moral and theoretical obligations often amounted to nothing. These complications of subinfeudation destroyed all proportion and symmetry in the ranks of the feudal nobility. There were knights who held small fiefs directly from the king; counts who held fiefs from petty barons; and untitled lords whose fiefs rivaled those of counts or dukes. The count of Champagne, to cite a well-known example, was the vassal of the king of France for part of his lands and of nine other lords, including the German emperor and the duke of Burgundy, for the remainder.

The Feudal Castle and Its Inhabitants

The site of the noble's castle was chosen for its defensibility rather than for convenience or ease of access. A hilltop, a rocky promontory, an island, or any similar position provided a suitable site. It was not common for castles to be built of stone until the eleventh and twelfth centuries. The defensive military techniques learned by the crusaders in the Holy Land during the twelfth century further influenced stone castle-building in medieval Europe.

Since many knights fought for their lord for only forty days a year, the duration of campaigns was strictly limited. Little fighting was done at night, and less during the harsh northern European winters. When threatening forces were sighted in the area, all local inhabitants, including peasants and the few merchants who might be nearby, retreated within the castle walls. Castles had storerooms for emergencies such as this. Many medieval castles were almost impregnable, but the introduction into Europe of artillery and gunpowder in the fourteenth century led to gradual but vital alterations in medieval fortifications.

Compared to the ingenuity expended on making the castle an impregnable fortress, relatively little thought was given to making it a comfortable habitation. Though the living quarters in a baronial castle of the better sort were a great improvement over the old keep and were more luxurious than the small castles of the lesser nobility, they were still dark, damp, and inconvenient. The windows in the outer walls were mere arrow-slits set deep in the masonry. They let in very little light but a good deal of wind, for they were without glass. There was little privacy in the castle. It was crowded with servants, men-at-arms, and transient guests, and had very few rooms.

The great vaulted hall was the center of the social life of the castle. The lord, his family, and their noble guests ate at a table that might be set on a raised dais at one end, while the less important folk sat at long tables stretching down

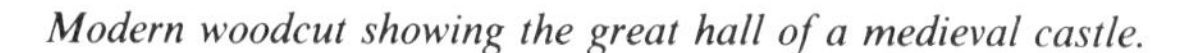

Modern woodcut showing the great hall of a medieval castle.

the hall. After the evening meal a wandering minstrel might sing or recite one of the interminable epic poems of medieval chivalry. When the lord had retired, those who had no other place to sleep spread their cloaks on a table or on a pile of straw on the floor. In winter a great fire was lighted in the huge stone fireplace, but the hall must have been cold and drafty beyond the range of its heat. The floor was flagged with stone and covered with rushes, which must have become rather foul by spring. Hunting dogs wandered about freely and gnawed bones thrown to them by the diners.

Besides eating and drinking, the castle offered few diversions in time of peace. The lord and his lady were occupied in looking after the business of the estate and overseeing the work of the servants. Still, they were left with a good deal of time on their hands. In fine weather, hunting with hounds or hawks was the favorite amusement of both sexes. The nobles loved the chase, second only to war, and guarded it as their exclusive privilege. Peasants who poached the lord's game were harshly dealt with. The young noble spent much of his time practicing the use of arms, and on special occasions there were tournaments. In winter, the noble inhabitants of the castle enjoyed a variety of indoor games, most of which sound remarkably familiar. Chess was very popular, as were checkers, backgammon, and various dice games. But reading, which fills so many hours for the modern man of leisure, was literally impossible for most of the medieval nobility. Small wonder that the noble, as he sat listening to the wind howling about the castle walls, longed for spring and hoped that when it came there would be a good war, with plenty of excitement and plunder. Sometimes the arrival of company broke the monotony.

We may ask where the baron found the money to pay for this picturesque, if somewhat comfortless, magnificence—the great castle, the host of servants, the horses and hounds, the tournaments, the open-handed hospitality, and the ruinous expenses of war. The modern French historian Achille Luchaire gives us part of the answer:

> In order to keep up this style of life, it was necessary to oppress subjects cruelly and take much booty from the enemy. Even so, one could not make both ends meet. And it is one of the striking and characteristic traits of feudal life that the noble, great and small, appears to be constantly in need of money, poor, on the watch for financial expedients, always indebted, and a prey of usurers of all kinds.

The growing prosperity which followed the revival of commerce and city life did, however, raise the standard of living of the landholding class generally. The nobles of the twelfth and thirteenth centuries had more money to spend than had their ancestors in the earlier period when the produce of the land could seldom be turned into cash. But, unfortunately for their solvency, there were also more things on which to spend money; the merchants and skilled artisans from the cities furnished them with goods which in the early Middle Ages had been unobtainable luxuries, but which, when made available, soon became necessities. Thus the expenses of noble life seemed always to rise more rapidly than did income. Economy was, in any case, never a characteristic noble virtue. Rapacious greed for money was common enough among the nobles, who sought to recoup their failing finances by grinding their peasants, extorting tolls from passing merchants, pillaging the lands of their enemies, or outright thieving, but what money they acquired they spent recklessly in conspicuous consumption.

We have hitherto said little about the lady of the castle. She was not, in contemporary opinion, as important as her husband or sons, yet her position was steadily improving throughout the High Middle Ages. Feudal society was becoming more civilized and, in the more cultured courts of the higher nobility at least, the feminine influence was strongly felt. The lady of the castle had, indeed, great responsibilities. When her husband was absent she took command, and if the castle were besieged she managed the defense, often as bravely and skillfully as her lord could have done. Under ordinary circumstances she was responsible for the work of the female servants, overseeing the spinning, weaving, embroidering, and sewing. She was also the hostess, and mingled freely with the knightly visitors to the castle. She had a good deal of social freedom, but in the most important event of her life she had no voice.

The feudal lady had no say in the choice of a husband, which was made for her by her relatives or her overlord. Feudal marriages were always marriages of convenience, involving the transfer of land or the union of two noble houses. If the lady had no brothers she inherited her father's fief, and it was vitally important to the overlord that the fief, and incidentally the heiress, were given to someone who would make a suitable vassal. If she were not the sole heiress, she at least brought a dowry of money or land to her husband. This was far more important than any romantic consideration.

In certain parts of feudal Europe, women did have a direct political voice. Thus, in some of the estates of southern France women took part in deliberations; this was atypical, however. The noble lady was far from enjoying equal rights with the men of her class in practical matters; in compensation, she "benefited"—to some degree at least—from the idealization of women that sprang from the ideals of chivalry, which were slowly transforming the barbarous noble warrior into a knight and giving him some of the manners and ideals of a gentleman. Both the powerlessness and the idealization of woman, which are under attack in our culture, have medieval origins.

The Church in the Feudal System

So far we have discussed feudalism only as it affected laymen—nobles and peasants. We must now consider the position of the clergy in the feudal system, for it would be impossible to understand the history of the medieval Church or of feudalism without understanding the intimate connection between the two. It was inevitable that the Church should become feudalized, since it was a great landholder and landholding on a large scale was possible only by feudal tenure. Landholding in the Middle Ages was accompanied by political, judicial, and military responsibilities and a complex of personal relations. As a landholder, the Church became of necessity an integral part of feudal society, bound to the secular world by innumerable personal and economic ties. It has been reckoned that during the twelfth and thirteenth centuries approximately one-third of the usable land in western Europe was controlled by the Church. Even as early as the ninth century, according to one historian's estimate, there were bishops and abbots whose lands covered more than one hundred thousand acres, while even the poorest held five thousand acres or more.

The lands had been accumulated as the result of generations of pious gifts, inspired more often than not by the desire of a dying king or lord to reconcile himself with God and to throw a good deed into the balance to outweigh his sins.

After the time of Charlemagne, most gifts of this kind were in the form of fiefs and were held in feudal tenure for the Church by bishops, as rulers of the dioceses, or abbots, as the heads of monasteries. So much land could not be held without making necessary the military service expected from all vassals. Since the bishops and abbots, as churchmen, were not supposed to fight, they were forced to parcel out part of their lands to lay vassals who owed them military service, which in turn they could pass on to the lords of the churchmen. There was little to distinguish an ecclesiastical fief from any other. The bishop or abbot gave and received military service and the usual relief and aids like any lay noble, save that election took the place of inheritance and that land once acquired by the Church could never be legally alienated from it. These ecclesiastical nobles were usually vassals-in-chief of the monarch, and their military support was often more important to the king than that of the lay lords, whose family ties and ambitions might interfere with their obedience.

Just as in lay society there was a clear distinction between peasant and noble, in the ecclesiastical hierarchy there was a social distinction, though not so rigid, between the lower and the higher clergy. The parish priests were mostly of peasant stock, and those who served the manorial churches were almost as dependent on the lord of the manor as were the other peasants. The bishops, abbots, and other high officials of the Church, on the other hand, were usually of noble birth. The younger son of a noble family might gain through such a position far greater wealth and power than he could expect from his share of the family estates. As a result, the great nobles frequently interfered in ecclesiastical elections to secure a vacant bishopric or abbacy for one of their relatives, thus establishing him comfortably and gaining for themselves a wealthy and powerful ally. Still more frequently, the king bestowed an ecclesiastical office as a reward for service and in order to guarantee the faithful performance of the clerical vassal's duties by placing the office in trustworthy hands. The men who thus rose to influential positions in the Church were not necessarily more religious in character or interests than ordinary lay nobles. Their training and tastes were very similar to those of their brothers who had remained "in the world." They loved hunting and fighting and took an active part in feudal politics. Many a lusty bishop led his mounted vassals into battle, lightheartedly swinging a mace in place of a sword and thus avoiding the sin of shedding blood.

The Early Feudal State

Marc Bloch has shown that feudal society was woven together in a vast complex of personal relations, wherein every man—peasant, noble, and cleric—owed obedience to some immediate superior. In this complicated and decentralized system, the idea of a state composed of citizens ruled directly by a central government ceased to exist. Yet, throughout the feudal period (roughly 900-1200 in France) kingdoms maintained their existence and kings continued to govern, though with diminished powers. There was no centralized system of taxation, coinage, laws or law courts, and no national army. But there were feudal, local equivalents of all these functions, and the monarchy survived in the midst of feudalism because it had itself become feudalized.

The theory of feudalism recognized the king as the supreme overlord of all lords and the final proprietor of all the land in the kingdom, though most of it was parceled out to his vassals-in-chief. He ruled, then, neither as an absolute monarch nor as a constitutional monarch, like modern kings, but as a feudal overlord. In place of state taxation, the king had to depend for the expenses of government on the income from his own lands—the royal estates—and on the feudal aids and other perquisites of the feudal contract with his vassals. He could not raise a national army, but could call upon his vassals to perform their military service, accompanied by their vassals and subvassals. He could not issue legislation binding on all inhabitants of the kingdom, but he could command his vassals and issue edicts in the pious hope that his vassals would pass them on to the people they ruled. He had no jurisdiction over the majority of citizens, but could hold a feudal court for the trial of his immediate vassals and dependents. In practice, it is true, the vassals-in-chief obeyed the king and performed their duties only when they felt it expedient to do so, and they seldom brought more than a fraction of their own vassals with them when called upon for military service. More often than not, in the early period of feudalism, they felt strong enough to ignore royal commands. Nevertheless, the king had an inestimable advantage over the other feudal lords by virtue of the theory of supremacy, which was recognized as valid even when ignored in practice.

Medieval kings were believed to have special powers—for example, the ability to heal scrofula by a touch of the hand. The magical qualities of kingship, embodied in the vial of chrism which was poured on the head of a French king anointed at Reims, was a transcendent mystery that enhanced the medieval concept of Christian rule. Thus, even when the French monarchy was at its nadir in the tenth and eleventh centuries, the Church safeguarded the theory of charismatic kingship. On a more pragmatic level, when the French Capetian monarchs attempted to augment their limited authority they had to make use of these spiritual advantages in conjunction with the realities of the feudal system. The creation of a relatively centralized French monarchy by the early thirteenth century was the work of determined, amazingly long-lived Capetians, generally working with the Church. The role of the Church was quite important, for it gave to the Capetian monarchy many of its greatest advisers, such as Suger, abbot of St. Denis during the reign of Louis VII. The French Church collaborated with the Capetians in order to secure peace and order in the land, and also because of a theological predisposition toward the theory of charismatic Christian kingship.

In the western Frankish kingdom, which became the kingdom of France, the century following the death of Charles the Fat and the dissolution of the Carolingian Empire was one of turmoil and disintegration—disintegration of the kingdom and also of the larger fiefs—and of the fullest development of feudalism. Across the blurred pages of French history pass the shadowy figures of the Carolingian and Robertian kings, good and able men some of them, but frustrated at every turn by the independence of their unruly vassals. Of these two royal families, the Carolingians depended chiefly on the traditional loyalty of the people to their house and on the respect of the clergy for the consecrated descendants of the great Charles. The Robertians, so called because they were descended from Robert the Strong, count of Paris, had no long-established hereditary claim to the royal title and had therefore to depend on their personal ability and on their strength as the most powerful feudal family in France. For a full century after the deposition of Charles the Fat, Robertian and Carolingian kings alternated on the throne until the Carolingian line finally came to an end with the death of Louis V in 987. The next king, Hugh Capet, belonged to the

Robertian family, but has generally been regarded as the founder of a new dynasty which bore his name.

The election of Hugh Capet (987–996), then, marks the beginning of the famous Capetian dynasty. For over three centuries his descendants passed the crown in unbroken succession from father to son, gradually changing the elective kingship to one clearly hereditary. During that period the average length of reign was nearly thirty years. In the beginning, however, they were merely nominal overlords of the feudal kingdom, less powerful than many of their vassals. Hugh Capet had been forced to give away a considerable part of his lands as bribes to secure his election. What little additional power he acquired through the royal title did not compensate for that loss. As king his authority scarcely extended beyond his own family land, shrunk now to a narrow strip of territory running north and south through central France, with Paris at its center. This was the beginning of the Île de France, the land over which the king was the immediate lord. Hugh's successors, Robert II (996–1031) and Henry I (1031–1060), were unable to control even this small territory. Unruly vassals, secure behind the walls of their fortified castles, defied the kings in their own domain. Throughout the remainder of the kingdom, the nobles went their independent way with no more than lip service to the king.

There were innumerable great and petty fiefs, whose boundaries and interrelations shifted constantly with the shifts of family fortune. To draw a map of feudal France in the eleventh century would have been a superhuman task even for a contemporary, and, in any case, it would not have remained accurate for any length of time. There were, however, a few great fiefs which remained fairly constant, though tending to disintegrate as the subvassals became more independent. To the north of the Île de France lay the half-independent counties of Vermandois and Flanders; to the west were the great duchies of Normandy and Brittany and the rich counties of Anjou and Maine; to the east were the county of Champagne and the duchy of Burgundy. Southern France was beyond the reach of the eleventh-century kings, for it was separated from the north by radical differences of language and culture. The largest fief there—and for that matter the largest in France—was the duchy of Aquitaine, which stretched clear across the country south of the Loire. The dukes of Aquitaine occupied an almost royal position in southern France, but, like the Capetian kings, they had very little power over their vassals. To the south of Aquitaine lay the duchy of Gascony and the county of Toulouse.

Most of these great fiefs were as large as the royal domain. What chance had the king of France to assert his authority over such powerful vassals? Very little indeed. The contrast with Germany during these same three centuries is thus most striking.

Suggestions for Further Reading

P. H. Blair, *An Introduction to Anglo-Saxon England** (1954).

F. L. Ganshof, *Feudalism,** trans. by P. Grierson (1964). A major study, giving the beginning student and the specialist fine insights into the nature of the feudal phenomenon.

*Available in a paperback edition.

C. H. Haskins, *The Normans in European History** (1959). Haskins, the master, at his best [AHA, 182].

C. E. Odegaard, *Vassi and Fideles in the Carolingian Empire* (1971). Important contribution to the vexed question of feudal origins [AHA, 184, in part].

S. Painter, *French Chivalry** (1940). Delightful reading, and still a sane and useful introduction to an elusive subject [AHA, 185, altered].

F. M. Stenton, *Anglo-Saxon England,* 3rd ed. (1971). Brilliant, detailed survey of the subject. Outstanding scholarship and graceful style. The book is part of the distinguished Oxford History of England series.

C. Stephenson, *Medieval Feudalism** (1942). Masterful condensation based on wide reading in the sources; the best brief introduction to a dangerously complex topic [AHA, 184].

Holy Roman Empire Against Reformed Papacy

11

> I forbid to King Henry, . . . who . . . has rebelled against the Holy Church, the government of the whole realm of Germany and Italy.
>
> POPE GREGORY VII

Germany, Italy, and the Holy Roman Empire

Medieval Germany grew out of that east Frankish kingdom which had fallen to Louis the German by the Treaty of Verdun in 843. The decline of Carolingian authority after Charlemagne's death meant that by the end of the ninth century most of the country was under the control of the dukes of Saxony, Bavaria, Franconia, and Swabia, and, after 925, of Lorraine. Despite their tribal designations, the five duchies were political and geographical rather than ethnic and linguistic entities. These German-speaking areas had been brought into Christendom by the military prowess of the Merovingians and Carolingians. Their dukes were not the descendants of ancient, pre-Carolingian Germanic leaders; rather, they owed their prestige to the Carolingian authority which had been conferred on them or their predecessors. The great question for these east Frankish lands early in the tenth century was whether a centralized authority could emerge out of the wreckage of the great Carolingian Empire. Could the dukes weld these far-flung administrative units into a relatively centralized and secure polity? By and large, the German kings of the tenth and eleventh centuries accomplished this great task, and the contrast with the feudal, near-chaotic conditions prevailing across the Rhine in France is striking.

When the German branch of the Carolingian line ended with the death of Louis the Child in 911, the dukes and other magnates of Germany gathered to elect a new king. They chose Duke Conrad of Franconia (911–918). The nobles felt it necessary to have a king, but they were not prepared to surrender any of their authority to him. As a result, the royal title carried with it little more than honor—and none too much of that. As king, Conrad's authority scarcely extended beyond his own duchy. Realizing that the king, to make his rule effective, must have the support of more than one duchy, Conrad planned to improve conditions in the next reign. Before his death he made his son promise to give up his own claims to the crown in favor of his rival Henry, duke of Saxony, and thereafter to support his government. Such at least is the story told by the contemporary chronicler, Widukind.

As a result Henry I, called Henry the Fowler, was elected in 919 and founded a dynasty that lasted for more than a century. Backed by Franconia as well as his own duchy of Saxony, Henry was able to force the other dukes to at least nominal submission. His success in defending the eastern frontiers against barbarian invaders also added considerably to his prestige. He defeated and drove back the heathen Wends—the Slavic people to the east of the Elbe—and the Hungarians, who were ravaging the central part of Germany. Henry also forced the duke of Bohemia to recognize him as overlord. On his death, Germany was still little more than a federation of duchies, but Henry had laid the foundation on which his brilliant son Otto was to build a stronger kingdom.

All the dukes concurred in the election of Otto I (936-973) and did homage to the new king. Almost immediately, however, his attempts to establish an effective authority over the dukes drove them into revolt. Within the next two years he had to suppress serious rebellions in Bavaria, Franconia, and his own duchy of Saxony, and to defend Lorraine against an alliance of its duke with the king of France. Following these revolts, Otto strove to bind the duchies more closely to himself by granting them to his own kinsmen and making marriage alliances between his relatives and members of the ducal houses. This policy was none too successful even in his own lifetime, and could have no permanent value. Even a king of so commanding a personality as the great Otto could not always depend on his kinsmen, and he had to put down another widespread and dangerous rebellion in 953-954.

Rather more successful was his policy, continued by most of his successors for a century, of granting large tracts of land and great administrative powers to the archbishops and bishops. While permitting the clergy to elect these officers in the usual manner, he reserved the right of approval and—to all practical intents and purposes—chose them himself. To insure their loyalty, he invested them not only with their fiefs but also with the symbols of their ecclesiastical offices. He thus surrounded himself with powerful and loyal vassals who, because of the rule of clerical celibacy, could not leave legitimate heirs and therefore could not establish an hereditary claim to their fiefs. For generations these ecclesiastical princes were the strongest support of the monarchy. In these various ways, Otto gradually extended and consolidated the royal authority. Meanwhile, he was continuing his father's work in defending his eastern frontiers and conquering his heathen neighbors, thus laying the foundation for the permanent extension of Germanic rule and Christianity to the east. Still more important, he administered a crushing defeat to the Hungarian invaders on the Lechfeld near Augsburg in 955. Thereafter they ceased to trouble the western kingdoms.

Like Charlemagne, Otto kept an interested eye on Italy. Otto and many of his German successors were interested in Rome nor merely or even primarily because of its ancient, universal, and Christian claims, but also because their own power in Germany depended in part upon securing the south German territories of Swabia and Bavaria. A strong political force in northern Italy could engender renewed separatist sentiment in southern Germany. Thus, Otto believed the guarantee of his rule in Germany to rest in large part upon control of northern Italy and Rome.

For half a century Italy had been in a condition of utter anarchy. The Lombard kings in the north were powerless against the great nobles; and in the central district, the Papal States, Roman nobles dominated the feeble popes and used the power of the Papacy for their own ends. The country was ripe for conquest. In 951, Otto invaded Italy on the pretext of rescuing Queen Adelaide, the widow of the former king in northern Italy, who was being imprisoned and mistreated by her husband's successor, Berengar II. The expedition was successful as far as it went. Otto defeated Berengar and married the beautiful Adelaide but was recalled to Germany by a rebellion there. He contented himself for a time with forcing Berengar to recognize him as his overlord, and ten years later again invaded Italy. This time he deposed Berengar and proclaimed himself king, as Charlemagne had done. Still following in the footsteps of the great Carolingian, he proceeded to Rome where, in February 962, he was crowned emperor by Pope John XII.

The coronation of Otto is at the heart of one of the most famous disputes in modern German historiography. Critics of Otto the Great and his imperial successors have argued that they diverted the energies of the German peoples from their historic task, the colonization of lands to the east, in a vain attempt to secure imperial primacy in Italy. Defenders of the Ottonians have pointed to the vital political connections between southern Germany and northern Italy. As is the case with so many all-encompassing modern historiographical theories, these divergent viewpoints reflect the times in which they were propounded. German historians who justified the imperial policy of Otto tended to be within the Catholic, universalist, Hapsburg tradition. Critics of the Ottonians were often partisans of the Prussian royal house in its struggle for a predominantly Protestant, Prussian north German state.

The connection between the Ottonians and Rome was not limited to the political sphere. Religion and ecclesiastical administration played a significant role in the reformist policies of the German emperors. The Papacy fell into profound degradation repeatedly during the tenth and eleventh centuries. Reformist impulses, in part stemming from imperial German abbeys endowed by members of the imperial houses, influenced pious German emperors toward direct interference in papal and north Italian ecclesiastical affairs. In addition, many of these emperors took the universal Christian aspect of their title seriously; they felt great responsibility for the Christian Church, the center of which was Rome. Thus, the policy of the German Holy Roman emperors in Italy had historical, ecclesiastical, and political bases. These motives are not always easy to disentangle, but before condemning these emperors for neglecting German affairs, we should take into consideration the complexity of the problems which confronted them.

Struggle Between the Saxon Empire and the Reformed Papacy

For nearly a century, from the imperial coronation of Otto the Great to the death of Henry III, the emperors were dominant in the papal-imperial partnership which claimed universal rule over all Christendom. It was, indeed, a dark age for the Church, reflecting the evils of a turbulent and disorganized feudal society. But there were signs of new life in this winter of the Church's discontent. Demand for reform was growing rapidly in many places, and the purification of the Papacy under Henry III made Rome the center of the reform movement. Thereafter, for more than two centuries, the popes strove to strengthen the Papacy and the Church by freeing them from outside influence. This policy brought the Papacy into conflict with all secular governments, for the attempt to gain independence soon led the popes to claim supremacy over worldly powers.

THE HOLY ROMAN EMPIRE IN 1050

The struggles between popes and emperors which occurred intermittently between 1075 and 1268 were not merely conflicts between a reformed, militant Papacy and a politically conscious German monarchy. They involved two forces which, as German historian Gerd Tellenbach has pointed out, both claimed primacy in the search for a just Christian order in the world. The Holy Roman Empire was as much a spiritual as a political conception, its theoretical antecedents reaching beyond the rise of the Roman Empire and Christianity to the prophecies of the Book of Daniel of the Old Testament. For many publicists and propagandists of the imperial ideals, the continued existence of a universal Holy Roman realm was assured until the coming of the anti-Christ and the end of the world. Thus the maintenance of such an empire was a guarantee that the Final Judgment, when trembling mortals would be confronted with their sins, was not yet at hand. The reformed Papacy claimed the right to take the lead in establishing Christian order in the world. Where it was blocked by the outrageous claims of an essentially secular authority, it claimed the prerogative to use all weapons at its disposal to crush that malignant power.

The death of Henry III in the prime of life was a disaster from which the Empire never fully recovered. The centrifugal forces favoring local independence in Germany and Italy were held in check only by the most alert watchfulness and by constant pressure on the part of the emperor. With Henry's death that pressure was lifted for a fateful period. Henry had planned to save the Empire from the dangers of a disputed election and to confirm the hereditary principle of succession by having his infant son crowned king while he himself was still alive. Henry IV (1056–1106) thus succeeded peacefully to the throne, but at barely six years of age. For the next thirteen years, until the young emperor-elect took active control of the government, anarchy ran riot. Neither his mother, who acted as regent until 1062, nor the faction of ecclesiastical and lay nobles who then seized the government and the guardianship of the young monarch, could maintain the pressure necessary to preserve imperial authority in either Germany or Italy.

In Germany, the nobles, who were technically royal officials responsible for local government, had actually acquired a hereditary right to their offices and lands, and hence were ever ready to assert their independence of royal control. More and more the emperor was forced to rely for aid and counsel in peace and war on his great ecclesiastical vassals, the bishops and abbots. These the emperors had generously endowed with land, since their fiefs could not be made hereditary. They were still royal officers and it was tremendously important to the central government to secure the election of men who would be loyal to the emperor. The German towns, too, most of which were ruled by bishops, were usually loyal. But these supporters of the monarchy were useless unless led by a strong emperor.

Even more in Italy than in Germany, the imperial authority depended on the constant activity of a vigorous ruler, and it was almost destroyed during the minority of Henry IV. Numerous towns in Lombardy, growing rapidly in response to reviving trade, were beginning to yearn for independence and growing restless under the rule of their bishops, who represented the imperial government. Milan was especially turbulent. There the citizens gained a powerful ally in the pope by protesting the emperor's interference in the election of their archbishop, thus giving a coloring of religious reform to their revolt. In central Italy the imperial position was further complicated by the pope's claims to rule over the Papal States, dating back to the eighth-century Donation of Pepin.

In the southern part of the peninsula and in Sicily a new menace to imperial rule in Italy had been slowly rising, and grew strong during the minority of Henry IV. This area had until recently been composed of a number of little independent states—Lombard, Byzantine, and Moslem—none strong enough to trouble the emperors seriously, though all attempts to conquer them had failed. In 1016, a band of Norman knights landed at Salerno on their way home from a pilgrimage and discovered the possibilities for fighting and plunder offered by the frequent wars between the rival states. Each year thereafter brought more adventurers of the reckless Norman breed, eager to fish in the troubled waters of southern Italy. In the course of time, as their numbers increased, Norman leaders built up small states of their own. At the opening of the reign of Henry IV, Robert Guiscard, a perfect examplar of the Norman conqueror, dominated most of southern Italy. He was the terror of the native populations of the south and a constant menace to imperial Italy. In 1059 Pope Nicholas II invested him with land, and Robert replied by doing homage to the pope and assuming a vassal's obligation to protect him. By thus aiding in the establishment of a strong Norman state to the south, the pope hoped to free himself from dependence on the emperor for defense and, at the same time, to acquire an armed ally to use against him if necessary. Here as elsewhere in Italy, the hostile attitude of the Papacy was to prove the most serious obstacle to the re-establishment of imperial domination.

The opposition of the popes to Henry IV grew out of a movement for the reform of the Church which had been active for some time before it gained influence at Rome. It had originated as a monastic reform in the Burgundian monastery of Cluny. This monastery, since its foundation in 910, had been exempt from the rule of the local bishop. Its abbot recognized no superior except the pope. Under a series of able and pious abbots, it acquired a great reputation for holiness and strict observance of the monastic rules of Saint Benedict. It was joined by a number of other monasteries, new and old, in all parts of Europe, all under the rule of the abbot of Cluny. This congregation of monasteries was a new departure in monastic organization. Through it the demand for reform, not only of the monasteries but also of the whole Church, gained a wide hearing. The pious Emperor Henry III and his appointee Pope Leo IX took up the reform movement under papal direction, but with the emperor still in full control.

From the Ascension of Gregory VII to the Concordat of 1122

When Hildebrand ascended the chair of Saint Peter as Gregory VII (1073–1085), the reform program was given a new impetus and wider scope. The character of Gregory dominates the history of Europe in these years. His rise proves that upward mobility was possible in the medieval Church; from a peasant home he had risen by sheer force of character and ability to the most important office in Christendom. Small and unprepossessing in appearance, he commanded respect for his integrity and the burning zeal that threatened to consume his frail body. He had an iron will and was inspired by an unshakable determination to do what he considered right for the Church. For two years he strove without much success to force the bishops, especially of Germany and northern Italy, to strict obedience. Then, in 1075, he published the first papal decree definitively forbidding lay investiture. It had long been the recognized right of the feudal overlord of a bishop or abbot to invest him with the insignia of his fief, just as he would any other vassal. The insignia representing an ecclesiastical fief, however, had a spiritual significance, and the pope now claimed that no layman had the right to bestow them.

There was an essential difference between the spirit of Cluniac monastic reform and that of revolutionary popes such as Gregory VII. The primary aim of monastic reform was to free this form of Christian life from the meshes of feudal, secular domination. The reform program of Gregory VII, which plunged the Empire into decades of civil war and hardship, involved nothing less than extricating the entire Church from the secular administrative world of German and north Italian feudalism. In so doing, the Papacy set itself up as a judge of secular political behavior.

The choice and investiture of bishops may, for example, appear to modern students to be a purely ecclesiastical question. Why was Gregory's opposition to lay imperial investiture so revolutionary? Precisely because the imperial administration in Germany relied heavily upon its own ecclesiastical appointees for the secular administration of the German kingdom. This new papal-imperial conflict struck at the heart of the political structure of the German kingdom. This practical issue brought to the fore the broader and more serious problem of supremacy, which had all along been inherent in the theory of the Holy Roman Empire, awaiting only an open conflict between a strong pope and a determined

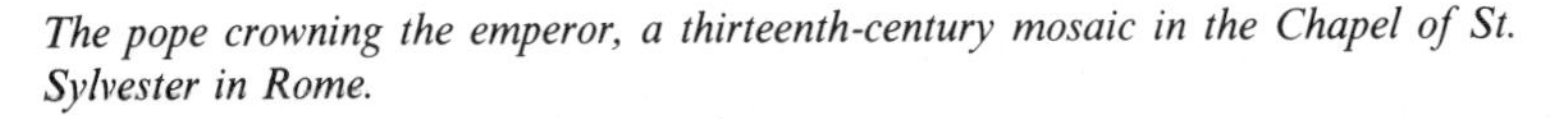

The pope crowning the emperor, a thirteenth-century mosaic in the Chapel of St. Sylvester in Rome.

emperor to become explicit. The emperor admitted the universal spiritual authority of the pope, while the pope in turn admitted the universal secular authority of the emperor. They had parallel powers, both divinely ordained. But in case of conflict, which had the higher authority? History weighed both equally. The popes had always given the crown to the emperors, but the emperors, including the pious Henry III, as guardians of the Church had frequently deposed bad popes and chosen their successors.

Propagandists for the Papacy supported the claims of Gregory VII by pointing to such diverse sources as the New Testament and the Donation of Constantine. Christ had told Peter that he was the rock upon which the Church would be built, and in this declaration papal apologists saw the legitimation of universalist papal claims. When Constantine the Great was on his deathbed in 337, he had supposedly bequeathed the western part of the Roman Empire to Sylvester I. Actually, this "Donation of Constantine" was probably forged in the papal chancery in the eighth century in order to help persuade the Frankish ruler to come to the aid of the Papacy, then beleaguered by Lombard dukes.

Henry's attempts to re-establish imperial authority in Italy had already caused a breach with the Papacy before Gregory was elected, but a rebellion in Saxony in 1073 forced him to make peace with the new pope. Henry did not reopen the conflict until two years later when he had restored peace in Germany. He then challenged the pope by investing his own candidate with the archbishopric of Milan, to which Gregory replied with the decree against lay investiture. With the aid of his bishops, most of whom were loyal and opposed to the pope's strict reforms, Henry took the offensive and declared Gregory deposed. But he had reckoned without the restless lay nobles of Saxony. When the pope replied by excommunicating the emperor and freeing his subjects from their oath of allegiance, many of the German nobles took the opportunity to rebel.

Henry was forced to conciliate the pope in order to have a free hand against rebellion at home. Hastening to Italy, he sought out the pope in the castle of Countess Mathilda of Tuscany at Canossa in January 1077. Henry pleaded for absolution as a penitent sinner—a plea that the pope, as a priest, could not refuse, especially when the emperor, as Gregory recounts, demonstrated his contrition by standing for three days barefoot in the snow before the barred gates of the castle. The absolution of Henry, freeing him from the ban of excommunication, caused a strong reaction in his favor. The pious returned to their allegiance and the insurgent nobles lost their excuse for rebellion. Nevertheless, the emperor had set a dangerous precedent in his dramatic recognition of the pope's spiritual authority, a precedent that was to have more influence on later generations than in his own day. Still, it was an immediate victory for the emperor, though the disaffected nobles persisted in their rebellion and elected Rudolf, duke of Swabia, as an antiking.

It was the pope who reopened hostilities. Henry had continued to invest his ecclesiastical vassals, and in 1080 Gregory took the decisive step of deposing him and recognizing Rudolf of Swabia in his place. This time general public opinion was against the pope. He was the aggressor and it was generally considered that he had exceeded his powers. With the aid of German and Italian clergy, Henry deposed him and procured the election of an antipope. The emperor then besieged Rome and entered it in 1084; there he was crowned by the antipope Clement III. Gregory was forced to flee to his Norman allies in the south and died in exile.

Gregory's successors, especially Urban II (1088-1099), continued his program of reform and his struggle with the emperor. They were generally recognized in the lands outside the Empire where reform had been effected without so much conflict; Henry's antipope was accepted only where the emperor could enforce obedience. Yet the schism (the split in the Church between the adherents of the rival popes) continued until the emperor's death. Henry's life ended in tragedy. His last years were embittered by the treachery and rebellion of his son Henry, in alliance with the papal party.

With the accession of Henry V (1106–1125), the schism was ended and for a time pope and emperor were at peace. But the new emperor was no more ready than his father had been to give up control of ecclesiastical elections, of which lay investiture was the symbol. Through the reigns of three popes the controversy continued, often accompanied by violence. At last, worn out by the long strife, both parties agreed to settle the investiture question by a compromise, effected at Worms in 1122.

According to the Concordat of Worms, signed by both emperor and pope, bishops and abbots were to be invested by the emperor with the insignia of their secular office only (that is, their fief), not with the ring and staff which symbolized their spiritual authority. In Germany the investiture was to precede consecration and the emperor was to be represented at elections. This left him still in practical control. However, in Burgundy and Italy, where the emperor had lost real authority, the imperial investiture was to follow consecration, and so was not a necessary preliminary to taking office. In France and England the question had already been settled: the monarchs gave up actual investiture but retained a dominant influence in elections. The emperor had retained what was most vital to him—control over the German clergy. But the compromise was really a papal victory. The emperor had given up a recognized right, while the pope had merely stopped short of the full assertion of his theoretical claims.

There was a certain irony implicit in this papal triumph, though it only became apparent during the next century. In their attempt to disentangle the

Henry IV on his knees begging Countess Mathilda of Tuscany and the abbot of Cluny to intercede for him with Pope Gregory VII. The miniature is from a manuscript life of Mathilda.

ecclesiastical administration from secular imperial rule, the popes descended into the political mud of Christendom. The politicization of the reformed Papacy only augmented its arrogance, and by the end of the thirteenth century there was widespread dissatisfaction with the Holy See. Such dissatisfaction was no longer confined to imperial enemies, occasional disgruntled reformers, and clannish Roman rivals.

But this backlash was still in the future, and at the end of the eleventh century papal prestige was at its height. Pope Urban II was the moral leader of one of the greatest expressions of the medieval epoch—the First Crusade.

Suggestions for Further Reading

G. Barraclough, *Medieval Germany,* 2 vols. (1948). Excellent and important. This work contains the writings of major German historians who have dealt with the medieval period [AHA, 183, in part].

G. Barraclough, *Origins of Modern Germany* (1946). The best English-language introduction to medieval German problems [AHA, 183].

R. E. Herzstein, *The Holy Roman Empire in the Middle Ages: Universal State or German Catastrophe?** (1966). Translations, with introductory comments and bibliography, of major modern interpretations of the medieval Empire.

C. H. McIlwain, *The Growth of Political Thought in the West* (1932). Best introduction to medieval political theory [AHA, 199].

J. B. Morrall, *Political Thought in Medieval Times* (1958). In spite of certain limitations, this book well meets the requirements for a brief introduction to political thought in the Middle Ages [AHA, 199].

G. Tellenbach, *Church, State, and Christian Society at the Time of the Investiture Contest** (1970). One of the most important studies of the investiture controversy from both the theoretical and practical views. Tellenbach's approach is that of an objective German scholar.

W. Ullmann, *Medieval Papalism* (1949).

*Available in a paperback edition.

The Crusades and the Counteroffensive Against Islam

12

> The Christian exults in the death of a pagan, because Christ is glorified.
>
> SAINT BERNARD OF CLAIRVAUX

The Great Popular Crusade

For centuries the great Moslem states had dominated the Mediterranean, firmly implanted in Spain, Sicily, North Africa, and the Middle East. But with the beginning of the eleventh century, the tide began to turn. Islam had lost its political unity, and the Moslems' aggressive driving force had begun to decline.

The Abbasid caliphs, who had once ruled a great Mohammedan Empire from Baghdad, had lost their power long before the crusaders invaded the East. In the middle of the eleventh century, the Seljuk Turks took over what remained of the Abbasid Empire, though continuing to recognize the nominal authority of the caliphs as religious leaders. The Turks gave new strength to the Moslem state and made it a greater menace to Christendom. Driving westward, they took Syria from the caliphs of Cairo and most of Asia Minor from the Byzantine Empire. They had defeated the Byzantine army at Manzikert in 1071, putting the Byzantine Empire in a hazardous position.

Since the tenth century, great numbers of Western pilgrims had traveled to the Holy Land to visit the sites of Christ's life and death, to worship at the Holy Sepulcher, and to do penance for their sins by the cost, toil, and danger of the long voyage. Such pilgrims had been welcomed and treated well by the tolerant Fatimite caliphs; but after Jerusalem was captured by the Turks in 1071, the pilgrimage became more hazardous. Thereafter the returning pilgrims brought tales of Turkish atrocities, probably exaggerated, and of the defilement of the holy places. Europe, then, was already aware of the Turk, and in a mood to be easily aroused, when the Byzantine emperor, Alexius Comnenus, appealed to the pope for aid against the infidel, who had been threatening Constantinople. The time seemed ripe for a counterattack. Three years before, in 1092, the death of the Turkish sultan had thrown the whole Turkish Empire into civil war and anarchy. Asia Minor and Syria were left under independent and antagonistic princes. Pope Urban II responded enthusiastically to the emperor's appeal. Indeed, it is possible that he would have embraced the idea of a crusade on his own initiative, without urging from the East.

Of all the Crusades, the first was unique in important ways. It was by far the most genuine mass movement of any of the Crusades, a true popular upsurge of sentiment and religion. Secondly, none of the other Crusades seemed, at least in the beginning, so unified in intent and in obedience to a single force. The reigning pope inspired universal respect. Third—and this could be said of no other Crusade—it achieved even more than it set out to. Jerusalem fell to the crusaders after they had suffered many losses and undergone many trials and tribulations. This great Crusade was set in motion by a speech delivered by Pope Urban II at a major Church council at Clermont. There are different and somewhat contradictory accounts of Urban's speech, but they tend to agree on most essentials, particularly the inspirational quality of the address and the enthusiasm with which it was greeted. The pope played upon the emotions of his audience, holding out every possible inducement to join the expedition—remission of sins, protection of their land until their return, the hope of plunder. He was answered by shouts of "God wills it!" Most of those present at once donned the cloth cross which signified that they were pledged to the Crusade. Preachers, of whom Peter the Hermit was the most famous, traveled through France and other parts of Europe, carrying the message and arousing great enthusiasm everywhere.

The pope's reasons for urging the Crusade are clear enough. The Papacy had gained greatly in prestige since the accession of Gregory VII. Save in Germany, where Henry IV was still in violent opposition, the pope's claims to universal supremacy were generally recognized. By placing himself at the head of a great international movement like the Crusade, Urban demonstrated that he, not the emperor, was the leader of Christendom. There was also a more powerful

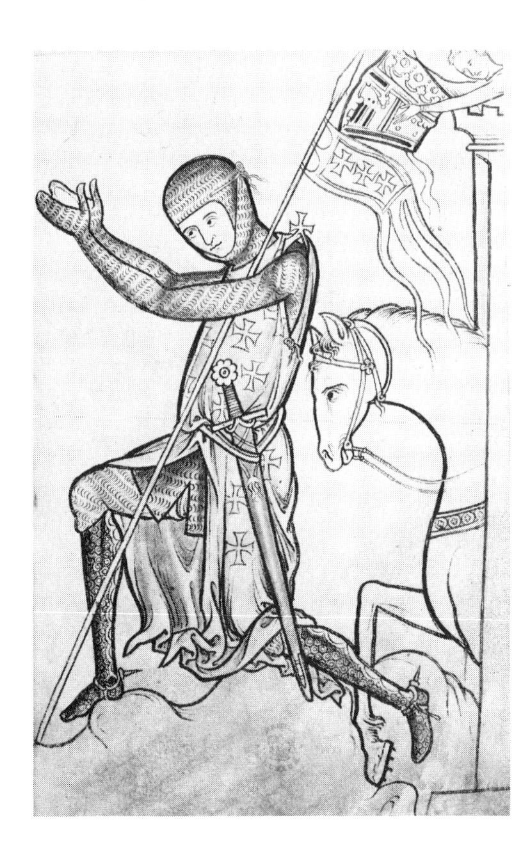

A crusading knight, identified as such by the crosses on his surcoat and pennon. The miniature is from a thirteenth-century psalter.

motive. Urban, like most of the popes after him, sincerely wished to expand the Church of which he was the ruler, and to make it a universal church.

Why were rough feudal barons, knights, and even merchants and peasants stirred by the pope's call to take part in such a perilous undertaking? In any great popular movement of the kind, many motives must work together. The prime motive was, of course, religious. The Cluniac and papal reform movements had done much to stimulate popular piety. It was an age of violence but also of strong religious feeling, with a decided bent toward asceticism. To the medieval man, the life of the monk was the only truly religious life. He was deeply conscious of sin; he feared eternal damnation; and he felt the necessity of performing some act of voluntary suffering as atonement for his sins. Great numbers of men, to whom the regular life of the monk was impossible, did penance for their sins by going on pilgrimage to holy places, even as far as Jerusalem. The Crusades were in essence super-pilgrimages. But the religious appeal went farther than that. The feudal warrior's conception of loyalty was simple. A man fought for his lord against his enemies. And how could a man show his devotion to God better—or more congenially to his natural tastes—than by fighting for Him against His enemies, the infidels who had defiled Christ's sepulcher? The crusader believed that God had called him to arms through His representative, the pope, and he answered gladly.

The adventurous spirit and love of fighting so characteristic of the medieval knight urged him on to a glorious enterprise in which fighting was no sin. Besides, feudal Europe was becoming somewhat overcrowded. There were many landless knights and younger sons who were short of land. The great examples of this feudal thirst for land and adventure were the famous sons of Tancred, Norman knights who conquered Apulia and Sicily, and took part in frequent wars in northern France and Flanders. Men of their type participated in the conquest of England in 1066. The descendants of these adventurous knights played a major role in the First Crusade. In the rich East, about which they knew little but rumor, there were tempting opportunities for plunder and land for the taking. It must not be forgotten that, from the practical point of view, the Crusades were expeditions for the conquest of Syria (present-day Syria plus Lebanon and Palestine). As for the Italian merchants who constantly aided the crusaders, their interests were obvious: they wanted to establish safe trading-posts in the Near East under Christian governments. The Emperor Alexius had hoped that an expedition from the West might aid him in recovering Asia Minor.

None of the great rulers of Europe—Emperor Henry IV, Philip I of France, or William Rufus of England—was sufficiently at peace with the Church or his own nobles to take part in the Crusade. Its leadership was left to a group of great barons, chiefly from France and the lands bordering it. Godfrey of Bouillon and his brother Baldwin led the Lorrainers. Raymond of Toulouse led the Provençal forces, while the most successful leader was Bohemond of Otranto, who led the Normans. Time was needed for preparation, so by mutual agreement the crusaders delayed their departure until the late summer of 1096, though some disorganized bands had already preceded them. They traveled by different routes, arriving in Constantinople during the following winter. Emperor Alexius, who was rather alarmed at the size of the army, persuaded the leaders to take an oath of allegiance to him, on the understanding that they would hand over to him any land they conquered or hold it as his vassals.

It is impossible to do more than guess at the size of the crusading army, but a recent authority estimates it at between 4,200 and 4,500 cavalry and possibly

30,000 infantry. From Constantinople, the crusaders passed over into Asia Minor. There they captured Nicaea. Moving on, they left the city, as well as most of Asia Minor, in the emperor's hands, thus accomplishing for him about as much as he could have hoped. Their next objective was Antioch, the most important town in northern Syria. On their way, they swung farther east through Armenia, where the friendly Christian population aided them in taking the Turkish strongholds. There Godfrey's brother Baldwin remained behind to found the county of Edessa. The siege of Antioch occupied the entire winter of 1097-1098. When at last, after great hardship, the crusaders broke into the city, they were themselves besieged by a Turkish army. They were in a desperate position, but their courage was revived by the miraculous discovery of the Holy Lance, or what they believed to be the lance that had pierced Christ's side on the cross. Heartened by this sign, they sallied out and defeated the Turkish army. Quarrels among their leaders and a dispute as to whether they should hand Antioch over to the emperor delayed them for some months. Finally, when Alexius failed to appear, they left Bohemond in possession of Antioch and moved on down the coast.

They met with no strong opposition, for the inhabitants of the country were accustomed to conquest and cared little who ruled them. When they arrived before Jerusalem in the summer of 1099, they found that it had been taken from the Turks by an Egyptian force and was not strongly garrisoned. The taking of the city was followed by scenes of pious joy and bloodshed. The celebration in the Church of the Holy Sepulcher, where men wept together in joy and grief, and the merciless slaughter of the inhabitants well expressed the spirit of the Crusade.

The Crusaders in Palestine

After the capture of Jerusalem, many of the crusaders returned home, feeling that they had accomplished their immediate purpose. The remainder stayed to extend their conquests and to organize the land they had taken as a feudal state. The first ruler chosen by the barons, Godfrey of Bouillon, refused the royal title, preferring that of defender of the Holy Sepulcher. His brother Baldwin, however, who succeeded him in 1100, took the title king of Jerusalem. The work of conquest continued for a quarter of a century, greatly aided by fleets from the Italian commercial cities and by a constant stream of fighting pilgrims from the West. The result was the Latin kingdom of Jerusalem, a feudal state stretching from the southern end of Palestine all along the Syrian coast and thence to the northeast. It was divided into four large units—the kingdom of Jerusalem proper (the royal domain) and three great fiefs: the county of Tripoli, founded by Raymond of Toulouse; the principality of Antioch, founded by Bohemond and Tancred; and the county of Edessa, founded by Baldwin I.

The lords of these great fiefs recognized the king as their overlord, but were practically independent sovereigns. Within the royal domain and the three large fiefs, there were lesser baronies and knights' holdings, granted to vassals in return for military service according to feudal custom. The Latin Kingdom of Jerusalem of the twelfth and thirteenth centuries is a major source of our knowledge of medieval feudalism. The Assizes of Jerusalem, or findings of the royal courts of the kingdom of Jerusalem, tell us much about feudal relationships during the High Middle Ages. These records reflect some of the unique conditions prevailing in the conquered Holy Land, but their legal terminology and feudal concepts provide us much information about the type of feudal society out of which the conquerers of the Holy Land emerged in the eleventh and twelfth centuries.

In the coastal towns, merchants from Venice, Genoa, and Pisa, whose fleets had dominated the Mediterranean since about 1050, built permanent trading-posts and were given special privileges. The original inhabitants, including numbers of Jews and Christians who had kept their faith through centuries of Moslem domination, still made up the bulk of the population. The crusaders who settled in the kingdom of Jerusalem were never more than a small minority. They made themselves at home in the new land, gradually adopting the clothing and many of the customs of the inhabitants as better suited to the climate, which was so different from that of the West.

The kingdom of Jerusalem was weak. It was little more than a narrow coastal plain, open to attack along the flank. Moreover, it was weakened by the rivalries and jealousies of its great lords, of the merchants from the different Italian cities, and of the two great orders of crusading knights, the Hospitalers and Templars, both of which had acquired a great deal of land since they were founded in the early days of the conquest. There was always hostility too between the older settlers and the new arrivals from the West. All that saved the crusaders was an equal lack of unity among their Moslem neighbors. The latter, however, were slowly uniting. In 1144, they reconquered Edessa without much difficulty. News of this disaster led to the organization of the Second Crusade. Moved by the preaching of Saint Bernard of Clairvaux, Louis VII of France and the Hohenstaufen emperor, Conrad III, led large armies to the East in 1147, accomplishing little or nothing. Their failure was due largely to the jealousy and bad faith of the Europeans in Syria whom they had come to aid.

By the late twelfth century the Crusader states had lost the vigor of their recent predecessors. Perhaps the amenities of life in the Holy Land and generally friendly relations with an alien population sapped the crusading will of the descendents of the first crusaders and of recent European arrivals. The harsh

THE KINGDOM OF JERUSALEM IN 1140

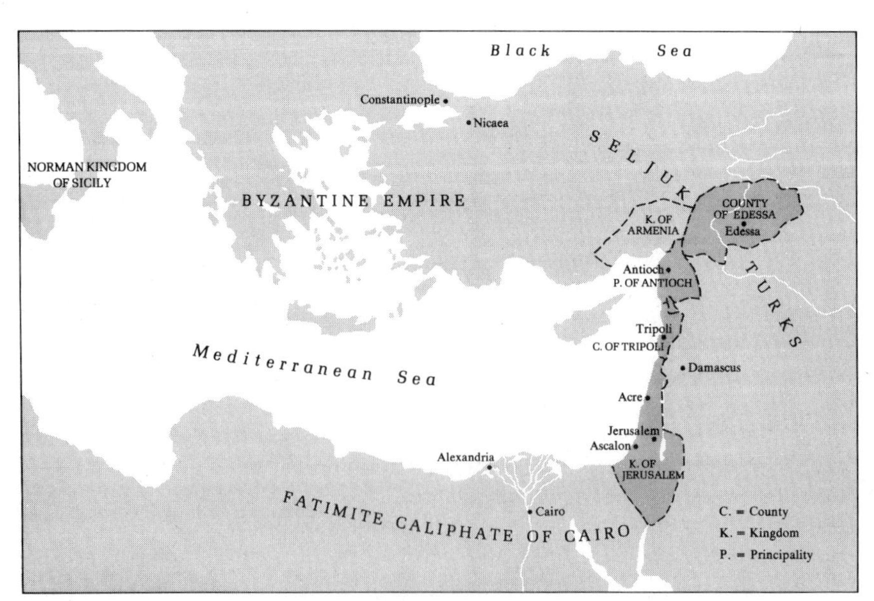

winters of northern Europe were a dim memory, if they were known at all to the generation of crusaders struggling to maintain its hold in the Holy Land in the late twelfth century. The permanently small number of crusaders made them largely dependent upon help from western Europe, and this aid depended in turn upon the whims and greed of Italian merchants. Each Crusade seemed to awaken less enthusiasm among the populace of western Europe. The Greek emperor was sometimes indifferent, sometimes hostile. The crusaders began as an isolated group of western Europeans, but they soon learned remarkably well how to coexist with the devotees of Islam, who made up the vast majority of the population of the Holy Land. A small Jewish minority continued to live in Palestine.

The emergence of a great new Islamic leader, Saladin, was the beginning of the end for Christian hegemony in Palestine. By 1187 Jerusalem itself had fallen. The fall of Jerusalem, after nearly a century of Christian rule, shocked Europe and aroused enthusiasm for a new Crusade. This time the three greatest rulers of Christendom took the cross and led their countrymen to the East. The aged emperor, Frederick Barbarossa, was the first to depart. He drowned while crossing a mountain stream in Asia Minor, evidently succumbing to a stroke or heart attack, and most of his followers returned home. The kings of France and England, Philip Augustus and Richard the Lionhearted, arrived later. It was not until 1191 that the latter, who had stopped on the way to conquer the island of Cyprus, joined the crusaders who were besieging the city of Acre on the coast of Palestine.

Philip and Richard, of very different characters, were natural enemies. Quarrels soon broke out between them, nearly destroying the effectiveness of the crusading army. One of the chroniclers of the period asserted that "the two kings and peoples did less together than they would have done apart." Philip returned home soon after the fall of Acre, leaving Richard to carry on the war against Saladin. Innumerable romances have been woven about the campaigns of these two warriors. Indeed, even today mothers in Arabia discipline their children by threatening that, if they do not obey, "Richard will get you." This suggests the strength of the impression King Richard I made on both friend and foe. Saladin was scarcely less renowned.

Both men were courageous and both could be magnanimous, but Saladin showed himself to be the more civilized of the two. Richard, a disturbed romantic whose reign was drenched in blood, won a place for himself in both Christian and Moslem legend by his reckless daring but was unable to capture Jerusalem. In August 1192, he concluded a truce with Saladin whereby the Christians gained a strip of the Palestine coast from Acre to Ascalon and the right to free entry for pilgrims going to Jerusalem.

The End of the Crusades

The thirteenth century, which opened with the great pontificate of Innocent III, might have been expected to produce some successful Crusades. There were five major crusading efforts during this period; but they were all rather inglorious affairs, and the very first one, inaugurated by Innocent himself, was shamefully diverted from its purpose. Germany at the beginning of the century was preoccupied with the civil war between the rival emperors. The knights who gathered at Venice in 1202, therefore, were mostly French. They had bargained with the

Venetians for transportation, but were unable to raise the stipulated price. After much discussion they arrived at a compromise: they would pay for their passage by capturing for the Venetians the rival trading city of Zara, across the Adriatic. Europe was shocked by the use of a crusading army against a Christian city and some of the crusaders refused to serve. But worse was still to come. Zara was taken, but the Venetians drove a hard bargain and the crusaders were still short of funds. The Doge of Venice, who seems to have been the evil genius of the Crusade, again tempted the crusaders by pointing out the rich plunder to be had from the sack of Constantinople, provided an excuse could be found for attacking it. The excuse was presented by a pretender to the throne of the Byzantine Empire, who promised the French knights everything they asked if they would aid him. Accordingly, they moved on to Constantinople, captured the city, and looted it amid scenes of wanton violence. Then, when the newly installed emperor was unable to fulfill his promises, they ousted him in turn and elected one of their own number, Baldwin of Flanders, as Roman emperor. Venice was given special trading privileges and a good deal of territory along the coast and on the islands as its share of the plunder. The Latin Empire of Constantinople lasted until 1261, when it was retaken by a Greek pretender who held Asia Minor.

What was left of the Latin states in Syria maintained a precarious existence until the last decade of the thirteenth century, but they were pitifully weak. The internal quarrels, factions, and jealousies that had proven so dangerous to them in the twelfth century were now multiplied. It was clear that they could not defend themselves for long without aid from the West—and the extent of that aid was steadily decreasing. By 1291, the last of the Latin possessions in Syria had been wiped out. The Latin Kingdom of Jerusalem had come to an end, after an existence of nearly two centuries. As wars of conquest, the Crusades had achieved no permanent results; but they had served an important purpose by checking the westward advance of the Turks.

The Crusades undoubtedly acted as a stimulus to the awakening economic, social, and cultural life of western Europe. They parallel a period of intellectual ferment and expanding social energy. But to what extent were the Crusades a cause, and not merely an outgrowth, of the rising civilization of the Middle Ages? This is a question to which many answers have been given. It is difficult to specify any single development that would not have taken place at all without the Crusades. The Italian cities, and through them the other towns of Europe, certainly benefited directly by the trade with the Christian states in Syria and by the transport of pilgrims and crusaders to and from the Holy Land. But trade with the Near East had begun before the Crusades and would have increased without them, though not perhaps so rapidly.

Europe in this period borrowed heavily from the science, philosophy, luxuries, and general culture of the Moslem world. But the most direct contact between Christendom and Islam was through Spain and Sicily rather than the East. The medieval popes undoubtedly gained prestige from their leadership of such great international enterprises as the Crusades. But their supremacy was won on other grounds. Almost the only innovations in the Papacy that can be traced directly to the crusading movement were the institution of the clerical tithe, a direct papal tax levied on all the clergy, and the sale of indulgences. Both of these methods of raising money were continued by later popes after the Crusades, which were their original rationale, had ceased. The monarchies in France and England probably gained from the diversion of the fighting energy of the feudal nobles to a distant field. But the rise of the monarchies was due far more to other causes.

Nevertheless, despite all possible qualifications, and even though it may have been more a stimulus to developments that would have taken place anyway than an original cause, a movement that involved so many people over a period of two centuries must have made a strong impression on the life of the age. The effects of travel depend entirely on the mental equipment and powers of observation of those who undertake it, and many who made that perilous journey probably learned little or nothing from it. Still, some among the many crusaders and pilgrims returned with a broader mental horizon and new ideas. Aside from what they may have learned from the infidel, knights from all parts of Europe met and learned the customs of one another's countries. The manners and customs of chivalry became more universal and more highly formalized. The romantic adventures of the crusaders were retold in song and story, giving rise to a new popular literature for the knightly class. Above all, the Crusades shook up a society and made it less provincial.

The Expansion of Catholic Europe

While the crusaders were carrying Christianity into the distant lands of the eastern Mediterranean, other Christian soldiers were waging a more permanently successful war against heathens and infidels within Europe itself. The conversion of the Slavs of Bohemia—the modern Czechoslovakia—was begun as early as the ninth century by Byzantine missionaries. But the Bohemians, unlike the Russian Slavs, did not remain in the Greek Orthodox faith. They turned instead to the Roman Church. After the middle of the tenth century, when the German emperor, Otto the Great, forced the Czechs to recognize him as their overlord, Bohemia faced westward. It became a fief of the Empire, though it always preserved a separate government of its own, and its duke, who after 1158 bore the title of king, had greater power over his people than had any of the emperor's other vassals. Poland, the other great Slavic country to the east of the Empire, was not converted to Christianity until the second half of the tenth century, through the work of Roman Catholic missionaries.

Unlike Bohemia, Poland did not become a permanent part of the Holy Roman Empire, though it did remain within the Roman Church. Poland covered a large territory, but seldom enjoyed strong government and was always open to attack from its powerful neighbors. Hungary, the Empire's eastern neighbor to the south of Poland, was still slower to receive Christianity. There were many Slavs in Hungary, but the dominant people was the Magyars, a nomadic nation which, like so many others, had drifted into Europe from western Asia. After ravaging Germany for years, the Magyars were defeated by Otto the Great in 955 and forced to settle down. Nearly half a century later, they were converted and brought into the Roman Church by their king, Saint Stephen. During the thirteenth century, Poland and Hungary formed an invaluable bulwark for Western Christendom against the attack of the fierce Mongols, who swept out of Asia across eastern Europe and founded the vast empire called the Golden Horde, which long dominated Russia.

Not until the eleventh century was Christianity firmly established in the Scandinavian lands to the north of western Europe. The Danes were the first to be converted by Catholic missionaries, but there were still many heathen in Denmark when the Danish king Canute (1017–1035) ruled a great empire that included England and Norway. Norway soon followed and finally Sweden, though not without stubborn resistance from the devotees of the old heathen gods.

Very different from this process of conversion was the expansion of Christendom to the northeast of the Empire during the period of the Crusades. Throughout most of the twelfth century the Germans of Saxony, Holstein, and the North Mark carried on a war of conquest against the heathen Slavs who dwelt to the south of the Baltic, between the rivers Elbe and Oder. As German authority moved eastward to the Oder, the land was resettled by German colonists, while adventurous German traders established new trading cities all along the Baltic coast. The final success of the struggle was largely due to the leadership of Henry the Lion, duke of Saxony.

Meanwhile, farther east in Pomerania, between the Oder and the Vistula, the Poles had extended Christianity to the Baltic by similarly forceful means. But the Prussians, a wild and warlike people of Letto-Lithuanian stock who occupied the territory between Poland and the Baltic beyond the Vistula, were still heathen and a constant menace to the Poles. Early in the thirteenth century, the Poles appealed to the crusading order of Teutonic Knights, who had already done good work in the Holy Land, to aid them against the heathen Prussians. The Poles came to regret the invitation—for the next seven and a half centuries. The knights were promised whatever land they could conquer, and the donation was ratified by the emperor. The knights began their campaign in 1230, and thereafter pressed the crusade, as they considered it, so strongly that by 1283 they were masters of Prussia. They thus founded a German state on the eastern Baltic, separated from the Empire only by the strip of Polish Pomerania.

Still greater interest attaches to the expansion of Christendom by the conquest of the highly civilized Islamic state in Spain. The collapse of the caliphate of Cordova in 1034, due to internal dissension, provided a good opportunity for the little Christian kingdoms in the north to expand at the expense of the

SPAIN, 1100–1248

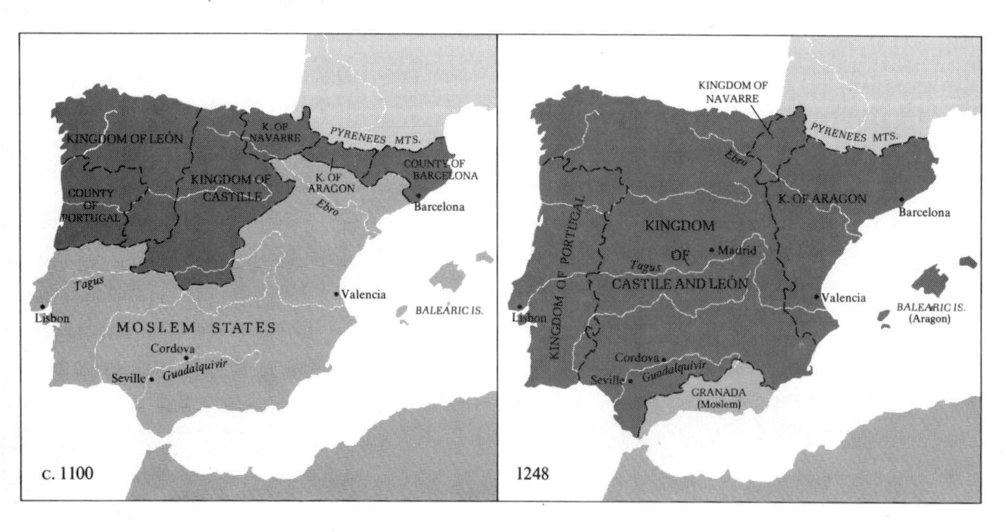

Moors, as the Moslems in Spain were called. For more than two centuries they continued the struggle with varying success, often aided by crusaders from France and other parts of Europe.

The success of the Moslem states' resistance to the Christian reconquest was attributable to military manpower that arrived in Spain from North Africa during this period. Without the arrival of Moorish forces the Christian reconquest might have achieved total success long before the end of the fifteenth century. By 1248, only the little kingdom of Granada in the south remained in Moorish hands. The rest of Spain was divided among four Christian kingdoms. Castile, to which León had been permanently united since 1230, was the largest, occupying most of the central and western part of the peninsula. Aragon, the next largest, occupied a triangle, of which one side extended along the Pyrenees from the east and the second stretched down the eastern coast below Valencia. In between Castile and Aragon on the northern border was the little kingdom of Navarre, which had been unable to expand because it was surrounded by two powerful neighbors. Finally, in the southwest was the newly founded kingdom of Portugal, an amalgam of Moorish and Christian elements, which influenced important aspects of the language and culture of Christians in Spain. Many Christian and Jewish scholars in western Europe traveled to Cordova and performed important works of translation, thereby furthering the reintroduction of Aristotelianism and Greco-Roman scientific knowledge into western Europe.

The age of the medieval Crusades lasted longer in Spain than in any other area of Europe or the Near East. The Spanish example, however, is particularly illustrative of the beneficent intellectual by-products of Islamic-Christian confrontation.

Suggestions for Further Reading

A. S. Atiya, *Crusade, Commerce and Culture* (1962).

A. Bailly, *Saint Louis* (1949).

A. Kelly, *Eleanor of Aquitaine** (1947). An imaginative work of literary distinction and sound scholarship [AHA, 182].

J. L. LaMonte, *Feudal Monarchy in the Latin Kingdom of Jerusalem, 1100 to 1291* (1932). Stands high among important books concerning crusaders. Divided into three parts: constitutional development of the Latin Kingdom of Jerusalem, its administrative machinery, and some political relationships of the kings of Jerusalem [AHA, 187, in part].

R. A. Newhall, *The Crusades,* rev. ed. (1963). Clear, scholarly sketch [AHA, 187, in part].

S. Runciman, *A History of the Crusades,** 3 vols. (1951–1954). Probably the last time a single historian will undertake to write a scholarly history of the entire crusading movement. Runciman shows great narrative skill—and also a pronounced bias in favor of Byzantium and the Eastern Christians.

K. M. Setton, ed., *A History of the Crusades* (1955). A cooperative work planned to cover all aspects of crusade history [AHA, 186].

*Available in a paperback edition.

Medieval Civilization: Greatness and Decline

THREE

The Medieval Town

13

If anyone shall have remained in the city of Lincoln for a year and a day without claim on the part of any claimant . . . he shall remain in peace.

ROYAL CHARTER GRANTED BY HENRY II OF ENGLAND

Stadtluft macht frei. (City air makes one free.)

GERMAN PROVERB

Aspects of the Medieval Town

The study of medieval civilization requires a consideration of the town life that emerged so dynamically between 1000 and 1300. The medieval city must have presented a picturesque appearance to the wandering merchant who plodded down the dusty road leading to the city gate. First he would see the high encircling wall of heavy stone, surrounded by a moat and surmounted by towers very like those of a baronial castle; strongly fortified walls were as necessary to the security of the townsfolk as they were to the feudal lord. At sunset the great gates were closed, and if the merchant were too late, he would have to stay outside until dawn. Inside the walls, he would see a mass of roofs, sloping at every imaginable angle, and crowned with chimney pots in which storks built their nests. Here and there would rise the thin spires of parish churches and, if it were an episcopal city, the tall cathedral tower would shoot up from the center above the surrounding roofs, dominating the whole town.

With the revival of relatively long-range commerce beginning in the eleventh century, it became common for traveling merchants to set up stalls displaying their wares outside the original walls of the city. The areas in which this was done were known as *faubourgs*. We can trace the expansion of many medieval cities by noting the demolition of old walls and the construction of new battlements which protected the newly prosperous faubourgs.

Cities had originally been built around the smallest possible spaces to make them easily defensible and to save labor and expense, hence the amazing congestion within any medieval city. Fires were frequent and often engulfed large parts of the city, for there was no way of fighting the flames except by a bucket line from the nearest well. Much of the city of Rouen was burned six times in the first quarter of the thirteenth century.

Churches abounded in every quarter of the city, for the burghers were pious folk. The great cathedral in the center of the city was the pride of the pious and patriotic burgher's heart. It was a magnificent edifice of solid stone adorned with intricate carvings, high-arched stained-glass windows, and soaring towers.

Cathedrals of the Gothic type were the artistic masterpieces of the Middle Ages. Within the cathedral there was an atmosphere of peace and a dim religious light, strongly contrasting to the noise and bustle of the marketplace outside. The only open space in the city was the square in front of the cathedral or the largest church. There the town market was held and the people congregated for all public ceremonies, making the great church the center of the life of the city.

Important as were cities in the civilization of the High Middle Ages, they were very small in comparison with their modern counterparts. The total area within the walls of medieval London was less than one square mile. By the end of the thirteenth century the more prosperous cities had grown enormously since the early Middle Ages and were becoming overcrowded, but their populations were still small by modern standards. Medieval population statistics are generally unreliable, but there is good reason to believe that even at the beginning of the fourteenth century none of the great Italian cities had more than 100,000 inhabitants. London had about 40,000 people, but no other English city had more than a quarter of that number. Ghent and Bruges, the two largest cities in the Netherlands, had between 40,000 and 50,000 inhabitants. No German city was as large as these; Cologne, the largest, had something over 30,000 people. Some historians have credited Paris with the rather unbelievable figure of 200,000 inhabitants; certainly it was the largest city in France. The great majority of cities in all parts of western Europe were in reality no more than small market towns of 1,000 or 2,000 inhabitants.

Commerce, Agriculture, and Towns

How did a thriving urban life come into being in the High Middle Ages? What force gave new life to old cities and created new ones? The answer is, in part, trade. Roman civilization, which had been largely urban, had depended on wide-ranging commerce. But Roman trade declined with the Empire, and the cities declined with it. Only in the part of the Eastern Empire around the great commercial city of Constantinople did trade continue to flourish. In the West, cities survived, with sadly diminished populations, as centers of episcopal or civil administration or fortified strongholds. In short, cities declined when trade di-

Defensive walls surrounding the French city of Carcassonne. The addition of a second, outer wall in the last half of the thirteenth century and the strengthening of the inner wall made this one of the most heavily fortified cities in France.

minished and began to grow again when trade was revived in the eleventh and twelfth centuries. However, they would not have developed as they did had it not been for great demographic and agrarian expansion after the tenth century.

In offering this interpretation, we should acknowledge that the development of cities was also the product of their own internal evolution. Cities which succeeded in achieving a degree of communal independence from local lords or kings often developed their economic, juridical, and administrative organs in a most precocious way. Yet those cities which were able to develop in harmony with a monarchy that provided the order necessary for the transaction of daily business benefited from this relationship. These factors should not be overlooked in examining the development of medieval urban centers against the background of long-distance trade and agrarian expansion.

Wide-ranging European commerce revived first in Italy, where Venice and the formerly Greek cities of the south had never entirely lost contact with the Byzantine Empire. When, in the eleventh century, Christendom began to take the offensive against Islam, their trade with the Near East increased rapidly. Finally, the First Crusade, at the end of the century, completed the opening of the Mediterranean to European traders. The ports of the Levant and the islands were now in Christian hands, and there was a clear road to the East. Venice, cut off from the mainland by lagoons and forced to make its living from the sea, took the lead in the mercantile revival. Venice was the trading city par excellence, the Queen of the Adriatic, the wealthiest city in the West. But before the end of the

The town of Loches in the Loire valley in France, its appearance little changed since the Middle Ages.

eleventh century, Genoa and Pisa, on the other side of the peninsula, were already formidable rivals. Like Venice, they acquired trading-posts in the newly conquered kingdom of Jerusalem.

Meanwhile in the north, the ports of Flanders, fortunately situated on the deep estuaries where the Rhine, the Scheldt, and the Meuse flow into the North Sea, were becoming centers of a similar revival of international trade. The original agents of this revival were the Northmen, who, after destroying the commerce of the western seas by piracy, restored it again when they turned to legitimate trade. Their long boats plied the coasts of the Baltic, the North Sea, and the Atlantic and called at English ports. This trade naturally centered upon Flanders, where the wine and other products of the interior could be exchanged for wool from England or wax, furs, and amber from the Baltic.

From these two focal centers trade gradually spread inland. During the eleventh century, commercial relations with Venice, Genoa, and Pisa were a great stimulus to the growing towns of the Lombard plain and Tuscany. By the beginning of the twelfth century, the commercial revival had spread to the ports of southern France and Christian Spain. From there and across the Alpine passes from Lombardy, merchants followed roads and rivers into France and Germany, until they met northern merchants traveling down the rivers from the Flemish coast. The penetration of trade into the interior proceeded slowly, but before the end of the twelfth century the main trade routes had been opened up, and merchants traveled constantly to all parts of Christian Europe.

The rise of territorial monarchies, which offered security, was important to the development of towns in Spain, France, and England. Agrarian expansion, allowing for the export of surplus grain to the towns, was a necessary prerequisite for their growth. The excess population of the countryside often provided adventurous emigrants to the towns. Town and country were thus linked in innumerable and crucial ways.

Medieval commerce was conducted largely by itinerant merchants, who carried their wares with them on long journeys. It was a hazardous life, but the profits, when fortune smiled, were proportionately large.

Throughout the High Middle Ages, annual fairs were the most important element of interregional trade. Without them, the exchange of foreign goods would have been greatly restricted, if not impossible. In the twelfth century, the fairs of Champagne were attended by merchants from all parts of Christendom, but there were innumerable others in every country of Europe. Fairs were normally held in cities, but were usually under a higher authority than the municipal government, such as the king, a bishop or abbot, or a great feudal lord, who guaranteed "the peace of the fair."

Not the least of the attractions of the fairs for foreign merchants was the prospect of speedy justice. Ordinarily, the mills of justice ground slowly in the Middle Ages, and they did not grind very fine. Moreover, each city had its own laws and customs, which strangers could not be expected to know. Above all else, the traveling merchant needed the protection of dependable courts, a law with which he was familiar, and speedy trials, so that his departure for other parts might not be delayed. All these he found in the jurisdiction of the lord of the fair and in the special merchant courts, called in England "pie powder" courts, a corruption of the French *pieds poudreux,* for the dusty-footed merchants who frequented them.

Burghers and Town Government

The burghers, the "bourgeois" of the eleventh and twelfth centuries, were generally individuals of peasant origin who lived in towns, drawing their livelihood from artisanry and commerce, rather than directly from the land or from warfare. They valued a more orderly form of existence, while feudal lords and their miserable peasants saw life as a bloody affair in which war was the dominant fact. The bourgeois valued his individual freedom, and appreciated the town as a bastion of order in a society torn by constant feudal turbulence. The bourgeois, gaining confidence, wished to control his own institutions, which led to constant struggles with other, more traditional, forces in the society: feudal lords, bishops, and sometimes emperors and kings.

This struggle achieved classical dimensions in northern Italy. The Lombard cities fought for freedom against their bishops and the emperors for a century and a half, until they forced even the powerful Frederick Barbarossa to recognize their right to self-government as practically independent city-republics. Nowhere else did cities achieve such complete independence, though the great Flemish cities came close to it and in Germany a few of the largest acquired the status of free imperial cities, subject only to the nominal authority of the emperor. In most places the burghers were content with less. They were willing to acknowledge the political authority of the king or their lord and to pay taxes. All they asked was that their obligations be defined and limited, that the town as a corporation and not individuals be responsible for them, and that, within the town, the burghers be left as free as possible to manage their own affairs. Often these concessions were obtained peacefully by the purchase of a charter from the

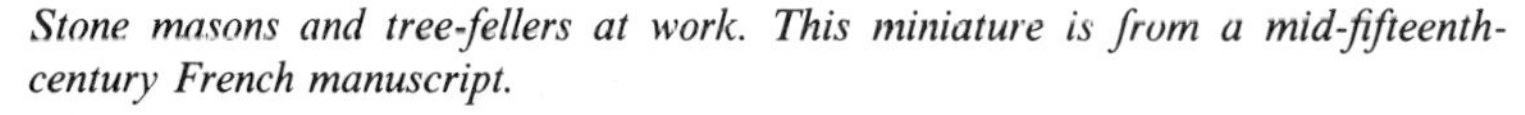

Stone masons and tree-fellers at work. This miniature is from a mid-fifteenth-century French manuscript.

king or one of the great lords. This was particularly true in England and on the royal domain and the great fiefs in France.

As a rule the nobles, save for a few rulers of great fiefs like the counts of Champagne, were less favorably disposed toward the cities than were the kings. But they were often forced by poverty to sell charters, and were gradually discovering that free cities were likely to be more prosperous and thus to pay them more taxes than those whose freedom of action was hampered by feudal restrictions. In France, many lords founded new towns on their estates, offering very liberal terms to attract settlers, in order to augment their incomes from the prospective taxes.

We may therefore speak of widespread internal colonization in western Europe during this period. All over France, lords interested in attracting new settlers issued charters authorizing the incorporation of *villes neuves,* or new towns. This process of colonization was not restricted to France. In Spain, for example, Christian lords fighting Moslem authority had a permanent interest in attracting new settlers to their lands, and acted accordingly. A rise in population meant new or greater towns. In the German border areas of central Europe, the process of colonization was continuous from the tenth to the fifteenth centuries.

The government of the typical medieval city was in the hands of a council and a number of executive officers or magistrates (they went by a variety of names), nearly always burghers of the city chosen by their fellow burghers freely or in collaboration with the lord. Their principal duty was to levy and collect taxes. There were usually direct taxes on income and indirect taxes on the sale of goods. With the money raised in this way, the city government maintained defenses, public works, and the administration of government, and paid whatever taxes the city owed to the king or its lord. The growing political power of the cities and their influence with the monarchy depended largely on this ability to raise money taxes, which had no parallel in the feudal system.

A tailor at work in a shop open to the street, from a fourteenth-century Italian manuscript.

The city also had its own system of civil and criminal law and its own courts and judges. City laws and judicial procedure were usually much more enlightened than the ancient customs still enforced in the feudal courts. At least they were better suited to the needs of those who made their livings from commerce and industry. The right to participate in the government of the city was seldom open to all inhabitants. It was ordinarily limited to men of property who were legally recognized as burghers, a privilege which they defended jealously against outsiders and the poorer classes.

Among the duties of the city magistrates were the supervision of the town market and the collection of market tolls, which were an important part of the city's revenues. Nearly all cities had the legal right to hold markets, though they often had to pay dearly for it. In thirteenth-century France, and earlier in England, the kings asserted their exclusive right to issue charters granting that privilege. Markets must not be confused with fairs. The former were purely municipal institutions for local trade, held for one day only once or twice a week. Here the peasants from the countryside displayed their produce for sale to the burghers. In some places, in order to augment the tolls, even the merchants of the city were forced to close their shops and sell in the market during market days.

It was not only in the markets that the municipal government supervised the city's trade. Since it was their duty to protect the interests of the whole body of citizens, the magistrates felt justified in exercising a minute control of all business within the city. Perhaps because the city existed in the midst of a hostile environment, and the citizens were forced to depend upon one another for aid, the medieval burgher felt that the interests of the individual should be subordinated to the welfare of the whole community. He had, therefore, no objection to a paternalistic government which set prices, supervised methods of manufacture, determined the quality of goods, regulated wages and hours of labor, and prevented any individual from taking unfair advantage of his fellow citizens. The purpose of medieval economic legislation was to guarantee to the worker and seller a fair living and to protect the consumer against fraud or undue cost.

Merchant and Craft Guilds

The practical result of these regulations was the grant of a monopoly to the guild, a producers' association which determined urban legislation relating to its area of production. In a time of relative economic scarcity, the protection offered to producer and consumer by such a monopoly outweighed the potential disadvantages of a restriction of trade. In a later age, medieval economic legislation would be associated with restrictive monopoly, and there would be agitation against such constraints.

The medieval person had no confidence in the economic law of supply and demand as the source of prices, nor in the principle that free competition is the greatest stimulus to trade. If he acknowledged them at all, he considered them immoral. Instead, he believed that for every commodity there was a just price, which should be the same in times of shortage and of plenty. This price was set by custom and based on the normal price of raw materials plus the reasonable profit necessary to permit the workers and merchants to live in the style recognized by public opinion as suitable to their status. The Church had a good deal to do with evolving and enforcing this theory, but secular authorities accepted it implicitly as the basis for all legislation regarding price. The statute books of every city were filled with laws designed to enforce the sale of goods at just or reasonable prices, and the guilds, too, did their share. Of course, this legislation did not always accomplish its purpose. The principle of the just price was too vague, and the severe penalties constantly re-enacted against "engrossing, forestalling, and regrating"—three kindred methods of cornering the market and withholding goods until the demand had raised the price—show that not all medieval businessmen allowed moral theories to interfere with their desire for gain. The condemnation of "usury"—that is, the charging of interest for money lent—arose from a similar principle. It was believed that money was not an active force, and that to exact a price for its use was to take unfair advantage of the needs of one's fellows. But this prohibition was even less rigorously observed than the theory of the just price.

Despite everything that the Church and secular governments could do, money continued to be lent at interest, in a thinly disguised form. But the rate of interest dropped in the late Middle Ages as money became more available. Gold coinage reappeared north of the Alps in the late thirteenth century, and when the sons of great banking families such as the Medicis became popes in the sixteenth century, the Church modified its hostility toward interest.

Aside from their obviously economic function, we should not overlook the fact that the earliest guilds were social and religious in character. They offered their members various social benefits, among the most important of which was the dignity of a decent religious burial, and also represented the corporate personality of a given trade. This personality was commonly expressed in the thirteenth century by the donation of a stained-glass window to a Gothic cathedral. The original Latin name of the guild, the *universitas,* reflects this corporative socio-religious function.

The manifold duties of the merchant guild were in many respects the same as those of the city government. There was, indeed, so close a connection between the two that it was often difficult to distinguish between them. The guildsmen were the most active burghers and frequently controlled the government of the city. Often the same men served as city and guild officers. But the city government had wider powers and was superior to the guild, which merely administered the economic side of government and exercised a monopoly of trade. In the course of time, as the merchant guilds began to decline, their powers were in many places assumed by the city administration. The twelfth century was the period of greatest power for the merchant guilds. When industry became more highly specialized, their place was largely taken by the various craft guilds. The merchant guilds or companies, which reappeared in the late Middle Ages, were of a different character, dealing usually with some particular line of trade.

The craft guilds were essentially industrial, but they also had a mercantile character. They were composed of artisans of a given trade or craft, who manufactured or prepared goods and sold them, usually directly to the consumer. The type of work which each guild could undertake was strictly defined. In the larger cities, where there were a great many craft guilds, they were very highly specialized. For example, there might be two separate guilds for the manufacture of men's and women's shoes. In smaller places, on the other hand, several allied crafts might be lumped together in a single guild. Each guild exercised a monopoly over its particular trade within the city. The right to sell its goods must have been transferred to it in some way from the merchant guild which had exercised a blanket monopoly on all selling. The history of the relationship between the two types of guild is very obscure and no doubt varied from place to place. In general, it seems that the monopoly and other powers of the merchant guild were parceled out to the craft guilds, and that the merchant guild either continued as a vague aggregate of all guilds or merged with the city government.

As the guilds developed and acquired more power by the thirteenth century, they became more rigid and exclusionist in structure. The justification for such policies was the maintenance of the high standards and training practices of the various trades. In fact, those guildmasters who had acquired positions of power in their guilds tended to make them hereditary. The boys chosen to be apprentices, and ultimately journeymen and masters, tended to come from families friendly or related to those of the masters. In a time of widespread economic contraction, such as prevailed in much of western Europe during the fourteenth century, existing guilds became even more exclusive and monopolistic in their practices. In some cases, the growth of far-flung commercial capitalism harmed local craft guilds and subjected them to intolerable social and economic pressures. Rivalry developed between craft guilds and merchant traders, and the great "capitalist" entrepreneur ultimately triumphed by controlling the political life of cities from Italy to northern Europe.

Suggestions for Further Reading

W. Beresford and J. K. S. St. Joseph, *Medieval England, an Aerial Survey* (1958).

E. M. Carus-Wilson, *Medieval Merchant Venturers** (1954).

P. M. Hauser and L. F. Schnore, eds., *The Study of Urbanization* (1965). Essays covering many areas.

J. H. Mundy and P. Riesenberg, *The Medieval Town** (1958). Good though brief introduction to medieval urban problems [AHA, 192, in part].

H. Pirenne, *Economic and Social History of Medieval Europe** (1937). An excellent survey covering the entire medieval period. Pirenne's sometimes controversial views enliven the book, which is especially effective when dealing with northern Europe during the crisis-filled late medieval period.

H. Pirenne, *Medieval Cities** (1925). A brief, eloquent statement of the "Pirenne thesis": the revival of Mediterranean long-distance trade led to the rise of south French, Italian, and Catalonian towns, which in turn, through the diffusion of prosperity, resulted in the growth of medieval towns elsewhere from the eleventh century.

E. Power, *Medieval People** (1935). The charm of these six lively essays has long held thousands of readers captive [AHA, 196, in part].

*Available in a paperback edition.

Christianity and Culture in Medieval Europe

14

Law is a regulation in accord with reason, issued by a lawful superior for the common good.

SAINT THOMAS AQUINAS, *SUMMA THEOLOGICA*

The Church as Institution

The growth of cities provided the setting for the major forces of institutionalized religion and learning in the central Middle Ages: the papal curia, the universities and cathedral schools, the court scholars, and the urban preaching orders of friars. As the administration of the Church became more highly centralized, a tremendous mass of business was referred to Rome, which the pope could not handle singlehandedly. He was assisted by a host of subordinate officers and clerks who made up the papal *curia* or court; he also had an advisory council in the College of Cardinals. The cardinals were appointed for life by the pope and ranked second only to him in the ecclesiastical hierarchy. Their importance depended largely on their exclusive right to elect the popes, which had been guaranteed to them by the decree of Nicholas II in 1059.

The codification of Church law (canon law) from the late eleventh century played an important role in the developing administrative structure of the medieval Church. Outside of Rome, the principal administrative officers were the bishops, each of whom was the head of the Church in his diocese. The diocese was the most important territorial unit of Church administration. A number of dioceses grouped together formed a province, and the bishop of the principal diocese of the province was called an archbishop.

In the principal city of each diocese there was a cathedral, which was the bishop's church. Here there was a "chapter" of canons, who were responsible for the conduct of the services. The cathedral canons had much the same relation to the bishops that the cardinals did to the pope. They assisted him in administration, acted as an advisory council, and had the sole right, according to canon law, of electing a new bishop, though their choice was in practice frequently dictated by the king or some other feudal superior. This right was nullified if a bishop died on his way to Rome. According to tradition, when this happened the pope had the sole right to appoint the diocesan successor.

The head of each chapter was the dean, elected by the canons. By the thirteenth century the cathedral chapters had acquired a good deal of land, which, with the support of the popes, made them fairly independent of their bishops. With each canon's prebend or office went the income from a particular piece of land. As a result, the prebends were often sought by young nobles who had no particular religious interests. The popes were forced to issue frequent edicts, usually in vain, ordering canons to remain in residence and to attend to their duties. As a measure of reform some chapters were organized on a monastic basis with a rule of communal life.

The smallest unit of ecclesiastical administration was the parish, and it was the parish priest who had the most direct contact with the people. In country districts the parish was usually identical with the village or manor. The parish church was endowed with a share in the cultivated fields of the manor. The land set aside for the sustenance of the priest on the manor was called the glebe. The priest drew his income from this land, from offerings and from the tithe. The last, which had originally been a free offering for any religious purpose, had become a tax on the income of all parishioners, enforceable by law. However, the priest was not permitted to keep all or even the largest part of his income. Part went to the bishop in various forms of ecclesiastical tax and part to the patron of the church. The latter was usually the lord of the manor, whose ancestors had originally endowed the church with its land.

In Germany in particular, the Church had to come to grips with an old tradition which severely limited ecclesiastical authority. The *Eigenkirche,* which literally means "one's own church," was a Germanic Christian tradition which assumed that the lord on whose land a church was situated was the proprietor of the church, with full authority to appoint its servants. As the authority of the Roman Church developed on the basis of its own legal traditions and claims from the eleventh century, such a concept became an intolerable affront to ecclesiastical independence, which was the aim of great popes like Gregory VII. In part, the struggle between Gregory VII and Henry IV was a contest between the corporative independent identity of the universal Roman Church and the right of a Germanic lord to control the ecclesiastical officials who served him and the churches within his lands. In a rough feudal age, the tendency toward local control of the Church was enhanced in Germanic areas by the tradition of the *Eigenkirche.*

Everywhere in Europe, the Church, with its lands and tithe, was a benefice or living which the patron bestowed upon the priest, retaining a share of its income for himself. Lay patrons often gave the living to favorites or sold it to the highest bidder, with little regard for the suitability of the candidate for his office. The clerical patron—bishop, abbot, or dean—might hold the office of priest himself and appoint as a substitute a vicar who did all the work and received only a small proportion of the income.

In this feudal age, when literacy was such a rare phenomenon, the low educational and moral level of the priesthood was a constant object of denunciation and scorn on the part of ardent reformers. We must beware of taking such strictures literally, however, for reformers focused on the most outrageous stories and rumors in order to substantiate their case. Nevertheless, raising the educational and moral level of the priesthood was one of the major aims of the Gregorian reform movement in the late eleventh century. In this, the Church seems to have been remarkably successful, although its achievement was probably as much due to the general strengthening of monasticism and the Roman ecclesiastical administration as to the concerted campaigns and denunciations of reformers.

Aside from all its other activities, the Church had wide judicial powers, exercised in the episcopal courts, which administered ecclesiastical or canon law rather than the civil law of the secular courts. The sentences prescribed in criminal cases by canon law, which always avoided the shedding of blood, were notoriously lighter than those of the civil courts. Hence, despite the opposition of secular governments, the episcopal courts were sought by all who could claim "benefit of clergy." Fines were the most common punishments inflicted, with the result that the courts furnished a considerable portion of the bishop's revenues. This fact also largely explains the opposition of the kings, especially in France and England, to the transference of cases from royal to ecclesiastical courts. Kings were increasingly conscious of their own prerogatives and by 1200 were in a position to assert them.

They were opposed—and in this they had the support of the bishops—to the increasingly popular custom of appealing cases from the local Church courts to the papal curia at Rome. Appeals to Rome not only drained a good deal of money out of the country, they also removed important cases from the jurisdiction of the bishops, whom the kings could more or less control, to a distant and independent court.

To the medieval person, religion and the universal Church, with its sacramental powers, were inseparable. He could scarcely imagine the bliss of heaven, but hell was a place of eternal physical torment as real to him as a neighboring county. Indeed, a Norman peasant probably had a clearer mental picture of the topography, climate, and general living conditions of hell than of Burgundy or Aquitaine. He believed that no man, because of the original sin inherited from Adam and the sins which he himself would inevitably commit, could by his own unaided efforts win salvation and avoid damnation. He must depend on divine grace, channeled to man through the sacraments of the Church.

The doctrine of the sacraments, which had developed gradually since the early days of Christianity, was not fully developed until the twelfth century. There were seven sacraments in all. Baptism, administered as soon as possible after birth, cleansed the child of original sin and signified his entry into the Church. Without it there could be no hope of salvation. The sacrament of confirmation was administered by a bishop during adolescence, and marked the communicant's conscious acceptance of the faith, confirming his baptism. Extreme unction was the final sacrament, the last rite performed to prepare a dying person's soul for eternity. These three sacraments were, in the normal course of events, administered to every man and woman once. The other two universal sacraments were more frequent. The sacrament of penance, following confession and proof of repentance, washed away the guilt of sin and left only the necessity of an act of penance in this world or in purgatory to prepare the soul for heaven. Finally, and most important of all, the Eucharist, or consecrated bread and wine, administered during the service of the Mass, was miraculously turned into the body and blood of the Savior (transubstantiation) and admitted the communicant to a share in the saving grace resulting from Christ's supreme sacrifice. The two remaining sacraments, marriage and ordination, were administered to laymen and clergy respectively. Each was considered indissoluble, the former so long as both parties lived, the latter for life, though under certain conditions the bond of marriage might be broken by a special dispensation from the Church.

From the time of the Council of Nicaea in 325 to the dogmatic assertion of the immortality of the individual soul early in the sixteenth century, the Church tended to concretize and make dogma that which had been long accepted but recently attacked. Dogma is an ecclesiastical doctrine which cannot be doubted without lapsing into error and heresy. Thus, three key elements of church dogma—the nature of the Trinity, transubstantiation, and the immortality of the individual soul—were all defined against the background of ecclesiastical and intellectual crisis.

When the Church confronted a political crisis—conflict with a king, for example—the pope had other weapons. An entire kingdom might be placed under an interdict, which meant that none but the most essential sacraments—baptism and extreme unction—could be performed by priests in that land.

Saints and Heretics

It is interesting to note how the image of Christ changed in the High Middle Ages. The Christ portrayed above the portals of Romanesque churches built in the eleventh century bears considerable resemblance to the Byzantine Christ, the remote world-creator. He is formidable, distant, and awesome. The Christ of later Romanesque and Gothic sculpture from the late twelfth century has taken on more human characteristics and appears to be a warmer being. In part this change reflected artistic evolution, in part the less harsh quality of European life after the end of the real feudal age. Another important phenomenon of the High Middle Ages was the rise of mariolatry, the cult of the Virgin Mary. This too was largely a Gothic phenomenon, coming to the fore in the sculpture of the twelfth and thirteenth centuries. To medieval people, Mary became virtually a fourth figure of the godhead. A warm human woman whose purity and access to the divine were faltering man's best hope, she interceded with God on behalf of penitent sinners. Some of the greatest medieval art reflects this cult of the Virgin.

Veneration of the Virgin and other saints focused on the relics of their mortal existence—their bodies as well as their clothing and personal belongings. The relics of famous people always have a sentimental value, such as we would attribute to the pen used by Shakespeare, and are always eagerly sought by collectors. But the relics of the saints meant much more than that, for they partook of the miraculous powers of the saints themselves. To touch them was enough to heal illness or to keep one from harm. The bones of one of the major saints were worth more than a king's ransom, and pilgrims came from afar to seek aid or comfort at the shrine that housed them. Pilgrimages too were often undertaken as full or partial performance of the penance prescribed by the Church. Throughout the medieval centuries, bands of pilgrims might be encountered daily on any of the main roads of Europe.

Toward the end of the Middle Ages there was a widespread reaction, particularly among scholars, against popular veneration of relics and pilgrimages. To many reformers, these acts connotated superstition. Chaucer portrayed this mocking attitude somewhat sympathetically in his *Canterbury Tales,* stories of human frailty and religiosity set in the context of true religion and true fraud.

Heresy was a problem for the Church throughout the Middle Ages. It was provoked by various tendencies—sometimes external religious doctrines, sometimes internal social stresses, sometimes a quest for a renewed Christianity. On certain occasions all these elements were combined. The two most important heretical sects, the Albigenses and the Waldenses, flourished chiefly in southern France, though they spread into neighboring countries. The former, also called Cathari, were the most numerous and made their appearance as early as the eleventh century. The doctrines of the Albigensians bore a marked resemblance to earlier forms of eastern dualism such as Mithraism and Manicheanism. Their central doctrine seems to have been a very literal and rather morbid identification of everything physical and material with the forces of evil in the universe. The Waldenses seem to have been much more "normal," and their doctrines were closer to true Christianity. Except in the south of France, where they were included in the mass persecution of the Albigenses, they were not rigorously pursued by the Church, and remnants of the Waldenses survived for centuries in Piedmont, Germany, Bohemia, Hungary, and even in orthodox Spain. Their founder was a rich merchant of Lyon, Peter Waldo, who about the year 1170 gave his property away to the poor and began preaching in an effort to recall people to the simple doctrine of Christ found in the Gospels. Neither he nor his followers at first had any thought of heresy, but their vigorous condemnation of the wealth and worldliness of the clergy soon led to their denunciation by the Church. Their protest against the clerical monopoly was never entirely forgotten.

Throughout the twelfth century the Church had made fitful efforts to suppress heretics, but it was Innocent III who first committed the full authority of the Papacy to the task of destroying enemies of the faith. In 1207, he summoned the chivalry of Europe to take part in a Crusade against the Albigenses. The northern knights laid waste the rich lands of southern France, slaughtering thousands. They struck a mortal blow against the flourishing culture of Languedoc and Provence as well as to heresy, but the latter at least would soon have revived had the work of the crusaders not been followed by the preaching of the newly founded orders of friars and by the steady persecution of heresy by the papal Inquisition or Holy Office, now for the first time firmly established.

Inquisitorial procedure—the identification and trial of heretics—was not new; it had been a regular part of the bishops' judicial duties. But the bishops were busy men and often none too zealous. In 1233, therefore, Pope Gregory IX gave a permanent commission, later more fully developed, to regular inquisitors who were to set up special courts, in formal cooperation with the bishops, for the discovery and trial of heretics. The methods of the Inquisition—the secrecy of the trials, the refusal to divulge the names of the accusers so that the accused might answer them, the full and accurate records kept by the court, and the use of torture to extort confessions—inspired dread wherever the institution was established, and in the long run succeeded in stamping out most heresy. The sentences imposed ranged from public penance to life imprisonment. However, stubborn heretics who refused to recant, and those who relapsed into heresy, were turned over to the secular government to be burned at the stake.

Monks and Friars

The rise of two great monastic orders in the thirteenth century was directly related to the social and religious turmoil of the age. They owed their existence to historical phenomena typical of that era: towns, heresy, and a longing for a purified, Gospel-oriented existence.

Saint Francis of Assisi (1182?-1226), who founded the Friars Minor or Franciscans, came from a background rooted in the wealth and luxury of the new northern Italian urban merchant class. The very name Francis is indicative of the future saint's background; his father gave him a French name because southern French or Provençal culture typified to this Italian merchant everything soft, courtly, luxurious, and elegant. The lush culture of southern France before the Albigensian Crusades influenced the Tuscan civilization that was to produce men such as Saint Francis and Dante.

Francis was one of the most lovable of the medieval saints. In his youth he lived a gay, irresponsible existence, loving poetry and gallant gestures. His conversion from this frivolous life occurred suddenly, when he was still in his early twenties. In his new way of life, Francis lost none of his joyous spirit, love of poetry and nature, or the personal charm that had always attracted others to him. His teaching in part represented an impulse toward a return to a simpler, more natural order in which man was at one with nature in a divinely blessed creation. Yet Francis' message was one not of escape from the prosperous cities of the thirteenth century but of the bestowal of the simple, natural word of the Gospels upon city people.

Historians such as Labande have argued that Saint Francis' concept of the divine harmony between man and nature was at the root of impulses which culminated in the naturalism of the Italian Renaissance. In noting this interpretation, however, we should not overlook the fact that in venerating nature Francis was adoring God and His work. He was not a pagan exulting in the glories of the natural order. The various Italian Renaissance poets who adopted this attitude were reviving an ancient Roman tradition, rather than following in the footsteps of Saint Francis.

Both the Franciscans and the Dominicans, in receiving their licenses from the pope, were exceptions to the new papal policy against the proliferation of monastic orders. A major cause of this prohibition was the frequency with which restless and wandering monks switched from one order to another. The more orders, the greater was the chaos.

Before long, gray-cloaked friars were familiar figures on every highway and in every crowded slum of western Europe. They were a universal order, exempt from the authority of the bishops, and their general was subject only to the pope. As they became more popular, the ideals of the friars began to change. They accepted gifts of houses and furniture, despite the vow of poverty on which Saint Francis had insisted so strongly, and their high standard of character gradually declined. A few, however, clung to the spirit of the rule, with the result that after a long and bitter controversy the order was finally divided.

The Spiritual Franciscans and Fraticelli of the fourteenth century attempted to carry on the spirit of Saint Francis. They became involved in controversies with popes such as John XXII largely because they insisted that apostolic poverty was the sine qua non for the salvation of the Christian individual.

Saint Dominic (1170-1221), founder of the order of preaching friars named after him, was a native of Castile. He was well educated and became a canon and later a subprior of the Augustinian order. In 1205, he accompanied his bishop on a mission into southern France, where he was shocked by the prevalence of heresy and soon began to preach in an effort to win back heretics to the orthodox faith. For the next eleven years he continued preaching, though often in danger from the violence aroused by the Albigensian Crusade. Like Saint Francis, Saint

Dominic gathered a group of followers about him. He received papal recognition for his order in 1216, though the final rule was not drawn up until four years later. Saint Dominic was a man of admirable character, gentle and kindly and absolutely fearless; but he lacked the rare spiritual charm of the Italian saint, and his main purpose was the more limited one of converting heretics rather than giving spiritual inspiration to the orthodox, who often needed it quite as badly. He, too, insisted on the vow of poverty, but valued it not as an end in itself, as Saint Francis did, but because it would increase the prestige and influence of the preaching brothers. When poverty seemed a disadvantage rather than an asset, the Dominicans departed from the rule without the conflict which beset the Franciscan order. Friars from both orders were frequently entrusted with the conduct of the Inquisition, but it was the Dominicans who devoted the most time to the grim task of suppressing heresy, earning for them the name of *domini canes* ("hounds of God").

The work of these new orders at first consisted of preaching and combating heresy, but they came to play a major role in the developing universities of the thirteenth and fourteenth centuries. Both Dominicans and Franciscans taught theology at such universities as Paris and Oxford. Both orders produced some of the great intellectuals of the age, but by the fifteenth century the former intellectual greatness of the orders had largely degenerated into squabbling over chairs, assertions of traditional authority, and constant repetition of pedantic theological disputes. The German Dominicans in particular became the butt and laughingstock of the German humanists in the period before the Lutheran Reformation.

The Culture of the Chivalric Order

In the spirit of Saint Francis there was a courtly and chivalric element which reflected the Provençal and Tuscan culture of which his father had been so enamored. What was the chivalric culture of the High Middle Ages?

Every noble, if he could afford it and did not enter the Church, was made a knight as soon as he came of age. He was then recognized as a member of that great international society of fighting gentlemen, the Order of Chivalry. The word chivalry, as applied to the Middle Ages, is often loosely used with a variety of connotations, but always in reference to the heavy-armed and mounted knights called in France *chevaliers* and in Germany *Ritter,* both words originally meaning horsemen. The word is sometimes used to denote an international order with fairly definite customs and rules, or again to refer to a band of soldiers of that class, as in "the chivalry of France." More commonly today, it is used to refer to ideals of honor, gallantry, and loyalty supposed to belong to men of the knightly class.

The education of the future knight was a formalized process begun when he was a very small boy. Prowess in battle, honor, and a sense of pride in the nobility played an important role in his education. The Church's emphasis on honor and religion as part of the chivalric code served to tame feudalism, originally a brutal and rough phenomenon.

But the refinement of chivalry was, in all probability, due more to the ladies than to the Church. It was their growing influence in noble society that imposed "courtesy," the manners of the court, on the knights. The twelfth and thirteenth centuries witnessed the first flowering of chivalric love. Gallantry took its place beside the more primitive virtues in the knight's code. Feudal marriage, in which the fief was the first consideration, left little room for romantic sentiment between man and wife. But any knight might swear devotion to a noble dame, wear her colors in the tournament, and fight in her honor without giving offense, provided he observed the conventions and maintained his devotion on a spiritual plane. The most extreme idealization of women, combined with a practical recognition of their inferior position in society, was characteristic of medieval chivalry. It found expression in, and was in turn encouraged by, the romantic literature of the age.

In the High Middle Ages, all serious writing was still done in Latin, but there was a growing popular literature in the language of the people. It was intended primarily for a noble audience and reflected their manners. Courtesy and the cult of chivalric love made their appearance in southern France earlier than in the rude northern lands. In the twelfth century, the *troubadours* or wandering poets, many of whom were knights of noble birth, composed and sang delightful little love lyrics for the delectation of the most cultured society in Europe. Though limited in scope, their lyrics treated courtly love with delicate subtlety, combining intricate rhyme and graceful meter. This southern poetry reached its fullest development at the end of the twelfth century, before much of the culture of Provence was destroyed by the terrible devastation that accompanied the Albigensian Crusade, but it continued to exert a stimulating influence on later generations. The pagan spirit of much of this poetry may have been of Eastern origin, brought to Catalonia, Provence, and Tuscany by merchants

Ladies watching a tournament, from a thirteenth-century manuscript. The victorious knight is the noble minnesinger Walther von Klingen, who proved his devotion to his lady, probably the central figure above, with valiant deeds as well as lyric verses.

familiar with Islamic and other non- or pre-Christian cultures. Dante and Petrarch later drew upon it for inspiration, as did the northern French songwriters of the fourteenth and fifteenth centuries.

A similar type of lyric poetry flourished during the High Middle Ages in the courtly circles of Germany, where the minnesinger, like the Provençal troubadour, sang of his eternal love for the high-born lady to whom he had pledged his devotion. In the courtly poetry of thirteenth-century Germany, the troubadour attempted to woo a woman of higher social status whom he could never attain. This glorification of spiritual love was a counterbalance to the strong element of rapine and plunder in feudal society. The Church, through the popular cult of the Virgin Mary, encouraged the troubadour to idealize the unattainable lady, thereby increasing respect for womanhood and combating the degradation of women in feudal society. No finer lyric poetry was written during this period than that of the noble Bavarian minnesinger, Walther von der Vogelweide (c. 1170–1230).

Meanwhile in northern France, and spreading from there to England and Germany, a different kind of literature was appearing. There the warlike *chansons de geste* were recited by professional *jongleurs* or ministrels for the amusement of the rough feudal barons. These long epic poems dealt with semi-historical characters, mostly attributed to the court of Charlemagne. Some seventy or eighty *chansons* made up what is known as the Charlemagne cycle. In fact, there was little historical truth in them. Their value to the historian lies in the description of customs contemporary to the authors. In the *chansons,* Charlemagne and his peers act in every respect like twelfth-century nobles. The earliest and finest of the *chansons,* the *Chanson de Roland,* composed before the end of the eleventh century, is a grand martial poem based on Charlemagne's invasion of Moslem Spain and the massacre of his rearguard in the pass of Roncesvalles. The spirit of these epics was purely feudal. They dealt with battle, feudal loyalty and rebellion, and hatred of the infidel. The spirit of the northern French epics was similar to that of Romanesque architecture. Rough-hewn in style, they reflected the warrior spirit of a constantly warring society. Strength rather than grace for its own sake is characteristic of both the *Chanson de Roland* and great Romanesque structures such as the original abbey of Mont Saint-Michel in northern France.

But the north too was coming under the influence of courtesy, and this delicate sentiment found expression in the "romances of adventure" centering around the court of the legendary King Arthur of Britain. These are tales in verse and prose of knights errant who fought bravely and often out of devotion to their ladies or to rescue distressed damsels from ogres and magicians, rather than for the simpler feudal reasons that motivated the heroes of the *chansons.* The legends of the knights of Arthur's Round Table are still the common property of all European literatures. Many of these romances were the work of accomplished poets like Chrétien de Troyes, who composed the romance of *Perceval* in the reign of Louis VII. The same story appeared again, in a more perfect literary form, in the work of the German Wolfram von Eschenbach. The romance of *Tristan and Iseult,* perhaps the finest of them all, appeared in French as well as in the German of Gottfried von Strassburg. Sir Thomas Malory later translated many of the romances into vigorous English prose. There were also other cycles of romances, dealing with the Homeric story of the siege of Troy and the adventures of Alexander the Great, as well as the more historical tales of the Crusades. Thus a wealthier, more urbanized civilization made the transition from the feudal and Romanesque to the chivalric and Gothic, from epic to romance, from the cult of war to the cult of love.

From Abelard to Aquinas: The Revival of Learning and the Universities

A self-confident western European civilization slowly emerged in the eleventh and twelfth centuries, partly as a result of the successful Christian counteroffensive against the Moslems in North Africa and the Holy Land. This expansion of the European horizon brought European merchants and clerics into intellectual contact with the more sophisticated civilizations of the Islamic and Byzantine East. That, in turn, broadened the European intellectual perspective to include more of the great classical works of Aristotle and Plato, as well as their important Arabic commentators. Constant contact with the Islamic culture in southern Spain and Sicily opened the Christian European mind to such new intellectual stimuli. Above all, the growth of cities after the eleventh century provided a secure setting within which individuals committed to the new learning might, under the protection of bishops and kings, develop centers for the dissemination of their ideas. The centers of western European learning were no longer the monasteries, with their ambiguous attitudes toward those classics which had been preserved, in however inaccurate a form, but the cathedral schools of the great towns, and eventually the specialized (postgraduate) universities in such cities as Salerno, Montpellier, Oxford, and Paris.

In order to prevent unqualified men from teaching, the chancellor of the cathedral was empowered to grant licenses to those who had passed a qualifying examination, which, of course, necessitated the specification of a curriculum so that the candidates would know the material on which they were to be examined. Those who were granted licenses were called masters of arts and formed the governing body of the university, the faculty of arts. Using the analogy of the guild, the students may be considered the apprentices and the bachelors the journeymen with a limited license to teach in certain elementary courses. The master's degree was accepted as a guarantee of proficiency, sought by all, even those who did not intend to use it for active teaching. After becoming a master of arts, the student who wished specialized training in one of the professions might pursue a further course of study leading to the degree of doctor and admittance to the faculties of theology, medicine, or law.

The University of Bologna, famous for its law school, was organized somewhat differently, for there the governing body was the society or university of students, who had organized for mutual protection against teachers and townspeople alike. The faculties were thus subordinate to the students. Most of the southern universities followed this model.

The universities were essentially clerical institutions. Both teachers and students were classed as clerics, and so were exempt from ordinary civil jurisdiction. The charter granted to the University of Paris by Philip Augustus in 1200 recognized this exemption from the jurisdiction of royal or municipal courts. Further independence of local authority was acquired shortly thereafter by papal edict. The university, as a corporation, was freed from the jurisdiction of the bishop, and disciplinary powers were vested in the faculty, subject only to the pope. The same arrangement was also made in regard to the other universities, giving them a remarkable degree of corporate independence.

The jurisdictional authority of the university was important, for the students were a riotous lot at times. Letters to parents requesting more funds to meet unexpected expenses, none too well itemized, were evidently as common then as now. So were letters from parents complaining that their sons were wasting their time and their parents' hard-earned money in irresponsible pleasures. The Victorian writer John Addington Symonds, in a delightful volume of verse called *Wine, Women, and Song,* translated some of the typical student songs of the twelfth and thirteenth centuries.

The course in the faculty of arts leading to the M.A. degree, normally a six-year program which awarded the bachelor's degree somewhere along the way, was the backbone of the university curriculum. It was taken by all students, including those who intended to enter the higher faculties later. The *trivium* (grammar, rhetoric, and logic) and *quadrivium* (geometry, astronomy, arithmetic, and music) formed the framework of the curriculum. By far the most time was devoted to the former, and in particular to logic. In the first half of the twelfth century, there had been a considerable revival of interest in classical Latin literature; but the introduction of Aristotle's *Logic* at about that time, and of his *Metaphysics* in the early years of the thirteenth century turned the attention of scholars increasingly to logic and philosophy, while grammar and rhetoric became merely a means of teaching Latin, the language in which all texts were

A university lecture by the fifteenth-century painter Lorenzo de Voltolino.

written and all lectures delivered. The Latin of the medieval universities was strictly utilitarian. It was used to convey information and hence remained a living tongue, changing and adapting itself to fit the needs of the age in a way that would have been impossible had it remained bound by classical precedent. Logic and philosophy were also used for practical purposes, furnishing a method of study applicable to theology, medicine, law, and science. They were the universal tools of the medieval scholar, who was more given to metaphysical speculation and close, hard reasoning from authoritative texts than to experiment or observation of natural phenomena. The method of teaching in the medieval university was authoritarian and expository, the scholar or master posing questions about a text and commenting on it. This exegetical method ultimately culminated in the methodology known as scholasticism.

Highly significant for the history of European civilization was the work of Islamic students of philosophy, who translated the Greek and Hellenistic philosophers into Arabic and in the twelfth and thirteenth centuries passed them on, enriched with commentaries, to the schoolmen of Western Christendom. The Moslem philosophers were transmitters of Aristotelian and Neoplatonic ideas, rather than original thinkers; but there was originality in their aim, similar to that of the Christian scholastics, of harmonizing rational Greek metaphysics and revealed religion. The Persian philosopher and scientist Ibn Sina (980-1037), known to the Latin West as Avicenna, exerted a strong influence upon medieval Christian as well as Islamic thought.

Many of the Moslem philosophers were interested in the natural sciences, bringing to their study an eager curiosity and keen powers of observation. They not only absorbed the works of Greek scientists, including many since lost, but added discoveries of their own. The works of the ancient Greek physicians, Galen and Hippocrates, were also translated into Arabic in the early Abbasid period. To this body of medical knowledge Moslem physicians later added the results of their own valuable clinical experience, collecting the whole into great encyclopedic works on the subject. The works of Avicenna were later translated into Latin, and he was long recognized in western Europe as one of the great masters of medicine. Finally, the Moslems made contributions of the greatest importance to the development of mathematics. Building upon the Greek heritage and borrowing from India the system of numerals still called Arabic, they laid the foundations for modern arithmetic, geometry, trigonometry and algebra.

Theology was the Queen of the Sciences in the Middle Ages, for it explained religion and revealed the way to salvation. Three problems especially interested the scholastic theologians. One was the problem of conflicting authorities; for all theological speculation was founded upon close study of unquestioned authorities, of which the Bible was the chief, with the works of the Fathers and the decrees of the Church ranking a close second. That these authorities did not always agree was brought forcibly to the attention of theologians in the first half of the twelfth century by a rash and brilliant young teacher, Peter Abelard (1079-1142), who is now remembered chiefly for his tragic love of Heloise. Abelard's exposition of authorities in direct conflict with each other in a work boldly entitled *Sic et Non* (*Yes and No*) challenged the logical subtlety of the schoolmen. Among the scholars who undertook to bring them into harmony the most successful was Peter Lombard, whose *Sentences* became the standard textbook of theology.

A second and more fundamentally important problem arose from the introduction of ancient Greek philosophy, with Moslem commentaries, into the world of medieval Christian thought. It not only furnished the schoolmen with a quantity of pre-Christian metaphysical speculation; it also inspired them to put their trust in natural reason guided by logic. During the period of the Roman Empire, the important Latin-speaking theologian Tertullian had supposedly answered pagan doubters of Christianity by saying, "I believe because it is absurd," thus asserting that traditional methods of logic had no place in the great Christian mysterium. This did not suffice, however, for a man such as Thomas Aquinas.

For many of the schoolmen, the problem of reconciling reason with revelation was solved by the formula, borrowed from Augustine and restated by Saint Anselm of Canterbury in the late eleventh century, "I do not seek to know in order that I may believe, but I believe in order that I may know." This was not a denial of the potency of reason. It merely asserted that reason can achieve valid results only when informed by revealed truth. The recovery in the thirteenth century of the complete works of Aristotle, together with the commentaries of the great Arabic philosopher Averroës, made it more difficult for many schoolmen to maintain this position. Deeply impressed by the logical coherence of Aristotle's philosophy, which they regarded as the supreme achievement of natural reason, the Christian followers of Averroës were forced to assume that Aristotle's conclusions might be true in philosophy but, where they conflicted with Christian dogma, untrue in theology. Averroës interpreted Aristotle in such a way as to be unacceptable to orthodox Christian belief, using Aristotle to cast doubt upon such doctrines as the immortality of the individual soul and the finite term of the earth's existence. Thus, early in the thirteenth century papal authority prohibited that type of Aristotelianism which bore the imprint of the Averroistic interpretation. By this time, the University of Paris had achieved a dominant position in the teaching of Christian theology, and Church authority was particularly concerned about the nature of the curriculum in that university.

The conflict between reason and revelation could thus be solved only by isolating philosophy and theology in separate airtight compartments. It was to confront this problem without falling back upon the Augustinian formula, that Saint Thomas Aquinas (1225–1274) undertook in his great *Summa Theologica* to construct a comprehensive synthesis of philosophy and theology. Reason and faith were for Aquinas merely different ways of reaching truth. There can be no conflict between them, according to Aquinas, since there is but one truth, which comes from God. Aquinas employed reason, aided by Aristotelian logic and metaphysics, as far as it would go, leaving to faith in revealed truth only such matters as were beyond the reach of reason. Thus he held, for example, that the existence of God and the immortality of the soul could be proved by natural reason, but that other doctrines were susceptible to proof only through revelation.

The controversy over the relation of reason to revelation was inseparably bound up with a third problem, that of the reality of "universals," which divided medieval schoolmen and was of fundamental importance to scholastic thought. The problem, in its simplest form, is whether absolute reality is to be found in individual things or only in the general ideas, or universals, which have existed from the beginning of time as forms in the mind of God. The philosophers who took the latter position under the influence of Plato and the Neoplatonists were called realists. For them the idea of man, for example, was an ultimate reality, a universal which predated individual men and which eternally exists distinct from men. Individual men are but imperfect reflections of the universal reality. The opposing or nominalist school, on the contrary, held that the individual entity alone is real and that universals are merely names given to groups of individual things which are sufficiently similar to be classified together for purposes of convenience. Between these extreme points of view there was room for compromise. Abelard held that both the individual and the universal had absolute reality. Aquinas too professed a modified realism, closer to Aristotle than to Plato. He argued that universals possess eternal reality, but also exist *in* individual things as their essence. It was by assuming the reality of essences as universals that Aquinas was able to organize all material and immaterial beings, natural and supernatural, into a great chain of being stretching upward from inanimate nature to God. Only through some form of realism could reason posit transcendental or supernatural beings as knowable and thus offer rational proof of the articles of religious faith. Realism also furnished a valuable support to the authority of the Church by placing emphasis on the Church as an eternal, ideal entity instead of upon the individual and fallible human beings who compose its membership.

The fourteenth century brought a reaction toward nominalism under the influence of Duns Scotus (d. 1308) and the more extreme William of Occam (d. 1349?). Believing that the human mind can grasp only the reality of particular things, Occam rejected the possibility of proving the truths of religion by reason. In theology, then, the triumph of nominalism in the fourteenth and fifteenth centuries destroyed that system of thought which made possible the logical proof of Christian beliefs, and threw people back upon faith, thus preparing the way for the ideas of Luther and the Protestant Reformation. The nominalist mode of thinking was a step toward the modern preoccupation with individual things, historians' interest in individual people and events, political liberals' emphasis upon the individual citizen rather than upon society as an ideal whole, and scientists' interest in the behavior of concrete things.

This dissolution of the realist synthesis early in the fourteenth century was also due to the spread of new mystic doctrines in the Church. Among the great proponents of the new mysticism was the German Rhenish preacher, Meister Eckhart, who had a profound impact on German thought up to and after the time of Luther.

Roman Law

The rebirth of interest in Roman law, so vital to both the civil and the ecclesiastical world, was the result of work begun in northern Italy. Late in the eleventh century, Irnerius and the Bolognese glossators, or commentators, began to lecture and comment upon Roman law. The Roman tradition, legal and otherwise, had always been stronger in medieval Italy than elsewhere in Europe. With the development of long-range trade and the revival of cities, Roman law, which was universal in spirit and based upon such concepts as the absolute ownership of property, was clearly more useful than the parochial feudal tradition. Classical feudalism had never been as deeply rooted in Italy as in northern France and elsewhere on the continent. The influence of Byzantium, which had close cultural ties with Italy during this period, was brought to bear upon the law school of Bologna, which borrowed heavily from Justinian's code.

Religious Art and Music

In an age when religion was a powerful factor in everyday life and the Church largely dominated society, it is not surprising that the art which best expressed the emotions and aspirations of the people should be religious art.

During the twelfth and thirteenth centuries, the gradual evolution of the Gothic style of architecture out of the older Romanesque brought about a radical revolution in the construction of churches and cathedrals and produced the finest examples of medieval architecture. The characteristic feature of Romanesque architecture was the use of round arches and vaults, which necessitated either very heavy walls to bear the weight of the roof or the substitution of wooden roofs for stone. The pointed arches characteristic of the Gothic style were not only stronger but also carried weight more directly downward, with less lateral thrust. What made the Gothic cathedral a masterpiece of engineering, however, was not simply the use of the pointed arch and vault but the combination of these with pillars and buttresses to form a skeleton framework which took the weight

The façade of the Cathedral of Angoulême. The rounded arches, heavy walls, and massive weight are characteristic of Romanesque architecture.

of the roof off the walls. As a result, almost all the wall space could be used for great decorative windows.

The late art historian Erwin Panofsky, in a brilliant little book entitled *Gothic Architecture and Scholasticism,* has pointed out several structural similarities between Gothic architecture and medieval scholasticism. Panofsky states, for example, that "the natural . . . fauna and flora of High Gothic ornament proclaimed the victory of Aristotelianism." Just as Aquinas' realist synthesis dissolved into the mysticism and nominalism of the fourteenth century, so the Gothic synthesis of the great cathedrals such as Chartres and Amiens evolved into the particularities of style and exaggerated, though beautiful, virtuosity of much fourteenth-century Gothic building. In classical Gothic architecture, Panofsky sees "the acceptance and ultimate reconciliation of contradictory possibilities." This was also the spirit of Thomist scholasticism (that originated by

The façade of Reims Cathedral. The pointed arches, soaring verticality, and abundant sculptural decoration are characteristic of High Gothic architecture.

Thomas Aquinas). Even before Aquinas, Gratian, the twelfth-century codifier of canon law, based his work upon the synthesis or reconciliation of opposing dialectical tendencies. In both Gothic architecture and scholasticism we see a synthesis of various dynamic tensions and tendencies, a vaulting idea which subsumes the wide-ranging but disciplined Christian intellect.

Another tendency common to Gothic architecture and scholasticism was the drive for absolute clarity, making apparent every aspect of the structure, and thus enhancing the beholder's awe before the complex totality. But it was not only through its beauty of line and color, carved stone, and stained glass, that the cathedral expressed and satisfied the artistic instincts of medieval people. The cathedral was also the scene of the colorful services of the Church and the drama of the Mass, accompanied by the soaring music and verbal beauty of the Latin liturgy.

The great musical innovation of the High Middle Ages was polyphony. Early Gregorian chants progressed in a single melodic line. In the polyphony of the twelfth and thirteenth centuries, we see a phenomenon akin to both Gothic architecture and scholasticism, the dynamic interrelationship of several melodic lines or voices. The thirteenth century witnessed the composition of many of the great hymns of the Church, such as the *Dies Irae,* or *Day of Wrath,* written by Thomas of Celano around 1265, a time of great turmoil in Christian Europe.

Gothic architecture, high medieval polyphony, and Thomist scholasticism were thus aspects of a Christian medieval synthesis, all of which changed in the fourteenth century. The political setting of such cultural developments differed in France, England, Italy, and Germany, but its common religion and common language for ecclesiastical and intellectual discourse—Latin—gave to medieval Europe the aspect of a Christian commonwealth.

Flying buttresses supporting the upper walls of the choir and apse of Notre Dame Cathedral.

Suggestions for Further Reading

F. B. Artz, *The Mind of the Middle Ages* (3rd ed., 1958). A survey of medieval learning and culture.

M. W. Baldwin, *The Medieval Church,** rev. ed. (1964). The many aspects of Church life and polity are succinctly described in this excellently balanced introduction. Good selective bibliography [AHA, 188].

M. H. Carré, *Realists and Nominalists* (1946).

E. Gilson, *History of Christian Philosophy in the Middle Ages* (1955). This has long been regarded as a standard reference work on the subject. Though dealing with a weighty subject, Gilson writes gracefully. His viewpoint is that of a modern French Thomist.

C. H. Haskins, *The Rise of Universities** (1957). A fine, brief treatment of an interesting subject.

C. H. Haskins, *The Renaissance of the Twelfth Century** (1927). An extremely influential study of the revival of learning in the twelfth century. This work treats the rise of the cathedral schools and universities, the study of law, medicine, and theology, and numerous other aspects of the new age of learning.

F. Heer, *The Medieval World: Europe, 1100–1350** (1964). A brilliant series of almost impressionistic essays, showing tremendous imaginative and narrative powers. Besides teaching a great deal, this book is an exciting reading experience.

D. Knowles, *Evolution of Medieval Thought** (1962). A clear, descriptive work by the British Dominican scholar.

D. Knowles, *The Monastic Order in England* (1940). Outstanding, detailed history of English medieval monasticism.

E. Panofsky, *Gothic Architecture and Scholasticism** (1966). A little gem of a book; an important and successful attempt to relate medieval architecture to medieval thought. Highly recommended.

E. K. Rand, *Founders of the Middle Ages** (1928). Fine portraits of early medieval intellectual and spiritual figures, men who molded the medieval mind.

Otto von Simson, *The Gothic Cathedral: Origins of Gothic and the Medieval Concept of Order** (1962). An important, detailed, illustrated study of Gothic architecture. For those with a particular interest in this area.

R. W. Southern, *The Making of the Middle Ages** (1953). One of the most brilliant and influential interpretations in the field. Southern deals with medieval style in its various forms and approaches the Middle Ages by asking major questions. A rich reading experience.

H. Waddell, *Peter Abelard** (1959).

H. Waddell, *The Wandering Scholars,* rev. ed. (1934). Delightful tales of medieval students, clerks, and scholars. The world of the medieval student—at once ribald and spiritual—comes alive in this standard work.

H. Wieruszowski, *The Medieval University** (1966). An excellent, brief study containing many useful documents.

P. Wolff, *The Cultural Awakening,** trans. by A. Carter (1969). A recent interpretation of medieval culture during its formative centuries, written by an outstanding French historian.

*Available in a paperback edition.

The Triumph and Crisis of the Monarchy in France

15

> Seek earnestly how your vassals and your subjects may live in peace and rectitude beneath your sway; likewise the good towns and the good cities of your kingdom.
>
> LOUIS IX TO HIS SON

> I tell you in the name of our Lord that you are the true heir of France and the son of the king.
>
> JOAN OF ARC TO THE DAUPHIN

French Kings Increase Their Prestige, 1060-1180

The most important accomplishment of the French kings in the High Middle Ages was not their romantic involvement in the Crusades but their use of feudal law—escheat of fiefs, marriages, courts of assize, conquest, and familial ties—to create a centralized feudal monarchy. Great medieval kings established monarchical states which guaranteed internal stability such as western Europe had not known since the second century of the Roman Empire. They thus provided much of the necessary security and inspiration for the urban and intellectual currents examined in Chapters 13 and 14. Drawing upon the charisma of Christian kingship and the crucial support of the Church, French kings had created an effective territorial monarchy by the end of the thirteenth century.

By the middle of the eleventh century the royal house of Capet was almost eclipsed in the midst of its great vassals—the lords of fiefs such as Normandy, Champagne, Anjou, Burgundy, Toulouse, and Aquitaine. The king's actual power was limited almost entirely to the royal domain, the Île de France, from which he drew his chief financial and military support. Even there, however, his authority was none too great, for rebellious barons defied him from behind their castle walls or sallied forth to prey upon the peasants or passing merchants and clergy.

The main work of the Capetian monarchs in the eleventh and the early twelfth centuries was the pacification of the Île de France. In this effort Philip I and his son Louis VI accomplished significant work, laying the foundations for the later extension of royal power to other areas in northern and central France.

The greatest danger to the French monarchy in the eleventh century came from the union after 1066 of Normandy with England, which is discussed in Chapter 16. Against this coalition Louis VI was able to do no more than hold his own. Henry I of England, the younger son of William the Conqueror, though in theory Louis' vassal for Normandy, was a much more powerful ruler than Louis. His kingdom and his duchy were better organized than France, and he had strong allies. His nephew, Theobald, count of Champagne, whose fiefs bordered the Île de France on the east and west, aided him in any action against the French king. The Emperor Henry V, too, was his son-in-law and on one occasion formed an alliance with him against France. This danger was averted by an unprecedented rising of the French nobles in support of their king, but until the death of Henry I in 1135 the situation was always tense. The weak French kings of this period were successful in preventing an alliance of all the great vassals against Capetian authority, however. One must marvel at the survival of the Capetian monarchy during these turbulent years of feudal warfare.

During the reign of Louis the Fat (Louis VI), the rise of the monarchy was checked, though not entirely stopped. Louis VII (1137–1180) was less wise, less decisive in action, and certainly less fortunate than his father. At the very beginning of his reign, he greatly enhanced the territory of the royal domain by marrying Eleanor, heiress to the duchy of Aquitaine. However, this was less of a gain than it might seem and proved to be only temporary. Aquitaine and its dependencies formed a huge fief, but its nobles were so independent that it did not add significantly to the king's resources. During his first years as king, Louis expended more energy than he did later, but it was sadly misdirected. After a long and useless feud with Theobald of Champagne, he left France to take part in the ill-starred Second Crusade. After his return in 1149, he settled down more seriously to the business of ruling; but by that time the Anglo-Norman menace had taken a new and more dangerous form as a result of alliance with the house of Anjou.

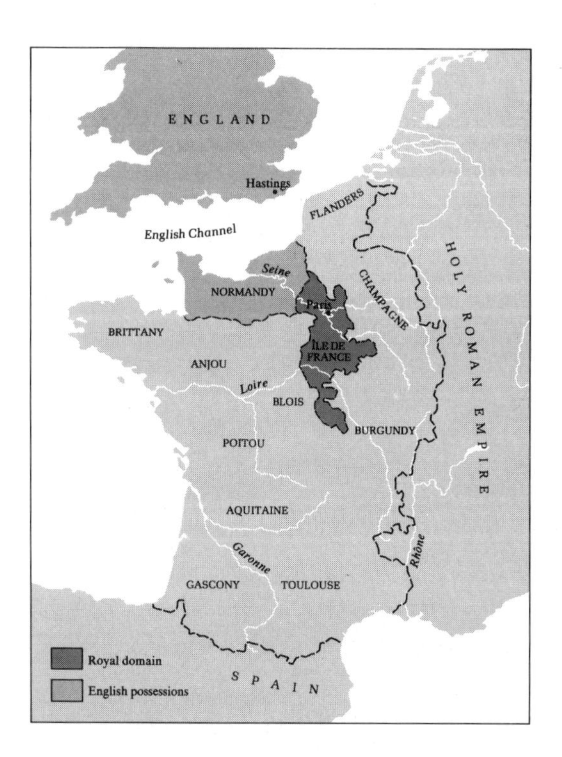

FRANCE IN 1100

In 1152 Louis VII, who was always swayed more by personal emotions than by motives of policy, divorced his flighty southern wife, Eleanor of Aquitaine. Henry Plantagenet of Anjou married her almost immediately, thus adding Aquitaine to his already formidable collection of fiefs. The acquisition of Eleanor's inheritance meant more to Henry than it had to Louis, since it bordered on his Angevin domain and formed with it a solid block. Including as it did the counties of Poitou, Aquitaine, and Gascony, it stretched down the western coast of France from the Loire to the Pyrenees, and in its central section eastward across France to the Rhône. In 1154, Plantagenet became king of England as Henry II, and four years later he acquired Brittany. He was now lord of more than half of France and much more powerful than his overlord Louis VII. For his part, Louis had weakly allowed this dangerous consolidation of fiefs to take place without effective opposition; later, when he realized the seriousness of the menace, his attempts to lessen Henry's power were feeble and irresolute. Henry remained the practically independent ruler of the lands he had acquired.

French Kings Expand the Royal Domain, 1180–1270

The reign of Philip II (1180–1223), surnamed Augustus, opened a new era in the history of the French monarchy by greatly expanding the royal domain at the expense of the English kings. The French kings had already acquired considerable moral authority. It was time to give that authority a solid backing, based on real power drawn from a wide domain under the king's immediate government. Philip was well suited to carry out that task, and fortune favored him. He had a far more decided character than his good-natured father, Louis VII, and, though he lacked the reckless chivalrous spirit of his grandfather, he had other qualities equally useful to a king in his difficult position. Sane, clearheaded, and unscrupulous, he kept his eyes fixed firmly on his most important objective and seized every opportunity to forward his schemes. Philip was a politician and a statesman.

In the first years of his reign, while he was still very young, Philip suppressed the rebellion of a powerful coalition of nobles, and thereby gained some territory. Then, by asserting a hereditary claim to Vermandois and a claim through his first wife to her fief of Artois, he paved the way for further expansion of the royal domain to the north. By steady pressure he gradually added to it until his lands stretched north in a solid block to the English Channel, including the ports of Boulogne and Calais.

By the early thirteenth century, the strong feudal territorial monarchy of Philip Augustus was able to confront successfully the Anglo-Norman Plantagenet claims upon French fiefs. By 1205 the feckless King John had lost Normandy, Anjou, Maine, and part of Poitou to Philip Augustus. Furthermore, a noble friendly to the French king now had control of the controversial fief of Brittany. John was left with large territories in southwestern France, but they were disorderly and rebellious, and did not compare favorably with those in the north which he had lost. Philip's perspective was not limited, however, to his claims over formerly independent fiefs within the borders of the French kingdom. Philip meddled in the affairs of the Holy Roman Empire and quarreled with the pope. However, Philip is of historical significance mainly for his establishment of

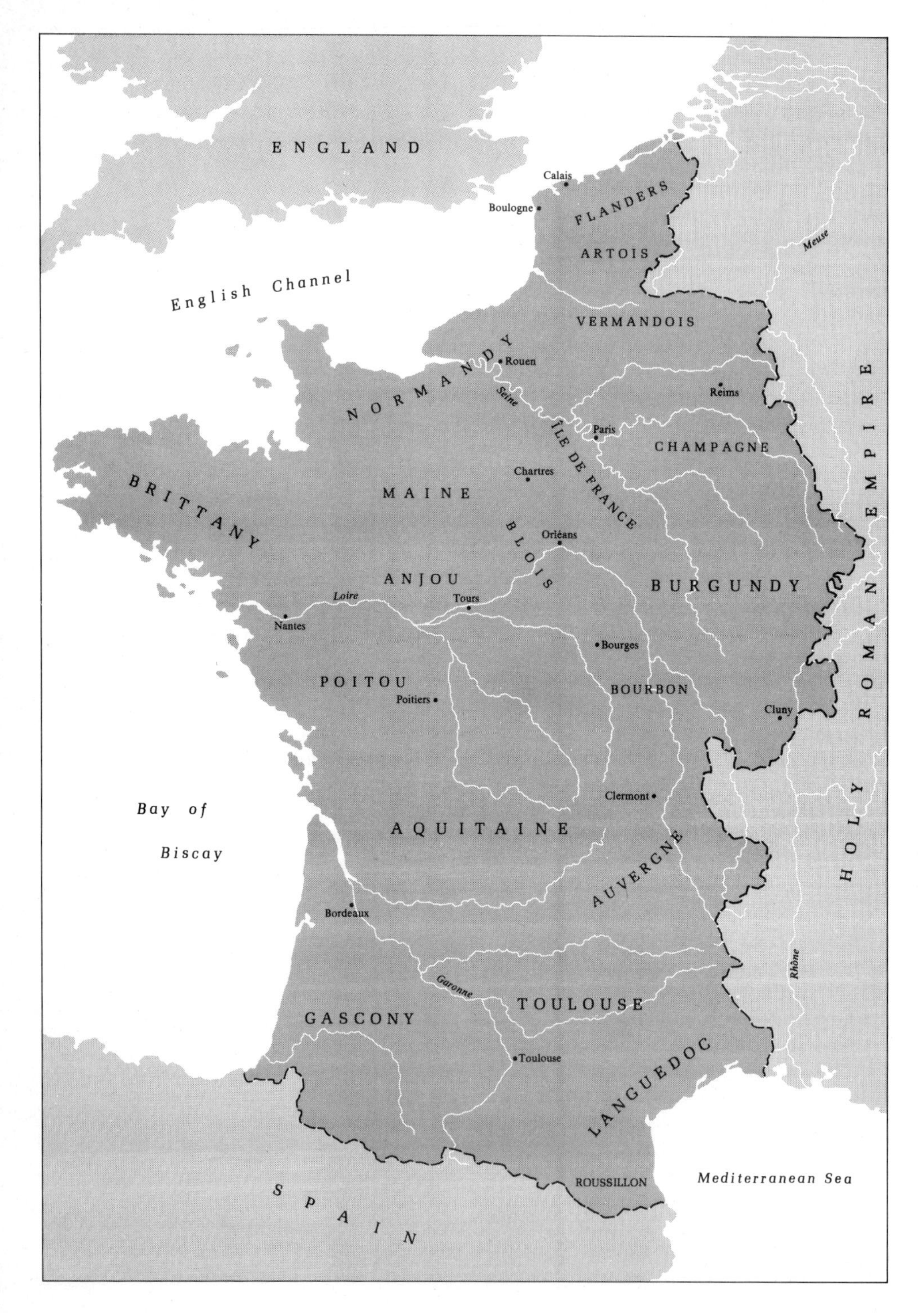

France in 1154

a broader territorial and institutional authority for his Capetian successors.

It was typical of Philip's attitude toward the Papacy that he refused to waste his strength by taking part in the crusade which Innocent had organized against the Albigenses of southern France in 1207—although he was later to profit by it. Knights and barons from all parts of Europe joined this crusade against the heretics. After years of fighting and bloody massacres, which destroyed the glorious culture of the rich southern land and left it desolate, the leader of the crusaders, a Norman baron named Simon de Montfort, succeeded in taking over nearly all of Languedoc from the count of Toulouse. In the last year of Philip's reign, Simon's son, Amaury de Montfort, unable to defend his lands, offered them to the king. Meanwhile, Philip had been gradually extending his domain south into Auvergne and Aquitaine.

The work of Louis VIII (1223-1226) during his brief reign was a continuation of his father's expansion of the royal domain. He made a triumphal march into Aquitaine and turned what was left of the Albigensian Crusade into a royal conquest of Languedoc. He died before his task was completed, but he had accomplished so much that his son, Louis IX, was able quite easily to add Languedoc and Poitou to the king's domain, leaving the King of England only Gascony and part of Aquitaine.

Louis IX (1226-1270) was only twelve years old when his father's death made him king of France. His mother, Blanche of Castile, ruled as regent until he came of age, and continued to have a great deal of influence until her death in 1252. Few kings have been as popular as Louis IX, and it is safe to say that no king ever impressed his subjects so strongly with his essential goodness. He was

France in 1180

popularly regarded as a saint during his lifetime, and the Church officially conferred upon him the title of Saint Louis shortly after his death. His mother, a sternly pious woman, may have been responsible for some of his strong religious devotion and strict sense of duty. He spent much time in prayer, fasting, and ascetic practices. Yet he was no pious recluse, shutting himself away from the world. Despite his saintliness, Louis was a very practical ruler, who performed his duty as king with unfailing energy, though he was constantly troubled by bad health. He had also a great deal of personal charm. In every way Saint Louis was the perfect representative of the ideals of his age—he was simultaneously the chivalrous knight, the just ruler, the ardent crusader, and the pious saint. He was true to the ideals of his age, too, in his fanatical religious intolerance. Louis persecuted heretics and Jews with the greatest severity, and would sacrifice anything to wage war against the infidel.

Royal Administration

During his long and peaceful reign, Louis was able to consolidate the gains made by the monarchy in the preceding century, win the affection and loyalty of the people, and strengthen the system of royal government. Louis himself, however, still clung to the old feudal principles of government. His administrative and judicial reforms were limited to the royal domain, and when he interfered in the government of the fiefs outside it, he did so in accordance with feudal law and custom. He even gave new life to monarchical feudalism by granting Artois, Poitou, Anjou, and other fiefs to his brothers as *apanages,* thus risking their separation from the royal domain. Yet Louis felt more strongly than any of his predecessors that his consecration as king gave him special sacred rights and duties. He never hesitated to assert his will in what he considered a just cause.

As his character suggests, Louis was greatly interested in enforcing order and justice. He tried to secure equal justice for rich and poor in his courts, and frequently acted as a judge himself. He did away with trial by combat, which he considered barbarous, and abolished the old custom whereby the defendant in a trial might challenge his judge to combat if he considered the sentence unjust. Deprived of this right, the defendant's only alternative was to appeal to the royal court to rehear the case, which added considerably to the king's power and prestige. Louis also prohibited private warfare among the nobles, but even he could not stamp out that most cherished right of the nobility.

During the thirteenth century a system of royal administration was gradually taking shape in France. Philip Augustus had done a great deal to systematize the government of the royal domain, by dividing it into administrative districts under royal officers, called bailiffs in the north and seneschals in the south. These royal officers had great powers, which they sometimes abused. Louis IX sent out representatives to supervise their activities more closely, somewhat in the manner of the English traveling justices.

The king's court, or *curia regis,* a vague body which aided the king in the central government, was also developing along more systematic lines during this period. There was a *chambre des comptes* (not so named until 1309), corresponding roughly to the English exchequer, and at least the beginning of a separate court of appeal, which later developed into the permanent *Parlement* of Paris. These specialized courts were not yet composed of a permanent set of ministers, but were parts of the curia regis, sitting to hear the bailiff's reports and to try cases. Still, each had some more or less permanent members, trained men who began to form the nucleus of a professional class of ministers and judges.

The Age of Philip the Fair

With the reign of Philip IV (1285–1314), called the Fair, we definitely enter the transitional period in the history of the French monarchy. The time was now ripe for the king to assert his position as monarch rather than mere feudal overlord, and to adopt what may be called a national policy both at home and abroad. This Philip the Fair did with momentous results; but how much of the credit or blame should be awarded to the king himself is still a matter much debated by historians. There seems good reason to believe that the real driving force behind the royal government was less the king than his ministers.

These men were professional administrators; unlike the great vassals and prelates who had filled the councils of the early feudal kings, they were of comparatively humble birth. Because they had been trained in the royal court and depended entirely on the king for their position, they were devoted to the king's interests. Most of them were lawyers, well versed in Roman law and impregnated with its statist principles. They were cool-headed, sagacious, and unscrupulous enemies of feudalism, the Papacy, and any other power that infringed on the king's rights. In the midst of their vigorous activity we can only dimly discern the enigmatic figure of the king.

Philip's assertion of royal authority over France soon brought him into

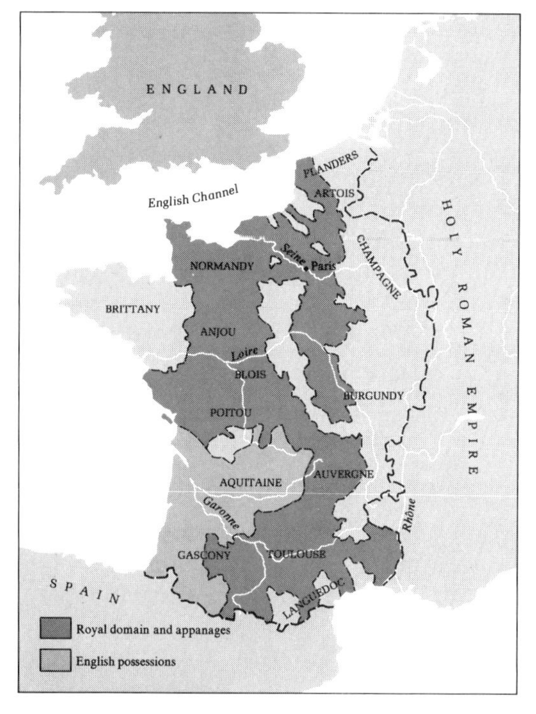

France in 1270

conflict with his two most independent vassals: Edward I, king of England, who held the fiefs of Aquitaine and Gascony in southwestern France as a legacy from his Angevin ancestors, and the count of Flanders, whose fief in the north included rich commercial and industrial cities closely connected by trade with England. War with Edward broke out in 1294. After four years of fighting, both parties agreed to a truce which was finally confirmed by treaty five years later. However, the count of Flanders, who had joined Edward in the war, was not included in the truce. Left alone, he was forced to submit, and his rich county was added to the French king's domain. Philip's success in this sphere was brief. In 1302, the Flemish burghers rose in revolt, massacring French residents, and their militia almost annihilated a feudal French army at Courtrai in Flanders. Three years of bitter fighting followed before Philip restored peace by giving Flanders back to its count at the price of a heavy indemnity.

These wars between French kings and Flemish cities and towns involved many factors of particular interest to the historian of medieval affairs: international trade, urban centers, feudal armies, feudal monarchy, and international diplomacy. They pointed simultaneously to an earlier era and to an age yet to come. The important Flemish weaving industry was largely dependent on English wool. The Flemish nobility was hostile to the centralizing tendencies of Flemish counts in the thirteenth century, and thus looked with favor on the work of the Capetian kings, which impinged upon the authority of the Flemish counts. Total French domination of Flanders, however, was detrimental to the trade and economic prosperity of the Flemish cities. While much of the Flemish aristocracy and urban patriciate was sympathetic to the Capetians, for both cultural and political reasons, the middling burghers and the proletariat resented French control for political and economic reasons. The result was a long period of strife.

His expensive wars with England and Flanders left Philip in great need of money, and the crusading religious order of Knights Templars was a tempting prey. The Templars had grown enormously rich in land and money, become great bankers, and lent large sums to the king. Moreover, since the conclusion of the Crusades, they no longer had any valid reason for existence. Philip, therefore, set about cold-bloodedly to accomplish their ruin, with a view to canceling his debts and confiscating their wealth. Their trial, begun in 1307, continued for five years. The knights were arrested and forced under torture to confess to the most horrible charges of immorality and blasphemy. The widespread propaganda that accompanied the prosecution was all the more effective because of the secrecy that had always shrouded the life of the order. The final act in this judicial farce was the abolition of the order in 1312 by Pope Clement V, who was completely under the thumb of the French king. Their lands were to be given to the Knights Hospitalers, but in France, at least, it was the king who profited.

As the government of Philip the Fair was more nearly national than that of any of his predecessors, it is not surprising that he broke with feudal precedent and made a bid for popular support by summoning representatives of the burgher middle class, as well as his feudal vassals and the clergy, to give consent to his decisions on matters of national importance. The Estates-General, as the new assembly of all three classes or estates came to be called, was summoned only at times of crisis, such as the attack on the Templars in 1307, or when unusual taxes were needed.

The latter was, indeed, the most important reason for the innovation. The greatly increased expenses of the royal government, particularly in time of war, could no longer be met out of regular income from the royal domain and feudal dues, or even by such extraordinary measures as the debasement of the coinage or the confiscation of property belonging to Jews, Templars, or Lombard bankers. New taxes on all classes were necessary; and these could be collected more easily if the people at large had given their consent through their representatives, even though such consent was only a matter of form and royal officers still found it necessary to haggle over details of collection with feudal magnates or smaller regional assemblies. French kings had long been accustomed to summoning their vassals-in-chief, lay and ecclesiastical, to court to give aid and counsel. Philip's new departure was the extension of that summons to representatives of the towns—that is, to the commoners who were his subjects rather than his feudal vassals—to meet with the Great Council.

Though a new departure for the French monarchy, the summoning of the Estates General was not an isolated instance of appeal by a ruling prince for support from representatives of the rising urban middle class, whose possession of money made it increasingly important from the point of view of a financially embarrassed prince. Other states—including England, the Spanish kingdoms, the Holy Roman Empire, and the territorial principalities of Germany—were following the same procedure at this time. Moreover, in France itself the great feudatories, the half-independent vassals outside the royal domain, were doing the same thing in summoning the estates of their own territories. The Estates-General was so named to distinguish it from the local or feudal estates, some of which maintained separate existences for centuries.

The Estates-General did not acquire its name or form at once, but with repeated meetings the new body gradually took shape. For consultation the assembly split up into three bodies, each made up of representatives of one of the estates of the realm—the clergy, the nobles, and the commons. The Third Estate was composed mainly of representatives elected in various ways by the burghers of the chartered towns. Later, at times, election was extended to the country districts as well. But as most of the land was owned by the nobles, the only commons important enough to be represented on most occasions were the urban middle class. The function of the estates was not to initiate legislation or to control the government. Their duty was to consent to the king's proposals, though they might present lists of grievances in the hope that the king would take steps to redress them.

The new institution was a means of bringing the royal government into closer contact with the most important classes in the state. That it failed to serve this purpose as effectively as it might have was due to the inability of the Estates to weld themselves into a really national assembly. The Estates-General seldom met as a single body representing the whole kingdom. Usually the estates of Languedoc and those of northern France met separately and some meetings represented still smaller areas. The resulting weakness of the Estates prevented them in the long run from exercising effective control of royal government and so left the way open to the continuing development of royal authority.

France and the Hundred Years' War: The First Phase, to 1380

Soon after the death of Philip the Fair, France entered an agonizing period of famine, dynastic crisis, and war. By 1350 war with England was a crucial and seemingly permanent aspect of French history. The Hundred Years' War had begun.

This great series of wars owed its origin to a variety of causes. It was in part a feudal struggle between French kings and their powerful English vassals, who held lands in southwestern France. Trade and economics also played a role, particularly in Flanders, a scene of Franco-English rivalry. French kings had patronized the Franco-Scottish alliance, particularly since the turn of the century, and this was viewed as dangerous by English monarchs. Finally, the death in 1328 of the last Capetian king, Charles IV, gave rise to the question of succession to the French throne. The first Valois king, Philip VI, claimed the right to the throne in 1328, and he made good his claim. At the time, Edward III of England was not in a position to claim the throne, though his lawyers pointed out that as the grandson of Philip the Fair he had as much right to the French throne as did Philip VI. Years later, publicists for Edward and the English cause in Flanders, England, and France pointed to this claim in order to justify the military efforts of the English and their allies.

Edward III (1327–1377) and Philip VI (1328–1350) had each ruled about a decade when England and France were plunged into a war that continued intermittently through the greater part of the reigns of five kings in each country. The war massively influenced the development of both countries, but because it was fought largely on French soil it had a much more immediate effect on the internal history of France than on England. The Hundred Years' War was in reality either more or less than that, since from beginning to end it covered more than a century, though there were less than a hundred years of actual fighting.

The English and Flemish established control over the English Channel in 1340, thereby laying the groundwork for future English victories on the continent. The Battle of Crécy in 1346 was not merely an overwhelming victory for the forces of Edward III; it also marked a transition in the history of medieval warfare. The heavily armored French feudal knights charged in vain against the dismounted English men-at-arms, while the English archers with their effective longbows spread death in the ranks of their adversaries. The English relied more heavily on mercenaries and footmen than did the French, and French chivalry seemed slow to learn the lesson of the Battle of Crécy. The reason for this was in part social. The French aristocracy—indeed, the European aristocracy—viewed its social prerogatives as closely related to its primacy in chivalric warfare and was loath to give up the panoply and ceremony which typified its concept of warfare. Thus, the first period of the Hundred Years' War, ending in the 1360s, was a series of unmitigated catastrophes for the French.

The British men-at-arms looted the French countryside. A French king, John II, was captured at Poitiers. The English king was given full possession, free of all feudal obligations, of Calais and Pontieu in the north, and of Gascony and Aquitaine in the south. The French had to pay a huge ransom for the release of King John. It was also during this period that the French people learned to dread the arrival of the brutal and ruthless English soldiers. The term "cry havoc," which springs from this period, represented a barbarous signal to the English soldiers to loot, rape, and burn villages and towns in France. Throughout the Hundred Years' War, the French were subject to such undisciplined barbarism by English and French mercenaries alike, the French *routiers* being scarcely less brutal than the English footmen.

To this general suffering was added a burden of taxation such as France had never known. Again and again the king called the Estates-General to secure their consent to the taxes needed to finance the war. But the people were sullen and discontented, and the estates were growing bolder. The estates called by Philip VI in the year of Crécy and the following year refused to consent and demanded reforms in the government. After Poitiers they threatened what amounted to revolution. Led by a Parisian merchant, Étienne Marcel, and backed by the armed citizens of Paris, the estates of northern France demanded and for a time secured practical control of the government, then in the hands of the Dauphin Charles. At this point the situation was complicated by that desperate rising of the peasants known as the Jacquerie for the name "Jacques," commonly applied to the peasant.

Recent empirical and theoretical work by scholars such as Norman Cohn and Chalmers Johnson helps us put the jacquerie in a broader perspective. Not just an aimless uprising, it was the peasants' reaction to the horrors of war, and embodied their hopes for a more just social order. Many peasants believed that the oppressive prerogatives claimed by their lord were justified neither by the teachings of Christ nor by the image of Eden they had seen in the stained-glass windows of cathedrals and heard described by priests and wandering preachers. The peasants did not forget that they or their immediate ancestors had lost age-old rights such as the use of common lands. Nor did they take kindly to increased exactions in an age when inflationary demands and the costs of wars caused the lords to oppress their peasants ever more heavily. The madness of war and the horrors of plague and violence also contributed to these messianic and desperate revolts for human freedom and social justice.

Although the burghers of the French towns were mostly of peasant origin themselves, their rapport with the peasant revolutionaries was minimal. This

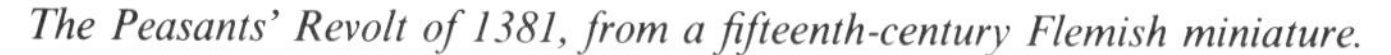
The Peasants' Revolt of 1381, from a fifteenth-century Flemish miniature.

failure of rapport between peasants and burghers will reappear in the great sixteenth-century peasant wars in southern and southwestern Germany. The townsman and the peasant lived in different worlds; although their interests, as opposed to those of the feudal nobility and a grasping monarchy, might coincide, the Middle Ages does not offer many examples of a level of political consciousness conducive to cooperation between them.

When Charles V (1364–1380) became king, he was prepared to profit by the lessons he had learned when acting as regent. He at once began the reconstruction of government finances and the reorganization of the army, whose success won him the title Charles the Wise. He called the Estates-General, which he had reason to distrust, as infrequently as possible, and when he did so was able to secure permanent taxes which made future meetings less necessary. These taxes fell chiefly on the commons, and so were readily agreed to by the first two estates, whose representatives formed a majority of the assembly. For the collection of the new taxes, Charles organized an administrative machinery that lasted for centuries. The army was put on a more regular footing, with knights and archers enrolled in companies and paid by the king.

After five years of preparation, Charles was ready to reopen the war. He himself took no part in the fighting, since he was more a scholar and statesman than a warrior. Instead, he entrusted the command of the army to the capable and popular Breton knight Bertrand du Guesclin. For the first time, the French enjoyed the advantage of superior generalship over the English. Du Guesclin may have been, as was commonly reported, the ugliest man in Brittany, but he was certainly a great soldier with years of practical experience behind him. Avoiding pitched battles, he occupied bit by bit nearly all the territory that had been ceded to Edward.

Joan of Arc

The French successes at the end of the fourteenth century preceded a generation of relative calm within the Hundred Years' War. Unfortunately, King Charles VI (1380–1422) was subject to fits of insanity at an early age and from the 1390s was incapable of consistently controlling the government. Powerful relatives, including the duke of Burgundy and Louis, duke of Orléans, rivaled each other in exploiting the royal government in their own interests. Although Louis was assassinated in 1407, his kinsman, the Count of Armagnac, continued the opposition to Burgundian domination over French affairs of state. By 1411, Burgundians and Armagnacs had come to blows in a civil war.

With the death of Charles VI in 1422, the question of succession to the French throne became more than a theoretical controversy. There was widespread suspicion, probably shared by the heir, or dauphin, Charles, that he was a bastard. One party, the Armagnacs, supported the young uncertain dauphin, the future Charles VII. The ambitious young king of England, Henry V, had taken advantage of the confused situation and had invaded France in 1415, routing the French at Agincourt in a battle remarkably reminiscent of the French disasters of Crécy and Poitiers in the preceding century. After 1419, the Burgundians entered into an alliance with the English, while the Armagnacs supported Charles. Henry V died in 1422. By 1429, the dauphin Charles had little authority north of the Loire River, where he was known derisively as "the King of Bourges," his temporary capital on the Loire.

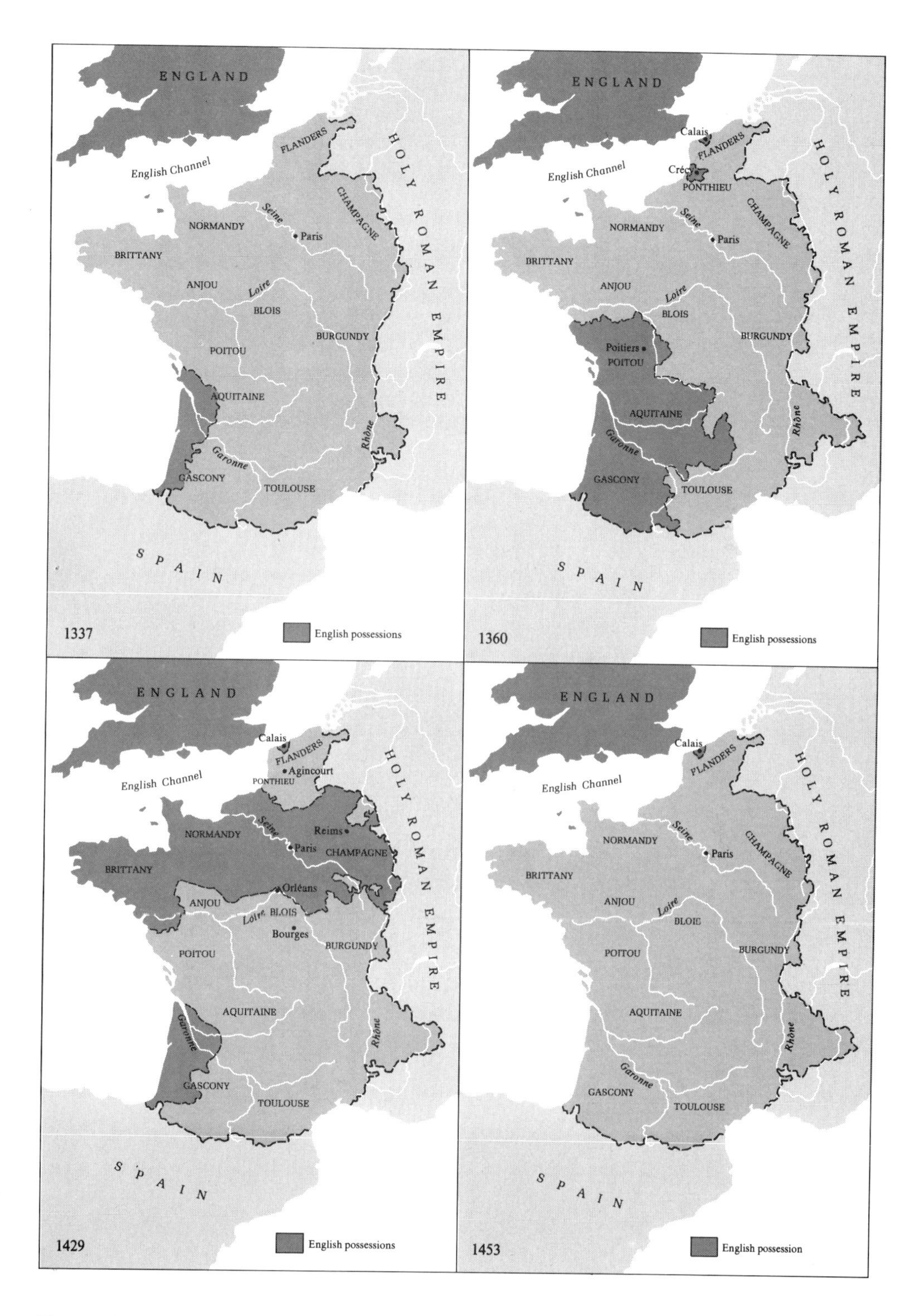

FRANCE DURING THE HUNDRED YEARS' WAR, 1337–1453

South of the Loire, the Armagnacs fought on under the leadership of the Dauphin, who now took the title Charles VII (1422–1461), though he had not yet been officially crowned and was widely rumored to be illegitimate. He was not a man of forceful character, but he had a few able and devoted followers and managed to hold his own fairly well against the duke of Bedford, who acted as regent for the young Henry VI in France. By 1429, however, Charles' position was becoming precarious, when the appearance at his court of that remarkable young woman, Joan of Arc, inspired Charles and his supporters with new confidence and energy.

The story of the peasant girl of Domrémy who believed, and made others believe, that God had chosen her to save France and win the crown for its rightful king is well known. For a year she led the French army, raising the siege of Orléans and cutting a path for the king to Reims, in whose ancient cathedral Charles was crowned and consecrated after the manner of his ancestors. It was a triumph quickly followed by tragedy. In May 1430, "the maid" was captured by the Burgundians, who sold her to the English. After months of imprisonment, she was tried on charges of heresy and witchcraft and finally burned at the stake. But Joan had not died in vain. She had given new spirit to the army and the king—who let her die without raising a hand to save her—and had aroused in the French people a patriotic fervor that has never died out.

The war lasted two decades longer, a period of slow but steady success for French arms. Charles VII made peace with Burgundy in 1435 and repelled the English step by step. The tactics of his general, Dunois, were much the same as those employed by Du Guesclin and were equally successful. By 1453, only Calais was left in English hands and the Hundred Years' War was over.

France had suffered terribly during the long conflict, but emerged from it a united state with a new national consciousness. It is too early to speak of "nationalism" in the modern sense. But the French now realized at least that they were not English, and that it mattered to French people of all classes and social backgrounds that France have a king of native rather than foreign origin. This was the major contribution of Joan of Arc and Charles VII to the growth of French national consciousness. The attempts of both the Estates-General and the great princes to control the government had failed. The way was now clear for the establishment of monarchical rule.

Suggestions for Further Reading

L. Fabre, *Joan of Arc* (1954).

R. Fawtier, *The Capetian Kings of France** (1960). The best work in English on the development of the increasingly effective Capetian monarchy. Covers the ninth through the fourteenth centuries.

M. L. Labarge, *Louis IX* (1968). Good study of Saint Louis.

A. Luchaire, *Social France in the Time of Philip Augustus,** rev. ed. (1957). A classic work dealing with life in France around 1200.

E. Perroy, *The Hundred Years' War** (1965). A detailed survey, particularly

*Available in a paperback edition.

strong in dealing with the war from the French viewpoint. Considered a standard work.

C. Petit-Dutaillis, *Feudal Monarchy in France and England** (1936). The best comparative description of Western feudal monarchies [AHA, 182].

J. R. Strayer, *The Administration of Normandy Under Saint Louis* (1932). One of the best studies of a province in medieval France [AHA, 182].

B. Vaughan, *John the Fearless: The Growth of Burgundian Power* (1966).

The Triumph of Medieval Monarchy in England

16

No freeman shall be taken or imprisoned or dispossessed or exiled or in any way destroyed, nor will we go upon him nor send upon him, except by the lawful judgment of his peers or by the law of the land.

MAGNA CARTA

The English continued shooting as vigorously and rapidly as before; some of their arrows fell among the [French] horsemen, who were sumptuously equipped, and, killing and maiming many, made them fall.

DESCRIPTION OF ENGLISH BOWMEN AT CRÉCY BY FROISSART

From Saxons to Normans

While feudal kingdoms were being formed on the Continent from the wrecks of the Carolingian Empire, a united Anglo-Saxon kingdom was taking shape on the island across the Channel. By 954 the descendants of Alfred, the great king of Wessex, became in fact kings of England. The Danish conquest was in the long run a blessing to England, for it made possible the unification of the whole kingdom under a stronger monarchy with a more systematic administration than had existed in the old Saxon kingdoms.

The new English kingdom was not feudal. Although it contained elements of feudalism, the king had effective authority. His power, indeed, was limited only by his dependence on the support of the nobles who made up his council, the Witan, with which he was bound to consult on all important matters. For purposes of local government, the kingdom was divided into shires. This system, begun in Wessex, was introduced into the rest of England after the conquest of the Danelaw. It was retained by the Normans after they conquered England, and has remained to the present the basic structure of English local government. The principal officer of each shire was the earl, usually a great noble, who was commander of the shire militia and occupied a position similar to that of the Carolingian counts, displaying a similar feudal tendency to regard his office as an independent hereditary right.

Royal authority was represented more directly by a less exalted but more useful officer, the sheriff, who took over more and more of the actual administration of the shire. He collected the rents due to the king from the royal estates and the fines assessed in the shire courts. He was also responsible for maintaining order and enforcing justice. Under the Saxon and, later, the Norman kings, the sheriffs furnished a link between central and local government, between the king and his humbler subjects, that had no parallel in the early feudal kingdoms on the Continent. The shire court was an important institution of local government which lasted through the period of Norman feudalism and had a permanent effect on the growth of English governmental and judicial practice. It was a periodic assembly of the more important landowners and freemen of the shire, presided over by the sheriff, in which administrative business was carried out and criminal and civil cases were heard, the final judgment being given by the members of the assembly. Similar courts for less important cases were also held in each "hundred," the smaller areas into which the shire was divided for purely local administration.

During this last century of Anglo-Saxon England, the Church and the monarchy worked closely together, raising the moral and educational standard of the monks and the secular clergy. This undertaking was in large part due to the efforts of reformers influenced by Cluniac tendencies on the Continent. The most famous of these English reformers was Dunstan, archbishop of Canterbury.

A new Danish conquest of England occurred in the eleventh century but had little demographic impact. It was a political conquest of twenty-five years' duration, not the mass migration characteristic of earlier Viking centuries. From 1042 to 1066, the English were governed by an Anglo-Saxon royal family. Upon the death of the last Anglo-Saxon king, Edward the Confessor, in January 1066, England became the political plaything of Danes, Normans, and Anglo-Saxons.

The Witan gave the crown to Earl Harold of Wessex, the strongest man in England though not of royal blood. His election did not go unchallenged. Across the Channel in Normandy, Duke William cast covetous eyes on the English throne. He was a distant relative of Edward the Confessor, and claimed that both Edward and Harold had acknowledged his right to the succession. His case was strengthened by the charge that Harold had broken a solemn vow to support him. Moreover, he was given the blessing and moral support of the pope, whom Harold had antagonized by exiling the Archbishop of Canterbury from England for political reasons.

William was no mean antagonist, for Normandy had become the strongest duchy in France in the century and a half since its founding, and was now almost an independent state. Though French in speech and manners, the Normans still possessed the wandering instincts and vigorous, adventurous spirit of their Viking ancestors. In the late summer of 1066, William crossed the Channel with an army of adventurers and landed near Hastings on the southern coast. King Harold, who had just defeated an invading army of Danes in the north, rushed south to meet him. The two armies met at Hastings in a hard-fought battle that decided the fate of England for centuries. The Saxons lost. Defeat in itself might not have been fatal to their cause, but Harold and his brothers had fallen, and England was left without a leader.

On Christmas Day, William the Conqueror was crowned king and a new era in English history opened. Thereafter England, with a population still overwhelmingly Anglo-Saxon and Danish in origin, was to be ruled by a dominant minority of Norman and French conquerors. This small group introduced new elements of language and culture, as well as new forms of government and administration, from the Continent.

Anglo-Norman Kings Organize a Royal Government, 1066-1154

The position of the English kings at the beginning of this period contrasted strongly with that of the kings of France. While Philip I was unable to exercise any authority outside the Île de France, and none too much even there, William the Conqueror was master of all England. He had the tremendous advantage that the whole country was his by right of conquest. William kept a large amount of land himself, and the rest he allotted to the Norman barons who had helped him in the conquest. This land was granted in the form of fiefs to vassals, who held it directly from the king as tenants-in-chief, giving in return a stipulated amount of military service. This military service was provided for by regranting part of the land to knights, who thus became subvassals of the king.

The land was given by the king to the barons not merely in theory, as confirmation of their hereditary possession of land won by their ancestors as in France, but in actual fact. Moreover, most fiefs were composed of pieces of land scattered throughout various parts of the kingdom. No single baron was strong enough to defy the king successfully. William collected all feudal dues to the last penny, and also instituted some sort of national taxation. This income, in addition to that from the extensive royal estates, guaranteed the financial independence and stability of the king's government. Finally, William and his successors insisted on the principle that vassals who held land from the barons owed their first loyalty to the king rather than to their immediate lords. From the first, Norman feudalism in England was a fairly centralized system.

William retained the old Anglo-Saxon system of shires and shire courts but added to it other institutions imported from the Continent. The most important of these were itinerant ministers from the royal court (somewhat like the old

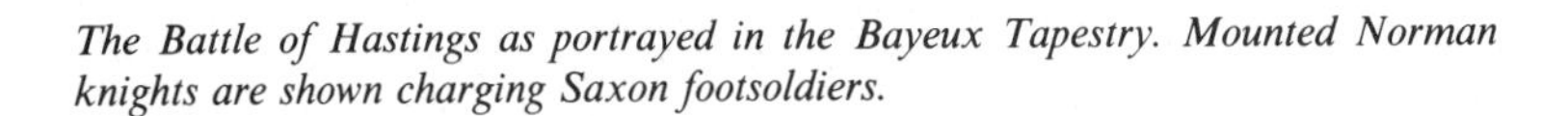

The Battle of Hastings as portrayed in the Bayeux Tapestry. Mounted Norman knights are shown charging Saxon footsoldiers.

Carolingian missi) and the sworn inquest or jury (so called for the French *juré*, because it was composed of men who had sworn to tell the truth). Both of these institutions were used to good effect in 1086 to collect information for the famous Domesday Book, an amazing survey of the land and chattels of the kingdom compiled for the purpose of insuring full payment of feudal dues and royal taxes. Ministers from the royal court, mostly educated clergymen, were sent out with writs empowering them to summon a group of freemen from each community to testify under oath as to the wealth of each estate. In later times, these itinerant "justices," as personal representatives of the king, and the sworn jury were to be used extensively for administrative purposes and for the prosecution of justice.

For thirteen years after the Conqueror's death, his son William Rufus (1087–1100) proved that royal power can be dangerous in the hands of a tyrannical king. However, his reign was not long enough to cause permanent damage. He died unlamented, shot by an arrow while hunting in the New Forest, and the crown passed to his younger brother, Henry I (1100–1135).

Henry was a hard, cool-headed, systematic man, of the true Norman breed, with a strongly legal turn of mind and a passion for order and justice. His primary motive, no doubt, was to strengthen his own power, but he did so in ways that benefited the whole kingdom. Traveling justices, sent out from his court, investigated complaints of feudal oppression, examined the conduct of the sheriffs, and heard judicial cases, which the king claimed fell within his jurisdiction as involving breaches of the king's peace. Henry was perhaps too interested in his continental possessions for the good of England—he spent more than half his reign in Normandy—but he chose able ministers to carry on his work in his absence.

The central government was regularly handled by the king, or his representative, and the king's court, the curia regis. This court was normally composed of a fairly small group of ministers and any of the barons whom the king chose to summon. On special occasions all the king's vassals-in-chief were summoned to it to form the Great Council. It was only natural in this shifting court that the specialized task of looking after the royal finances should be given to a more or less permanent group of experienced men who received the taxes, audited the sheriffs' accounts, and noted expenditures. These men came to be known, for the checkered table at which they sat to reckon their accounts, as the lords of the exchequer. The court of the exchequer was the first of several such courts which later grew out of the shifting and formless curia regis. Like his father, Henry I kept a firm hand on the English Church, but the abolition of lay investiture had become the primary point of papal policy. The question was finally settled in 1107, in England as in France, by a compromise wherein the king gave up nothing but the formal investiture with the ring and staff.

The Age of Henry II

Henry II (1154–1189) acquired his great feudal dominion in France before he became king of England at the age of twenty-one. Though he continued to spend much of his time in his continental fiefs, it was his work in England that justified his reputation as one of the greatest of medieval rulers. Henry's energy was remarkable, even in a family noted for that quality. His superabundant vitality exhausted the ministers who were forced to keep pace with him. He was constantly active, traveling from end to end of his domains; a terror to evil-doers, he had despite his violent temper his grandfather's love of order and justice. Every part of England knew the short sturdy figure, powerful shoulders, and bow legs, warped from a lifetime in the saddle, of the homely red-headed king. He kept in personal touch with the sheriffs whenever possible, and by developing the powers of the exchequer brought them under closer control by the central government. Though he introduced very little that was actually new to the system of administration, Henry II developed the machinery of government until he had established a permanent centralized system that would survive the neglect or mismanagement of weaker kings.

Henry II had inherited the legal mind of that "lion of justice," Henry I, and his most permanent contributions to English institutions were in the field of judicial and legal procedure. He greatly extended the jurisdiction of the royal courts by augmenting the list of cases recognized as "pleas of the crown" or breaches of the king's peace, and by throwing open his courts to all freemen involved in civil suits regarding the possession of land. At the same time he used the itinerant justices in a much more systematic way than before, so as to make royal courts easily available in all parts of the country. The regular use of these traveling justices led to the transference of a large number of cases from the local feudal or shire courts to the royal courts.

Royal justice was surer and more fair than that dispensed in the local courts and so became more popular. The king had sound financial reasons for doing everything in his power to extend the jurisdiction of his courts, since fines, payments for writs, and the like were an important part of the king's income. At the same time, the royal courts did much to raise the king's prestige and unify the

Medieval England

kingdom, for the king's justices were gradually developing a system of common law for the entire country which would eventually supplant varying local systems. No parallel to this development was occurring anywhere on the Continent.

Perhaps the most important of Henry's innovations was the regular use of the jury as part of the machinery of justice in the royal courts. This was an evolution from the sworn inquest used by earlier Norman kings and now put to a new judicial use. In Henry's time the jury was used chiefly for the accusation or indictment of criminals. Freemen in each locality were summoned by the king's justices and forced to tell, under oath, if they knew of any criminals in their neighborhood. Criminals thus accused were summoned to the king's courts for trial, no matter who would otherwise have had jurisdiction over them. A further use of the jury, which to some degree foreshadowed the later development of the trial jury, was the assize, a trial in a royal court to settle disputes over the possession of land, in which the jury not only gave evidence but also rendered a verdict on the basis of its previous knowledge of the circumstances.

Henry's desire to extend as far as possible the jurisdiction of royal courts caused his one serious conflict with the Church, when he tried to encroach on the jurisdiction of the ecclesiastical courts and canon law. Some conflict was almost bound to occur between the Church and a king as absolute and legal-minded as Henry II, though the pope himself was too busy with his fight against the German emperor Frederick Barbarossa to press the issue in England. Henry claimed that "criminous clercs" (clergymen who had committed crimes), after being convicted in an ecclesiastical court, should be degraded and turned over to royal officers to be punished as though they were laymen. He also objected strongly to the appealing of cases to the papal court at Rome.

In 1162, he secured the election of his most trusted minister, Thomas à Becket, to the archbishopric of Canterbury, in the hope that he would be a pliant tool. Henry was disappointed. Once he was head of the Church in England, Becket became the most violent opponent of royal encroachment. He denounced the Constitutions of Clarendon—a statement, drawn up by the king in 1164, of the restrictions to be placed on ecclesiastical courts and on papal interference in England—and for six years the quarrel dragged on. It was ended only when Becket was murdered before the altar of his cathedral, possibly with the foreknowledge of Henry II. For this act a remorseful and frightened Henry II, who in a fit of anger had seemingly desired Becket's death, did penance.

The Road to Magna Carta

Richard I (1189–1199), the Lionhearted, who succeeded his great father, Henry II, on the English throne, was an absentee king. However, the royal government, under the justiciar Hubert Walter, who was also archbishop of Canterbury, continued to function as efficiently as if the king had been present, though the justiciar often had a hard time raising the large sums of money demanded by the king for his campaigns. Many towns took advantage of the king's need and purchased charters giving them greater freedom of self-government. The Great Council (the full meeting of the barons in the curia regis) took advantage of the king's absence to assert a little more authority. Otherwise, the strong system of royal administration created by Henry II continued with very little change.

Richard was succeeded by his brother John (1199–1216), who is portrayed in popular legend as one of the worst and most unpopular of medieval English kings. According to contemporary accounts, John was indeed an unattractive personality: avaricious, lecherous, untrustworthy, and flighty. He was the kind of king who, by his own actions, brought about great coalitions against his policies.

The first disaster of John's reign was the loss of most of his continental fiefs to Philip Augustus. Immediately thereafter, he rushed into an unnecessary quarrel with the powerful Pope Innocent III, who until that time had been very favorable to him and supported him against Philip. The occasion of the quarrel was a dispute over the election of an archbishop of Canterbury to fill the place of Hubert Walter, who had died in 1205. Two candidates were elected, one secretly by the canons of the cathedral, the other openly by the clergy, but under the command of the king. Innocent set both elections aside and gave the post to Stephen Langton, an able and learned English cardinal. John refused to accept him. The pope applied pressure by imposing an interdict on England in 1208, and by excommunicating the king the next year. John retaliated by taking over the lands of the Church, thus alienating the English clergy. The nobles were also becoming discontented under his oppressive government and excessive taxation, and there were threats of rebellion. Finally, in 1213, when Philip Augustus prepared to invade England in his own and the pope's interest, John was forced to submit. He not only accepted Stephen Langton, but did homage to the pope for his kingdom, which he agreed to hold as a fief from the Papacy.

John's submission to the pope did not end the discontent in England. In 1214 he joined Emperor Otto of Brunswick in a war against Philip Augustus,

The murder of Thomas à Becket before the altar of Canterbury Cathedral.

who was supporting Frederick II in his bid for the imperial crown. John hoped to recover some of his lost lands while Philip was occupied with Otto. After Otto was defeated at Bouvines, however, John was unable to stand alone against the French king and returned empty-handed to England to find the nation united against him. The barons, who were the fighting force of the kingdom, took the initiative, actively supported by the clergy and the citizens of London.

In June 1215, they forced John to set his seal to the famous Magna Carta or Great Charter. By this time the pope was sympathetic to King John, who had made England a fief of the Holy See, further antagonizing the great English potentates. But Innocent III was far away, involved in other struggles, and unable or unwilling to help John in this situation.

The importance of Magna Carta was much greater for later times than for its own day. The charter was merely a promise that the king would observe the law in dealing with his vassals, though some vague phrases mention the rights of all free men. Perhaps the greatest significance of the charter for future times was the implication that the law was above the king, and that the barons, as representatives of the whole nation, had the right to force the king to obey it. The American system owes much to this assumption.

The Turbulent Age of Henry III

When John died in 1216 he was succeeded by his young son Henry III, who reigned ("ruled" is too strong a word to describe a large part of his tenure) for the next fifty-six years. Given his father's nature, it is not surprising that Henry III was for long periods unstable and foolish. He reigned at a time when England's population, trade, and cities were rapidly growing, a period of great cultural efflorescence in medieval England as well as elsewhere in western Europe. The Anglo-Norman aristocracy was becoming less French and more English. Despite all of this, Henry's reign was a disaster from the viewpoint of English kingship. It was significant mainly because it brought into being a coalition of towns, prelates, and nobles which laid the foundation for parliamentary government in medieval England.

Henry's insane foreign policy—which included a promise to aid the pope in crushing the Hohenstaufens, and to pay all the expenses of the war, in return for the recognition of his second son, Edmund, as king of Sicily—and his defeats in Scotland and Wales finally aroused the barons to definite action to control the king's irresponsible government. The Provisions of Oxford, which the king was forced to accept in 1258, bestowed the real powers of government on a small group of the greater barons. This provisional government failed because it gave too much power to a small feudal group that did not represent the nation. The opposition party then tried to put into effect a much more sweeping reform under the leadership of Simon de Montfort, a younger son of that Simon who had led the Albigensian Crusade. He had come to England years earlier, been made Earl of Leicester, married the king's sister, and had become thoroughly English in his sympathies.

After defeating the royalist army at Lewes, Montfort controlled the government for a year (1264-1265), until he in turn was defeated and killed. During that time he convened a meeting of the Great Council to approve his administration. To it were summoned not only two knights from each shire, which was customary, but also two citizens from each chartered town. Aside from the representation given to the towns, this "parliament" was not a great innovation. That term was already in common use for such meetings of the Great Council. Nor did it accomplish much for the present. De Montfort's experiment failed because he tried to force changes too rapidly. However, it did bear fruit in the next reign, for Edward I learned that it was easier to govern with the cooperation of the people's representatives than to confront the opposition of the nation.

The Growth of Constitutional Government, 1272-1327

Only the work of a wise and strong king was needed to complete the first step in welding England into a strong constitutional state, and for such a purpose Edward I was ideally qualified. His appearance and character were well suited to capturing the popular imagination and making him a national hero. He was tall and well built, a good soldier, and at least every other inch a gentleman. He had, moreover, a sound legal mind and a genius for organization. Before he came to the throne Edward had had a good deal of experience as the most active force in the government of his feeble father Henry III. Non-Welsh historians have hailed him not only as the conqueror of Wales but, more important, as a great legislator and organizer, the English Justinian and the father of the English Parliament.

Edward made his eldest son titular prince of Wales, a title which has normally been conferred upon the heir to the English throne ever since. Edward succeeded in making Wales a permanent part of the English state, but his successors were less successful in their attempts to annex Celtic Scotland to the growing English kingdom. Their military attempts to overcome Scotland only drove the kings of that fiercely independent land into cooperation with anti-English French diplomacy. For a good part of the next three centuries, this Scottish-French alliance profoundly influenced English foreign policy and politics. Not until the early seventeenth century were Scotland and England united in a personal union, and not until the early eighteenth century was this union recognized as permanent.

The reputation of Edward I as a great statesman rests more securely on his contribution to the formation of English governmental institutions than on his conquest of Wales or his brief successes in Scotland. Institutions that had been vague and fluid took definite shape under his hands. In the interest of good government and the unity of the state, Edward undertook to make the royal administration more efficient and to centralize authority under the crown at the expense of the barons, who might still be dangerous if their wings were not clipped. Depending on middle-class ministers, trained by service for their duties, and on the new class of professional lawyers, he built a well-ordered machine of government and justice entirely responsible to the king. The curia regis was now fairly clearly divided into special courts with well-defined functions—the exchequer for financial matters, the courts of common pleas and the king's bench for civil and criminal cases respectively, and the king's council, which not only assisted the king in the general business of government but also took cognizance of all cases that did not fall under the jurisdiction of special courts. All England was beginning to look to the king and his courts for government and justice.

Edward was more than a great administrator. He was also the first great English legislator. Under him the English common law—that is, the law applied in the king's courts and hence common to the whole country—was given the form it was to retain with very little change for centuries. This law had been created by custom rather than legislation. Hitherto, the work of the king's courts had been confined to interpreting it in judicial decisions. Now the king began to legislate. Working with his council, Edward I issued statute after statute, supplementing or altering the common law to give it definite form and bring it into touch with contemporary needs. No single accomplishment, perhaps, has done more to make England a unified state than the development of the common law. It was the king's law and the law of the whole kingdom; in the face of it feudal and local customs faded away.

Last but not least of Edward's contributions to the development of English institutions was his establishment of Parliament, including representatives from the middle class of town and country, as a permanent part of the government. Here too, his work consisted not so much in creating something absolutely new as in combining and giving more definite and permanent form to earlier institutions. Neither Parliament nor representation was new in Edward's reign; but the two had never been combined on a national scale, or at least not with sufficient frequency to give the new institution which resulted from the combination a permanent status; the parliamentary experiment of Simon de Montfort in 1265 had failed and other summonses of representatives had been only partial and irregular.

To this assembly were now added representatives from the middle class, but unlike the Third Estate in France they included knights from the country as well as burghers from the towns. For the origins of this type of representation we must look to a uniquely English institution, the shire court, to which representative knights and burghers had for generations been summoned to give information for administrative and judicial purposes, to serve on presentment juries, and even to pass judgment. They were summoned because they knew local conditions and customs. When Edward I summoned two knights from each shire and two burghers from each chartered town to meet with the Great Council, he was, from one point of view, merely centralizing the representation in the shire courts for the whole kingdom; from another point of view he was enlarging the Great Council to include representatives of his subjects throughout the state as well as his great vassals.

While the medieval Parliament was a peculiarly English institution, its thirteenth-century origins reflect that union of Norman and Anglo-Saxon elements which was typical of a good deal of medieval English culture. The Great Council, for example, was very similar to the curia regis of the Capetian kings of the thirteenth century. But whereas the Capetian curia regis became departmentalized into the nucleus of a future administrative bureaucracy, the Great Council of Edward I in the late thirteenth century became a judicial and consultative body in conjunction with an older tradition of Anglo-Saxon representation of shires and towns.

The representatives of the commons, as they were called, were not yet permanent members of Parliament, but after 1297 it became evident that their presence was necessary when nonfeudal taxes were to be proclaimed. Taxation, however, was not the only purpose of Parliament. It was also a court for the redress of grievances outside the jurisdiction of the common-law courts. By including the representatives, the king opened the way for petitions of grievances from the middle class, which it was the duty of Parliament to redress. Finally—and this is perhaps the most important motive for summoning the commons—Edward desired a broader and more genuinely national basis for his government than was provided by the barons alone. The knights of the shire and the burghers could furnish invaluable information regarding local conditions, and on returning home could explain the acts of the government to their neighbors. Under Edward I, Parliament was not yet organized in its present form. When the representatives were present, they stood at the back of the hall and took no part in the proceedings, save to give consent or to express opinions when asked. However, they were already in the habit of conferring separately as to the decision they would give, and were thus paving the way for the formation of a separate House of Commons.

From Edward III to Henry VI, 1327-1461

Edward II (1307-1327) was a weak, corrupt monarch whose impact upon history was not great. Edward III (1327-1377), on the other hand, was a successful and popular king in his vigorous youth and middle age, but failure and popular discontent accompanied his premature and undignified senility. While he still retained his strength of mind, Edward was absorbed heart and soul in the war with France, and was prepared to sacrifice royal rights and prerogatives to Parliament and to give the people good government in order to secure the financial support necessary to military success. He was always a good politician as well as a brilliant general. When his powers began to fail, his son, the Black Prince, for a time took his place as a national hero. But, unfortunately, he too fell prey to premature illness and death, leaving his unscrupulous younger brother, John of Gaunt, to act as regent for the old king and later for the prince's infant son, Richard II (1377-1399). During the twelve years of Richard's minority, Parliament took advantage of the weakness of royal government to press its claims more strongly than ever, and after the king came of age he was forced for a time to accept a constitutional regime. Richard II, however, was arrogant, hot-headed, foolish, and determined to exercise an absolute authority that was no longer practicable. He eventually was forced to abdicate in favor of Henry of Lancaster, son of John of Gaunt.

Henry IV (1399-1413) owed his crown to Parliament. He was not the next heir to the throne, and so could not claim it by direct descent. Moreover, the fall of Richard II had demonstrated the folly of ignoring Parliament. Under the Lancastrian kings, therefore, that body acquired a larger share in government than ever before. The greater part of the reign of Henry IV was spent suppressing rebellions and making good his claim to rule. His efforts were eventually successful. He left the power of his house so firmly established that his son Henry V (1413-1422) was able to renew the French war with startling success and to threaten the power of Parliament. But at the height of his career Henry V died and the royal government was again weakened by a regency for an infant king. Even when Henry VI (1422-1461) grew up, the government remained weak, for he proved to be an utterly incompetent ruler. The country was torn by the strife of baronial factions and disturbed by the lawless violence of returned soldiers who were maintained by wealthy lords. Parliament took a larger share in government than ever, but it was too often dominated by noble cliques. Meanwhile, the war with France was lost and before the end of Henry's reign England was thrown into the chaos of civil war.

The effect of the Hundred Years' War on England, socially and constitutionally, was different from its effect on France. The English people had not suffered so much. It was always Frenchmen who were plundered and Englishmen who profited, a situation well calculated to arouse patriotic enthusiasm. Popular support for the war finally began to die out during its last stages in the fifteenth century when English kings, in a losing and dilatory struggle, attempted to raise taxes and armies in order to hold the small bits of France they still controlled.

During these decades of war, the steady evolution of the English constitution continued. A new court, the chancery, was established to hear the civil cases referred to the king's council from the common-law courts. These cases were mostly outside the scope of common law. An equally significant innovation was made in the administration of local justice during the reign of Edward III. In every county prominent knights or landowners were given power to judge minor criminal cases. They were called justices of the peace. Being men of respectable social position who were thoroughly acquainted with conditions in their neighborhoods, their judgments were usually respected and in agreement with local opinion.

The most important constitutional development of this period, however, was the gradual evolution of Parliament from the rather vague body founded by Edward I to something like its modern form, and its firm establishment as a permanent and necessary part of government. The commons made especially good use of the kings' need for money to carry on the war. They had learned to bargain. Before giving consent to taxes they would present petitions for the redress of grievances, and these petitions were often made into statutes by the king and given the force of law. The commons were thus acquiring the practical ability to initiate legislation. Parliament, and particularly the House of Commons, still had a long way to go before reaching its present position, but all the essential factors were present before the end of the Hundred Years' War. Later kings might dictate to Parliament or try to override it, but none could afford to ignore it.

France and England in the Late Middle Ages

The history of the English Parliament is highly dissimilar to that of the French Estates-General, which never succeeded in becoming an essential part of the government, and, on the contrary, was called less and less frequently after the middle of the fourteenth century, eventually almost ceasing to exist. One fundamental cause of the difference between the two institutions was the earlier centralization of government in England while both countries were still largely feudal. The tremendous difference in size between France and England in the fourteenth century further accounts for the retardation of parliamentary development in France. France's population was several times that of England during this period, and, geographically speaking, the territory to which the French king laid claim was considerably larger than that over which his English counterpart reigned. Given the difficulty of communications during the medieval period, it is not surprising that geography played a negative role in the development of centralized French institutions such as the Estates-General or the Parlement.

The English kings were strong enough to compel barons from all parts of the country to attend the Great Council even before it evolved into Parliament. In France, on the other hand, the great lords outside the domain remained strong enough to ignore the king's summons almost to the end of the feudal era. From the very beginning, then, the English Parliament was more truly national in scope than the Estates-General. There was an equally fundamental difference in the composition of the English House of Commons and the French Third Estate. The latter was composed almost entirely of representatives of the urban middle class, who had no interest in the country districts and nothing in common, socially or economically, with the nobles and clergy in the other two estates. The English Commons, on the other hand, included landowning knights from the shires as well as burghers, and these knights had much the same social and economic interests as the members of the House of Lords. Indeed, many of the knights from the shires were related to the lords by family ties, for in England, unlike any continental country, the younger sons of barons were excluded from the family inheritance and lost their status as nobles. Together with the numerous knights who held only one or two manors but who would have been classed as nobles on the Continent, they formed the peculiarly English class of gentry. From the social point of view, then, the English Parliament was more genuinely representative than the Estates-General, and the two English houses could work together to influence the monarchy as the three estates never could.

The end of the Hundred Years' War found both England and France on the verge of becoming united monarchical states. Both countries had yet to pass through a period of civil war (the Wars of the Roses in England and the war with Burgundy in France), but subsequent to that, each country's king became the direct ruler of the whole state by virtue of his royal title rather than as a feudal lord. In England, however, the king still had to rule by constitutional means through Parliament, whereas in France, once the great nobles had been suppressed, the king was left absolute and uncontrolled.

The rise of these great feudal monarchies was closely related to the development of urban life in western Europe. Indeed, the extension of trade and the growth of cities, due in part to phenomena such as the early Crusades, made possible the development of cadres trained in Roman, canon, and common law. Men of bourgeois origin proved vital to Capetian or Plantagenet kings in their centralizing work. The relative order and stability which these new monarchies could, at their best, provide to the towns was crucial to the further development of that rich urban life which was so typical of large areas of western Europe from the twelfth century.

Suggestions for Further Reading

F. Barlow, *William I and the Norman Conquest** (1965).

H. Cam, *England Before Elizabeth** (1960). A good introduction.

D. C. Douglas, *William the Conqueror: The Norman Impact upon England**

*Available in a paperback edition.

(1964). Outstanding, detailed institutional and biographical study, providing much information about Norman and Anglo-Norman feudalism.

G. Holmes, *The Later Middle Ages** (1962). A fine survey.

J. C. Holt, *Magna Carta* (1965).

P. M. Kendall, *Richard III* (1956). Highly readable, sympathetic study of a much maligned monarch.

B. D. Lyon, *A Constitutional and Legal History of Medieval England,* 2 vols. (1960). An outstanding, readable survey of vital aspects of British history.

M. McKissack, *The Fourteenth Century* (1961). Volume 5 in the Oxford history of England. An important, scholarly work, dealing with all aspects of English society in an era of war, revolution, and social change.

A. R. Myers, *England in the Late Middle Ages** (1952). A relatively brief but scholarly survey by an outstanding student of the period. A good, solid introduction.

S. Painter, *The Reign of King John** (1949). A detailed, readable account of the reign.

M. Powicke, *The Thirteenth Century* (1953). Volume 4 in the Oxford History of England. A scholarly and detailed work.

B. Wilkinson, *Constitutional History of Medieval England,* 2 vols. (1948-1952). A widely respected constitutional history.

Failure of the Holy Roman Empire in Italy and Germany

17

Austria est imperare orbi universo. (Austria is to rule the whole world.)

MOTTO OF FREDERICK III

The Era of Frederick Barbarossa

While medieval monarchies in France and England succeeded, in however tortuous and uncertain a fashion, in building relatively centralized states, Germany and Italy plunged into long eras of political decentralization. During the three decades of uneasy peace between the Empire and the Papacy which followed the Concordat of Worms in 1122, the chief interest in German history centers on the rivalry of two great feudal families, the Welfs and the Hohenstaufens. Later this feud was to spread to Italy, where the party which favored the Papacy and fought for local independence called themselves Guelfs from the German name Welf, while the imperial party were called Ghibellines from the German Waiblingen, the name of one of the Hohenstaufen family possessions. This Italian feud persisted for centuries, long after the rivalry of the two German families had subsided. Innumerable family feuds and private wars added to the general anarchy. The disturbed state of the Empire during the investiture controversy had given new impetus to feudal independence. Strongly fortified castles had sprung up everywhere.

The Empire was rescued from disintegration by the Hohenstaufen emperor Frederick I (1152–1190), called Barbarossa (Italian for "red beard"). From the first the new emperor inspired hope and confidence in all who longed for the restoration of peace, order, and strong government. Well built, handsome, and genial, the red-bearded monarch charmed all who knew him. Frederick was the epitome of the chivalrous ruler of the Middle Ages. He was a first-class soldier with a full-blooded love of battle, but he was also a just and conscientious monarch, bent on enforcing law and order in his harassed realm. In one respect only did he fail to appreciate the needs of his age: he did not understand or realize the importance of the growing commercial and industrial life in the towns. For feudal Germany, however, his reign marks an era of imperial authority and of comparative peace such as had not been seen for a century.

The feud between Hohenstaufen and Welf was buried, to be resurrected for a brief period only toward the end of his long reign. Frederick was himself half Welf, a nephew of Henry the Proud through his mother and of Conrad III through his father, and the head of the Welf family, his cousin Henry the Lion, duke of Saxony and Bavaria, was his friend and comrade in arms for twenty years. Lesser feuds were suppressed, at least so long as the emperor was present in Germany, by the enforcement of a "land peace" forbidding private wars. Since, however, the emperor could not be confined to Germany, his rule did not have as permanent results there as it might otherwise have had. He strove to recover imperial control of Italy—there to meet the only failure of his career.

Frederick's first expedition into Italy in 1154-1155, for the purpose of receiving the imperial crown, brought him face-to-face with two powers which were to unite in successful defiance of his authority—the Papacy and the Lombard cities. With the former he was at first friendly enough, for the pope needed his aid against the citizens of Rome, who had tried to revive the ancient freedom of the city under the leadership of a reformer named Arnold of Brescia. Frederick showed his willingness to aid the pope by securing the execution of the heretical rebel before his own arrival in the papal city. However, the first meeting between the ambitious emperor and the equally strong-minded and determined pope, Adrian IV (1154-1159), proved that their friendship was no more than skin deep. Frederick haughtily refused to act as squire to the pope and to hold his bridle and stirrup. The two potentates almost parted in anger. Frederick finally submitted to what he had considered an affront to his imperial dignity only when it was pointed out that there was ample precedent for the act.

The popes found allies against the emperor in the Lombard cities. Since the middle of the eleventh century, the Italian towns had been growing rapidly as the result of a great revival of international trade. The Crusades had further stimulated trade, and by the middle of the twelfth century the numerous cities that dot the Lombard plain were busy centers of industry and commerce. Originally these cities had been governed by their bishops, acting as imperial officers. But with increasing prosperity the citizens began to demand freedom and self-government. During the investiture controversy, both emperors and popes had sought their aid and had paid for it with concessions of liberty. When Frederick made his first expedition into Italy he found the cities and the land around them organized as communes, practically self-governing republics. He found them also in a shocking state of anarchy, each city divided into turbulent political factions and engaged in feuds with other cities. The emperor was surprised to find these burghers as independent and aggressively warlike as the feudal nobility, and realized that he must crush their independence before imperial government could be re-established in Italy.

In 1158, Frederick made a second expedition into Italy with a large army. After capturing Milan, the strongest of the Lombard cities, he called an Imperial Diet at Roncaglia. There he publicly asserted his imperial rights, as defined by the jurists on the basis of Roman law and medieval precedent. Disregarding the privileges of the communes, he claimed all rights of sovereignty, called the regalia, including the appointment of officers and collection of taxes from tolls, markets, mints, law courts, and the like. Never had the medieval Empire seemed so strongly established in Italy. But the imperial officers were unpopular and taxes oppressive. Milan revolted and with it several other cities, supported by the pope. At this point Adrian IV died and there was a hotly disputed election. A majority of the cardinals elected Alexander III (1159-1181), while a minority declared for Victor IV. It was the latter, more favorable to him, whom the emperor chose to recognize, thus assuring the continuance of the schism, since Victor was not accepted as pope anywhere outside the Empire.

ITALY IN THE TWELFTH CENTURY

Meanwhile, Frederick continued the war against the rebellious communes. In 1162 he destroyed much of Milan, banishing its citizens. But the discontent in Lombardy persisted. In 1166, Frederick had to make a third expedition to Italy to crush a league of cities which had united against him and had so forgotten their jealousy of Milan as to aid the Milanese in rebuilding their city. Alexander III, now in possession of Rome, was the heart and soul of the resistance to the emperor. Frederick, therefore, marched on Rome and captured it. His success was immediately followed by disaster, so typical of German imperial adventures in Italy, in the form of an epidemic that destroyed his army and forced him to retire to Germany, where domestic affairs kept him busy until 1174.

The Lombard League, led by Milan, used the years the emperor spent in Germany to gain the adherence of nearly all the north Italian cities. The war dragged on until 1176, when the emperor was disastrously defeated by the Lombard army at Legnago. Frederick accepted defeat with as much grace as possible. He made peace with Alexander III, ending the schism, and the following year he arranged a truce with the Lombard League, later confirmed by the Peace of Constance in 1183. The emperor surrendered the regalia, leaving the cities almost complete self-government. They in turn recognized the imperial sovereignty and swore allegiance. It was a decided triumph for the Lombard communes. As far as the pope was concerned, however, the results of the struggle were indecisive. Frederick had been forced to abandon his antipope and to recognize Alexander; but he had retained control of the Church in Germany, and neither emperor nor pope had surrendered his claims to supremacy.

Having failed in Italy, Frederick was free to concentrate on Germany, where only one serious problem arose to mar his declining years. A breach in his long friendship with Henry the Lion revived the old Welf-Hohenstaufen feud. Henry had been building up a strong feudal state in Bavaria and Saxony and in the Slavic lands north and east of the Elbe. Unlike the emperor, Henry was much interested in the rising commercial towns, and he laid the foundations for the commercial greatness of Lübeck and Munich. His government was enlightened but it bore heavily on the lesser nobles, who brought charges of oppression against him in the imperial courts in 1179. Frederick, who had been estranged from his cousin for a number of reasons, summoned him to appear to answer the charges. Henry refused. After a year he was outlawed on a charge of treason and his fiefs were confiscated. Of all his vast possessions he was allowed to keep only Brunswick and some other allodial lands in the north. His duchies of Saxony and Bavaria were partitioned into smaller units. This event marks the end of the dominance of the great duchies, and the rise in their place of a number of smaller principalities. What remained of the duchy of Bavaria was given to Otto of Wittelsbach, whose descendants held it until 1918.

Frederick's reign was brought to a close by the Third Crusade. Like so many of his contemporaries the aged emperor was fascinated by the hope of recovering the Holy Land, and in 1189 he set out with a large army. The gallant old fighter did not live to meet the Moslems, perishing in the icy waters of a stream in Asia Minor.

During his brief reign, Henry VI (1190–1197), Frederick's unprepossessing son, revived his family's feud with the Papacy and achieved a remarkable, though brief, success. Cruel and treacherous, Henry had none of the personal charm that had made his father so popular, but he had qualities of astuteness, learning, and determination that made up for the lack. With him the struggle for supremacy enters a new phase. The emperor's goal was now the political isolation of the pope in central Italy. Northern Italy had been won over by the grant of practical independence to the Lombard cities. Having married Constance of Sicily, heiress to the kingdom of Sicily, Henry also possessed a claim to all of southern Italy below the Papal States, although he was unable to overcome the resistance of the Sicilian nobles until 1194. Then, however, he was in a strong strategic position. The papal domain was completely surrounded by lands under his control or allied with him. Henry proceeded to establish his own vassals in the Papal States, reducing the land subject to the pope to the duchy of Rome. Hohenstaufen power was growing steadily in Italy when it was suddenly destroyed by the premature death of the emperor, not yet thirty-three years old.

The Deceptive Triumph of the Papacy

Seldom has history seen a more abrupt and thorough reversal of fortune than that which followed the sudden death of Henry VI. While rival candidates were disputing for the imperial crown, the Papacy came into the hands of the strongest of all medieval popes, Innocent III (1198–1216). His pontificate marks the highest point of power ever exercised by the Papacy. Trained as a jurist in the schools of Bologna and Paris, Innocent was thoroughly versed in canon law and ecclesiastical tradition. He was thirty-seven years old, unusually young for a pope, and in the full vigor of his youth. For eighteen years he influenced the nations of Western Christendom as the successor of Saint Peter, to whom God had given authority, "not only over the universal Church but also over the whole world." Never before had the papal claims to sovereignty over Church and secular governments been stated with such absolute conviction.

Yet Innocent did not regard himself as an innovator. He based his position on the time-honored theory of the Papacy, embodied in tradition and canon law, which had been codified so carefully during the twelfth century. His position was different from that of Gregory VII by the measure of the legal and institutional growth of the Church in the century and a quarter that lay between them. In claiming a potentially unlimited universal sovereignty, Innocent felt that he was merely asserting the recognized rights of the Papacy. He did not, it is true, claim direct authority over secular government in all cases. But he did assert a spiritual authority which might incidentally include secular authority, since it was his duty to judge the sins of all Christians, including rulers, and any act that had a moral significance (as what human act does not?) came within his jurisdiction.

Upon the death of Henry VI, Innocent immediately assumed a major role in imperial affairs. The pope eventually supported the imperial candidacy of Otto IV. As guardian of the young son of Henry VI, Frederick, Innocent wished to prevent any imperial claimant—including Frederick—from ruling Italy in any real sense. The defeat of Otto in 1214 by the French left Frederick as his logical heir, and an uncertain Innocent III was forced to accept him as emperor. Frederick's power was based in his mother's kingdom of Sicily, however.

Once rid of his rival, Frederick II restored peace in Germany by making concessions to the princes and to the Church, and in the year 1220 he returned to Italy, the land he had always considered his real home, to stage the last act of the Hohenstaufen drama. It is difficult to estimate the character of this last great member of a great family, so contradictory and even hysterical are some of the judgments passed on him by his contemporaries and by later writers. His enemies in the papal party saw in him an arch-heretic and a monster of depravity, while his admirers hailed him as "the wonder of the world" (*stupor mundi*). Even modern scholars have been moved to superlatives in describing him. Some have referred to him as "the first modern king," and one, writing in the *Cambridge Medieval History,* has asserted that "among the rulers in the centuries between Charlemagne and Napoleon he has no equal." Certainly there was genius in this descendant of German emperors and Norman kings.

Brought up amid the plots of a turbulent court, Frederick had learned to trust no one but himself. He had learned all the uses of deceit and had acquired a self-confidence based on a fairly just assurance of his own mental superiority to those around him. Sicily, where he passed his youth, was a cosmopolitan country made up of mixed Italian, Norman, Greek, and Moslem peoples, including every possible shade of social and religious opinion. As a product of that varied society, Frederick had developed a keen, skeptical mind, with little religious or moral conviction but an enthusiastic interest in literature, science, and philosophy, and a sanely enlightened appreciation of the needs of his kingdom.

Whenever he was free to do so, Frederick devoted his attention to his Sicilian kingdom, which included southern Italy, and it was there that his genius as a ruler showed itself most clearly. His first concern was to recover the royal domains, which had been lost during his youth. Frederick then took stringent measures to re-establish absolute government, building a system of administration by royal officers who would be superior to the feudal nobles. He reorganized the royal courts and councils, recruiting his ministers from men of common birth trained in law rather than from the nobility. In 1231 he issued a new legal code, the Constitutions of Melfi, based on the principles of Roman law, to supersede the prevailing tangle of feudal laws and local customs. He reformed the system of taxation, to increase his income. This bore heavily on the people, but they were compensated by Frederick's encouragement of industry, commerce, and agriculture. Frederick also did much to raise the intellectual level of Sicily. He founded the University of Naples, and his liberal patronage of writers and scholars made his court the intellectual center of the West. Under his rule, despotic though it was, Sicily became the most prosperous and civilized kingdom in Europe. Frederick is still remembered there as "il gran Frederigo."

As a true Hohenstaufen, Frederick could not concentrate all his attention on Sicily. He seems to have cared little for Germany, which during most of his reign he left in the hands of his son Henry, but he was determined to keep Sicily and the Empire together, and to unite Italy, if possible, under his rule. This intention brought him into conflict with the two ancient enemies of his house, the Papacy and the Lombard cities. The latter were still, as in the days of Barbarossa, independent, disorderly, and constantly at war with one another. Like his grandfather, Frederick II felt it necessary to enforce order upon them through imperial authority. But despite their mutual jealousies, they could still unite to defend their freedom, and the emperor's first attempts to rule them were met by the formation of a new Lombard League in 1226. Again the pope joined the Lombards in opposition to the emperor. The grounds of disagreement, however, were not quite the same as they had been in the previous century. Innocent III had triumphantly vindicated the papal claims to universal sovereignty, and the emperor had practically lost control of the German Church.

The issue of supremacy was still present, but the struggle was in reality for territorial rule in Italy. Despite his promises, Frederick was threatening the pope's control of the Papal States, while the pope, for his part, could still assert his feudal overlordship over Sicily. The pope had a weapon against Frederick in the latter's rash vow, made in 1215, to go on a Crusade. Pope Gregory IX (1227-1241) demanded the fulfillment of the vow immediately after his election. Frederick agreed to sail that year, but, falling sick at sea, he turned back. Gregory thereupon excommunicated him. In 1228, the emperor finally went on the Crusade and by diplomatic negotiations won Jerusalem, but this did not mollify the pope, since Frederick had undertaken the holy war while under the ban of excommunication and had, moreover, treated peacefully with the infidel sultan. Only after another year of warfare did pope and emperor sign a peace treaty, which enforced an uneasy truce for eight years.

Meanwhile, Frederick continued with varying success his attempts to suppress the Lombard cities. In 1235, he was called to Germany to put down a rebellion led by his son Henry. Returning to Italy with German troops, he announced his intention of establishing his authority over the whole peninsula. By 1238, the pope was openly allied with the Lombard League, and in March of the following year he again excommunicated the emperor. From that time on, Gregory and his successor Innocent IV (1243-1254) were relentless leaders of the opposition to Frederick. Both were canonists, fighting for the rights of the Church; they defined those rights more absolutely and made greater claims to secular power than even Innocent III had done. The war dragged on indecisively until the death of Frederick in 1250 brought final ruin to the imperial cause.

The Papacy still continued its implacable enmity to Frederick's descendants, while the Empire fell to pieces. Pope after pope carried on a ruthless war to stamp out "the viper brood of the Hohenstaufen." For four years Frederick's second son, Conrad IV, last emperor of the Hohenstaufen line, continued the struggle, but after his death Sicily was separated from the Empire. In 1265 the French-born Pope Clement IV called in a powerful French prince, Charles, Count of Anjou, younger brother of Louis IX, to win the kingdom of Sicily from Frederick's natural son Manfred. The following year Manfred was defeated and slain. Two years later, the last Hohenstaufen, Frederick's grandson Conradin, was captured and executed.

In Germany, meanwhile, the imperial government had completely collapsed. While Frederick II was busy in Italy, the nobles had successfully asserted their independence. Rebellion after rebellion had marked the last years of his reign, and when, the year after his death, his son Conrad IV left to carry on the war in Italy, the country was in a state of complete anarchy. After the death of Conrad IV in 1254, there was no generally recognized emperor for nineteen years, until the election of Rudolf of Hapsburg in 1273. During this stormy period, called the Great Interregnum, the German nobles acquired an independence that they were never again to surrender to any emperor. The German cities banded together for mutual protection, and their great prosperity was not destroyed by the political chaos of the Empire. German society, however, was fragmented—it was each for himself.

The Papacy had at last triumphed in the long and bitter struggle with the emperors—at least to the extent of disrupting the Empire, and leaving it permanently weakened. In these two centuries of conflict, the popes had also built up a great international sovereignty, with sweeping claims to spiritual and secular authority, and with a territorial state in central Italy under their immediate rule. At the same time, the struggle had prevented the development of a strong centralized government, or even of national unity, in both Germany and Italy. But the papal victory was not as permanent as it seemed. For, while the popes were fighting with the emperors, the kings of France and England had been steadily increasing their power and gradually building centralized territorial states out of feudal chaos. In the late Middle Ages, the popes were to find these national monarchs more dangerous enemies than the emperors had been.

Political Disintegration of the Empire

The German princes had made good use of the opportunities provided by the Interregnum to establish their independence, which they intended to keep. Nevertheless, they felt the need of a ruler strong enough to suppress the worst confusion and lawlessness, though not strong enough to interfere in the government of their own states. The tradition of the Empire was still powerful, though not so effective as to establish an orderly method of election of the emperor until the next century. Only an emperor could complete the formal structure of the feudal state and give a semblance of legality to the princes' authority. They therefore agreed on the election of Count Rudolf of Hapsburg (1273–1291), who seemed to fulfill all their requirements to perfection. His family was an ancient and honorable one, with large estates on the northwestern slopes of the Alps, but it was not one of the great princely houses. He himself was popular, a fine upstanding figure of a man with a reputation for amiability and knightly valor. On the whole, Rudolf made a satisfactory emperor. He used his prestige to suppress lawlessness and to re-establish peace wherever possible through diplomatic negotiations. At the same time, he made no attempt to interfere with the rights of the princes, and sold privileges freely to both princes and cities. Only one thing alarmed the electors. Rudolf was bent on acquiring land and power for his family. He seized the German fiefs of King Ottokar II of Bohemia, who had refused to recognize his election, and from them granted Austria, Styria, and Carniola to his own son Albert, thus founding a strong domain in southeastern Germany which the Hapsburgs were to retain until the present century.

The next significant emperor was Henry VII (1308–1313), who displayed a romantic though anachronistic sense of the imperial office, a sense he shared with his Florentine contemporary Dante. The desire to be crowned at Rome and to reassert imperial authority in Italy, which had lured so many medieval emperors to destruction, led him to purchase temporary peace in Germany by scattering privileges among the princes and to embark on an expedition across the Alps. In Italy he was hailed with delight by many, who hoped that he would be able to end the struggle between the Guelf and Ghibelline parties and restore peace. He himself became involved in the party feud, however, and died after three years of fruitless strife.

During all this time, the passing of the imperial crown from family to family (Hapsburg to Luxemburg and so on) with each generation prevented the emperors from taking any consistent steps to strengthen their authority outside their family domains, and even from developing any strong desire to do so. Any move in that direction would have met with strong opposition and would have had to be carried out at the emperor's own expense; for neither princes nor cities could be forced to pay taxes or furnish military service with any regularity. No emperor could afford to undertake seriously such a colossal task, especially since the crown, and whatever increased authority he could give it, would in all probability pass to some other family at his death. Had the monarchy been hereditary, as in France and England, there would have been a stronger incentive to make its power effective. As it was, the chief value of the imperial title was the right it gave the emperors to regrant escheated fiefs—that is, fiefs that had reverted to the crown through lack of heirs. The emperors used this right to enhance their own domains. In the middle of the fourteenth century, the imperial title was given back to the House of Luxemburg (Charles IV), where it remained with one short break for nearly a century.

With unusual realism, Charles IV recognized the futility of trying to establish an effective monarchy in Germany. All that he could do, he thought, was to take steps to prevent further disintegration. He had no confidence in the Diet of the Empire as an institution of government. This body, which was made up of all the princes as vassals of the emperor, was always hopelessly divided and had shown itself to be quite powerless. Charles turned instead to the princely electors, who, he hoped, might cooperate to prevent war and keep order if their own position was sufficiently secure. With this in mind, he published the Golden Bull at the Diet of 1356. The bull carefully defined the method of election and the personnel of the electors so as to prevent further disputes over the imperial title, such as had so often split Germany into warring factions in the past. There were to be only seven electors, including three ecclesiastical princes (the archbishops

The Golden Bull. The entire document was originally fastened together by a silk cord and seal.

of Mainz, Cologne, and Trier) and four secular princes (the count Palatine of the Rhine, the margrave of Brandenburg, the duke of Saxony, and the king of Bohemia). The rest of the bull was addressed to provisions for protecting the power of the electors. They were to have full sovereign power within their states; their territories were not to be divided for any reason; those of the secular electors were to be inherited according to the rule of primogeniture; and the title was to remain attached to the territory.

The Golden Bull was the nearest approximation of a written constitution the Empire ever had, and it was immensely important for the later history of Germany. It prevented many possible civil wars over elections and checked the subdivision of the larger states through divided inheritance, since other princes soon followed the example of the electors in adopting the rule of primogeniture. The electors, of course, gained most from the bull. They became practically independent sovereigns, ruling well-defined territorial states as allies rather than subjects of the emperor.

The elections of Albert II (1438–1439) and Frederick III (1440–1493) of Hapsburg in succession restored the imperial crown to the house of Hapsburg, where it remained as long as the Empire lasted. The change, however, brought about no improvement in imperial policy. The policy of the Hapsburgs was an entirely selfish one; they were interested primarily in their own family fortunes.

The Empire was by this time little more than a geographic designation or, as one contemporary writer put it, the shadow of a great name. The Empire had lost all unity, but this was to some extent compensated for by the growing power of the rulers of territorial states like Austria, Bavaria, Hesse, and the electoral principalities. In these areas the development of strong centralized government and, in some cases, of representative institutions, was very similar to that which was taking place during the late Middle Ages in France and England. The *Landtage* or Estates of Bavaria and Bohemia in particular acquired a share in the government comparable to that of the Estates-General in France. Outside these great principalities, however, all was hopeless confusion. There were a number of ecclesiastical states, ruled by archbishops, bishops, or abbots, and innumerable small territories under the jurisdiction of independent barons or free knights of the Empire, who recognized no superior except the emperor. There were also some sixty free imperial cities, which were independent city-states save for the emperor's nominal authority. In this tangled mass of petty independent jurisdictions there was no single power strong enough to enforce law and order or to protect life and property.

The Hanseatic League, the Teutonic Knights, and Poland-Lithuania

Despite the political disintegration of the Empire and the frequent petty wars that resulted, Germany was on the whole more prosperous than ever during the late Middle Ages. Commerce and industry flourished in the cities. The failure of the central government was undoubtedly a great handicap, but the people of the Empire did not accept a state of anarchy with resignation. Many parts of the Empire were forming independent states or associations. Leagues of knights, districts, and cities were formed for mutual defense, while great territorial principalities guaranteed order within their own borders.

While the Swiss, for example, were forming a confederation for mutual defense on the southern border of Germany, the rich merchant cities of the north were joining in a still more powerful association to protect their commercial interests. The land along the southern shores of the Baltic had been acquired from the pagan Prussians and other tribes and settled by Germans only recently, during the twelfth and thirteenth centuries. Here the emperor's authority had never been strong, and with the decline of the Empire it ceased to function altogether. The merchants in the new German cities of this district, as well as those in the hopelessly disorganized northwestern section of German-speaking portions of the Empire, were forced to depend on their own efforts to ensure their safety when traveling and to secure trading rights abroad. Only by pooling their resources could they maintain a fleet large enough to suppress the pirates who swarmed in the Baltic and the North Sea, or bring sufficient pressure to bear on foreign states to make them grant favorable commercial treaties.

From this necessity grew the league of north German cities, generally known as the Hansa or Hanseatic League. The first step toward such an association had been taken by the cities of Hamburg and Lübeck about the middle of the thirteenth century. Other cities joined them in rapid succession. By the end of the century, the Hansa had secured trading privileges of a very favorable kind in London, Bruges, Bergen, and Novgorod. These cities remained the chief foreign markets for north German trade in England, the Netherlands, Norway, and Russia respectively.

The formal organization of the Hanseatic League, however, was not completed until the middle of the fourteenth century. Even then it was no more than a vague and loosely defined confederation of cities, some seventy in all; the number varied owing to frequent desertions and realliances. The member cities were subdivided into four general territorial divisions: those of the eastern Baltic, the western Baltic, northwestern Germany, and the lower Rhine. In these districts the cities of Danzig, Lübeck, Brunswick, and Cologne were recognized as holding positions of rather vague leadership. On important occasions, representatives of all the cities met to decide questions of foreign policy or to make trade regulations. Despite its loose organization, the league was strong enough to play an important part in the politics of both northern Germany and the Scandinavian countries, and to maintain an almost complete monopoly of the Baltic trade.

Relations with the three Scandinavian countries, Denmark, Norway, and Sweden, were also an important aspect of the history of the Hanseatic League. Since the disintegration of the Danish empire of King Canute in the eleventh century, the Scandinavian countries had taken no active part in European affairs and were in general more backward than their southern neighbors. In the fourteenth century, Denmark was the most active of the three, and an attempt on the part of its king to encroach on Hanseatic trade led to a war with the league that lasted from 1361 to 1370. The league was finally successful, and the Treaty of Stralsund gave the Hansa complete freedom of trade in Danish territory.

For a generation the league dominated Scandinavian politics as well as trade, but toward the end of the fourteenth century its influence was endangered by the union first of Denmark and Norway, and finally of Sweden also, under one ruler in the Union of Kalmar, 1397. The union, which lasted until the end of the Middle Ages, was never a very strong coalition, but it was a standing menace to the Hanseatic monopoly of northern trade.

The history of the Hanseatic League is closely bound up with that of the order of Teutonic Knights. It was these crusading warriors who had made possible the expansion of German colonies and trade to the eastern Baltic by their conquest of heathen Prussia in the thirteenth century. The knights encouraged German peasants, nobles, and burghers to migrate to their newly conquered territory. Numbers of new German cities sprang up along the coast and the riverbanks. Danzig, Marienburg, Königsberg, and a score of others became flourishing commercial centers. They formed one of the quarters of the Hansa, and the league could always count on the knights as allies in its wars with the other Baltic powers. The decline of the order in the fifteenth century was thus a serious blow to the league. By that time, prosperity had begun to undermine the discipline and religious character that had made the knights so effective an organization during their period of conquest. In 1410, the Poles invaded the territory of the knights and defeated them disastrously in the Battle of Tannenberg. The order retained its land for another century, but in a weakened and impoverished condition. A second and more disastrous war with Poland ended in the Peace of Thorn, 1466. The western part of Prussia was annexed to Poland and the Grand Master of the order had to do homage as vassal of the Polish king for the remainder of his territory.

Throughout most of the fourteenth century, the Slavic kingdom of Poland, which was the Empire's largest eastern neighbor, was engaged in a long conflict in alliance with the Teutonic Knights against the heathen Lithuanians, whose territory stretched along the eastern frontier of Poland from the Baltic to the Black Sea. In 1386 this situation changed abruptly. By the marriage of a Polish princess to Jagiello of Lithuania and the election of the latter as king of Poland, the two states were united and Lithuania formally adopted Christianity. The territory of Poland was thus more than doubled and included an outlet to the sea

CITIES IN THE HANSEATIC LEAGUE AND THE DOMAIN OF THE TEUTONIC KNIGHTS, c.1400

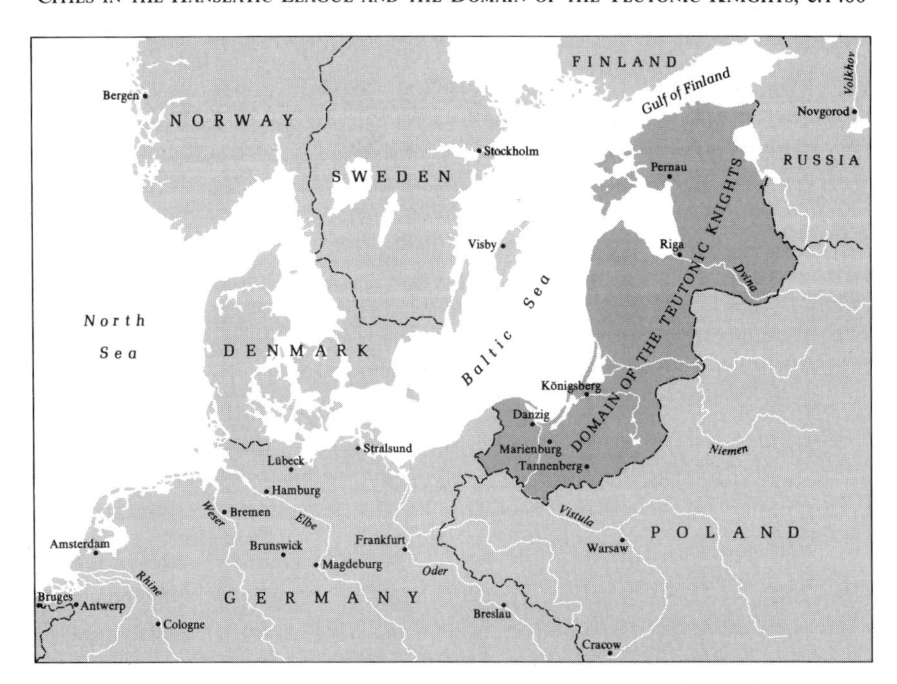

both to the north and the south. The new power of the combined countries was turned immediately against the Teutonic Knights, whose religious rationale for existence had disappeared with the conversion of the Lithuanians.

Poland was now one of the largest territorial states in Europe; but it was never able to make full use of its potential power. It lacked unity and stability. In old Poland the cities had been largely Germanized while the country districts had remained Slavic, and in the new acquisitions the population was a mixture of Lithuanians and Russian Slavs who had little in common with the Poles. Moreover, the elective monarchy and the selfish independence of the Polish nobles prevented the development of a strong central government. Anarchical feudalism lasted in Poland long after it had died out in the western states, just as political decentralization was a fact of life in Germany until the nineteenth century.

Suggestions for Further Reading

G. Barraclough, *Origins of Modern Germany** (1946). The best English-language introduction to medieval German problems [AHA, 183].

O. Halecki, *Borderlands of Western Civilization: A History of East Central Europe* (1952). Useful information on Poland and other areas of east central Europe during the central and late medieval periods.

R. E. Herzstein, *The Holy Roman Empire in the Middle Ages: Universal State or German Catastrophe?* (1966). Translations, with introductory comments and bibliography, of major modern interpretations of the medieval Empire.

E. Kantorowicz, *Frederick the Second, 1194–1250* (1931). The author was a prominent German Jewish writer influenced by the mystic interests of the Stefan George circle of poets and *littérateurs.* The book reflects great learning and an intuitive feel for the subject.

J. W. Thompson, *Feudal Germany,* vol. 2 (1962). Especially useful on German expansion to the east.

*Available in a paperback edition.

Economic Change and Social Conflict, 1350–1500

18

In the name of God and of profit.
MOTTO ON THE LEDGER OF A FOURTEENTH-CENTURY ITALIAN MERCHANT

The Growth of Capitalism in Italy

At the end of the Middle Ages, Western civilization began the worldwide expansion that was to make it the dominant factor in world history until at least the last third of the twentieth century. The economic dynamism of this society took on a recognizably capitalistic form by the late fifteenth century. As old medieval usages fell into decay in many parts of Europe, the entrepreneur and the banker played increasingly important roles in the life of the state. The leader in this development, as in so many other modern phenomena, was Italy. But although it was a pioneer in the development of early modern capitalist forms of business, Italy did not ultimately profit from their introduction as much as did other states in Europe. Those states that faced the Atlantic, rather than the Mediterranean, were to profit most from the expansion of European economy.

Adventurous traders from Venice, Genoa, and Pisa had long monopolized the trade between the eastern Mediterranean lands and western Europe, exchanging western textiles, metals, and other goods for the products of skilled Byzantine and Moslem industry or the still more priceless goods brought by caravan or vessel from the fabulous East. Much of this trade dealt in articles of very high value in proportion to their bulk and weight, so that a single boatload might carry a fortune.

The position of the Italians as middlemen between the East and the West presented unusual opportunities for the accumulation of capital far beyond the merchants' needs for living expenses, capital that could be reinvested in larger enterprises with a view to still larger profits. Many Italian merchants had accumulated great fortunes long before the end of the thirteenth century. They had also begun to work out the basic techniques of commercial capitalism, and, above all, to regard the reinvestment of their profits in larger enterprises as the major aim of business.

The essential element in the growth of Italian capitalism during the late Middle Ages was less the continued expansion of the volume of trade than the further development of capitalist forms of business organization and the perfecting of techniques for the handling of credit, exchange, and large-scale enterprises. One of the important factors that helped to accelerate this change in business practice around the year 1300 was the introduction by the Venetians and Genoese of large galleys for carrying valuable freight. These galleys were seaworthy even in the open ocean, and since they carried both oars and sails, they did not have to wait for a favorable wind to move in and out of port. Moreover, since they usually sailed in fleets and carried large crews, they could repel piratical attacks. Technological advances were important in the development of sea commerce. The introduction of the compass and better cartography were indispensable to long-distance journeys such as that of Columbus at the end of the fifteenth century.

From the beginning of the fourteenth century, galley fleets sailed regularly from Italy to England and Flanders, thereby establishing direct contact with the centers of northern trade and bypassing the Champagne fairs. They also sailed regularly from Italy to Egypt, Syria, and Constantinople. With relatively safe and regular transportation thus established to both the Near East and the West, the Italian merchants gradually ceased to travel with their goods, finding it more economical to stay at home in their counting-houses and direct through correspondence the activity of their partners or agents abroad. The traveling merchant, so characteristic of medieval trade, was thus replaced in Italy by the sedentary merchant, the prototype of the modern businessman. And like the modern businessman, the Italian merchant of the late Middle Ages extended the scope of his enterprise by doing much of his business on credit, and by pooling his capital with that of other merchants in various forms of partnership or corporate organization.

The great banking and entrepreneurial families of northern Europe and Italy in the late Middle Ages were often landholders as well. Land was still the major source of wealth in Europe, and in many ways the successful bourgeois emulated the gaudy aristocracy of the late Middle Ages. The epoch under discussion (c. 1350-1500) preceded by some centuries such modern capitalist phenomena as the divorce of the individual from the land and the concentration of workers in large-scale industries.

The Techniques of Early Capitalism

The temporary partnership was one of the commonest devices by which the sedentary merchant extended his range of activities and minimized his risks. Such partnerships enabled him to engage in a wider variety of enterprises than would have been possible on his own capital and credit alone. However, the form of organization which offered maximum continuity and operating capital was the family firm. Most large operations in international commerce and finance were, in fact, carried on by organizations of this type, which consisted of members of a family group who pooled their resources and worked under the direction of the head of the family. The firm might include relatives by marriage as well as trusted employees who were not actually members of the family. Though acting under the direction of the home office, junior partners frequently took up residence or founded branch offices in the foreign countries with which the firm traded.

Such firms, although essentially commercial, were also active in moneylending, banking, and handling foreign exchange, activities in which a large international organization, reserves of capital, and a well-established reputation

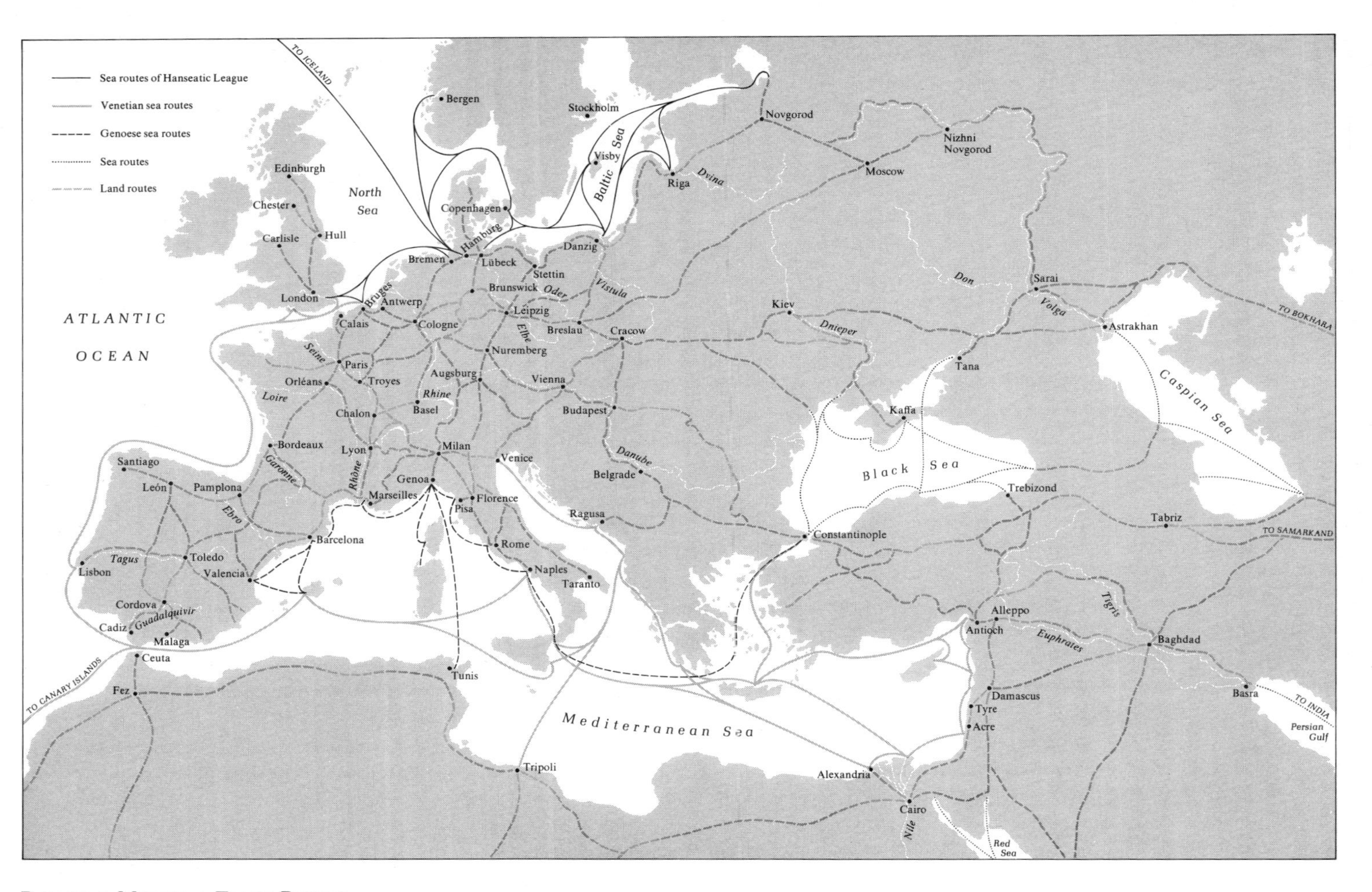

PRINCIPAL MEDIEVAL TRADE ROUTES

were needed. Since a good deal of the business of this period was conducted on borrowed capital, commercial firms and individual merchants were able to keep their surplus capital employed by lending it at interest. The Church's prohibition of usury, or lending at interest, was still in effect, but there were numerous ways of circumventing it. The doctrine of usury had developed in the precapitalist period when there were few opportunities for the profitable investment of money. The theologians who formulated the doctrine, therefore, were not thinking of money borrowed for the purpose of making money. They were thinking chiefly of consumer loans and regarded the charging of high rates of interest for such loans as immoral exploitation of the needs of one's fellow men. With the growth of capitalism this situation changed, but the condemnation of usury was too deeply embedded in canon law to be abandoned. However, popes such as Clement VII, himself a product of the Medici banking family, showed themselves to be tolerant of capitalist practices.

Merchants who needed borrowed capital found ways of circumventing the letter of the law, and moneylending flourished at interest thinly disguised. In addition to commercial loans, the large firms frequently lent money to kings, princes, popes, and prelates. These were usually large loans, which often brought in return commercial or other privileges as well as high rates of interest. They might, however, prove hazardous. Two Florentine firms, the Bardi and the Peruzzi, who between them had lent Edward III of England a million and a half gold florins, were forced into bankruptcy when the king repudiated his debts.

Most of the firms with foreign branches or associates were also engaged in the profitable business of transferring money from place to place by means of bills of exchange. It was frequently necessary for merchants or governments to convey money quickly and safely to distant countries, which they could accomplish by purchasing a bill of exchange from a banker who had international connections. The bill operated very much like a modern bank draft. The money was transferred on the banker's books without any actual shipment of coinage, the banker meanwhile making a profit through his expert knowledge of the rates of exchange between countries using different systems of coinage. The Italians, with their far-flung network of branch offices and agencies and their vast experience, were able to hold a virtual monopoly of this lucrative business until almost the end of the fifteenth century.

The growing complexity of commercial and financial dealings required much more systematic and accurate bookkeeping than had been needed in the early days of the revival of trade. During the fourteenth century double-entry bookkeeping gradually replaced single-entry and in the following century became standard practice among Italian merchants. The double entry under debit and credit, the basic principle of all modern accounting, served not only to simplify bookkeeping but also to point directly to profit or loss on each enterprise and so to encourage more careful calculation of risks.

Opportunities for the investment of capital were considerably more limited in industry than in commerce or finance, since most industrial production was still carried on by master craftsmen who manufactured goods on a small scale and sold them retail across the counters of their shops. In a few large industries, however, where the raw material was imported and the bulk of the finished product exported for sale abroad, the merchants who handled the import-export business found it profitable to assume control of the industry, and thus became industrial employers and entrepreneurs.

Large-Scale Capitalist Industry: Florentine Woolens

Florentine wool-weaving furnishes the most notable example during this period of a large capitalist-controlled industry. It grew rapidly once the establishment of an orderly and dependable sea-route to England enabled the Florentine merchants to import directly the fine English wool regarded as essential for cloth of the highest quality. By 1338, according to Giovanni Villani, the Florentine

Saint Joseph at work as a carpenter, by the Master of Flémalle, a fifteenth-century Flemish painter. A finely detailed view of the city can be seen through the window of the shop.

historian who was himself a wool merchant, there were two hundred woolen-cloth manufacturing firms in Florence, employing some thirty thousand workers, or about one-third of the population of the city. The manufacturers were organized in a special merchant guild, the Arte di Lana, or wool guild, which completely controlled the industry. The division of labor and the variety of skills involved in the production of fine cloth necessitated the development of a highly complex form of industrial organization. The raw wool had first to be beaten, washed, and carded in the merchant's warehouse. It was then given to spinners, mostly women who worked in their own homes, to be spun into thread. The thread was then transferred to weavers, most of whom also worked at home. From the weavers, the cloth passed in turn to fullers, dyers, stretchers, shearers, finishers, and other workers with special skills. Throughout the process the merchant employer retained ownership of the material and paid wages, usually by the piece, to the whole series of workers.

The Florentine wool guild thus differed essentially from the craft guilds, in which independent artisans undertook the manufacture of their product from beginning to end and sold it themselves at retail. The members of the Arte di Lana were not master craftsmen but merchant employers, while the workers were not members of the guild but subject to the guild's authority. The powerful guild could always gain the support of the city government in enforcing its regulations and in preventing the workers from forming any sort of organization to strike for higher wages or better working conditions. The workers, who in the best of times lived on the barest margin of subsistence, seethed with impotent fury in their class struggle against the economic and political powers that oppressed them; at least once, in 1378, they rose in a wild and briefly successful revolt. However, the rising of the Ciompi, as the wool workers were called, was savagely suppressed.

At one end of the social scale, industrial capitalism created a new class of propertyless wage-earners, akin to the modern industrial proletariat, who enjoyed none of the privileges or security that the medieval guild system guaranteed to the craftsmen. By making it possible for men with inherited wealth to invest their money without themselves participating actively in business, the growth of capitalist forms of business organization also created a leisured class, the members of which were free to devote themselves to the learned professions, the cultivation and patronage of literature and the arts, or simply the enjoyment of life. To this leisured class Italy owed much of its brilliant culture, and it owed a special debt to those whose great fortunes enabled them to patronize and support scholars, poets, musicians, and artists.

The Growth of Capitalism in the Netherlands

In the countries to the north of the Alps, capitalism developed later and more slowly than in Italy. The wealth of the northern countries was drawn largely from agriculture. Most northern cities were essentially market towns, serving the needs of the landholding classes of the surrounding countryside. Small-scale production and sale at local markets carried on through guild organization and city regulation much as in preceding centuries. True, some aspects of capitalism were beginning to be manifest even within the retail guilds, especially in the larger cities. During the long recession that occurred after c. 1348, the masters in many guilds set up barriers to the entry of journeymen, other than their own sons or sons-in-law, into mastership so as to avoid undue competition for what remained of the market. Later, when the recovery began and the market was once more expanding, these restrictions were retained, allowing the masters to take advantage of their monopoly to expand their individual businesses.

In some areas, such as Flanders, the urban patriciate which controlled the affairs of the great cities acquired the arrogance of the old feudal aristocracy. Class lines were tightly drawn, and class struggle was common in fourteenth-century Flanders. Throughout the late Middle Ages, the Netherlands (which included present-day Belgium and Holland) were the focal point of northern trade. Early in the fifteenth century, the Netherlands began to benefit from a strange natural phenomenon which greatly undermined the Hanseatic cities along the Baltic: the herring left the Baltic and began to make their home and nesting area in the North Sea.

In the low country ports of Bruges and Antwerp, spices purchased in Cairo might be exchanged for furs brought from Novgorod, and Rhine wines could be

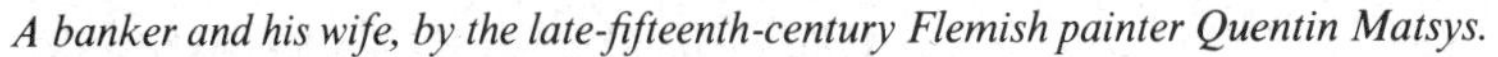

A banker and his wife, by the late-fifteenth-century Flemish painter Quentin Matsys.

exchanged for English tin. These ports were the northwestern terminus of the trade carried by Italian galleys from the Mediterranean, and the southwestern terminus of the trade carried from Scandinavia, North Germany, and Russia by merchants from the cities of the Hanseatic League. They were thus the connecting link in a semicircular trade route that ran from the Levant to the eastern Baltic. They were also the principal outlets for the river-borne trade of northern France and the Rhineland, and the bulk of England's foreign commerce.

This international trade brought great wealth to the Netherland cities, but in the late Middle Ages the merchants of the Netherlands took relatively little part in the carrying trade that radiated from their ports. Instead they conducted a profitable business as brokers or agents for the foreign merchants. This form of business brought prosperity to a fairly large merchant class, but did not as a rule create large fortunes. Even the business of handling foreign exchange, which made Bruges one of the great financial centers of Europe, was left largely to the Italian colony, composed of members of the great Italian banking firms.

The solid prosperity of the Netherland cities depended more on industry than it did on commerce or finance. All through the Middle Ages the Flemish cities, especially Bruges, Ghent, and Ypres, maintained a large wool-weaving industry based on the use of imported English wool. At the beginning of the fourteenth century, the Flemish wool workers revolted and gained the right to organize independent guilds to protect their interests. They also secured a voice in the city governments. But political agitation and economic legislation could not give the workers economic independence. By its very nature, a large textile industry was doomed to control by merchant employers who farmed out the wool to be worked and paid wages to the workers.

Though somewhat better off than the Florentine proletariat, the Flemish wool workers remained in a state of social unrest, and launched violent revolts at intervals throughout the fourteenth century. Toward the end of the century their economic situation was made more desperate by increasing unemployment. The growth of a weaving industry in England, which absorbed more and more of the English wool, caused a decline in the great Flemish industry and finally, in the fifteenth century, reduced it to ruin. Its place was taken, however, by new textile industries in both Flanders and Brabant, which made fine linen cloth, laces, tapestries, and carpets. These new industries, in which no established guilds existed to protect the workers, were organized along completely capitalist lines, being wholly controlled by merchant industrialists. They flourished particularly in the towns and cities that had not been great industrial centers in the Middle Ages and so did not have the firmly established tradition of economic regulation that existed in old cities like Bruges and Ypres.

The Growth of the English Cloth Industry

The economies of England and the Netherlands had been closely interlocked for centuries. The English government tightly controlled the export of wool in order that it might provide funds for the monarchy through heavy taxation. The staple, or warehouse and export control point, for English wool export to the Netherlands assured Flanders of a steady source of wool for its textile industry. But with the development of a widespread weaving industry in England in the fourteenth and fifteenth centuries, the English economy took an important step toward expansion. England became an exporter of woolen products, thus enlarging the vistas of English capitalists and encouraging the development of the shipping trade in England.

An unforeseen result of the staple system was to encourage the growth of this weaving industry in England, since it enabled English manufacturers, who did not have to buy taxed wool, to undersell their Flemish competitors. By the mid-fifteenth century, cloth had almost entirely replaced wool as an export product, and before the end of the century a new regulated company, known as the Company of Merchant Adventurers, was formed to handle the cloth trade with the Netherlands.

During this period England's foreign trade was concentrated increasingly in the city of London. Though a good deal of it was still handled by foreigners, especially Italians and the German merchants from the Hanseatic cities, the greater part had been taken over by English merchants well before the end of the fifteenth century. This phenomenon paralleled developments elsewhere, such as in Russia, where native merchants replaced German Hanseatic merchants in the following century.

These English merchants imported wine from Gascony and a great variety of manufactured goods from the Netherlands; in return they exported wool, cloth, tin, iron, and pewter utensils. Medieval London was a guild-ridden city, and membership in a guild was essential for the conduct of business. With the growth of foreign trade abroad, however, the character of the greater guilds began to change. Wholesale merchants were no longer restricted to dealing in the goods from which their guild took its name. The vintners still handled most of the wine trade, the fishmongers still specialized in fish, the grocers in spices and drugs, and the mercers in silk, fine fabrics, and other luxury imports. But members of any of these guilds might import or export any goods that promised a profit, and they all dealt in cloth.

Meanwhile, within the merchant guilds a clear distinction was developing between the wholesalers, who practiced all the techniques of capitalist enterprise, and the small retail shopkeepers. Before the end of the fifteenth century the wholesalers had formed separate organizations within a dozen or so of the more important guilds. These were known as livery companies because their members wore special and expensive costumes or livery on public occasions. Thanks to their wealth and corporate organization, the merchants of the livery were able to control the policies of the guild and reduce the poorer shopkeepers to subjection.

Mining and Banking in Germany and France

Toward the end of the fifteenth century an extensive and complex form of capitalist enterprise developed in Augsburg, Nuremberg, and other south German cities, largely as a result of a boom in copper and silver mining in the neighboring mountain country. During the Middle Ages, small independent miners had exhausted the veins of ore that could be reached easily from the surface, and after the middle of the fourteenth century production had fallen off.

What was needed to revive it was the investment of sufficient capital to pay for the labor required to sink deep shafts and the machinery to keep them drained and in working condition.

This capital was furnished in the second half of the fifteenth century by commercial family firms, which had grown prosperous from the trade that flowed through Augsburg along the overland route from Venice north to Leipzig and the Baltic ports. Once the copper and silver mines had been put into profitable production, the next step was to organize and control the smelting and metal-working industries and the sale of the finished products. All the various branches of the metal industries thus tended to come under the control of a few great firms of merchant industrialists, while miners and metal-workers tended to lose their independence and sink to the position of a wage-earning proletariat. Interest in mining also involved these firms in state finance. The German princes, including the Hapsburg emperors, claimed certain regalian rights over all mines situated on their lands. These were profitable rights, and the princes, who were perennially in need of ready cash, were frequently willing to turn them over to financiers as security for loans. The great firms with mining interests were thus forced to become moneylenders on a large scale to the German princes; they went on to found banking and finance operations on an international scale comparable to that of the great Italian houses.

The importance of mining in Austria and southern Germany led to a significant scientific interest in its techniques. Agricola produced his famous work on metallurgy in the sixteenth century. Martin Luther's own father was a man of peasant stock who had become a moderately wealthy miner with legal ambitions for his son. The development of capitalism was breaking down old barriers. The use of new technology in the late Middle Ages paralleled the increasingly widespread adoption of Roman law in countries as far-flung as Germany and Scotland. Roman law seemed more suited to the capitalist property concepts of the late medieval period than did the more haphazardly codified and land-oriented feudal law. Furthermore, Roman law could be used in widely separated lands, whereas feudal law tended to be parochial and particularistic.

Of the dozen or so great south German firms which rose to international prominence in the last years of the fifteenth and the beginning of the sixteenth century, the Fuggers were the most famous, though two other Augsburg firms, the Welsers and the Hochstetters, controlled enterprises almost as large and widespread. The great period of Augsburg finance coincided fairly closely with the lifetime of Jacob Fugger the Rich (1459-1525), under whose direction the family became the wealthiest in Europe, with a capital of some 2 million gold gulden. Driven by an insatiable thirst for profit, Jacob expanded the scope of the firm's activity, opening branches in Venice, Rome, Lisbon, Antwerp, Lyon, and other centers, and dealing in commodities of all kinds, in international exchange, and in public and private loans. In 1519 he lent Charles V the half-million gold florins that enabled him to bribe the Electors and win the imperial title.

Aside from lending money to royal governments, these new capitalists found many ways in which service to kings could be profitable. In the late Middle Ages, the rulers of the consolidated territorial states were using every means to increase their revenues by taxation, but the expenses of war and government and the cost of maintaining a splendid court were also rising. Government, in short, was becoming a big business, and neither kings nor nobles had the training to handle complex financial problems with any degree of efficiency. It was natural, then, that rulers turned for aid to the merchants and bankers whose success in business was a guarantee of their financial ability. And it was perhaps equally natural that many of the businessmen who became finance ministers of the crown took advantage of their positions to increase their own private fortunes by means that would not have stood close investigation.

Aside from pure graft, there were fortunes to be made from army contracts, the purchase of supplies for the court, tax-farming, and numerous other more or less legitimate uses of political influence. The spectacular career of Jacques Coeur (1395-1456), the wealthiest merchant of fifteenth-century France, furnishes a classic example of the opportunities—and risks—that royal service offered an aspiring financier. Coeur had already made a great fortune from a wide variety of investments in Mediterranean commerce, copper and silver mining, moneylending, and banking before he became for fifteen years master of the mint and royal treasurer to Charles VII. In this position his fortune increased notably, but he eventually fell from royal favor, having perhaps lent the king too much money. He was condemned on a number of charges, for which there was apparently little foundation, and imprisoned. His wealth was confiscated by the king, who thus simultaneously rid himself of his largest creditor, wiped out his debt, and filled his treasury in one shady transaction. One of the most significant things about the career of Jacques Coeur was his total lack of political power.

Jacob Fugger the Rich and his bookkeeper Matthäus Schwartz in a painting done in 1516 by the bookkeeper. The cabinet in the background bears the names of the cities where branch offices of the great Augsburg firm were located.

Such early capitalists were often totally dependent upon a monarch or other powerful man. The European middle class rarely had direct political power until the end of the eighteenth century.

The Disintegration of the Medieval Agrarian Economy

The rise of a money economy profoundly affected town and country. Both peasants and lords' agents sold produce in the city markets, introducing money into the agrarian economy and gradually changing its internal organization. There were many signs of its disintegration in the twelfth and thirteenth centuries, but not until the late Middle Ages did it change so fundamentally as to be no longer recognizable as feudal.

The Middle Ages witnessed many social revolts by the peasantry, some so widespread and destructive they might almost be called revolutions. To the medieval peasant who had heard of the Garden of Eden and the simple communal life of Christ's early disciples, the worldly splendor of the Church and the inequality of the classes appeared to be travesties of true religion. When preachers such as Wat Tyler and John Ball in England and Arnold of Brescia in Italy combined religious messianism with real social grievances, their impact upon both poor peasant and poor townsman could be revolutionary. Thus, in describing the role of the peasantry in medieval Europe, we should not overlook the times of profound stress and turbulence that marked its history. When peasants revolted, as they did in France in the late fourteenth century during the Hundred Years' War, they often took a terrible toll of their tormentors and masters.

In the thirteenth century, while Europe was colonizing internally and its economy was rapidly expanding, many lords commuted labor service owed them by their serfs in favor of cash payments by the serfs. The service involved farming the lord's demesne. When labor became scarce in many areas, however, wages rose, and many lords could no longer afford the labor needed to farm their demesnes. Such was the case, for example, during the long depression after the Black Death in the mid-fourteenth century. With the commutation of labor services, one of the major props of the old manorial system collapsed. This was the case in many areas of western Europe. Commutation—one vital factor among several others in this situation—opened the way for the development of what we might call late medieval or early modern agrarian capitalism. Gradations of social and economic status among the peasantry became more common in countries such as England and France. The commutation of labor to cash payment was instrumental in introducing money into the agrarian economy, promoting the process we have just described. The growth of capitalism on the land tended, in the long run, to undermine the position of the aristocracy. Most nobles could not compete with the new bourgeoisie in a capitalist economy, and they were further undermined by the expense of their social pretensions.

When the labor services owed by an unfree tenant were commuted, he was a long step closer to obtaining his freedom. Not only was he relieved of the most onerous and degrading duties resulting from his servile status, but it also became much less important to his lord to keep him in bondage. The lord could still require from his serfs or villeins the payment of heriot or merchet and other servile dues, but once he had lost his claim on their labor he was more easily persuaded to sell them their freedom for a lump sum or for an increase in what was now the money rent they owed him for their land.

In this way serfdom disappeared in England, except in occasional rare instances, before the end of the fifteenth century, and though there were still serfs in France and Germany at that time, they were no more than a small minority. The advantages of freedom, however, were often more spiritual than material. The emancipated serf was not necessarily richer, and he was often less secure. But freedom was a boon that could not be measured in economic terms.

On the whole, the economic condition, as well as the legal status, of the peasants seems to have been improving during these last centuries of the Middle Ages. The labor shortage that followed the Black Death put the peasant in a strong bargaining position. The commutation of services to fixed payments also worked to the peasants' ultimate advantage because of a persistent decline in the value of money, due to debasement of the coinage in most European countries. Thus peasants who owed fixed payments rather than labor services were actually paying less and less rent for their land. But improvement in the peasants' lot was neither steady nor uniform. In a transitional period of this kind, some profited and others suffered. Perhaps the most significant result of the collapse of the manorial structure was that the more fortunate or enterprising peasants were able to increase their holdings and become prosperous farmers, while the less fortunate or able lost their land and sank to the position of hired laborers.

The dislocation of the old system created a great deal of social unrest, as much among those who were impatient at the slow improvement of conditions as among those who actually suffered from the changing conditions. The immediate causes for such unrest varied, as did the setting. But unrest was well-nigh universal, and the Peasants' Revolt of 1381 in England was only one of many similar expressions of agrarian discontent during these centuries. In Italy, on the other hand, the great social changes of the late Middle Ages generally took place against a more urban background.

Suggestions for Further Reading

C. M. Cipolla, *Money, Prices and Civilization in the Mediterranean World, Fifteenth to Seventeenth Centuries* (1956). Brief introduction to a complex, major historical problem [AHA, 173].

M. Dobb, *Studies in the Development of Capitalism,* 2nd ed. (1963). Studies by a British Marxist.

F. C. Lane, *Venetian Ships and Shipbuilding of the Renaissance* (1934). Technical study on economic and naval history based on research in the Venetian archives [AHA, 541].

B. N. Nelson, *The Idea of Usury: From Tribal Brotherhood to Universal Otherhood,* 2nd ed. (1969).

R. de Roover, *Money, Banking, and Credit in Medieval Bruges* (1948). Presents a vivid and lifelike picture [AHA, 196].

*Available in a paperback edition.

R. de Roover, *The Rise and Decline of the Medici Bank,** rev. ed. (1963). A major study of the banking practices of Renaissance Florence, relating these to broader problems of the era.

S. Thrupp, *The Merchant Class of Medieval London** (1948). Reference is made primarily to members of the greater companies in the City [AHA, 194, in part].

Renaissance and Reformation

FOUR

Italy and the Papacy During the Renaissance

19

> Greeting: It is possible that some word of me may have come to you, though even this is doubtful, since an insignificant and obscure name will scarcely penetrate far in either time or space.
>
> FRANCESCO PETRARCH, LETTER TO POSTERITY

Renaissance Society

The late Middle Ages witnessed the disintegration or transformation of many institutions of medieval civilization: feudalism, the traditional agrarian economy, Empire and Papacy, and a predominantly religious orientation in art. The urban society of the Italian Renaissance in northern and central Italy pioneered in this subtle transformation from late medieval to early modern politics and culture.

Renaissance, a French word, means rebirth. The term originally signified a rebirth of appreciation of classical Greek and Roman art and literature. To the Italian artists who used it in the sixteenth century, Renaissance meant the rebirth of realistic perspective in painting; to the Italian humanists it signified a revival of the pure Latin used in the Ciceronian age of the Roman Republic. In the nineteenth century historians began to broaden the concept of the Renaissance to include such phenomena as the emergence of egotistical power politics in the Italian city-states. The practice of such politics was unaffected by the theoretical Christian principles of the medieval period. Around 1860 Jacob Burckhardt described the Renaissance as the birth of the esthetic, subjective orientation of modern man. Even as early as the seventeenth century it had become common for historians to divide history into ancient, medieval, and modern periods, the modern period generally commencing in the fifteenth century with the "Renaissance."

Institutions that were typically medieval had never been as strongly rooted in Italy as in northern Europe. The sense of the classical legacy became more pervasive in Italy as a result of the growth of self-assured Italian city-states and communes from the eleventh century.

The Renaissance was characterized by the merchant's quest for profits, the prince's lust for power, the patron's desire to immortalize himself through portraiture, the humanist's rejection of medieval Aristotelianism, and a spirituality centered upon man and his fate rather than upon the medieval divine comedy of Dante and Saint Thomas.

The changes in society brought about by wealth and city life gave rise to equally significant changes in the interests and mental attitude of at least the wealthy and leisured classes. The methods of capitalism demanded literacy of all who engaged in business, while the wealth it produced enabled an increasingly large number of laymen to secure a good education. To a far greater extent than had been possible in the Middle Ages, laymen participated actively in literature and learning, and their worldly interests enhanced the secular content of Renaissance culture. At the same time, the busy life of the cities and the new possibilities for enjoyment of life and the satisfaction of aesthetic tastes and intellectual curiosity provided by luxury, wealth, and leisure tended to push thoughts of religion and the hereafter farther into the background of many people's minds. Growing disrespect for the Papacy and the organized Church heightened this tendency.

The Italian people of the Renaissance, however, were seldom irreligious. Few if any were atheists or even unorthodox. Perhaps they had fallen into the "forgetfullness of God in time of prosperity" against which medieval preachers were wont to warn their flocks. Certainly the world and the flesh had no terrors for this generation, even though they might still fear the devil. This was the extent of the secular spirit of the Renaissance people who threw themselves heart and soul into the full enjoyment and eager exploration of the world about them.

In this vital urban society people awoke to a new consciousness of themselves as individuals. Of the modern characteristics that were making their appearance in this chaotic age of transition, few are more significant or difficult to define than the individualism that so many historians have contrasted to the medieval outlook. People have always known that they are individuals. But in the stratified society of the Middle Ages, in which social status depended on membership in a closed corporation—whether guild, monastery, or manor—or on rank in the feudal system, people were inevitably more conscious of their ordained place in the scheme of things than of their own individual personalities. As the medieval social structure began to crumble, however, careers became accessible to men of talent.

In the rapidly shifting politics of the Italian cities, nobility of birth was not essential to power; the new capitalist methods of business enabled some men to accumulate wealth far beyond that of their fellows; and generous patronage of art raised low-born artists high above the level of the ordinary artisan. There seemed no limit to what any man might accomplish, aided only by fortune and his own ability. In the new secular spirit, too, men found a double incentive for the full development of their individual powers. Immortal fame in this world came to seem more important than immortal life in the next, and the eager enjoyment of all that this world had to offer stimulated men to the development of all sides of their personalities, so as to wring the maximum experience and pleasure out of life.

This new recognition of individual potential brought to life a new social ideal—that of the well-rounded personality—to take the place of the medieval ideal of the man who perfectly represented the qualities of his class or group. It was an ideal that found practical expression in the amazing versatility that characterized so many Italians in the fifteenth century. Statesmen like Cosimo and Lorenzo de' Medici, the bankers who ruled Florence, soldier-despots like Duke Federigo of Urbino, and businessmen like the Florentine Palla Strozzi were also scholars and cultured patrons of the arts, while innumerable examples might be cited of artists who practiced painting, sculpture, and architecture with equal facility and still found time for the pursuit of scholarship and philosophy. Such versatility of interest was not limited to people of unusual genius. The average man or woman of culture now sought consciously to acquire at least an adequate familiarity with all branches of human activity so as to develop his or her personality to its fullest extent.

The Renaissance in Italy was above all an age of confusion and contrast in politics, in religion, in morality, and in individual characters. Medieval and modern characteristics existed side by side in the same society and the same person, producing violent contradictions and startling incongruities. As the fifteenth century drew to a close, the people of Florence, who for years had followed the leadership of Lorenzo de' Medici, most cultured and worldly of statesmen, fell suddenly under the spell of the ascetic monk, Savonarola (1452–1498), only to repudiate and burn him a short while later.

The despots, who ruled by force and cunning, recognized the binding power of no law, human or divine. The development of all man's faculties too often meant the development of the baser as well as the higher instincts. Princes like the Visconti of Milan might combine inhuman cruelty with the most delicate appreciation of art, and artists like Benvenuto Cellini (1500–1570) might be little better than thugs in their private lives. The most enlightened and rational Italian statesmen made policy guided by the auguries of charlatan astrologers. In every court in Italy the veneer of refined and learned society covered dark stains of immorality, and lavish magnificence paraded the streets of every city in glaring contrast to the most wretched poverty.

Evolution of the Italian States to 1494

The Italian Renaissance was born in the midst of political chaos. Italy was not yet a nation in the political sense. Only in the south, in the kingdom of Naples was there any political unity. The rest of the peninsula was divided into small city-states, which had acquired almost complete independence from the overlordship of emperor or pope. Each was torn by hostile factions and was frequently at war with its neighbors. The traditional feud between the Guelf and Ghibelline parties gives slight coherence to Italian politics in the thirteenth and early fourteenth centuries, but that ancient quarrel later lost almost all its original meaning in the tangle of local interests and antagonisms. Cities fought for control of trade routes or to destroy commercial rivals; country districts rebelled against domination by the cities; and within the cities classes and parties fought for control of the government. In the midst of this confusion, two general tendencies may be observed: the destruction of republican governments at the hands of despots and the expansion of the larger city-states at the expense of the less powerful ones. The first of these processes was under way at the beginning of the fourteenth century.

Nearly all the cities of northern and central Italy had begun their independent careers as republican communes dominated by an upper class of mixed merchant and noble families. Toward the end of the thirteenth century, this old ruling class was challenged by the newly rich capitalists and also by the middle class of craftsmen and shopkeepers, so that class warfare and frequent revolutions threatened to destroy the internal peace and order that were essential to the prosperity of business. The only possible solution seemed to be government by a dictator or despot, who would be strong enough to keep order and would impose peace at the cost of political liberty. Some few states, like Venice and Florence, escaped actual despotism, but they were scarcely more democratic, since their government was controlled by a small group of wealthy families. The manner in which the despots acquired their absolute power differed from place to place. Some turned temporary authority, legally delegated to them as officers of the state, into extra-legal power; others were mercenary soldiers or local feudal lords who seized the government by force of arms; still others used their wealth to gain control of the republican governmental machine.

The despots, like men of any other class, differed widely in character, but certain characteristics were common to almost all of them. Most were men of unusual ability and force of character, for only such individuals could have risen to power without the support of legal or constitutional claims. They regarded themselves as above the law and, having broken with all traditional forms of government, they were free to reorganize the state to serve their own wealth and power. They had something of the calculating spirit the new capitalist entrepreneurs. They were often ruthless, cruel, and treacherous, because they had to rule by force and fear. Nevertheless, they frequently gave their cities wiser and more stable government than they had enjoyed under the old republican communes.

As Machiavelli pointed out in his justly celebrated handbook for despots, *The Prince* (1513), it was in the interest of the despot himself to maintain the prosperity of the city he ruled, and no despot could rule for long unless he did so. Most of the despots were intelligent enough to realize that they must win the respect, and, in some measure, the gratitude of their people. This desire, as well as genuine love of culture, caused many of them to lure poets, scholars, and artists to their courts by the promise of generous rewards. No small part of the artistic and literary glory of the Renaissance was due to their liberal and remarkably discriminating patronage.

Machiavelli and other Italian patriots often denounced a phenomenon common throughout Renaissance Italy, the *condottieri.* These mercenary bands of soldiers under the command of famed warriors fought for different princes and despots, switching sides according to the whims of monetary fortune. Occasionally, the condottiere leader won political power for himself. More commonly, these troops ravaged the countryside; they were often more dangerous when in search of an employer than when in the service of one. Certain condottiere leaders have been immortalized in Renaissance sculpture, and their faces are those of hardened, mercenary men, the scourge of Italy. To the *condottiere* war was a business; in this he had something in common with the Italian urban merchant, who was otherwise his opposite.

The expansion of the greater states at the expense of the less powerful ones began later than the rise of the despots and was not completed until the fifteenth century. But by 1454, the year the Peace of Lodi ended the long conflict between Venice and Milan, it had progressed so far that only five great states and some three or four lesser ones remained of the scores that had dotted the map of Italy at the beginning of the Renaissance. Let us examine three of these states: Venice, Florence, and the Papal States.

The great merchant city of Venice, built over lagoons, commanded the Adriatic Sea. Since the revival of long-distance trade in the post-Carolingian age,

Venice had been one of the richest cities in Europe. Its geographic position made Venice the natural middleman in the trade between the eastern Mediterranean and western Europe, while the lagoons which separated the city from the mainland gave it a security that enabled it to remain aloof from the tangled feuds of Italian politics. Moreover, unlike the other Italian republics, Venice had evolved a stable system of government that prevented revolutions and party strife. Since the thirteenth century most of the people had been entirely excluded from the government, which was monopolized by an oligarchy of wealthy families. From these families the doge (president) was elected for life, as were the grand council, the senate, and the powerful council of ten, which after 1310 kept check on the doge and the senate.

Alarmed by the expansion of Milan under the Visconti family in Lombardy, the Venetians early in the fifteenth century changed their policy and embarked on the conquest of a land empire beyond the lagoons. Thus, Venice became more deeply involved in the fickle international politics of the following centuries. By 1454, Venice ruled a mainland state stretching from eastern Lombardy to the Adriatic and was a permanent factor in the uneasy balance of power that prevailed in Italy until the French invasion forty years later.

On the western coast of Italy, to the south of Lombardy, lies the district of Tuscany, bounded on the east and south by the Papal States. This entire territory, except Siena and Lucca, was gradually brought under the rule of the expanding republic of Florence, which conquered even the great mercantile city of Pisa in 1406. Florence had grown tremendously rich from its woolen and other industries. It was also one of the greatest banking centers of Europe and the recognized leader of Italy in all branches of culture. But despite their unusually high level of intelligence and the amazingly large number of men of genius to be found among them, the people of Florence had never succeeded in working out a sound republican constitution. Throughout the fourteenth century and the first

Andrea del Verrocchio's equestrian statue of the condottiere Bartolomeo Colleoni. Commissioned by the Venetian Senate, the bronze monument (c. 1483–1488) stands by the Church of Saints John and Paul in Venice.

part of the fifteenth, the city was a prey to frequent revolutions and party feuds and was dominated most of the time by a small group of wealthy families.

This system caused so much disturbance and injustice that in 1434 the majority of the Florentine people accepted without protest the control of their government by Cosimo de' Medici, whose great banking family was to rule the city for the next sixty years. Florence remained a republic in form, but Cosimo and his successors were in reality despotic rulers. They held no official title and merely controlled the republican machinery from behind the scenes. After thirty years of wise government, which won him the title of *pater patriae* (father of his country), Cosimo died and was succeeded by his son Piero (1464–1469). Under Piero's rather uncertain guidance the power of the Medici seemed to be slipping, but it was fully restored by his brilliant son Lorenzo "the Magnificent" (1469–1492).

ITALY IN 1494

With Lorenzo the prestige of the Medici name reached its apex. He was a man of complex character and versatile genius, at once poet, patron of art and learning, statesman, and diplomat. It was in no small measure due to his diplomatic skill that Italy enjoyed a state of relative peace during his lifetime. His son Piero, however, proved unfit to carry on the family tradition. His weakness in dealing with the French invasion of 1494 roused the Florentine people to drive the Medici out of the city, though they were to return later.

The Papal States stretched across central Italy and included the Romagna, which extended up the eastern coast beyond Ravenna. This large territory was in theory ruled by the pope, but petty despots had established practically independent governments in nearly every city except Rome, and even there the pope was not very secure. The fifteenth-century popes had the task of bringing these independent lords to obedience, no easy undertaking because most of them were professional condottieri. Greater progress might have been made had not some of the popes been more eager to replace the despots with members of their own families than to subject them to papal authority.

Engrossed in these familial and political interests, the Renaissance popes became increasingly worldly until there was little to distinguish them from the other Italian princes. They formed diplomatic alliances, made and broke treaties, and hired armies of mercenaries for wars of conquest or defense. Like the other princes, they maintained luxurious courts and spent huge sums of money on magnificent buildings and patronage of the arts.

The most notorious pope was probably the famous Borgia, Alexander VI (1492–1503). His son, Cesare, did much to strengthen the pope's hold over the turbulent Papal States, and Alexander's successor, the warlike Julius II, built up a strong secular state. The Medici popes, Leo X and Clement VII, were great patrons of the arts. During this era, the Papacy was the degraded plaything of various ambitious Spanish and Italian families; it had become a Renaissance state. In the eyes of many Europeans it was no longer worthy of the great task which Saint Peter had presumably conferred upon it. The crisis of the Papacy had begun much earlier, however.

The Babylonian Captivity of the Medieval Papacy

The Papacy, which popes from Gregory VII to Innocent IV had raised to great heights, reached its point of lowest prestige between the early fourteenth and early fifteenth centuries. It still made universalist claims, which were interpreted in some quarters as assaults upon the authority of secular powers. But its prestige had diminished; in an age of growing territorial monarchies, the universalist claims of the Papacy met with increasingly open and arrogant resistance.

When Boniface VIII (1294–1303) ascended the throne of Saint Peter, he had no reason to believe that the prestige of the Papacy had been in any way impaired. There had been no pope strong enough to put its power to the test since the end of the war with the emperors, and possibly no one could gauge the subtle changes in popular opinion that had taken place in the interim. The character of the new pope was certain to make his pontificate a crucial one in the history of the Church. He was already in his late seventies and had spent his lifetime in political and diplomatic activity. Boniface had been one of the most vigorous and capable of the cardinals, but his great capacities were offset by equally great failings of character. He was arrogant, ruthless, and immensely vain and gave little evidence of deep moral or religious conviction. His policies seem to have been motivated more by personal and familial pride than by devotion to the welfare of the Church. The early years of his reign were spent in crushing the powerful Roman family of Colonna in the interest of his own less powerful house, the Gaetani. At the same time, his love of power drove him to an uncompromising assertion of all those claims to universal supremacy with which his long training in canon law had made him thoroughly familiar.

His conception of papal authority soon brought Boniface into conflict with the kings of France and England. The first crisis arose from the much-disputed question of the relation of the clergy and Church property to the state. In 1296, Philip IV (the Fair) and Edward I were at war and both demanded subsidies from their clergy to help meet the unusual expenses. They argued that the clergy, as subjects of the state, should contribute to the defense of the realm in return for the protection afforded them by the royal government. The pope, on the other hand, asserted that no secular ruler had the right to tax churchmen or Church property. That right could be exercised only by the pope as ruler of the Church. This view Boniface expressed in a famous bull, called *Clericis laicos* from the first two words of the text. The bull forbade the clergy of any country to pay subsidies of any kind to secular rulers without the pope's consent. Philip promptly replied by forbidding the exportation of money from the country; ostensibly a war measure, this decree had the effect of cutting off the papal income from the French Church. Edward also took vigorous action, virtually outlawing the English clergy who refused to pay the subsidies. Faced with this decided opposition, and finding that the clergy would not support him strongly against their king, Boniface was forced to withdraw the bull.

The pope, however, soon recovered confidence. The crushing of the Colonna in 1298 made his position at Rome secure, and in 1300 he celebrated the first jubilee year. Immense crowds of pilgrims—their number has been reckoned as high as 2 million—flocked to Rome to take advantage of the special indulgences and spiritual benefits promised to all who came to the Holy City and contributed to the papal coffers. The success of the jubilee gave Boniface economic independence and an exaggerated confidence in the loyalty of the people to the Church. He was ready again to assert his authority over his royal opponents.

It was the king of France who bore the brunt of the second conflict with the haughty pope. The immediate cause of the quarrel this time was the question of clerical exemption from civil jurisdiction. Philip the Fair had condemned the bishop of Pamiers in Languedoc for treason and other serious crimes, apparently on ample grounds, and asked the pope to degrade him from office prior to the execution of his sentence. As might have been expected, Boniface refused to recognize the right of a secular court to try an ecclesiatic. In December 1301, he called the case to Rome for a new trial, at the same time issuing two bulls, one renewing the prohibitions of *Clericis laicos*, the other taking Philip to task for misgovernment. Feeling that the independence of his government was at stake, Philip decided to make an unprecedented appeal for popular support. In April 1302, he called the first Estates-General and stated his own side of the case to them, with the result that all three estates, including the clergy, addressed letters of protest to Rome.

This opposition merely spurred Boniface to a more extreme statement of his authority, extending the controversy into the wider field of the supremacy of Church over state. The bull *Unam sanctam,* published in November 1302, contained the most absolute statement of supremacy over secular rulers issued by any pope. Most of the arguments were not new, but the whole tenor of the bull was without precedent in its uncompromising force. It concluded with the flat statement that "for every human creature it is absolutely necessary for salvation to be subject to the Roman Pontiff." The bull was followed by an ultimatum to Philip demanding his complete submission under threat of excommunication. The tragic conclusion of this struggle shocked European opinion, for it was consummated in a way that would have been unthinkable a few decades before.

Feeling that submission was impossible, Philip decided that his only alternative was to take the offensive. He called an assembly of the barons and higher clergy of France, before which his ministers accused Boniface of heresy, simony, and a host of other crimes. Meanwhile his chief minister, Guillaume de Nogaret, was dispatched to Italy to arrest the pope and bring him back to answer the accusations of the king before a general council. On his arrival in Italy, Nogaret discovered that the unsuspecting pope had gone to the little mountain town of Anagni to escape the summer heat. The French minister followed him there, accompanied by an armed band raised by the pope's bitter enemy, Sciarra Colonna. They had little difficulty breaking into the town and seizing Boniface, whom they found deserted by his court but arrayed in all the dignity of his pontifical robes. They did not hold him long, for the people of the countryside rallied to his rescue and freed him, but the damage was already done. The aged pope died within the month as a result of shock and chagrin, and with him died the medieval Papacy.

For two years after the death of Boniface VIII, the outcome of his struggle with the French monarchy remained in some doubt. The next pope lived only a few months, and in the long interregnum that followed, Philip the Fair was able to bring sufficient pressure to bear on the cardinals to force the election of a French pope, who took the name Clement V (1305-1314). Clement was in France at the time of his election, and Philip used every means possible to keep him there. The disturbed condition of Italy, torn by the strife of the Guelf and Ghibelline factions, offered the pope an excuse not to take up residence in Rome. Instead, after four years of wandering about France, he established the papal capital at Avignon. There the popes remained for nearly seventy years. The city was not actually in French territory—it was in Provence, then a fief of the Angevin king of Naples—but it was just on the border of France. The popes were doubtless safer there than in Rome, but it was mainly French influence that kept them from returning to their proper home in the ancient capital of Western Christendom.

Clement's acquiescence in crushing the Templars at the request of Philip the Fair, and in other matters, demonstrated the importance to the French kings of keeping the popes at Avignon. And the popes, being French themselves, were willing enough to stay. Twenty-five of the twenty-eight cardinals appointed by Clement V were French, thus ensuring the election of another French pope—and so it continued through seven successive reigns. To some people it seemed that the rulers of the Church were being held captive under the domination of France, whence the term "the Babylonian Captivity of the Church" generally applied to this period in papal history.

Effect of the Babylonian Captivity

Until the middle of the fourteenth century, the strong French territorial monarchy was the dominant power in Europe, the work of successive Capetian kings having increased monarchical authority in a way that was without parallel elsewhere on the Continent. French influence on papal policy was especially evident in the relations of the Avignonese popes with other European powers. During the first half of the fourteenth century, it was the policy of the French kings to keep the Holy Roman Empire weak and divided, in the hope that they might be able to expand their domain eastward at the expense of the imperial lands in the Rhône and Rhine valleys. To this policy Clement's successor, John XXII (1316-1334), lent hearty support, the more willingly because he was eager to restore papal authority in Italy and wanted no imperial interference there. He therefore did nothing to help settle the disputed election between Louis of Bavaria and Frederick of Hapsburg, which had caused a civil war in Germany. Even after Louis won a decisive victory in 1322, John refused to recognize him and ordered him to cease acting as emperor until he had received papal confirmation. When Louis refused to admit the pope's right to confirm or reject a successful candidate for the imperial crown, John excommunicated him. The quarrel dragged on, keeping Germany in a state of unrest, until the death of Louis IV in 1347. John's successors would have been willing to make peace, but were prevented from doing so by fear of the French king.

Meanwhile, in 1338 the German Diet proclaimed the principle that the emperor's election was valid without the consent of the pope. This principle was later confirmed by the Golden Bull of 1356. The popes thus lost one of the rights which supported their claim to supremacy over the emperors, a right which their medieval predecessors had asserted vigorously and used on more than one occasion as a pretext for interfering in imperial affairs.

John XXII, like other Avignonese popes, actively furthered Christian missions. John believed the most immediate threat to Christendom to be Turkish and Islamic. The Mongols' great conquests in the East in the thirteenth century seemed to offer an opportunity to Christianity. If Christian missions could convert the Mongol ruler or khan to Christianity, Islam would be outflanked and Christendom would be dominant in the world. Thus by the end of the thirteenth century Christian missionaries, usually Franciscans, were traveling to the East in a promising but ultimately vain attempt to convert the Tartars. John XXII carried on this work.

The heavy weight of papal taxation aroused grave discontent in the countries outside France. In England it led to open opposition on the part of the government, for the English kings, who were at war with France, felt an especially keen resentment at seeing so much English money going to a French pope. Edward III even went so far as to protest that "the successor of the apostles was commissioned to lead the Lord's sheep to pasture, not to fleece them." Papal provisions, or appointments, to English benefits were particularly unpopular because they were so often given to officials at the papal curia and other foreigners. In 1351, Edward III had Parliament pass the Statute of Provisors making this practice illegal. Two years later he sought to curtail papal interference in England still further by issuing the Statute of Praemunire, which made the appeal of cases from the local ecclesiastical courts to the papal court illegal without the king's consent. In the long run, however, these statutes had little effect save to force the popes to share some of the spoils with the king.

More serious, however, than the opposition of state governments was the popular discontent aroused by the demoralization of the clergy as a result of the financial and administrative policies of the Avignonese popes. As time went on it became increasingly clear that the Papacy was losing both popularity and prestige, and that this was due in part to the continued residence of the popes at Avignon, which had become a symbol of all the papal abuses of the age.

A brief visit to Rome by Pope Urban V in 1367 ended in disillusionment. Ten years passed and a new pope was elected before the project was renewed. At last, in 1377, Pope Gregory XI decided to make the long-deferred move, lest Rome and the Papal States should be lost beyond recovery. He was welcomed with delirious joy by the Roman populace.

The Great Schism, Heresy, and the Councils

No one could have foreseen that the death of Gregory early in 1378 would plunge the Church into a situation infinitely worse than any that had preceded it. The papal court was scarcely settled in Rome when a new pope had to be elected. The majority of the cardinals, who were French and homesick for Avignon, undoubtedly wanted another French pope. The Roman people, on the other hand, were determined to keep the Papacy now that they had recovered it, and they clamored wildly for a Roman pope, or at least an Italian. The election was held amid scenes of mob violence that terrified the cardinals.

They hastily chose an Italian, who took the name Urban VI (1378-1389). Urban was a Neapolitan who had risen to the rank of archbishop through the favor of some of the French cardinals at Avignon. But if the cardinals hoped that he would be grateful and thus amenable to their control, they were bitterly disappointed. From the first he treated them with a brutal contempt that led some observers to suspect his sanity. Finding their position intolerable, the cardinals withdrew from Rome and held a new conclave. Declaring the election of Urban invalid because it had taken place under threat of violence, they elected in his place a French cardinal, Clement VII (1378-1394). The new pope with his cardinals then returned to Avignon.

In Rome, meanwhile Urban excommunicated Clement and the rebellious cardinals, and appointed twenty-eight new cardinals of his own. There were now two popes and two colleges of cardinals, and the people of Christendom were faced with the problem of deciding whether the pope at Rome or the pope at Avignon was the true successor of Saint Peter. The Church was split from top to bottom and the schism was not to be healed for nearly forty years.

The validity of the elections of Urban VI and Clement VII might honestly puzzle any impartial observer. The various states of Europe, however, made the choice of adherence to one or other mostly on political grounds. Italy—with the exception of Naples, which was traditionally allied with Avignon—rallied to the Roman pope. France, naturally enough, recognized Clement. National enmities and alliances dictated the positions of the other powers. Scotland, Spain, and those of the German princes who were friendly to France adhered to Clement, while England, Flanders, Portugal, the Empire, and the Scandinavian countries gave their obedience to Urban.

The schism had disastrous effects on both the prestige of the Papacy and the spiritual health of the entire Church. The rival popes thundered against one another, denying each other any claim to authority, so that conscientious people did not know which way to turn. Rival claimants fought over ecclesiastical offices, and the clergy everywhere was demoralized. Moreover, both popes were in desperate need of money, since each could draw revenues only from the part of the Church that adhered to him. As a result, all the financial abuses of the captivity were multiplied, with correspondingly evil effects. Popular discontent was redoubled and criticism of the clergy and the Papacy became bolder.

The growth of open heresy in England and Bohemia demonstrated in the most forcible fashion the disastrous results of the schism of the Papacy. But even without that object lesson, the evils of the schism were so apparent that laymen and clergy in all parts of Christendom realized that it must be brought to an end lest the whole structure of the universal Church be destroyed. The popes and cardinals on both sides loudly proclaimed their eagerness to end the schism, but none was willing to make the first move or to sacrifice his position. Even the deaths of the original schismatic popes did not bring about reconciliation, for new popes were elected to fill their respective places. Under such circumstances, the only hope of decisive action seemed to lie in a general council which could coerce the popes.

The hope of effecting significant changes through such a council proved somewhat chimerical. In an age of rising territorial states, national political jealousies prevented coordinated attempts at political reform, and clever popes were able to play off one faction in the council against another. Though councils might be useful in solving particularly embarrassing problems, such as the existence of more than one pope, they proved useless in the attempt to effect general ecclesiastical reform. Any sustained cooperation, except against a particularly glaring heresy that appeared to threaten everyone, was quite beyond their capacity.

Eventually, a group of cardinals met and took upon themselves the responsibility of summoning a general council to meet at Pisa in 1409. Despite the doubtful legality of the council, an imposing array of churchmen attended. The first act of the council was to depose the two reigning popes, the Roman Gregory XII and his rival Benedict XIII. The cardinals present then proceeded to elect a new pope, who took the name Alexander V. The latter, however, died within a few months and was replaced by Cardinal Baldassare Cossa as "John XXIII," an able but unscrupulous man who had risen to prominence by methods more worthy of an Italian despot than a churchman. Meanwhile, Gregory and Benedict had refused to accept their deposition and had both found some support in the conflicting interests of the European states. The council had merely made matters worse. Instead of two popes there were now three!

This impossible situation lasted five years. Emperor Sigismund found the only solution by asserting his right as Roman emperor to call a council of the Church, as the great Constantine had done at Nicaea. The new council, attended by representatives from all parts of the Roman Church, assembled at Constance in 1414. After much negotiation the three popes were deposed or forced to abdicate, and in 1417 a Roman cardinal of the Colonna family was elected as Martin V (1417–1431). The schism was ended and the Papacy was restored to Rome. In dealing with other pressing problems, however, the council was less successful. The attempts of the council to reform the abuses in the Church, which had grown during the period of the captivity and the schism, were almost fruitless. The council did, however, issue two very important decrees, one asserting the superiority of a general council over the pope, the other providing for the convocation of future councils at frequent intervals.

In this conciliar theory, the Council of Constance left a legacy dangerous to the authority of future popes, but on the whole its action strengthened rather than weakened the Papacy, at least insofar as it restored the pope to Rome and left him without rivals. Martin V and his successor Eugenius IV (1431-1447) were able to establish themselves in a position of some political security in the Papal States, to regain some measure of control over the clergy, and, in the long run, to withstand the menace of conciliar authority. In this they were aided by the political weakness of the greater European states.

Martin V and Eugenius IV did much to restore the papal authority, but the popes were still far from regaining the powers they had possessed before the fall of Boniface VIII. Never again could they exercise effective supremacy over secular rulers, and even within the Church their control was limited by the practical power of the great state governments. This was particularly true in France where, in 1438, King Charles VII published a law, the Pragmatic Sanction of Bourges, which set definite limits on papal interference in ecclesiastical elections, papal taxation, and appeals to Rome. In short, it established a sort of national church under the control of the French monarchy. The governments of England and Germany took less radical action, but were moving in the same direction, and later the Spanish monarchy gained almost complete authority over the Church in Spain. Much of the papal victory in the investiture struggle evaporated by 1500.

The Literary Renaissance in Italy

While the Papacy was becoming an Italian state, the foundations of an Italian national literature were being laid. This literature gave Italy a language that served as a bond of unity never achieved in the political realm. Some signs of this development are evident in the last years of the High Middle Ages, in the adaptation to Italian uses of forms taken from the lyric poetry of southern France and in the synthetic court language fostered by Frederick II in Sicily. But the close relation between spoken Italian and Latin, which was the general literary medium, as well as the great variety of dialects spoken in the numerous Italian states, had prevented the growth of a universal Italian literary tongue. Literary Italian was largely the creation of three fourteenth-century writers who were sufficiently typical of their age and confident in their own creative genius to abandon old traditions and strike out on new paths.

Dante, Petrarch, and Boccaccio were the triumvirate who created the literary language of modern Italy. All three were Florentine by descent, although the first two were exiles, and they used the Tuscan dialect as the basis of their literary language. In other respects, however, they were very dissimilar, and the differences in their characters are illustrative of the gradual drift away from medieval modes of thought.

The first and greatest of the three, Dante Alighieri (1265-1321), seems to belong more to the Middle Ages than to the Renaissance. The idealized love poetry of his *Vita Nuova* is nearer to the troubadour tradition of medieval

Provence than to the worldly verses of the Renaissance poets. His greatest work, the magnificent *Divine Comedy,* presents, in its breathtaking voyage through hell, purgatory, and paradise, a panoramic survey of medieval thought.

The second of the triumvirate, Francesco Petrarca, or Petrarch (1304-1374), was considerably less medieval. His introspective absorption in his own personality, his longing for immortal fame, and the intensely human quality of his lyric poems addressed to Laura, together with his passionate interest in classical antiquity, mark him as a man of the Renaissance. His influence on the forms of Italian poetry, especially the sonnet and brief *canzoniere,* is second only to Dante's, whose use of the Tuscan dialect he reinforced and purified.

We should not establish a false dichotomy between medieval spirituality and Renaissance secularism. Petrarch revolted against medieval styles in a quest for *spiritual* sustenance. He rejected the Aristotelian Aquinas in favor of the Platonist Augustine, and turned away from Aristotle because of the materialism that had been read into the Greek philosopher by certain students of the Arabic Averroist school. There is something modern and romantic in Petrarch's unbridled literary exploitation of his own personality, but his quest was an ethical and spiritual one, not to be confused with the rampant materialism of later, modern ages.

The chief contribution of Giovanni Boccaccio (1313-1375) was the shaping of an Italian prose style. Lacking the depth of character and spiritual insight of his two great fellow citizens, this amiable and worldly Florentine burgher was perhaps more typical of his city and his age than either of them. He observed the surface of life with keen enjoyment and described it with a clarity that made the stories of his *Decameron* models for later novelists and motion-picture directors.

The rapid development of Italian literature was cut short with the death of Petrarch and Boccaccio, and it was not revived again until the second half of the fifteenth century. The new language could not compete with the amazing revival of interest in the classic literature of ancient Rome. Even Petrarch and Boccaccio were far more interested in their Latin than in their Italian writings, and for two full generations after their death Latin thrust the vulgar tongue completely into the background.

The Latin classics were not a discovery of the Renaissance. Many were in common use, though chiefly as models of grammatical construction, throughout the Middle Ages; but the deep chasm which separated medieval ideals from those of pagan antiquity made any real understanding of the ancient writers impossible. In the fourteenth and fifteenth centuries, however, there was growing up in Italy a society, essentially urban, secular, and based on wealth, which was not far removed from the civilization of ancient times, though it was not yet nearly so perfectly formed. It is not surprising, then, that Italians of this age should discover a new meaning in the classics. In these pre-Christian writings they found a culture that seemed to embody everything for which they were blindly groping. They applied themselves with devout enthusiasm to the study and imitation of antiquity, inspired by the conviction that the road to progress lay in a return to the glorious past that had preceded what they considered the Gothic barbarism of the Middle Ages.

The men who devoted their lives to the study of the classics were called humanists, that is, those who sought to acquire *humanitas.* The word "humanism" is based upon a German term coined in the early nineteenth century. By the fifteenth century the humanist was a man who had a firm grasp of classical Latin and knew something about ancient thinkers such as the Stoics and Cicero. Humanism might also mean an appreciation of nature and society, of the arts, and of the individual personality and its potential. There was no necessary conflict between humanism and Christianity. Indeed, most humanists continued to think of themselves as Christians, and some went so far as to try to harmonize the wisdom of Socrates and that of Christ.

The humanists were indefatigable workers. They were driven by their reverence for antiquity to undertake the double task of restoring the works of classical authors to their original form and perfecting their own knowledge of classical Latin style, including correct spelling, inflection, syntax, and scansion, which had been almost forgotten during the Middle Ages. The only copies of the ancient authors they could find were the work of medieval scribes, who were often careless and ignorant of the niceties of grammatical construction. Every manuscript was filled with errors. The humanists had, therefore, to learn the rules of classical grammar from the study of imperfect manuscripts and then to apply the knowledge they acquired to the correction of the errors. This could be accomplished only by constant and painstaking comparison of all the manuscripts available and led to a frantic search for old manuscripts. Petrarch led the hunt and inspired his friend Boccaccio and others to take it up. Monastery libraries were ransacked and every new fragment was greeted with delirious

Sandro Botticelli's painting The Birth of Venus *(c. 1480), an example of Renaissance interest in classical pagan antiquity. According to a Greek myth, Venus emerged from the foam of the sea and was wafted along the waves to the shores of Cyprus by Zephyr, the west wind. On land, she was greeted and dressed by Spring.*

enthusiasm. Often the searchers found that they were too late, for many old monastic foundations had degenerated and their libraries had been allowed to moulder from neglect.

The revival of ancient Greek literature in Italy occurred later than that of classical Latin. Knowledge of Greek had died out completely in the West, and it was hard to find instructors who could teach even the rudiments of the language. The beginning of the revival may be dated from 1397, when a competent Greek scholar from Constantinople, Manuel Chrysoloras, was persuaded to come to Florence to teach. In the fifteenth century the humanists of Italy eagerly absorbed all the Greek classics, but they reserved their greatest enthusiasm for the philosophy of Plato, made available for the first time in its original form. Cosimo de' Medici even found time amid his manifold duties to found a Platonic Academy in Florence.

Not all the humanists were inspired literary figures. By the sixteenth century many were political hacks who for a price ground out polemics against the enemies of their patrons. Humanist rhetoric became increasingly stylized and bombastic, and most scholars agree that between the sixteenth and the nineteenth centuries the further development of an Italian national literature suffered because of the humanistic preoccupation with Latin classical form and precious rhetoric. Yet the humanists performed a service of immense and lasting importance to modern civilization by making the body of ancient literature fully available, and as a by-product of their philological studies they developed an independent critical spirit which was carried over into other fields. However, they were often as prone to accept without question the validity of anything found in the ancient writers as their medieval predecessors had been to accept the authority of the Bible, the Church Fathers, and Aristotle.

By the opening of the sixteenth century, Italian was also beginning to hold its own with the ancient languages as a medium for serious prose. The works of Niccolò Machiavelli (1469–1527), the shrewd Florentine historian and political theorist, have furnished every European language with a synonym for the cynical sacrifice of moral means to political ends. Like most educated Italians of his generation, Machiavelli was well versed in the classics. His original ideas, however, were based on his own observation of Italian politics during some fifteen years as a secretary and diplomat in the service of the Florentine republic. When the Medici returned in 1512, he was driven into exile, and in the following embittered years he wrote his most famous book, *The Prince.* Here he analyzed, with little regard for medieval Christian moral considerations, the methods by which a prince might rule successfully. His maxims, illustrated with references to the ruthless policies of Renaissance princes such as Cesare Borgia, have both shocked and fascinated generations of readers.

The Artistic Renaissance in Italy

The great unknown medieval artists responsible for the stained-glass windows of Gothic cathedrals and the sculpture around their portals were masters of naturalistic art. Indeed, they reveled in the realistic delineation of flora and fauna. This isolated naturalism was displayed, however, within the Christian context of the Gothic cathedral, and the medieval artist was a craftsman working within a corporate endeavor. His naturalism was not meant to stand by itself as a tribute to either the genius of the artist or the realism of his work. It was a portrayal of one part of the creation, undertaken to give meaning to the spiritual totality that was Gothic architecture. We do not know the names or histories of many medieval artists or sculptors, but the aesthetic and creative individualism of the Renaissance has left us a rich panorama of knowledge about individual artists.

In the late Middle Ages and the Renaissance, the development of a wealthy educated secular society with a keen interest in artistic portrayal of the beauties of this world gradually changed the status of the artist and the conditions affecting his art. The artist of outstanding and immodest genius was in great demand. He might receive from princes, merchants, and bankers rewards far beyond those of the ordinary artisan. His name and the individual character of his work became assets of high value. Working for men who were losing their respect for medieval traditions, the artist was free to strike out along new lines and to develop his individual genius to its fullest extent.

Of the major arts, painting was most characteristic of the Italian Renaissance and was developed to the highest degree of perfection. Until almost the end of the period, Florence was the greatest center of painting, as well as of literature

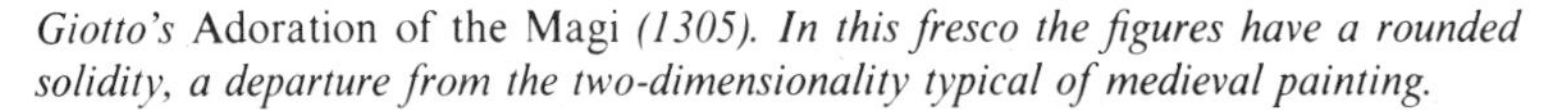

Giotto's Adoration of the Magi *(1305). In this fresco the figures have a rounded solidity, a departure from the two-dimensionality typical of medieval painting.*

and most of the other arts. There, in the opening years of the fourteenth century, Giotto (1276–1336) took a long stride away from the stiffly formalized Byzantine technique of earlier religious painting toward greater naturalism. Throughout the rest of the century his successors moved steadily in the direction he had indicated, though their work was still primarily religious and they had not yet acquired the technical knowledge or skill required to accomplish their objective fully.

The fifteenth century was a period of adventurous experimentation and rapid progress in technique. Art was increasingly devoted to secular subjects, although religious themes still predominated. Driven by the desire to copy natural beauty and the outward appearance of men and women as accurately as possible, the fifteenth-century artists mastered the laws of perspective and shadow, discovered how to give their figures modeling and depth, and greatly improved methods of blending colors. Their figures stand freely and easily in three-dimensional space. Portrait painting, the result of the desire to be remembered by posterity, became for the first time a fashionable art form. The rediscovery of Roman, and to a much lesser extent, Greek painting led Renaissance artists and their biographers to assume that this new three-dimensional, aesthetic phenomenon represented a continuation of the classical tradition. Actually, it was something quite new, reflecting the technology and spiritual needs of a different age.

The generation of the great masters of the High Renaissance spanned the end of the fifteenth century and the beginning of the sixteenth. The first of these was the Florentine Leonardo da Vinci (1452–1519), the most versatile man of his age. He was a master of all arts, a poet and a musician as well as a practical

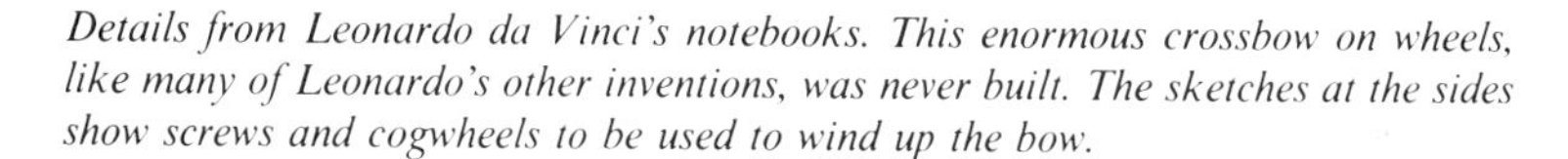
Details from Leonardo da Vinci's notebooks. This enormous crossbow on wheels, like many of Leonardo's other inventions, was never built. The sketches at the sides show screws and cogwheels to be used to wind up the bow.

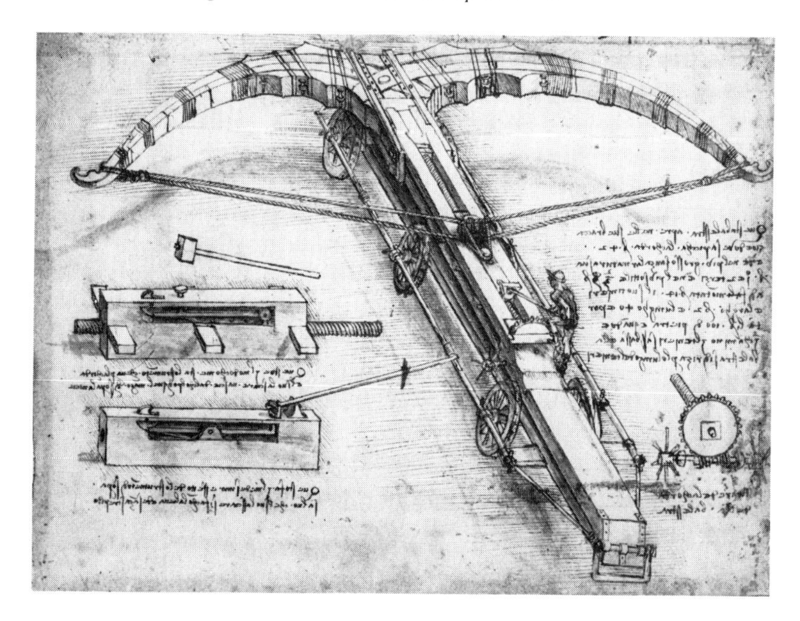

engineer and an experimental scientist of the first rank. This enigmatic genius had a driving curiosity that impelled him to discover what lay beneath the surface of things. His *Mona Lisa,* whose mysterious smile has puzzled and fascinated generations of spectators, and the disciples grouped about Christ in *The Last Supper* are studies in character as well as works of compelling beauty.

It was Pope Julius II who early in the sixteenth century subsidized some of the best work of Michelangelo (1475–1564), having persuaded him to turn from sculpture to painting for the decoration of the Sistine Chapel. The result was a magnificent fresco, covering the entire ceiling of the chapel, which for all time secures Michelangelo's place among the master painters. In it, as in everything he did, one can see the tragic driving force, the grandeur of design, and the deep religious emotion that make Michelangelo both unique among the artists of the Renaissance and an example of the contradictory drives of the Renaissance itself.

Suggestions for Further Reading

H. Baron, *The Crisis of the Early Italian Renaissance: Civic Humanism and Republican Liberty in the Age of Classicism and Tyranny** (1966). A crucial, sophisticated work on a critical period of Italian humanism and politics (c. 1400). Baron has a thesis to present, and it relates to the legacy of classical thought in terms of its living political and moral relevance to the men of the Renaissance.

M. B. Becker, *Florence in Transition* (1967). A study by a major American Renaissance scholar.

B. Berenson, *The Italian Painters of the Renaissance** (1968). A sensitive aesthete and gifted historian of art and culture, Berenson is a pleasure to read. He is always stimulating and sometimes brilliant.

G. A. Brucker, *Florentine Politics and Society, 1343–1378* (1962). An important scholarly monograph on a key Italian city during a time of social strife and economic change.

J. Burckhardt, *The Civilization of the Renaissance in Italy** (1958). This is one of the books that molded modern Renaissance studies. It is a work of art and views the Italian Renaissance as such, seeing analogous style in social life, politics, and art. Every educated person should read it. Burckhardt was a Swiss scholar who lived in the late nineteenth century.

W. K. Ferguson, *Europe in Transition, 1300–1520* (1963). The best contemporary survey of the Renaissance and Reformation eras.

J. R. Hale, *Machiavelli and the Renaissance* (1963). A brief but effective introduction to the Italian Renaissance.

P. O. Kristeller, *Renaissance Thought: The Classic, Scholastic, and Humanistic Strains** (1961). Kristeller is a leading contemporary historian on the intellectual currents that dominated Italian thought in the fifteenth and sixteenth centuries. His presentation is clear, his thought incisive.

G. Mattingly, *Renaissance Diplomacy** (1955, reprinted 1971). The best work in the English language on the techniques and major themes of Italian Re-

*Available in a paperback edition.

naissance diplomacy. Mattingly knew the Italian archives as did few other scholars, and he had a writing style that many of us envy.

G. Mollat, *The Popes at Avignon, 1305–1378* (1963). Detailed, highly regarded study of the Avignon papacy.

E. Panofsky, *Renaissance and Renascences in Western Art,** 2nd ed. (1965). Erwin Panofsky was one of the most scholarly, productive art historians of the twentieth century.

B. Tierney, *Foundations of the Conciliar Theory* (1955). Good exposition of the theory of Church government [AHA, 188].

W. Ullmann, *The Origins of the Great Schism* (1948). Masterful work by a distinguished student of medieval Church history and political theory.

The Waning of the Middle Ages in the North

20

> Dost thou adore the bones of Paul preserved in a shrine and not adore the mind of Paul made manifest in his writings?
>
> DESIDERIUS ERASMUS

Decay of Feudal Institutions

The period of transition from medieval to modern civilization began later in northern Europe than it did in Italy, and once begun it developed more slowly and along somewhat different lines. In the north, feudalism was more firmly entrenched behind its moats and castle walls; religion lay closer to the hearts of people far removed from the classical beauty of the sun-drenched Italian land; and in the quadrangles of Oxford and the dusty halls of the Sorbonne, the ghosts of Thomas Aquinas and Duns Scotus walked undisturbed, long after Italian scholars had deserted them to follow the still older ghosts of ancient Greece and Rome. But throughout northern Europe the same leaven was at work that had transformed society in the more prosperous south. Commerce and industry were creating wealth and with it thriving urban centers and an aggressive, self-confident new middle class whose energy was to disrupt medieval society. Yet the product of the transformation was not altogether the same as in Italy, for in the north cities were fewer and farther between, and the new society was to find its political focus in the centralized territorial state rather than the city.

In the fifteenth century, feudalism was fading fast. Some of its economic and social forms would survive for three centuries and more, but of its independent existence as a political force there remained only a shadow by the beginning of the sixteenth century. As in Italy, it was the power of money that wrecked the older forms of society. But in the great territorial states of the north, the influence of money was less direct; there it worked through the growing power of the rulers of the states, and the state absorbed feudalism into itself.

Throughout the Middle Ages, the political independence and privileged position in society of the nobles had depended in large part on their exclusive monopoly of the arts of warfare. But in the fifteenth century the introduction of gunpowder as an effective instrument of battle and siege placed a weapon in the hands of common men which enabled them to meet the heavily armored knights on relatively even terms. At the same time, the increase in the amount of money available through taxation and loans gave the rulers of the states a tremendous advantage over the less wealthy nobles in the use of this new and expensive weapon. Incomes sufficient to pay troops also freed monarchs from the necessity of depending on the services of their feudal vassals. The kings of great states like England, France, and Spain, and even the princes of smaller territorial states such as those of Germany, could now raise and maintain armies composed largely of common soldiers, against which the nobles were helpless. As early as the fourteenth century, the English kings had used the plebian longbow to good effect and demonstrated the superiority of a disciplined army over a feudal levy on the fields of Crécy and Poitiers. The use of gunpowder made the state army a universal institution. Unable to ignore or oppose their king, the nobles enlisted in the royal army and took the king's pay. They still fought, such being their nature, but they fought at the bidding of the twin powers of monarchy and money.

In yet another way, money—or the lack of it—was working to deprive the nobles of their cherished independence. While the businessmen, who were beginning to discover the profitable uses of capital, and the monarchs, who were acquiring greater powers of taxation, were growing wealthier, the nobles were becoming poorer, for the feudal system had never been designed to produce fluid wealth. Confronted with failing resources and rising expenses, the nobles were forced to seek aid from the royal purse. And the kings were well content to aid them with pensions, sinecure offices at court, or positions in the army and Church, thereby establishing a system of patronage that made the nobles more dependent than ever upon them. The feudal noble, in short, was becoming a royal courtier.

The decline of political feudalism left the rulers of the territorial states without serious rivals. Economic and social factors had contributed to this outcome, but from the constitutional point of view it was accomplished by a double process of consolidation of territory and centralization of governmental authority in the hands of more or less absolute princes. The growth of France as a united monarchical state is the most perfect example of this dual process. The French monarchy during the Hundred Years' War won the right to tax all its subjects directly, going over the heads of the feudal lords. For a time the Estates-General had seemed a possible rival to royal power, but when feudalism collapsed, the Estates proved too weak to exercise an effective check on the authority of the king. With variations due to differences in their past histories, most of the other states of Europe were undergoing a similar development as the late Middle Ages drew to a close.

Religious Revolt and the New Piety

The decay of feudal institutions was not the only major social change of the time. Religious life in the north was in the throes of a massive crisis: a movement for renewal was taking place. The leader of the movement in England was John Wyclif, a distinguished scholar and professor at Oxford. His first protests against papal supremacy and the wealth of the clergy, published in 1375, won him the friendship of John of Gaunt, who was already acting as regent for the aged Edward III. They also elicited an official condemnation from Gregory XI in 1377. The scandal of the papal schism, which occurred in the next year, prompted Wyclif to a more fundamental and far-reaching attack on the whole ecclesiastical system. Like the later Protestant reformers, whose doctrines he foreshadowed, Wyclif appealed to the authority of the Bible against that of canon law or the customs and dogmas of the medieval Church. He felt that the ills of the Church, most of which sprang from the wealth and temporal power of the clergy, could be cured only by a return to the simpler life and teaching of the early Christians. It was the duty of the state to disendow the clergy when they failed to use their wealth for spiritual ends.

Relying on the authority of the Bible, Wyclif denied the validity of pilgrimages, the veneration of saints, and the power of the clergy to grant absolution for sins, and even attacked the fundamental doctrine of the material presence of Christ's body in the sacrament of the eucharist. His doubts regarding the sacramental power of the priests, especially those who were living in sin, struck at the very heart of the Church's power over the lay world. However, Wyclif was traveling too fast for the thought of his age. It was only the weakness of the Papacy and the doubtful support of John of Gaunt that enabled him, after he had been expelled from Oxford, to pass his last years in peace as a parish priest at Lutterworth. Wyclif died in 1384. His followers, called Lollards, preached his doctrines throughout England for some years until they were stamped out as dangerous heretics by Henry IV. But Wyclif's trenchant criticism of the Church could never be wholly suppressed. Many of his ideas were to be asserted again at a more favorable time by the Protestant reformers of the sixteenth century, and in the meantime his teaching had spread to the distant land of Bohemia, where it received an enthusiastic welcome.

The movement for reform of the Bohemian Church in the early years of the fifteenth century was not entirely due to the influence of Wyclif. For some time before they learned of him, reforming preachers had been protesting the wealth and immorality of the Bohemian clergy, which seems to have been unusually corrupt. It was Wyclif's teaching, however, that provided the great Bohemian reformer John Huss with the weapons he needed to gain popular support for his attack on the Church. Like Wyclif, Huss was a scholar and professor—he taught at the University of Prague—but he was less a theologian and more a conscious teacher of his nation than the English reformer. To his moral indignation against the corruption of the Church was added a strong patriotic resentment of the German clergy, which had secured most of the important posts in the Bohemian Church. This combination of views made Huss popular among the native Bohemians and a dangerous opponent of the Papacy and the Empire.

In 1414, Huss was summoned to appear before the general council called by Emperor Sigismund at Constance to answer charges of heresy. He was tried and condemned and after refusing to recant was burned at the stake in July 1415. The emperor had treacherously repudiated the safe-conduct he had given Huss. The burning of Huss made it impossible to reconcile the Bohemian rebels to the Church. The Hussites formed a separate sect, fiercely loyal to the memory of their martyred hero. Their resistance ended only after years of furious fighting, and then only as a result of compromise on the part of the Church.

In the fourteenth and fifteenth centuries there developed a powerful movement of awakening piety in Germany and the Netherlands which was to have a strong influence on both the Renaissance and the Reformation in the North. But it was not piety of a kind to strengthen the loyalty of the people to the organized Church. This movement originated with a group of religious mystics who, though orthodox sons of the Church, cherished ideals that were not altogether in keeping with its practices, and strove to transcend, without repudiating, its mechanical organization.

From our vantage point, the important effects of this revival of mysticism were, first, the increase in fervid piety in an age that had begun to take religion for granted and, second, a growing indifference to the sacramental system in an age when that system, though of vital importance to the authority of the Church, was becoming formal and mechanical in its operation. The mystics did not doubt the necessity of the sacraments, as did the Lollards and some other heretics. But they placed less emphasis on their importance. The mystics' aims were too personal and immediate for them to rely much on formalized observances, or to feel the need of a priest to act as an intermediary between the individual soul and God.

The new mysticism began in Germany. Its influence on popular piety came about through the work of Johann Tauler (c. 1300–1361), who preached to the common people and gained a wide hearing. Unlike most preachers of the time, he did not represent salvation as the aim and end of religion, but emphasized the love of God as an end in itself. To this end any person, no matter how poor or ignorant, might aspire through simple faith, prayer, and purity of life. This was a kind of mysticism within the comprehension of the masses. Tauler was the leader of a group known as the Friends of God, who did a great deal to raise the

John Huss being burned at the stake as depicted in an early-fifteenth-century German chronicle.

standards of German morality and piety. The essence of the mystics' teaching was published toward the end of the fourteenth century in a little anonymous volume which Luther, who admitted its great influence on his thought, named *The German Theology.*

In the Netherlands, mysticism flowered later and exercised a more direct influence on the thought of the new age. Here as in Germany it produced one great book, the *Imitation of Christ* by Thomas à Kempis, written in the first quarter of the fifteenth century and still popular after more than five hundred years. The doctrine of this most widely read expression of the new piety, or *devotio moderna,* as it was called, was very simple: he who would be a true Christian must live as Christ lived, think as he thought, and imitate him in every possible way. This was an ideal with which the Church could not quarrel, yet this aspiration ignored the elaborate system whereby the clergy was made indispensable to salvation. In the Netherlands too the mystics formed a society, known as the Brethren of the Common Life, devoted to the education of boys. Throughout the fifteenth century, their schools, especially the large school at Deventer in Holland, were important in spreading the new learning of the northern Renaissance, and did much to shape the ideals of many of the most influential humanists.

The Renaissance Crosses the Alps

Religious inspiration was a more important factor in the work of northern humanists than of their Italian predecessors and counterparts. Northern humanists were more interested in the uses of ancient Greek for a better edition of the Bible than were the Italian humanists. Northern painters tended to use Florentine techniques and Venetian colors to portray a spiritual quest and torment that reflected the unique contradictions of a changing society. There was mutual borrowing in oil techniques, however, and the Florentine school derived some of its skill in oils from Flemish painters. If the pagan Roman spirit had never completely died out in Italy, the northern pagan gods of the skies and the earth had never completely vanished from the heartland of Germany. The quest for salvation was more obvious in the work of the painter Albrecht Dürer, the humanist warrior Ulrich von Hutten, and the great humanist scholar Desiderius Erasmus than in the ethereal classicism of the painting of Botticelli or the eclectic intellectualism of the great Italian humanist Giovanni Pico della Mirandola. The contradictions of late medieval northern society inspired the intellectual and spiritual quest of many Germanic souls: among these contradictions were the tradition of the Holy Roman Empire, the crises of the Church, and the social upheavals and dislocations caused by the rise of capitalism in metallurgy and agriculture.

The spread of the new classical learning in the north was greatly aided by the rapidly increasing use of printed books, which followed the invention of movable type by Johann Gutenberg of Mainz about the year 1447. The effects of the printing press on the general intellectual development of Europe can scarcely be overestimated. Its immediate effect on the spread of humanism in the north was to place the classics and the writings of Christian antiquity at the disposal of all who could read them, at a moderate price, and to afford the humanists themselves a far wider audience than would have been possible before. Hitherto all books had been written by hand and were often inaccurate as well as expensive. Even in Italy manuscripts were scarce and dear. In the north, where there were proportionately fewer wealthy bibliophiles and where the distance between libraries was greater, the study of ancient writings would have presented enormous difficulties. The spread of the Reformation after 1517 would have been much slower had it not been for the printing press. Typical publications of this age were polemics and woodcuts disputing Martin Luther's theology.

The northern humanists had all the reverence for antiquity and all the scorn for the Middle Ages that were characteristic of their Italian counterparts. But above all—and this was their unique contribution—they found in the Scriptures and the writings of Christian antiquity a simple, vivid religion, which they felt had been distorted by long centuries of involved theological argument and buried beneath the accumulated mass of medieval Church tradition. It was their task to restore this early evangelical faith in all its purity.

In Germany, the outstanding leader of the new movement was Johann Reuchlin (1455-1522). He had studied in Italy and after his return to Germany devoted his life to the study of Hebrew as an aid to the understanding of the Old Testament. As a preliminary step Reuchlin published the first Hebrew grammar north of the Alps in 1506, a work of great service to the new scholarship. His open opposition to a scheme for the suppression of Hebrew books caused him to be charged with heresy by the inquisitor of Cologne, backed by the Dominican teachers in the university there. The resulting trial, which lasted six years, roused a storm of controversy. It was one of the first cases in which both sides appealed to public opinion through the medium of the printing press. On Reuchlin's side

A Florentine printer's shop, from an engraving made around 1570. Workers at the left are sorting and setting type. At the rear of the shop, one man inks a press, while at the right another lowers a press to print.

were the humanists; on the other side were the monks and conservative theologians along with the converted ex-Jew Pfefferkorn.

In their literary debate, the humanists, equipped with a far superior Latin style, had the best of it. When argument failed, they resorted to ridicule with devastating effect. One work in particular remains an immortal monument to the wit of the humanists. *Letters of Obscure Men,* written anonymously early in the sixteenth century by one of the young humanists at the University of Erfurt, is still good reading for its hilarious humor and biting satire. It takes the form of a series of letters addressed to one of Reuchlin's principal opponents, presumably by his humble admirers. Written in comically barbarous Latin, the letters ex-

Knight, Death, and Devil *(1513) by Albrecht Dürer, a fine example of the art of copper engraving, developed soon after the invention of printing to illustrate books. The subject was apparently suggested by Erasmus'* Manual of the Christian Soldier.

posed the ignorance, superstition, and naive gullibility of the obscure monks and priests who rallied to the defense of tradition. A supplement, even more bitter, appeared shortly after from the pen of the bellicose German knight and poet, Ulrich von Hutten.

By far the most influential of all the Christian humanists was Desiderius Erasmus of Rotterdam (c. 1469–1536). He more than anyone else formulated and popularized the reform program of Christian humanism. Erasmus was born in Holland, educated by the Brethren of the Common Life in their school at Deventer, and entered a monastery at an early age. However, he soon escaped from that narrow environment and thereafter led a wandering existence, living for years in France, England, Italy, Germany, and Switzerland, equally at home wherever there were learned men who could converse with him in the classical Latin that was almost his mother tongue. Not until the time of his first visit to England in 1499, during which he met the great humanists John Colet and Thomas More, who became his lifelong friends, did he turn seriously to the religious studies that were to occupy his attention for the rest of his life.

The chief aim of Erasmus' work in religious thought was the restoration of Christianity to its early simplicity as taught by Christ and His disciples. This conception of religion made a thorough understanding of the original meaning of the Scriptures necessary. Erasmus believed that the Vulgate, as the official Latin version of the Bible was called, could not be entirely trusted, since it was a translation and had been repeatedly recopied, making errors possible. Erasmus, therefore, undertook the task of editing the Greek text of the New Testament from the earliest available manuscripts. After years of labor he finally published it, with extensive annotations, in 1516. This was the first time that the New Testament had been printed in its original language. The conservative theologians, accustomed to accepting the Vulgate as the final authority and largely ignorant of Greek, were profoundly suspicious of the new edition and attacked Erasmus bitterly.

Meanwhile, Erasmus was also working busily for the reform of the practices in the Church that seemed to him out of harmony with the Christian spirit. He had a devastatingly satirical wit and had early discovered that ridicule can sometimes be a more effective weapon than heavy argument. Because of his command of Latin style, wit, and humor, everything he wrote was widely read. In his reformism and learning Erasmus typified intellectual northern Europe on the eve of the Reformation.

Suggestions for Further Reading

H. S. Bennett, *The Pastons and their England** (1951). A rich portrait of late medieval England, using as the source the famous Paston Letters.

J. L. A. Calmette, *The Golden Age of Burgundy* (1963).

M. P. Gilmore, *The World of Humanism, 1453-1517** (1952). A well-written, broadly inclusive study. Gilmore is especially effective in presenting the social and theological background of the Lutheran revolution. A volume in the Rise of Modern Europe series edited by William L. Langer.

*Available in a paperback edition.

J. H. Hexter, *More's Utopia: The Biography of an Idea* (1965). Hexter uses More's famous work as a way of presenting the intellectual history of an important humanist and his era.

J. Huizinga, *Erasmus and the Age of Reformation** (1957). A highly readable, scholarly study by the great Dutch historian.

J. Huizinga, *The Waning of the Middle Ages** (1955). A work of genius; the Dutch scholar has portrayed the decaying age of chivalry in stark colors. Huizinga, like Burckhardt before him, had the ability to portray an entire age through the ideals and traumas reflected in its art and stylized life-forms.

A. Hyma, *Brethren of the Common Life* (1950). Fine study of the background of humanist Christian reform in northern Europe before the Reformation.

H. Kaminsky, *A History of the Hussite Revolution* (1967). The Hussite rebellion was really a social, national, and theological revolution. It threw central Europe into a revolutionary turmoil that prepared the way for the dramatic events of the Reformation a century later.

P. M. Kendall, *Louis XI* (1972). Masterful study of the mysterious but effective "Spider King," Louis XI, a French monarch whose work laid many of the foundations of the old regime.

P. H. Lang, *Music in Western Civilization* (1941). Highly readable, detailed social history of music. A standard reference work.

G. Leff, *Heresy in the Later Middle Ages,* 2 vols. (1967). An interesting, detailed study of late medieval heresy, with attention paid to its social and ecclesiastical environment.

M. M. Phillips, *Erasmus and the Northern Renaissance** (1950). Good, brief introduction to the northern Renaissance.

The Reformation and Counter Reformation

21

I neither can nor will recant anything, since it is neither right nor safe to act against conscience. God help me. Amen.

MARTIN LUTHER AT THE DIET OF WORMS

Saint Dominic did this; I, too, will do it. Saint Francis did this; therefore I will do it.

SAINT IGNATIUS LOYOLA

The Torment and Triumph of Martin Luther

Desiderius Erasmus was a man of moderate temper. He could never accept the break with Rome heralded by Martin Luther in 1517. Erasmus wished to reform and purify Christianity, in terms both of the Church and of the Scripture, and to reconcile Socrates and Christ, but he did not want a religious or social revolution. Like most other humanists, Erasmus the intellectual detested the violence and social turbulence which might put an end to his quiet studies.

The most devout churchmen recognized that reform of the Church was necessary and hoped to bring it about in ways that would leave the outward structure intact. They were too late. Before they could accomplish anything, the explosive forces of the new German patriotism of the knights and the statism of the princes, the new ethical and moral interests of the bourgeois class, and the new humanistic piety, combined with old grievances against Rome and discontent with the clerical system, were ignited by the fiery preaching of Martin Luther. The resulting explosion split the ancient Church beyond all hope of reconstruction. What occurred was a religious revolution, generally referred to by historians as the Protestant Reformation, or simply the Reformation.

In 1516 Erasmus greeted the accession of the Medici pope, Leo X, as a joyous occasion for humanist reformers. In a famous letter to the new pope, he expressed the sentiments of this group when he argued that a fundamental reform of the Church was necessary. It is ironic that on the eve of the Protestant Reformation the moderate humanist reformer was reduced to appealing to this son of a wealthy Florentine banking family in the name of ecclesiastical reform. Erasmus was unrealistic in his hopes.

By the second decade of the sixteenth century, Germany was ready for a religious revolution. All that was needed was a leader who would unite men of varied interests and show them the way. That leader was Martin Luther (1483-1546). Luther's parents were Saxon peasant folk, stern, hard working, pious, and somewhat better off than average, for they were able to give their son an excellent education. In 1501, at the age of eighteen, young Martin entered the Saxon university at Erfurt. For four years, he studied the nominalist philosophy that still dominated the old school, but he also read the classics and talked to an enthusiastic group of young humanists known as the Erfurt poets. Having completed his course in the faculty of arts, Martin began the study of law in accordance with the wishes of his practical father.

The psychoanalyst Erik Erikson, in his famous study *Young Man Luther*, has suggested that Luther's abrupt decision to enter a monastery in 1505 was an overt sign of a crisis of early manhood through which the twenty-two-year-old Saxon was then passing. For the next twelve years Luther was tormented by a sense of his own unworthiness and by fear of damnation. His solution to this problem, the doctrine of justification through faith alone, came to him only toward the end of his dozen years of existential agony. Luther's tortured quest for a sense of certainty (or identity) was the motivating force behind the theological tracts he published from 1517 onward.

Luther was ordained a priest, and in 1508 he moved to the house of his order at Wittenberg to teach at the new university recently founded there by the elector of Saxony, Frederick the Wise. There followed nine years of outwardly peaceful academic activity, during which Luther lectured to students, preached in the castle church, and began to acquire a considerable local reputation. But quiet though they seemed, they were years of mental turmoil for the young friar, until the discovery of the doctrine of faith brought peace to his soul and, before long, strife to all Christendom.

Since his entry into the monastery, Luther had been tormented by the fear than nothing he could do would be sufficient to merit salvation. Indeed, it was this fear that lay behind his sudden decision to become a monk. Luther had acquired from the peasant environment of his childhood a conception of God as a stern, unforgiving judge, and he had accepted the current teaching of the Church that salvation depended on good works, which included observance of the sacraments, prayer, fasting, and, if one would be sure, the ascetic practices of monasticism. But, though he devoted himself to an excessive asceticism, Luther still found no assurance that he had merited salvation. Saint Augustine's suggestion that only those who are predestined to receive divine grace will be saved further shook his faith in his own efforts. Who can know that he is among those chosen?

The answer to all Luther's problems came to him suddenly from the reading of a verse in Saint Paul's Epistle to the Romans on which he was lecturing to the university students. It contained the phrase, "The just shall live by faith." Luther had often read it before, but now he saw in it a new meaning—that man may be justified, i.e., saved, by faith and by faith *alone*. Doubtless only those predestined for salvation are given faith, but to possess faith, which is the means of salvation, is also to possess the conviction that one will be saved. It took some time for Luther to work out all the logical consequences of his doctrine, for he was not a systematic thinker. Eventually, however, he was forced to conclude that, if faith alone is needed for salvation, the good works of the Church, fasts, pilgrimages, and even the sacraments, are unnecessary, and that no one is dependent upon the services of pope or priest for his salvation.

With these ideas running through his mind, it was inevitable that Luther should begin to criticize some of the practices of the Church arising from the doctrine of good works. As it happened, the issue that first aroused him to open protest was represented by the papal indulgence proclaimed by Pope Leo X to obtain money for the construction of St. Peter's Church in Rome. The granting of indulgences had been a common practice in the Church for more than two centuries; it was an integral part of the Church's scheme of salvation and had become an important source of papal revenue. In theory it was an elaboration of the penitential system, the origins of which date back to the early days of the Church. Following confession and proof of contrition, the sinner received absolution for his sins through the sacrament of penance. He was then free from the guilt of sin and the fear of eternal damnation. But he still owed further atonement in the form of penance or punishment in this world and, after death, in purgatory. The first indulgences or remissions of further penance were granted by the popes, acting as the successors of Saint Peter, to the crusaders. Later, pilgrims and other penitents earned indulgences, until in the fourteenth century the Avignonese popes set the precedent of accepting money payments as constituting good works.

To Luther, however, convinced that faith alone could save people from the consequences of sin, it seemed clear that indulgences were not only useless but actually harmful, for people were encouraged to put their trust in something that could be of no help to them. He felt bound to issue a warning. As the simplest method of securing a hearing, he prepared a list of ninety-five theses or propositions on the subject and announced his willingness to defend them in public debate. Following the usual academic practice, he posted these theses on the church door at Wittenberg where all could read them, and he awaited developments. To his surprise the theses aroused a perfect furor of interest. They were

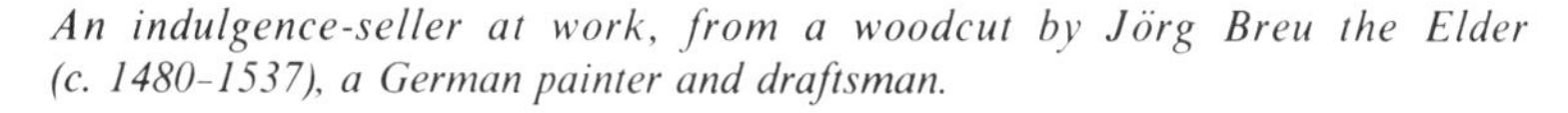

An indulgence-seller at work, from a woodcut by Jörg Breu the Elder (c. 1480–1537), a German painter and draftsman.

soon printed and circulated all over Germany. That they convinced their readers was attested to by a sharp decline in the sale of indulgences.

In 1517, Luther had no thought of breaking away from the Church, but the events of the next three years forced him step by step away from it. In order to meet the arguments of the papal legates who were sent to demand that he recant, he had to work out his ideas to their ultimate conclusion. Almost against his will, for he had a natural respect for authority, the Wittenberg friar was forced to realize that his beliefs were contrary to many of the doctrines of the Church and that there was no place for him within the Roman communion. He had, however, found in the Bible a firm support for his convictions, and resting on that divinely inspired authority he confidently defied the authority of the pope.

Leo X was delayed in taking decisive action against Luther by what seemed to him the more important business of the imperial election in 1519. This hotly disputed election worked doubly to the advantage of Luther: his prince, Frederick the Wise, was able to secure from the future emperor, Charles V, as the price of his support, a promise that the rebellious friar would not be condemned without a hearing before the imperial Diet. This meant further delay, and Luther used the time to good effect by writing a series of pamphlets to publicize his beliefs and win the support of the German people. He was amazingly successful. The *Address to the Christian Nobility of the German Nation on the Improvement of the Christian Estate* was a stirring appeal to German patriotism against the tyranny of Rome. In it he called on the German princes to reform the Church and outlined a comprehensive program.

Luther's appeal fell upon fertile ground. German patriotism had been growing in the preceding few decades. It focused on the old imperial idea and on a humanist revival of interest in the supposed virtues of the ancient Germans. It was popularly believed that Germany was the "milk cow" of the Papacy—that is, that the virtuous Germanic nation was being bilked by the greedy, decadent Roman Papacy. The contrast between sturdy German virtue and corrupt Romanism remained embedded in the German consciousness well into the twentieth century.

In a second pamphlet, *The Liberty of a Christian Man,* Luther explained in popular fashion the practical implications of his doctrine. These two pamphlets, directed primarily to laymen, were written in forceful German and so reached a far wider audience in Germany than they would if they had been written in the Latin normally used by scholastics and humanists for serious discussion. The invention of printing from movable type immensely aided Luther in his quest for popular allies. Luther reverted to Latin, however, in a third pamphlet, *The Babylonian Captivity of the Church,* a more scholarly exposition of his views on the sacramental and sacerdotal system, designed to appeal to a more learned audience of clerics trained in theology.

When at last Luther was summoned to appear before the Diet of the Empire at Worms in the spring of 1521, he went with the assurance that he had the sympathy of the majority of the German people. He was at the height of his popularity. All who nursed grievances against the Church or hoped for reform wished him well, for the split in the Church had not yet proceeded so far that it was necessary to take definite sides. Nevertheless, it took real courage to walk into the lions' den, with the fate of John Huss at Constance representing a warning of what might happen. It was a dramatic moment when the Saxon peasant friar faced the assembled dignitaries of state and Church and firmly refused to recant. The next day he left Worms. Within a few days he was proclaimed an excommunicated heretic by the Church and an outlaw by the Empire. But by that time Luther was safe in the castle of the Wartburg near Eisenach, where he had been taken on the orders of Frederick the Wise.

Luther passed a year in enforced leisure, which he put to good use by translating the New Testament into German. The Old Testament he translated later, completing it in 1532. Since his whole program rested on the authority of the Bible as against that of Church tradition, it was essential to Luther's success that the Bible be readily accessible to the people. The importance of his German Bible can scarcely be overestimated. It has often been called the most powerful Reformation tract, and it had almost as much influence on the development of the German language as on German religion. Luther was a master of his native tongue, and his Bible was as important to the standardization of German as was Dante's *Divine Comedy* to that of Italian.

The peaceful interlude in the Wartburg marked a turning-point in Luther's career as a reformer. Hitherto he had been a sturdy rebel against Church authority and a champion of individual liberty of conscience. He was now to become the organizer of a church of his own and an increasingly conservative defender of established authority. Returning to Wittenberg in the spring of 1522, he began at once the task of reconstruction. His first action was to moderate the extreme changes put into effect by some of his more radical followers during his absence. Luther then set about the business of organizing a new church on as conservative a basis as possible. In the Lutheran Church, as it finally took shape, a good deal of Catholic doctrine and practice was retained. Nevertheless, changes of vital importance were made.

In accordance with Luther's denial of the doctrine of good works and hence of the validity of the sacramental and sacerdotal system, all of the sacraments were abolished except baptism and the Lord's Supper, which are specifically mentioned in the Bible, and even these lost their status as good works. Pilgrimages, fasts, veneration of saints and relics, and the other traditional practices based on the doctrine of good works were also rejected. The clergy, no longer considered to have special sacramental powers, were permitted to marry and live the lives of ordinary men. The monastic orders were entirely dissolved. Luther himself married a former nun, fathered children, and lived out his days happily with his wife. Thus was broken down the barrier that had separated the clergy from the laity and made it a separate caste with unique privileges. Finally, the Lutheran Church, in everything save questions of belief, was placed directly under the control of the state government. The superintendents, who replaced the bishops, were practically state officers.

Luther had not intended to establish a new church, much less one so completely under the administrative control of the various German states. His work was altered by circumstances, some of which were apparent even before Luther's death in 1546. Luther's early dependence upon the Saxon state as his sole ally in the struggle against pope and emperor was thus fateful, if inevitable. The subsequent reliance of the Lutheran Church upon the various German states brought about a close alliance between organized religion and political authority, thus thwarting the sense of individual freedom that large elements of the German nation might otherwise have developed. While the reliance of the Lutheran Church upon the state is not the sole reason for the strong authoritarian strain in modern German history, it certainly did not deflect German politics from this evil path.

Within Luther's lifetime, nearly half of Germany officially adopted his

Church. The princes found in it a valuable support for their governments, while the burghers discovered in Luther's teaching a moral and ethical ideal as well as an individual spiritual life more in harmony with their character than those provided by the medieval Church. The victory of Lutheranism was in part the triumph of the territorial state over the universal Church, but it was also the triumph of a new lay-bourgeois ethic over the feudal-clerical-monastic ideals of the Middle Ages. Not the least important result of the Reformation was that the good citizen—the pious layman who was a good spouse and parent, honest, hard working, and thrifty—supplanted the ascetic monk or nun and the crusading knight as the ideal Christian.

The founding of Lutheran state churches inevitably caused grave political complications in Germany. Church and state were too closely united to admit of any degree of religous tolerance. The Lutheran princes claimed the right to determine the religion of their states as Catholic rulers did, and when at the emperor's dictation the Diet of Speyer in 1529 passed a resolution denying that right, the Lutheran princes drew up a formal protest. It was as a result of this that they came to be called Protestant, a name later applied to other non-Catholics. Shortly thereafter, both Lutheran and Catholic princes formed leagues for mutual protection, and Germany was divided into two armed camps.

Frederick the Wise shielding Luther (far left), Zwingli (right, wearing cap), and other leaders of the Reformation, a painting by Lucas Cranach the Elder dating from 1530.

Protestantism and Class Warfare in Germany

How did Lutheranism affect different social groups in Germany? In the case of the free imperial knights, a resurgence of German patriotism often merged with humanist objections to the Church, as in the works of Ulrich von Hutten. This class of knights had been pushed to the wall by economic developments in late medieval Germany. The free imperial knights, small landholders and free-lance warriors, were theoretically responsible to no one but the emperor, but with the rise of commercial capitalism and strong territorial princes, not to mention technological changes in the nature of warfare which promoted the use of mercenary armies, the free knights were in grave difficulty. As imperial knights responsible to the Empire rather than to any particular city or prince, men like Von Hutten and Goetz von Berlichingen were natural bearers of the German patriotic idea. They were anti-Roman and potential allies of German reformers in their struggle against the Holy See. Despite their impressive titles, the imperial knights were generally a pauperized class by the time of the Reformation. They were closer to the common people in their humor and their legends than were the great patrician burghers, the territorial princes, or the imperial court. The knights absorbed and disseminated the kind of ribald anticlericalism that the English writer Geoffrey Chaucer had earlier displayed in his *Canterbury Tales.* The free knights, now largely Lutheran, rose in revolt early in the 1520s, but they were crushed by their more powerful lay and ecclesiastical enemies.

The Lutheran Church was scarcely founded before it lost the support of another and larger class, the German peasants and poor city workers, who were alienated by Luther's conservative attitude toward the great social revolution which swept across Germany in 1525. The Peasants' War, as it was called, was a general rising of the downtrodden peasants, frequently joined by the discontented working classes in the towns, to demand justice and relief from crushing economic and social burdens. This uprising had been foreshadowed by a long series of similar revolts, extending over the preceding two hundred years and becoming increasingly frequent after the turn of the sixteenth century. The earlier risings, however, had been confined to limited districts. What made this rebellion at once more general and more radical was that the peasants had found, in Luther's assertion that the Bible is the only real authority, a justification for revolt and a program of social reform that would unite the discontented elements of different parts of the country in a common movement. Their dream of restoring the social conditions of evangelical Christianity was impractical, but it gave the necessary religious coloring to their demands. Beginning in Swabia, the revolt spread rapidly through central and southern Germany. For a time the old order seemed seriously threatened.

Luther was as alarmed as the princes at this revolt against established authority. With a singular lack of sympathetic insight, he urged the peasants to remember the biblical injunction to obey the magistrates. Then, when they refused to listen, he called on the princes to crush and slay the "thievish, murderous hordes of peasants." The lords needed no such encouragement. The revolt was put down with appalling savagery. The peasants and artisans sank back into a hopeless economic slavery and no longer looked to Luther for guidance.

In Germany the revolt unleashed by Luther's actions gave rise to a great variety of sects, which differed widely in creed as well as in moral and social teaching. Nevertheless, they shared a few common characteristics, and since most of them refused to recognize the validity of infant baptism and insisted on rebaptizing their converts, they were known collectively as Anabaptists. They refused obedience to the state church and sometimes to the state. They founded their doctrine, whatever it might be, on a literal, unhistorical interpretation of the Bible with a view to restoring the simplicity of primitive Christianity. They were cruelly persecuted everywhere by Catholic and Protestant states alike. Fanatical they may have been, but they were deeply pious, and their history is ennobled by an inspiring record of heroic constancy in the face of persecution. Despite every effort of the persecuting state churches, they continued to exist, and their modern descendants are to be found in the Baptist, Mennonite, Moravian and other churches.

The Anabaptists, who generally came from the lower classes, combined religious messianism with social revolution. Whereas Martin Luther was profoundly conservative in his views on the social order, men such as John Leyden and Thomas Muenzer were religious and social revolutionaries. Indeed, when Karl Marx's closest collaborator, Friedrich Engels, wrote his book *The Peasant Wars in Germany* in the early 1850s, Luther emerged as a hypocritical upholder of the social status quo, while Thomas Muenzer was portrayed as a visionary revolutionary who wished to unite oppressed urban and rural classes in a struggle against the establishment.

Zwingli and Calvin in Switzerland

Luther's doctrine seems to have been peculiarly suited to northern Europeans. Outside of Germany and Scandinavia, pure Lutheranism never gained any permanent hold, though Luther's influence and example played a major part in the spread of the Reformation to other lands. Except in England, where the Anglican Church grew under a variety of influences, the Protestants in other countries—Switzerland, France, the Netherlands, and Scotland, to name the most important—followed the leadership of Zwingli and Calvin. The Protestant churches founded in these countries were generally known as Reformed Churches, to distinguish them from the Lutheran.

In the fourteenth century three Swiss cantons had revolted and established the nucleus of what was later to become the Swiss Confederation. In the late fifteenth century the thirteen cantons of the Swiss Confederation provided some of the finest footsoldiers available to various armies operating in France, Germany, and Italy. Swiss cities such as Basel and Zürich, whose atmosphere was more democratic than that prevailing in neighboring states, were important in the development of Christian humanism. The Swiss reformer Huldreich Zwingli (1484-1531) had been profoundly influenced by Erasmus, and around 1519 he began to read Luther's early pamphlets. By 1525, appealing to the general desire for reform and the patriotic Swiss resentment of Roman domination, Zwingli converted the city council and a majority of the people of Zürich to his reformed views. Zwingli's Reformed Church regarded the Eucharist as a symbolic commemorative service, whereas Luther interpreted the Eucharist as consubstantiation, believing in the real presence of the body and blood of Christ in the bread and wine.

John Calvin (1509-1564), the new leader who did more even than Zwingli to form the spirit of the Reformed Church in Switzerland and the other countries that adopted it, was by birth and training French. He was born of moderately well-to-do parents in Picardy and educated at the University of Paris and in the law schools of Orléans and Bourges. At Paris he received a thorough training in the classics, which provided him with an excellent Latin style and may have been in part responsible for the skill in his native tongue that made him one of the greatest masters of French prose in his century. Calvin's legal training was equally important, for to the end of his days his thought on all religous and moral questions retained a strongly legal cast. Shortly after he had completed his studies, Calvin was converted to the new doctrine of the Reformation through reading the works of Erasmus and Luther. But France at that time was unsafe for heretics and he was forced to flee. He took refuge in Basel in 1534 and there began his first theological writing.

Two years later, Calvin published the first edition of his *Institutes of the Christian Religion*. From time to time thereafter he added to it in new editions and also translated it from the original Latin into French. In its finished form, this work contained a complete summary of that system of theology and morals generally known as Calvinism. More than any other book it was responsible for the spread of Protestantism to the non-Lutheran countries. Its clarity of thought and remorseless logic induced conviction more inescapably than did the mystical fervor of Luther. Though there was little that was really original in Calvinism, for the fundamental doctrines were almost without exception Luther's, the total effect was very different from Lutheranism. The chief difference, aside from the more logical and consistent development of Calvin's thought, lay in a decided shift in emphasis.

Starting with the belief in man's inability to save himself by good works,

John Calvin, portrayed by a contemporary artist.

Luther placed the greatest emphasis on the saving power of faith, whereas Calvin thought much more about the majesty and power of God, who predestines certain souls for salvation and assigns the rest of mankind to damnation. Calvin's was a sterner doctrine, and its sternness was reflected in his moral teaching and legislation. He considered it the duty of church and state to make men moral in the strictest legalistic sense. No aspect of his teaching had a more profound influence on the life of the Calvinist countries than this.

Emphasis on strict morality was the source of the one apparent logical inconsistency in Calvin's doctrine. Yet if it did not follow logically from his doctrine of predestination, it was psychologically necessary. No serious person—and Calvinism appealed to the serious—contemplating the awful majesty of God and the foreordained alternatives of eternal salvation and damnation could remain indifferent to his own fate in eternity. And since no one could be sure that he was of the elect, and nothing he could do of his own will could change the immutable decree of predestination, the Calvinist lived under the shadow of a terrifying uncertainty. According to all logic, the fact that he could do nothing to change his fate should have made him indifferent to his conduct in this world, but the doctrine of predestination had instead exactly the opposite effect. For it might safely be assumed that those whom God has chosen to be saved are people who lead good moral lives. The fact of living a strictly moral life did not prove that one was of the elect, but an immoral life did prove that one was not. Hence there was at least a partial assurance in the former case, and it was a bold individual who could spurn even such uncertain comfort.

Calvin and his followers tended to take their conceptions of God and of morality more from the Old Testament than from the Christian New Testament. To the Calvinist, moral laws were truly laws, such as Jehovah had handed down to Moses on Mount Sinai; in enforcing moral laws, including the strict observation of the Hebrew Sabbath, Calvinist rulers and ministers felt that they were carrying out the will of Jehovah. To understand the spiritual atmosphere of any Calvinist place, whether Geneva, Scotland, or New England, one must be familiar with the atmosphere of the Old Testament prophets and the Pentateuch.

The laboratory in which Calvin worked out the practical application of his doctrine was the city of Geneva. Situated in the French-speaking district on the borders of Switzerland, Geneva was not yet a full-fledged member of the Swiss Confederation when Calvin entered it in 1536, though it was closely allied with the Protestant canton of Berne, which was supporting the Genevan citizens in their struggle for freedom from the rule of their bishop and count, both of whom were members of the House of Savoy. The Reformation in Geneva, therefore, began partly as a political expedient for freeing the city from episcopal control. The chief Protestant preacher, Guillaume Farel, was encountering grave difficulties in organizing the Reformed Church among people who were not all converts by conviction. Such was the situation when Calvin came to Geneva for a brief visit and was commanded by Farel in the name of the Lord to stay and help him. For three years Calvin and Farel strove to organize and purify the new church, but their unbending discipline aroused so much opposition that they were finally driven out. The new church, however, was hopelessly divided without their leadership, and in 1541 the people of Geneva begged Calvin to return.

For the remainder of his life Calvin was the ruler of Geneva, though opposition to him was not crushed until 1555. Under the new constitution, which

Calvin helped to write, the government of Geneva was a sort of theocratic republic; the administration of state and church were so closely interwoven that it is difficult to determine which was responsible for the legislation that made Geneva the most "moral" city in Europe.

We may mention here the influence of the Genevan prototype on the organization of the Calvinist churches in other countries. Without exception the Calvinists opposed control of the church by the state and, as far as possible, avoided a hierarchical church organization through which authority could be imposed from above. They maintained the equality of all ministers and hence opposed any episcopal system. The church in Geneva was not in spirit democratic, having evolved in an aristocratic republic under the despotic will of John Calvin, but it contained the seeds of democracy, which were to bear fruit under more favorable conditions. In southern France, for example, Calvinism was soon adopted by large segments of the provincial aristocracy, but it furthered a broad sense of community between townsmen and aristocrats fighting against royal (Catholic) domination.

In most of the countries to which Calvinism spread, the Reformed churches began as persecuted minorities, and the Calvinists were forced into rebellion against the royal government by their belief that they must obey the laws of God rather than those of man. Under these circumstances each congregation organized as a separate unit, choosing its own minister, and only later was there formed a larger national organization, a synod or presbytery consisting of the ministers and elders of the various congregations. Authority in the Reformed churches thus derived originally from the congregations. The ministers, as the interpreters of God's word, exercised immense moral authority. They examined and ordained new ministers, but the congregation retained the right to select its own minister from those duly ordained.

This democratic form of church organization was more firmly established in Presbyterian Scotland than elsewhere, and it was one of the reasons for the antagonism James I displayed toward the Calvinist Puritans in England. During the course of the seventeenth century, many English Puritans seceded from the Anglican Church and formed Congregational churches. Because many of the early colonists who settled in America were Puritans, Congregationalists, and Presbyterians, they established the democratic form of church government in the new land, thereby contributing to the later development of democratic political government in the colonies which were to become the United States.

The German sociologist Max Weber and the British economist and social critic R. H. Tawney have argued that Protestantism, particularly Calvinism, was instrumental in the growth of democracy and capitalism in western Europe and America from the sixteenth century. They theorized that Catholicism had been oriented toward an older social order emphasizing security and hierarchy. These characteristics were inimicable to the adventurous, egalitarian spirit of early modern capitalism. The Catholic Church never overcame its hostility to "usury," or interest, the essence of capitalist economic life, whereas Calvin took a more lenient position toward this phenomenon. Further, Catholicism was based on an agrarian, aristocratic medieval society, whereas Calvinism grew up amid and appealed to an urban constituency. This thesis, though it has been modified and attacked from many angles, is a useful starting-point for evaluating the social and historical significance of the Reformation.

The Reformation in England

In the English Reformation the same factors were present that have been noted in the revolt from Rome in the continental states, but in a very different ratio. National, political, and economic motives played a much more important part than did religion in the early stages of the movement in England. Under Henry VIII, little more was accomplished or aimed at than the transference of the political control and temporalities of the English Church from the pope to the king. The religious reformation followed the political. Not until after Henry's death did England become in any real sense Protestant.

Henry VIII was as absolute a ruler as England had ever had, and his will was the determining factor in bringing about the break with Rome. Yet Henry could never have forced his people to abandon their ancient obedience to the pope had not a great many of them been prepared to welcome the move.

In the early years of the reign of Henry VIII, there was little to indicate his future role in the history of the English Church. He was a strong champion of orthodoxy. In 1521 Henry published a violent attack on the Lutheran heresy, for which the pope awarded him the title Defender of the Faith. Besides, Henry was much too engrossed in his ambitious foreign policy, in which he was encouraged by his chief minister, Cardinal Wolsey, to pay much attention to the reform of the Church at home. Though Henry apparently realized that clerical privileges, ecclesiastical courts, and papal jurisdiction were the only remaining obstacles to his complete control of his kingdom, Wolsey, who was papal legate in England and hoped to be pope, was able to distract the king's attention and stave off any action against the rights of the Church. More than once, papal ambassadors warned the pope that if Wolsey fell, the Church in England would suffer, and by 1527 Wolsey was slipping. His foreign policy had accomplished nothing except to waste the accumulated treasure of Henry VII and to burden the English taxpayers.

During this period Cardinal Wolsey and Thomas Cromwell originated in dim outline the policy which was to guide English diplomacy for the next four centuries, that of the balance of power. According to this policy, no one power was to be allowed to dominate the continent of Europe, and no great power was ever to dominate the mouths of the rivers emptying into the North Sea opposite southeastern England. It may be too much to claim that these men consistently adhered to such a policy, however, for at times Henry seemed to be guided more by adventurism and the desire for prestige than by the considered opportunism of the balance-of-power concept.

In 1527, Henry had been married to Catherine of Aragon for eighteen years and, but for one daughter, Mary, had no heir. Therein lay the immediate cause of the momentous events of the next few years. Henry needed a male heir to preserve the Tudor line. The death of all Catherine's sons in infancy began to seem to the king a divine judgment upon him for having broken the biblical injunction against marrying a deceased brother's wife (Catherine had previously been married, briefly, to his elder brother Arthur). Henry had secured a papal dispensation at the time of his marriage, but conscience and inclination combined to convince him that the marriage had not been valid. He was eager to marry again and had already chosen as his future wife Anne Boleyn.

Henry therefore instructed Wolsey to secure a divorce—or rather an annulment—from Pope Clement VII. But in 1527 the pope was in no position to take action against Catherine. She was the aunt of Emperor Charles V, and Charles was master of Italy. The imperial troops had just sacked Rome, and the pope was in their power. Negotiations dragged on until Henry lost all patience. In 1529 he called a Parliament to declare the English Church independent of Rome. Wolsey was deprived of his office and the following year was arrested on a charge of treason. Meanwhile, Parliament had begun to pass act after act reducing clerical privileges and papal authority. By 1533 it had so far separated the English Church from Rome that the new archbishop of Canterbury was able to annul the king's marriage.

The next year Parliament took the final step necessary to establish the complete independence of the English national church. All relations with the Papacy were severed, and the king was declared by the Act of Supremacy the supreme head of the Church of England. One more kingdom had been lost to the once universal Church. This was one more example of the triumphs of central government over separate interests, of state over church, and of the nation over the unity of Christendom.

Henry's was a conservative revolution. Except for the substitution of royal for papal authority, there was no marked change in the outward organization of the Anglican Church. The most radical change was the gradual dissolution of the monasteries and the confiscation of their lands. Parliament willingly lent its authority to the king's will, for the monks had long been unpopular and confiscation enriched both the state and the wealthy burghers and gentlemen who purchased monastic properties from the king. The sale of the monastic lands at well below their normal price gave a considerable number of people from the most influential classes in England a material incentive to oppose any reconciliation with Rome. Such a reunion might lead to a restoration of the confiscated lands to the Catholic Church.

There was even less change in doctrine than in organization. Henry was still a champion of orthodoxy, as far as was possible. A few earnest Catholics, like Saint Thomas More (canonized in 1935), were executed for their refusal to accept the king as supreme head of the Church in England, but there were as many martyrs on the other side who suffered because they were too Protestant. Parliament authorized the use of the English Bible, and some changes were made in religious practice, but Henry was determined to keep the essentials of the Catholic faith. In 1539, as a Catholic reactionary party gained ascendancy at court, Henry passed through Parliament an act defining the faith of the Anglican Church in six articles, all quite Catholic in tone; this act was enforced by severe persecuting laws. The political break with the Roman Catholic Church, however, inevitably opened the way for criticism of Catholic doctrine and, despite everything Henry could do, Lutheran and Calvinist opinions spread rapidly in England.

When Henry VIII died in 1547, he left his throne to his infant son Edward VI (1547–1553) and the government to a Council of Regency headed by the Protector Somerset, the young king's maternal uncle. During the next six years a doctrinal reformation was accomplished to supplement the political and constitutional reformation of the previous reign. There can be no doubt that Protestants, whether Lutheran or Calvinist or a compromise between the two, were still a distinct minority, but they were an influential minority strongly represented in the Council. The repressive laws of Henry VIII were repealed almost at once.

The next step was to prepare an English liturgy and enforce its use by an Act of Uniformity in 1549. This liturgy was the first Book of Common Prayer, the work of Archbishop Cranmer, whose grand English cadences are still heard in the services of the Anglican Church. Three years later it was revised to make it more acceptable to the extreme Protestants, and at the same time the official creed of the church was defined in the Forty-two Articles of Religion. These were made as vague and general as possible to enable those who were almost Catholics, as well as Lutherans and Calvinists, to remain within the church. England was still far from unanimity in religion. All that the government was working for at the time was a decent outward uniformity, while at the same time favoring a steady drift toward Protestantism. But the question was still an open one when the premature death of Edward replaced his Protestant government with the Catholic regime of his half-sister Mary Tudor.

El Greco's Burial of Count Orgaz. *The huge canvas, 16 feet in height, was completed in 1586. In the painting are signs of the gloomy formalism of the Spanish court and the religious aspirations of the Counter Reformation.*

Rome's Response to the Reformation

For half a century after Luther nailed his theses on the church door at Wittenberg, the Protestant Reformation continued to spread, until the very existence of the Roman Catholic Church seemed threatened. At the end of that half-century, one or another of the three great Protestant churches was firmly established, with the active support of the state, in the three Scandinavian kingdoms, in about half of Germany and Switzerland, and in England and Scotland. Calvinism was in open rebellion against a Catholic monarch in the Netherlands and was fighting on fairly even terms in France, while the Catholic states of Germany, as well as Poland, Bohemia, and Hungary, were honeycombed with the Protestant heresy, and signs of it had appeared even in Italy, the home of the Roman Church. Indeed, it has been estimated that in Germanic Europe around 1555 90 per cent of the population had renounced its allegiance to the Roman Church, though Rome had probably won back 50 per cent of the population by the early seventeenth century. The dramatic reversal was the work of the Catholic Reformation.

The spontaneous Catholic Reformation achieved its first and most complete success in Spain, and the Spanish spirit dominated the movement later as it became the Counter Reformation. The state of religion in the Spanish peninsula at the end of the Middle Ages was in many respects unique. The long crusade against the Moslems had tended to identify defense of the orthodox faith with the growing sentiment of patriotism, so that there was not a country in Europe where heresy was regarded with greater abhorrence. Spain had been relatively unaffected by the Renaissance revolt against medievalism and by the social changes that helped to diminish the piety of the Italian and prepare the peoples of the North for new religious ideals and beliefs. The spirit of Spain was unquestioningly orthodox and its piety of a type wholly in keeping with the ideals of medieval Christianity. Moreover, the monarchy had won control of the Spanish Church and the interests of state and Church were closely identified. Everything, therefore, favored the purely orthodox reformation begun by Cardinal Ximenes in the closing years of the fifteenth century with the full support of the monarchy. The result was a marked improvement in the morals and educational standards of the clergy, which in turn led to a strong revival of piety among the people under their care. But the Spanish reform also had its darker side of persecution and intolerance. The Inquisition was introduced into Spain in a new and more effective form, to crush by force and terror all deviation from the strict lines of medieval orthodoxy.

In Italy too, during the early decades of the sixteenth century, Catholic reformers were working earnestly to revitalize the spiritual life of Church and people, but their efforts were isolated and did not meet with the immediate success achieved by the reform in Spain. Indeed, in this late period of the Renaissance, Italy did not present a very likely field for either clerical reform or religious revival. The great mass of the people were orthodox enough, but superstitious rather than pious, and in Italy, more than anywhere else, the papal curia was a perpetual stumbling-block to reform. Most of the abuses in the Church had a financial rationale; their abolition would cause a sharp decrease in the revenues of the pope and the members of his court. Hence the vested interests at Rome were opposed to reform. At the same time, Italy had received too many material benefits from the Italian Papacy to rebel against it, as the northern states did, and there was no state government strong or independent enough to take the initiative in reform, as occurred in Spain.

There were in Italy in the second quarter of the sixteenth century many earnest and devout men, some of them high officials in the Church, who were sincerely interested in reform. All were united in their hope of a Catholic reformation, but as time went on they drifted into two fairly distinct groups, separated by divergent ideas on the policy to be pursued in regard to Protestantism. One group, best represented by the Venetian humanist and statesman Contarini, hoped for reconciliation with Protestant reformers on the basis of practical reform and a liberal interpretation of Catholic doctrine; the other, typified by the Neapolitan Bishop Caraffa, were equally eager for reform but rejected change or compromise in doctrine or usage, and favored the suppression of heresy by the means that had proven so successful in Spain.

Meanwhile, though efforts for practical reform were thwarted by lack of papal cooperation, considerable progress was made in the revival of religion among the masses of the people. Much of the credit for this work was due to new or revived religious orders, of which the most influential was the Capuchin order, founded in 1526 as a reformed branch of the Franciscans. The spirit of the new order was medieval rather than modern; its inspiration was a return to the ideals of Saint Francis. Like the early Franciscans, the Capuchins devoted themselves to preaching a simple piety among the poverty-stricken masses, and no group did more to gain popular support for the early Catholic Reformation than these kindly enthusiasts, whose pointed hoods soon became familiar sights in every marketplace.

With the accession of Pope Paul III (1534–1549), following the death of the harassed and vacillating Clement VII, the Catholic reformers at last began to receive some cooperation from the Papacy. Several of the most distinguished leaders of the reform party, including Contarini and Caraffa, were made cardinals, and a committee of cardinals was appointed to investigate conditions in the Church. Their report identified so many abuses in the papal curia and throughout the government of the Church that it was thought wise to suppress it, lest it give aid and comfort to the heretics. The pontificate of Paul III marks an important turning-point in the history of the Church, the end of the Renaissance Papacy and the beginning of the Counter Reformation.

In the early years of Paul's reign, liberal reformers led by Cardinal Contarini seemed to be in the ascendancy at Rome. They were prepared to make some compromise with the spirit of the new age represented by both the Renaissance and the Reformation, and they still hoped to re-establish the unity of the Catholic Church through reconcilation with the Protestants. That accomplished, a general Catholic Reformation, free from the distractions of partisan strife and dogmatic controversies, would be possible. This was the policy proposed much earlier by Erasmus, and it was doomed to failure now as it had been then. Contarini and his friends failed to realize the fundamental nature of the differences separating the new churches from the old. They had, however, powerful support in Charles V, who was determined to restore religious unity to Germany and would have been glad to do so by peaceful means. In 1541, a serious effort was made to establish a mutual understanding at a religious colloquy held at Regensburg. Contarini was the chief representative of the Catholic Church, and the liberal and conciliatory Melanchthon the principal spokesman for the Protestants. Thanks to Contarini's tactful diplomacy, both sides made surprising concessions, yet they failed to come to any agreement on the fundamental question of the sacraments. The net result of the colloquy was to prove the impossibility of reconciliation even under the most favorable circumstances. The party of conciliation was discredited and quickly lost influence. Its place was taken by the conservative reformers under the leadership of Cardinal Caraffa.

Loyola and the Jesuits

Of the various agencies through which the Counter Reformation was brought about, possibly none had a wider influence in retaining the loyalty of members of the Roman Church, or winning back those who had deserted it, than the devoted preachers and skillful teachers who made up the Society of Jesus. The Jesuits, as they were popularly called, placed the most powerful missionary organization the world has ever seen at the disposal of the Papacy.

In 1521, the year Martin Luther faced the Emperor Charles V at the Diet of Worms, the man who was to organize the Church's best defense against Luther's teaching was fighting as an officer of Charles' army in the besieged city of Pampeluna in northern Spain. He was a noble from the Spanish Basque province of Guipuzcoa, one Don Iñigo Lopez de Recalde de Loyola, better known to history as Ignatius Loyola (1491–1556). He was wounded before the city was taken, and in the months of anguish that followed, his whole attitude toward life was changed. Loyola determined to abandon his career as a soldier of the Spanish king for that of a soldier of Christ. He realized that for his missionary purpose he would need more education, especially in theology.

Though Loyola never became a great scholar, he had other qualities that made those more learned than he follow his leadership. Aside from absolute sincerity, unswerving determination, and those indefinable gifts of personality that any leader must possess, Loyola's most valuable asset was his uncanny insight into the workings of the human mind. This was abundantly proven by his *Spiritual Exercises,* the book that helped to win his first followers and later maintained the character of his order. Based on a detailed, introspective study of Loyola's own experience in the early days of his conversion, it gives directions for a period of intensive contemplation, lasting normally about four weeks, and designed to produce in the participant those soul-shaking emotional experiences that Loyola had undergone over a much longer time. The *Exercises* left an indelible impression on the minds of those who passed through the course faithfully, and it transformed them into devoted and obedient soldiers of the Church.

After some delay, the little group of companions who gathered about Loyola at Paris received confirmation from Pope Paul III in 1540. The following year Loyola was elected first general of the order. The new order was called the Society of Jesus, but a more accurate translation of the Latin *societas* would be "company of Jesus," for Loyola intended the word to be used in the military sense.

The purpose of the society was set forth clearly in its constitution, which Loyola completed just before his death, and in the bull of 1550. The best brief description is from the latter: "The company is founded to employ itself entirely in the defense of the holy Catholic faith." The method to be employed to this end was fourfold: to educate the young in orthodox schools, to win influence with the doubtful through service as confessors, to carry on missionary preaching in heathen or heretical lands, and to acquire diplomatic influence in international affairs by serving in the courts of nobles and princes. Unlike earlier monastic orders, the society was founded not primarily for the salvation of its members, though that aim was taken for granted, but to accomplish a definite purpose.

All members took the customary monastic vows of poverty, chastity, and obedience, but an inner circle of the most experienced members took an additional vow of special obedience to the Papacy. From these "Professed of Four Vows" the executive officers were chosen. The head of the order was the general, elected for life, with absolute authority over all members. Under him were the provincials and a descending hierarchy of inferior officers, very much like that of a modern army. The Jesuits were a mobile as well as disciplined body. Any member could be dispatched at a moment's notice to whatever field seemed most in need of his services. As a further innovation in the interests of efficiency, Loyola freed his order from restrictions of dress, ascetic practice, regular hours, and the like which were common in the monastic orders but might interfere with the duties of missionary preachers and teachers.

The society thus formed grew with amazing rapidity and soon spread to every country of Europe as well as to the heathen lands beyond the seas. At Loyola's death there were twelve provinces and fifteen hundred members. Preaching and hearing confessions made up the largest part of their work, but their service as educators was perhaps more important. Jesuit schools and colleges were established in every Catholic country and were regarded as among the most efficient of their age. The influence of the Jesuits upon Catholic education has continued into the twentieth century, particularly in the teaching of law and in primary and secondary education.

The Council of Trent

The Jesuits had barely begun their work when the rulers of the Church took steps to strengthen its defenses against Protestant heresy by convening a general council to determine the character of the Counter Reformation. It met in the imperial city of Trent, just north of the Italian border, for three separate periods. The first period, 1545-1547, was in the reign of Paul III; the second, 1551-1552, in that of Julius III; and the last, 1562-1563, in the reign of Pius IV.

From the beginning of the Lutheran movement, there had been frequent demands for a general council. At first Luther and his followers had appealed from the authority of the pope to that of a general council, and later the Catholic reformers who hoped for reconciliation, as well as Emperor Charles V, took up the cry. The popes, however, were loath to call one, for they had unhappy memories of the councils of Constance and Basel and feared that the chief result would be an attempt to limit their authority. When Paul III finally agreed to summon a council, he did so as the result of a policy that few of those who demanded it would entirely approve.

Since the failure of conciliation with the Protestants, the pope and the Counter Reformation party, now in the ascendancy at Rome, had determined on a new policy, to recognize the loss of the Protestants as a whole as irremediable and to concentrate on the defense of what remained, with the hope of winning back individual heretics. This policy appealed to the Spanish churchmen but not to the majority in France and Germany, who hoped for a compromise with the new ideas. Even the Spanish reformers opposed one very important point: they had little hope of the Papacy reforming itself and felt that reform should be carried out by the council, whereas the papal party felt that this part of the task should be left to the authority of the pope.

With all these divergent ideas about the work the council was to do, it is not surprising that its meetings were stormy and that there were long gaps between them. The political interests and animosities of the various states helped to complicate the situation still further. On the whole, however, the papal party was able to carry through its policy. At the beginning, the pope secured working control of the council by obtaining a decision that only bishops and heads of religious orders, present in person, should have the right to vote. This enabled him to maintain a loyal Italian majority, for Trent was close to Italy and prelates from distant countries were usually prevented by wars, expense, and other inconveniences from attending in large numbers. Still, papal control was never very secure, and papal legates were forced to compromise on the matter of reform, permitting its discussion on the condition that the definition of doctrine should be taken up at the same time.

All through the council (1545–1563), the Jesuits Laynez and Salmeron exerted a great influence on the members and were often instrumental in winning them over to agreement with the wishes of the papal party. During the last session, the diplomatic pope, Pius IV, took pains to secure the agreement of the great Catholic monarchs before submitting his projects to the council, and so won control of what seemed an almost impossible situation. The final triumph of the papal authority was assured when the council in its closing session voted to present all its decrees to the pope for confirmation.

The most important result of the Council of Trent was the final definition of Catholic doctrine. At a time when all religious opinion was in a state of flux, and Protestantism was splitting up into antagonistic churches with irreconcilable differences in belief, the Roman Catholic Church was given a coherent and authoritative statement of orthodox faith which was to prove a powerful instrument for the preservation of unity. The council decided that the Bible and the tradition of the Church were of equal authority, and that both could be interpreted only by the Church, which in practice meant by the pope as head of the Church. In addition, the traditional Latin translation of the Bible, the Vulgate, was declared the only authoritative version. This adherence to tradition as the best weapon against the innovators was the keynote of all the major doctrinal decrees of the council. By establishing the authority of tradition, the Council of Trent bound the modern Catholic Church to medieval precedent and made later changes in doctrine and practice extremely difficult. Still, the insistence on tradition had value, for it gave to the Roman Church the prestige and authority of unbroken continuity with the past, which the newer Protestant churches necessarily lacked.

The work of practical reform, so far as it was actually accomplished by the council, was of secondary importance. It did outline a comprehensive program of reform, abolishing the worst abuses and making provision for better discipline and higher educational standards among the clergy. The execution of these decrees, however, was beyond the power of the council, which ceased to exist as soon as its work was done. Enforcement had to be left to the executive authority of the pope and his successors. Fortunately, the majority of the later popes proved worthy of the trust. The Catholic Church never again suffered from the immorality, lax discipline, or corrupt worldly leaders that had left it so open to criticism during the period of the Renaissance.

With the conclusion of the Council of Trent, all the forces of the Counter Reformation swung into action, under the leadership of reforming popes and orders. They carried the war into the enemy's country. The Papacy under Sixtus IV (1585–1590) took its place once more as the leader of the Catholic world, though it no longer made the implicit claim to secular power that had hampered rather than enhanced its spiritual authority in earlier times. In the Latin countries of Italy and Spain, where the Counter Reformation triumphed most completely, the work of reform was accompanied by savage repression of heresy.

In 1542, when the Counter Reformation had first gained headway at Rome, Cardinal Caraffa persuaded Pope Paul III to reorganize the papal Inquisition in Italy on the Spanish model. The cruel but effective Spanish Inquisition had been founded in 1478. Throughout the remainder of the Counter Reformation period, the Holy Office, as the Inquisition was officially named, with its secret trials and its power to turn over condemned heretics to the secular government to be burned at the stake, maintained a reign of terror, completely successful in stamping out all overt signs of heresy in Italy and Spain. North of the Alps and the Pyrenees it never gained a firm foothold, though Philip II tried to introduce it into the Netherlands.

A second and almost equally important agent for the suppression of unorthodox opinion was the Index of Prohibited Books, an elaborate system of censorship of the press designed to prevent the publication or circulation of any book that might suggest to the people ideas derogatory to the Church or to orthodox belief. The effect of this rigid control of the press in suppressing the thought of the Spanish and Italian people can scarcely be overestimated.

The persecution of heresy and the censorship of heretical books were by no means confined to the Catholic Church. Tolerance of varying opinions in matters of religion found few champions in the sixteenth century. Nevertheless, the persecution of heretics was never as widely enforced in the Protestant countries as it was in Italy and Spain, for in none of them was there a distinct institution with the terrible powers of the Inquisition dedicated to that purpose. Protestant regions, such as Calvin's Geneva or Puritan New Salem, went in more for burning or drowning dissenters and witches, but such campaigns lacked the consistency generated by a powerful institution such as the Inquisition.

By 1648, the Counter Reformation, like the Protestant Reformation, had spent its aggressive force. By that time the religious map of Europe was fairly definitely fixed. In each country the church, whether Protestant or Catholic, had become closely identified with the political interests of the state and could count on it for permanent support when the wave of religious enthusiasm died down.

Suggestions for Further Reading

R. H. Bainton, *Here I Stand: A Life of Martin Luther** (1955). A popular biography, extremely sympathetic to Luther and his theology. Very readable, written by an outstanding American scholar.

R. H. Bainton, *The Reformation of the Sixteenth Century** (1952). A fine overview

*Available in a paperback edition.

of the Reformation era, written from a sympathetic viewpoint by the distinguished Yale historian.

H. Boehmer, *Road to Reformation* (1946). Standard work dealing with the origins of Luther's revolt against Rome.

J. Brodick, *The Origins of the Jesuits* (1960).

O. Chadwick, *The Reformation** (1964).

H. Daniel-Rops, *The Catholic Reformation* (1962). A favorable account by a famous Catholic historian.

A. G. Dickens, *The Counter Reformation* (1969). A useful survey by a British scholar. Readable and up-to-date.

A. G. Dickens, *The English Reformation* (1964). The work of a highly regarded historian.

J. P. Dolan, *The Essential Erasmus** (1962). Excellently selected and presented writings of Erasmus.

J. P. Dolan, *History of the Reformation* (1965). An excellent survey.

R. S. Dunn, *The Age of Religious Wars, 1559–1689** (1970).

G. R. Elton, *The Reformation* (1953). New Cambridge Modern History volume. Various specialists deal with different aspects of the Reformation era. Reliable and well edited.

E. H. Erikson, *Young Man Luther** (1958). A provocative, novel approach by a distinguished psychoanalyst. Erikson knows his history, and his portrait of Luther does not ignore cultural and historical factors in delineating the origins of his revolution.

H. Grimm, *The Reformation Era* (1965). Widely used American textbook survey.

H. Hillerbrand, *The Reformation* (1964).

J. Huizinga, *Erasmus and the Age of the Reformation** (1957). The fine work of the great Dutch historian.

H. Jedin, *A History of the Council of Trent*, 2 vols. (1957–1961). The standard study, by a great scholar.

R. Kingdon, *Geneva and the Coming of the Wars of Religion in France* (1956).

J. Lortz, *The Reformation in Germany*, 2 vols. (1968).

J. Ridley, *Thomas Cranmer** (1962).

J. Rillet, *Zwingli: Third Man of the Reformation* (1964).

F. Wendel, *Calvin: The Origins and Development of His Religious Thought* (1963).

G. H. Williams, *The Radical Reformation* (1962). Interesting study of the radical Reformation sects, which were persecuted by Catholics and Protestants alike.

The Emergence of Early Modern States

22

> A prudent Prince neither can nor ought to keep his word when to keep it is hurtful to him and the causes that led him to pledge it are removed.
>
> NICCOLÒ MACHIAVELLI

Hapsburg Domination

While religious struggles were tearing Europe apart, the authority of the state reached new heights in parts of the Continent. The two phenomena were related. The Catholic Church encouraged the strengthening of the states which were monolithic in their support of the old religion. In other areas, Protestantism had to turn to a sympathetic state authority in order to prevent its own destruction at the hands of militant Catholic forces. When we speak of a state, we do not necessarily mean national state. Certainly, the authority of the English state was strengthened by the Reformation, but in Germany the territorial princes benefited from the religious split. In the long run, the collapse of the universal Christian church could only redound to the benefit of secular power and the secular spirit. In many areas, however, this was not clear until a great deal of time had passed.

In discussing the sixteenth and seventeenth centuries, historians often refer to the emergence of a modern European state system. By this they mean that fully secular states, guided by a sense of their own economic and political well-being, emerged against a background of a continental balance of power and far-flung commercial and colonial rivalries. Machiavelli's state self-interest had been the vision of an ambitious politician and theoretician in 1512. By 1630, however, such concepts as state self-interest were taken for granted in the chancelleries of monarchs like Charles I of England and Louis XIII of France.

Germany in this period is one great exception, outside of Italy, to the general rule of national political consolidation and the rise of strong central government. Lack of unity in the Empire, however, was compensated for to some extent by the consolidation of the larger states within Germany. In these individual states, duchies, margravates, and the like, a tendency toward centralization similar to that we have noted in the large monarchical states was taking place.

The most striking development in German political history during this period, one that was to have a tremendous influence on the whole history of Europe, was the phenomenal rise of the Austrian house of Hapsburg. After the election of Albert II (1438–1439), the imperial title remained in the Hapsburg family generation after generation until it came to be considered almost a hereditary right. Albert was followed by Frederick III (1440–1493) and Maximilian I (1493–1519). Maximilian was chiefly responsible for bringing into the Hapsburg family the vast collection of lands outside Germany that would make his grandson, Charles V, the most powerful ruler in Europe in the next generation. His participation in the Italian wars brought him nothing but grief, and his devotion to family interests and foreign projects ruined his chances of building a strong imperial government in Germany. Maximilian's only success was due to the skill and good fortune with which he arranged a series of marriage alliances with other dynasties. But that alone was enough to make his house the greatest in Europe. With his vast accumulation of Burgundian, Spanish, Austrian, and imperial lands, Charles V, at the age of nineteen, became the ruler of a larger territory than had been collected under one monarch since the break-up of Charlemagne's empire.

THE HERITAGE AND EMPIRE OF CHARLES V

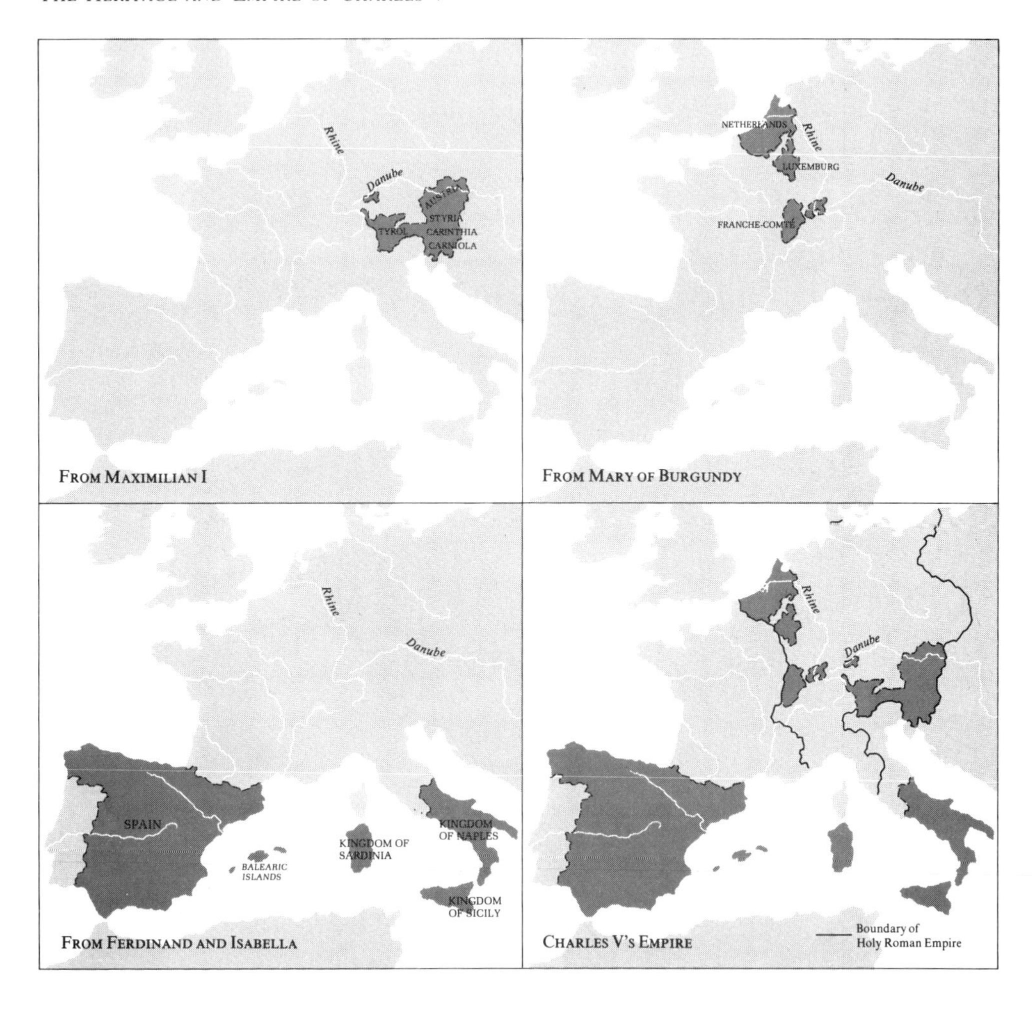

EUROPE IN 1520

Before the accession of Charles V, national and dynastic rivalry had embroiled the European countries in a greedy struggle for the spoils of Italy. That rivalry now took on a new character. Francis I of France stood pitted against the mighty Hapsburg as his sole rival for the hegemony of Europe. They had too many conflicting interests to remain at peace with each other, and the destruction of either would have meant the domination of Europe by the victor. The other states, therefore, were drawn into the struggle in the hope of maintaining a balance of power, that is, a state of international equilibrium. Meanwhile, within each territorial state the rulers continued to centralize the government still further and to develop unhampered sovereign power.

This major new theme of European history was replicated in miniature among the German states that made up the Holy Roman Empire. There Charles' ambitions for centralized control and dynastic aggrandizement encountered the similar ambitions of the territorial princes, who feared Hapsburg domination as much as did the rulers of the other European states. In Germany more than elsewhere, the situation was complicated by the religious revolution and the constant threat of Turkish aggression from the East. The result was the establishment of a temporary equilibrium among the German states that matched the larger equilibrium of Europe.

His imposing array of possessions made Charles V the most powerful monarch in Europe, but he was not so powerful as he appeared, for the available strength of his empire was always considerably less than the total strength of its component parts. It was a purely dynastic empire, accumulated through a series of family alliances, lacking both national and geographic unity. The person of Charles was the only bond holding the scattered dominions together. To utilize the full resources of each to advance a common policy or to satisfy their varying interests would have taxed the genius and energy of Charlemagne, and the nineteen-year-old ruler who inherited that appalling task was not a brilliant youth. He was not personally attractive, being of a somewhat stolid nature and having inherited the more unfortunate Hapsburg features. But, as time went on, he proved that he possessed a large measure of common sense and industry, patience and a degree of determination verging on stubbornness. These qualities served him better in the long run than the more brilliant and attractive traits of Francis I, his rival of the house of Valois.

Francis I of France was a little older than Charles and had already won military glory. He had a good deal of surface charm and culture, but his character was frivolous, without depth or substance. Had he possessed any of the qualities of greatness, he might have fared well in his contest with the Hapsburg, for, though he ruled less land, his holdings were united in one compact national state over which he had absolute control. However, he was vain, inconsequential, absorbed in selfish pleasures, and gifted with a fatal genius for snatching defeat from the jaws of victory.

French kings such as Francis I and Henry II struggled to prevent the destruction of their power by the encircling Hapsburgs. In the pursuit of this goal they were opportunistic enough to make alliances with both Protestant princes and Turkish potentates. They wished to take advantage of the religious struggles within the Hapsburg realms in order to nibble away at the rich Netherlands, western German fortress cities, and Italian lands. The long struggle between Valois (and, later, Bourbon) and Hapsburg did not really end until the middle of the eighteenth century, but its first phase was over by 1559, when France emerged unconquered and even enlarged by the seizure of the important eastern fortress cities Metz, Toul, and Verdun.

Charles V and His Empire

Though the contest with the Valois kings was the central theme of the reign of Charles V (1519–1556), the emperor also had to deal with a host of problems involving the internal government of his various states. He was born and brought up in the Netherlands, yet his empire was too large to allow him to tailor his major policies to Flemish interests. He was always a foreigner in Germany and Italy. In the latter he worked for Hapsburg domination rather than Italian unity, and in the former he allowed the interests of the Austrian Hapsburg states and the distractions of his dynastic war with France to thwart his efforts to rebuild a united imperial state. So far as Charles identified politically with any country as a base, it was with Spain. But Charles loved wealthy Flanders and the Flemish language.

The long period of warfare with the Moslems and the gradual expansion by conquest had left a permanent impress on the character of Spanish Castile. The Castilian people had grown up a fighting race, rigidly orthodox. Castile was mostly an agricultural and pastoral country, none too rich, though its industry and commerce were soon to be stimulated by the opening of exclusive markets in

Charles V as painted by Titian, one of the great portraitists of the late Renaissance.

the New World. The importation of gold and silver from Mexico and Peru would also bring about for a time a false prosperity. Aragon had a stronger central government, though there too the king was hampered by feudal nobles and the Cortes (the assembly or estates of the notables). Thanks to its position on the eastern coast, it had a more highly developed commerce than did Castile. The acquisition by the ruling family of Aragon of Sicily in the thirteenth century and the islands of Majorca and Sardinia in the fourteenth gave it a considerable share of the Mediterranean trade.

The foundations of the future greatness of Spain were laid by the union of the entire peninsula except Portugal under the rule of Ferdinand of Aragon and Isabella of Castile, who were married in 1469. When they inherited their respective kingdoms a few years later, the two greatest states in Spain were united under a single government, though for another generation they remained separate in theory. The combined power of the two monarchs made further conquest possible. In 1492, the year in which Columbus carried the flag of Castile to the New World, they conquered the kingdom of Granada, thus wiping out the last independent Moslem state. Thereafter Ferdinand launched an ambitious and astute foreign policy, designed to make Spain a power to be reckoned with in European affairs and to add to the territorial possessions of his family. In the Italian wars he acquired the kingdom of Naples from the lesser branch of the Aragonese dynasty in 1503, and in 1512 he conquered Navarre south of the Pyrenees.

The reign of Ferdinand and Isabella accomplished not only the territorial consolidation of Spain but also the centralization of authority in the hands of a strong royal government. This was especially necessary in Castile, where the independence of the feudal nobles had sadly weakened the government and produced a frightful degree of lawlessness and disorder. The monarchs began by restoring order and security for life and property and went on to strip the feudal nobles and the great crusading orders of their independent powers and subject them to the crown. In this task, Ferdinand and Isabella could count on the support of the common people, who preferred a strong government to feudal anarchy. Finally, Ferdinand and Isabella began the process of whittling away the authority of the Cortes of Castile and Aragon, the sole remaining check on the authority of the crown. Rebellions against Ferdinand's rule in Castile occurred after Isabella's death, but the two monarchs had done their work so well that their successors were able to establish the most absolute monarchy in Europe.

In the sixteenth century, Spain was the most powerful state in Europe, with the possible exception of France. It was certainly the strongest of the states ruled by Charles, and he made his permanent residence there, leaving it only when the pressing needs of his other possessions demanded his presence. He became in time a thorough Spaniard, winning the loyalty of the Spanish people by convincing them that their country was the center of his empire and that their interests were his.

In Germany Charles encountered his most difficult problems and met with least success. Although it was the ancient home of the Hapsburg family, Charles was always a foreigner in Germany. He spent little time there and constantly put off dealing with German problems until he had leisure from his more vital interests elsewhere. At his first imperial Diet in 1521, Charles took steps to meet the two most important problems of the Empire, the reform of imperial government and the suppression of the Lutheran heresy. In neither was he successful. A solution of the former problem was attempted through the creation of a council of regency, which would rule during the Emperor's absence and which he and the electors hoped would hold the Empire together. After Charles left, however, the council proved powerless to act on any important matter. It had no adequate military or financial power, and even the princes on the council ignored its decisions. It was completely discredited by its failure to suppress either a rebellion of Rhineland knights led by Franz von Sickingen in 1522 or the Peasants' Revolt three years later, both of which were crushed by the independent action of the princes most directly affected.

The emperor's legislation against Luther was no more effective than the attempt to reform the imperial constitution, and largely for the same reason. Imperial authority was not strong enough, especially with Charles engrossed in affairs elsewhere, to coerce the princes or the governments of the free cities. During his long absence no serious effort was made to enforce the Edict of Worms. The Lutherans were left free to organize their church wherever they had the support of the local government. Even when Charles finally returned to Germany in 1530, after concluding a temporary peace with Francis I, he was unable for long to give his full attention to the growing Protestant menace. After an attempt at reconciliation had failed, the emperor gave the heretics six months in which to return to the Church, after which, he declared, he would suppress them by force. But before Charles could put his threat into effect, he was forced to temporize by the necessity of gaining all the support he could muster against the Turks, and the opportunity for decisive action was lost.

For more than a century, Christian Europe had lived in fear of the Ottoman Turks, who in 1453 had completed the conquest of what remained of the Byzantine Empire by capturing Constantinople. During succeeding generations their conquests had continued at the expense of both their Christian and their Moslem neighbors. Their armies seemed invincible. When Charles V was elected emperor, they held all southeastern Europe, and before long the West was shocked by the news of a further Turkish advance up the Danube under the command of the new Sultan, Suleiman II, "the Magnificent" (1520-1566). In 1526 his army defeated the Hungarians and killed their brave king on the field of Mohács. In 1529 the Turks laid siege to Vienna but were driven back; in 1532, they advanced on Austria again. The Turkish threat to central Europe prevented Charles from taking firm action against the Lutherans before the 1540s.

As early as 1531, when there still seemed a chance of immediate action by the emperor, the chief Protestant principalities and free cities had joined together in the League of Schmalkalden for mutual defense. As other princes were converted to Lutheranism, they too joined the league. When Charles at last opened war on the League of Schmalkalden in 1546, he had fair prospects of success. His army was smaller than that of the league, but it contained a large number of Spanish footsoldiers, who had proven themselves the finest fighting men in Europe, and it was commanded by the able and ruthless duke of Alva. Charles' chief advantage, however, lay in the lack of unity among the leaders of the league and their equally fatal lack of military strategy. As the chief Protestant princes separated to protect their own lands, the emperor attacked them singly and forced one after another to submit to him. Charles then set about the suppression of Protestantism in the states of the vanquished princes. The next five years proved that it was easier to defeat the princes than to reconvert their people. They had been Lutheran too long to give up their religion even at the command of a victorious emperor. In 1552 the Protestant princes rebelled, aided by an alliance with Henry II of France. Three more years of anarchy at last persuaded the emperor to abandon all hope of crushing Lutheranism in Germany and to make peace.

The final settlement of the religious strife in Germany, at least for the sixteenth century, was arranged at the Diet of Augsburg in 1555. Known as the Religious Peace of Augsburg, it kept Germany free from religious war for more than sixty years. But there were terms in the compromise that maintained a constant tension between the Protestant and Catholic parties and promised serious trouble for the future. Four major principles laid down by this treaty are worth remembering:

1. The princes of the various German states and the governments of the free cities were to be free to choose between the Lutheran and Catholic faiths. The princes were to have the right to enforce the religion of their choice upon their subjects, but the free cities on the Lutheran side could not expel their Catholic minorities. This principle, which made the religion of the state that of its ruler, is generally identified by the phrase *cuius regio eius religio.*
2. The principle was to apply only to Lutheran and Catholic governments. It did not extend to Calvinists, though their number was increasing.
3. An "ecclesiastical reservation" made an exception of ecclesiastical princes (archbishops, bishops, and abbots) who ruled territorial states. Any of them who became Lutheran would surrender their states, which would remain under the control of the Church. Lutheran subjects of such princes were not to be forced to give up their religion.
4. Protestant states were to retain whatever Church property they had confiscated prior to 1552.

The Peace of Augsburg marks a definite stage in the disintegration of the Empire, not only because it determined that Germany would remain divided between two religions, but also because it recognized the sovereign authority of the princes in the important matter of religion. It was as much a victory for the princes in their struggle for independence as for the cause of Protestantism.

Spain and the Netherlands Under Philip II

For more than forty years, from 1556 to 1598, Philip II of Spain occupied a place in European affairs scarcely less influential than that of his father, Charles V. The first half-dozen years of Philip's reign marked the opening of a new era in the history of most of the states of Europe. Scenes shifted and new figures replaced the old on the European stage. The strife of Lutheran and Catholic in Germany had been settled by the Religious Peace of Augsburg. In the next few years, Protestantism was permanently established in England and Scotland. The Netherlands were drifting toward open revolt against Spain. France gave up its claims to Italy, thus ending the first phase of the long Hapsburg-Valois wars. The French Huguenots opened the Wars of Religion, which were to devastate France with civil strife for more than a generation, and in 1563 the leaders of the Catholic Church met in the final session of the Council of Trent.

Philip II inherited the crown of Spain with its dependencies in the Netherlands, Italy, and the Americas. Throughout his life he clung to a consistent policy and to the conviction that his policy was God's purpose for the people of Europe. Charles had been a cosmopolitan emperor, to whom family interests meant more than any country; Philip was a Spanish king, with a Spaniard's narrow patriotism, rigid orthodoxy, and relentless hatred of heresy. A baffling variety of tasks demanded his constant attention, and his efforts, like his father's, were hampered at every turn by the utter inadequacy of the financial means at his disposal.

Certain of Philip's domestic policies were highly unwise. After 1492, many Jews, who had been important in Spanish culture and commerce had been driven out of the country. Those who converted to Catholicism (the *conversos*) were allowed to stay in Spain, but the suspicion that many of them were actually *marraños*, or ostensibly converted Jews who secretly practiced Judaism, led the Spanish monarchy and its ally the Inquisition on a relentless hunt for lapsed Jewish converts. Such persecutions under Philip II helped to produce a deadening uniformity in the Spanish nation and in the long run further crippled Spain's development.

The net result of Philip's financial policy was to kill the goose that laid the golden egg. The *alcabala*, a tax of 10 per cent on every sale of goods—to mention but one of many burdensome taxes—was in itself enough to strangle Spain's commerce and starve its industry; to these were added innumerable hampering

Philip II, son of Charles V. Titian's portrait suggests the cold and enigmatic character of the Spanish king.

regulations and prohibitions, which in the end drove most of Spain's trade to the English or Dutch and drained the country of its gold and silver.

The results of Philip's unwise policy in Spain were not immediately discernible. Thanks to the apparent strength acquired through union with the great Hapsburg Empire, Spain had become the most powerful of the European nations during the reign of Charles V. For a time after his death, Spain was able to maintain the appearance of greatness and undiminished prestige, but under Philip Spanish power finally began to crumble. Two important successes, however, helped to hide this fact. In 1571 a partly Spanish fleet administered a decisive defeat to the Turks at Lepanto. In 1580 Philip succeeded in making good a hereditary claim to the kingdom of Portugal, thereby uniting the whole peninsula under his rule and adding the great Portuguese colonial empire to that of Spain. Nevertheless, in summing up the results of Philip's government of Spain over nearly half a century, one must note more failure than success. He left his people orthodox and proud, but his country impoverished. Economically and socially backward, Spain still seemed great, but before long internal decay would destroy its prestige.

In almost every respect the Netherlands was very different from Spain and could not be made to accept the same policies or methods of government. It was one of the tragedies of Philip's reign that he never fully understood or became reconciled to that fact. The seventeen provinces that made up the Netherlands were Philip's by hereditary right, but there was no political bond to hold them together. Each province had its own cherished institutions and ancient privileges. Even national and linguistic unity were lacking; the northern provinces were predominantly Germanic and Dutch-speaking, while the southern were more nearly French in tradition and language.

Early in the sixteenth century, the Netherlands was one of Spain's most lucrative possessions. It included great trading and banking cities such as Antwerp. Its people were hard working, prosperous, and independent, and its geographical position at the crossroads of northwestern Europe was of great strategic interest to the Spanish Hapsburgs. The Netherlanders were open to all the cultural and religious influences of the age and, despite persecution, many had adopted one or another of the Protestant faiths. Lutheranism and Anabap-

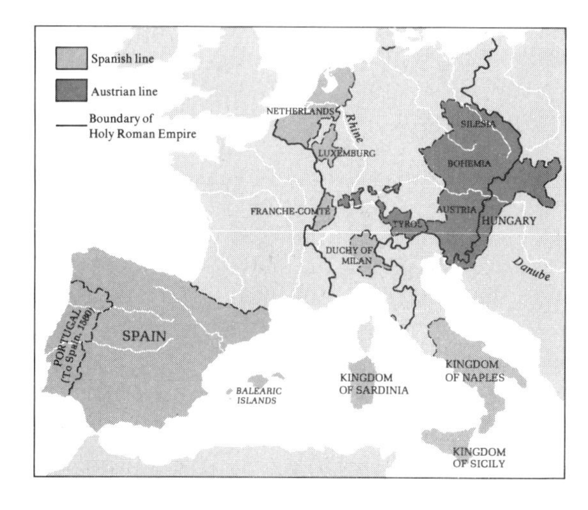

HAPSBURG LANDS AFTER 1556

tism had been the first to make an impression, but at the time Philip began to rule, Calvinism was spreading rapidly in the northern provinces.

The government of a people so divided, yet so prosperous and independent, required tact and understanding. Charles V, a native of the Netherlands and their own prince, had possessed those qualities in sufficient degree to retain their loyalty, though there was a good deal of discontent in his later years. Philip had neither tact nor understanding—and he was more of a foreigner.

The causes of the Netherlands' eventual revolt against Spain were inherent in the characters of Philip and his Dutch subjects. The irreconcilable opposition between his policies and their economic, political, and religious interests further alienated the Dutch. From the beginning they distrusted him as a foreigner who did not speak their language and had no sympathy with their point of view. Philip regarded the Netherlands as satellites of Spain, to be used to advance Spanish interests. Economic grievances soon gave a focus to Dutch resentment of this attitude. Philip was in desperate financial straits. He was forced to begin his reign by increasing the burden of taxation, already high under Charles V, and most of the money wrung from the Netherlanders was spent in Spain. Still worse, he strove to restrict Dutch commerce to give the advantage to Spanish merchants.

Political grievances fed resentment still further, as Philip tried to force upon the Netherlands a centralized absolute government like that of Spain, disregarding the ancient constitutional rights and traditional privileges of the separate provinces. Finally, Philip's determination to crush out heresy in all his dominions permanently alienated the growing number of Dutch Protestants, while his arbitrary reorganization of the Church government (including the creation of a number of new bishoprics) aroused the opposition of many Catholics. Philip's rigid Catholic policy was not the sole cause of the revolt, but once the revolt had begun it was the factor that made impossible any reconciliation of the provinces that were predominantly Protestant.

Provoked by Philip's policies, important elements of the Dutch aristocracy, urban patriciate, and proletariat revolted against Spanish domination. The story of the revolt is filled with heroism and brutality. By the 1570s, under the leadership of William of Nassau, prince of Orange, the northern provinces of the Spanish Netherlands had won their freedom and in 1581 formally declared their independence of Philip II. The southern provinces, known as the Spanish Netherlands (the future Belgium), were overwhelmingly Catholic, and Philip's regent, the diplomatic Alexander Farnese, duke of Parma, succeeded in detaching them from those in the north. Flanders and Wallonia remained in Spanish or Austrian Hapsburg hands until the late eighteenth century.

The northern provinces, known as the United Netherlands, achieved Europe-wide acknowledgment of their freedom in 1648. This achievement of independence marked the beginning of a great age for Dutch commerce and culture. Amsterdam became the great banking center of the West, and artists such as Rembrandt reflected the inspired sense of freedom and creativity unleashed by heroic struggles against the alien Spanish domination.

Monarchical Decline and Religious Wars in France

As in Spain, the territorial consolidation of France was accompanied by the centralization of power in the hands of an absolute monarchy. The nobles were deprived of almost all their political authority and the Estates-General was reduced to a negligible position. Meanwhile, the middle class in France, as elsewhere, profited by the restoration of order and the gradual assumption of economic control by a strong government. At the end of the fifteenth century, France was prosperous and all classes looked to the king as the embodiment of the state.

The most powerful and independent of the French fiefs still extant after the end of the Hundred Years' War was the duchy of Burgundy. Although descended from the French royal family, the Burgundian dukes had by the fifteenth century acquired extensive territories outside of France and gradually ceased to regard themselves as subjects of the French crown. In addition to their original duchy, they held Franche-Comté, Luxembourg, and the rich counties and duchies that make up the Netherlands. To these possessions Duke Charles the Bold (1467–1477) added Alsace and Lorraine. Charles ruled what was practically a kingdom in that debatable land between France and Germany, reminiscent of the ancient kingdom of Lothair, and it is not surprising that he desired the title of king. His ambitions inevitably brought him into violent conflict with Louis XI. For a time he seemed to be gaining the ascendancy, but he had also aroused the enmity of his warlike neighbors, the Swiss, and it was they who finally brought about his defeat and death.

Charles' daughter Mary kept up the struggle with France, aided by her husband Maximilian of Hapsburg, until her death in 1482. Maximilian then made peace with Louis. The duchy of Burgundy was surrendered and brought directly under the French crown. Alsace and Lorraine were returned to their former owners, but the rest of the Burgundian states were kept by Philip the Handsome, the son of Mary and Maximilian, to make a formidable addition to the lands of the House of Hapsburg.

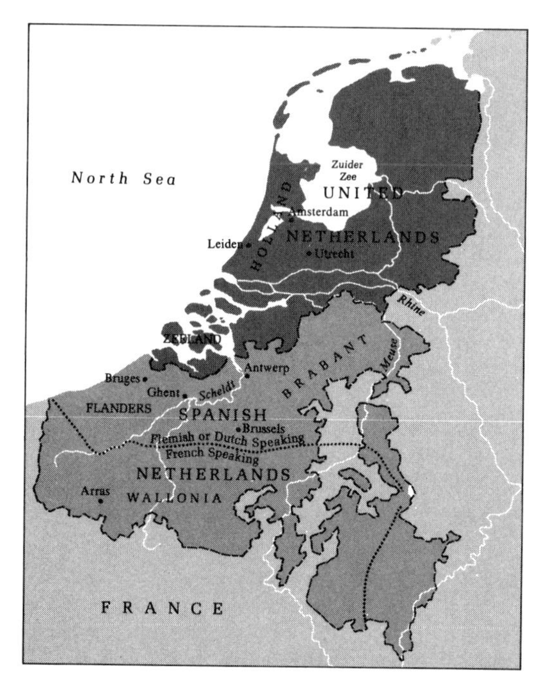

THE DIVISION OF THE NETHERLANDS IN 1581

Meanwhile, Louis XI was using his talent for diplomacy and intrigue to good effect in subjugating other semi-independent feudatories of France. The character of this strange, cunning, and unscrupulous man will always be an enigma to historians. He was superstitious, treacherous, and cruel; yet he must be given credit for his invaluable services in making France a united nation. When he died in 1483, the duchy of Brittany was almost the only fief outside the royal domain. Anne of Beaujeu, sister and regent for the young Charles VIII (1483–1498), secured the union of Brittany with the royal domain through the marriage of the king to Anne, duchess of Brittany, in 1491. This acquisition practically completed the consolidation of France into a united territorial state.

The collapse of political equilibrium opened Italy to a series of foreign interventions and invasions after 1494. These proved catastrophic, leading to the occupation of much of Italy by mercenary Valois and Hapsburg armies. In 1494 Charles VIII decided to make good his claim to Naples. His successor, Louis XII, pursued the same chimerical dreams. Ultimately, the French claims in Italy cost the French monarchy a great deal while achieving nothing in terms of territorial expansion. They succeeded only in weakening the Italian states to such an extent that Hapsburg domination became a reality early in the sixteenth century. The failed ambitions of Charles VIII and the costs they inflicted upon the French kingdom taught his grandson Francis I very little. This ambitious and extravagant young monarch had ambitions that exceeded even those of Charles VIII.

Both Francis I (1515–1547) and Henry II (1547–1559) were often hard-pressed for money to carry on their foreign wars. What income the government had, however, was entirely at the disposal of the king, and with reasonable care it should have been sufficient, though the expense of a standing army was considerable. Royal finances and authority were strengthened by the power Francis I acquired over the Church in France. The Concordat of Bologna (1516) left the king almost complete control of appointments to the higher ecclesiastical offices in the country. He used this power freely to reward the loyalty of the nobles and also to pay the diplomats and ministers who served him, thus relieving the royal treasury of a considerable drain. A further extension of royal power over the Church occurred in 1539, when Francis I transferred jurisdiction over the great majority of cases from the ecclesiastical courts to the royal courts.

The fact that the king had already acquired as much control of the national church and its wealth as he desired was one of the most important factors deciding the fate of the Reformation in France. Otherwise, Francis might easily have followed the example of other northern rulers in breaking with Rome. As it was, he remained strictly orthodox and persecuted heresy whenever he was on good terms with the pope, though neither he nor his son hesitated to ally themselves with the Protestant princes of Germany. Henry II was much more severe than his father in the persecution of French heretics, and, indeed, he had more to work on, for despite persecution the Calvinist faith spread rapidly in France.

The Reformation came to France as an importation from Germany and Switzerland, though the way had been prepared by early French humanists. The secret of its success was the influence of John Calvin and the shift among French Protestants from Lutheranism to Calvinism. Calvin was French and a master of French prose. He maintained personal supervision of the struggling French Protestant communities from his Genevan stronghold on France's eastern frontier, giving them the benefit of his genius for organization. Moreover, the Calvinist form of church organization was especially well adapted to the formation of a church in opposition to a hostile state government. In the year 1559, which saw the death of Henry II, the first French Protestant synod met secretly in the king's own city of Paris to work out a national organization for the Reformed Church in France.

In 1560 the crown passed to Henry's second son Charles IX (1560–1574), who was still a child. His mother, Catherine de' Medici, promptly took control of the royal government as regent. Hitherto this daughter of the famous Florentine family had played a secondary role as the wife of Henry II and mother of the late king, Francis II (1559–1560), but from this time on she was to be a principal participant in a hectic French drama. For nearly twenty years she directed the government and wielded whatever power was left to the French crown. She clung to a consistent policy, though one that had every appearance of inconsistency. Her aim was simply to retain control of the government for herself and her sons and to keep the kingdom at peace. To do so, she played off extreme Catholic against Huguenot (around 1560 French Protestants came to be known as Huguenots). Catherine strove to build up a center party of moderate Catholics who would be loyal to the crown and would help to keep the peace.

Her first action was to stop the persecution of the Protestants and to issue an edict granting them limited freedom of worship. This moderate edict failed to satisfy them, however, and it aroused strong opposition from the extreme Catholics. Fanaticism on both sides flared to fever heat. Catholics and Protestants rioted and desecrated each other's churches in every corner of France. In 1562, the duke of Guise, placing himself at the head of a group of Catholic nobles, seized control of the government and forced Catherine to recall the edict of toleration. The Protestants took up arms to defend their faith. The Wars of Religion had begun.

During the first decade of the religious wars in France, Catherine de' Medici occasionally pursued her goal of arranging a moderate peace between the two sides. In order to retain control of the government, she negotiated with Admiral de Coligny, a Huguenot leader, and planned to marry her daughter Margaret to young Henry of Navarre, who in time would become the leader of the Huguenots. As usual, however, Catherine failed to reckon with the fanatical passions on both sides, which she could never understand. The Huguenots were still unsatisfied, and the Catholics were developing a strong opposition under Duke Henry of Guise, the son of the old Catholic leader. Moreover, Catherine began to fear the influence of Coligny with the king, now of age, whom he was trying to persuade to help the Protestant rebels in the Netherlands and to seize the opportunity provided by the revolt to annex the French-speaking provinces.

Peace seemed as far away, and Catherine decided to throw in her lot again with the Guises. She persuaded herself that the admiral and the few remaining Huguenot leaders were the principal obstacles to peace and that if they were removed, Huguenot resistance would collapse. Their presence in Paris for the wedding of Henry and Margaret provided the opportunity, and on St. Bartholomew's Eve in 1572, Catherine and the Guises laid the plans that led to a terrible massacre on the following day, August 24, 1572. They had probably intended the murder of Coligny and the other chiefs, which Henry of Guise supervised himself, but, as news of the killing spread, the fanatical Parisian mob rose and before morning two thousand Protestants had been slain. Similar massacres in other cities accounted for thousands more deaths.

Between the St. Bartholomew's Day massacre in 1572 and the death in 1589 of the last of Catherine's sons, Henry III, France endured a period of religious wars compounded by an emerging dynastic struggle. Many nobles used religion as an excuse to attack the centralized monarchical system they had always disliked.

Henry of Navarre came from a small southwestern French kingdom in which the Huguenots were the majority. He was also the leader of the entire Huguenot party in France. When Henry III had a falling-out with Duke Henry of Guise, leader of the fanatical Catholic League, he caused Duke Henry to be murdered. This decision provoked his own assassination by a fanatical member of the league in the same year. At the death of Henry III, Henry of Navarre proclaimed himself king of France as Henry IV.

His religion was the chief obstacle in Henry's path to the throne. Except for that, the French people would have accepted him willingly enough, for they were weary of war. After four more years of fighting, Henry IV finally realized that the obstacle was insurmountable and formally adopted the Catholic faith. He is supposed to have uttered the cynical words, "Paris is worth a Mass." He had little trouble reconciling the leaders of the league, though he had still to fight a war with Spain, for Philip II was loath to give up his dream of dominating France through the Catholic party. The war ended on terms favorable to France in 1598, the last year of Philip's reign.

England's Path to Greatness

England had scarcely emerged from the Hundred Years' War in 1453 when it was plunged into long, intermittent civil strife between rival factions in the royal family and the nobility. The frequent and rather petty civil wars are known collectively as the Wars of the Roses for the white and red roses that were the badges of the houses of York and Lancaster respectively. The Hundred Years' War had left a dangerous legacy of disorder. The great nobles had become accustomed to keeping large bands of armed retainers, as well as to violence and bloodshed. The Wars of the Roses dragged on for several decades, thinning the ranks of the old nobility and destroying the form of neo-feudalism typified by the "livery and maintenance" or retainer system. A widespread desire for order provided the popular basis for a strong Tudor monarchy after 1485.

A new era in England's history opened in 1485 with the reign of Henry VII (1485-1509), first of the Tudor sovereigns. Having no very sound hereditary claim to the throne, Henry knew that his only hope of keeping it lay in giving the people the kind of government they wanted, and they wanted above all peace, security for life and property, and an opportunity to carry on their business under favorable conditions. A task of this magnitude takes time, and much was left to be done by his successors, but when Henry VII died England was in a reasonably orderly condition, with the royal authority unquestionably supreme in the state. His unabrasive centralization, further extended by Henry VIII and Thomas Cromwell, renewed and remolded English judicial and administrative institutions. It has aptly been called the "Tudor revolution in government" by the great contemporary British historian G. R. Elton.

Henry VII never forgot the interests of the merchants. English commerce, especially the rich trade in wool and woolen goods, had been growing rapidly during the fifteenth century, but with very little help from the central government. A large part of English trade was still handled by foreigners, some of whom, like the Hanseatic merchants, had greater privileges in English ports than did the natives themselves. Moreover, lacking strong support from the state, English merchants could not always secure favorable treatment in other countries. Henry undertook to change all this. At the beginning of his reign he passed legislation through Parliament designed to give English ships, manned by English sailors, a monopoly on the transport of certain types of goods. Wherever possible, he limited the privileges of foreign traders in England to give the advantage to their native competitors; where the foreigners still held privileges in England, he sought treaties with their home governments to secure reciprocal privileges for English merchants.

Henry VIII (1509–1547) inherited a government that was almost as absolute as that of the Valois kings. Confronted with this all-powerful monarchy, the old feudal nobility faded into insignificance. They were excluded from the king's council, which was the chief instrument of the central government, in favor of middle-class men and the new nobility created by the crown—men trained in legal and administrative service and wholly devoted to the king. At the same time, their local jurisdiction was superseded by that of justices of the peace recruited from the country gentry.

Although Tudor government was absolute, it was also popular and scrupulously constitutional. Parliament never died out in England as the Estates-General was dying out in France. Under Henry VIII, Parliament might seem little more than a tool in the hands of the king, but it was a tool that he used constantly and kept in good condition. Henry's major policies, such as his radical alteration of the government of the Church and his dissolution of the monasteries, were carried out by act of Parliament. Henry VIII was, indeed, a master in the art of handling Parliament. The success of the great Tudor monarchs, Henry VII, Henry VIII, and Elizabeth I, depended in large part on the fact that they understood their people, and never forgot the economic interests of the gentry and the middle class.

The task of administering an absolute government in England was made

Henry VIII, painted in 1540 by Hans Holbein the Younger. The painting shows the English king at the age of forty-nine, seven years before his death.

easier by the fact that it was relatively inexpensive. The English monarchs did not need to maintain a standing army, as did the continental rulers whose borders were always open to invasion. Though Henry VIII was frequently drawn into continental complications, the number of English troops employed on the Continent was never large. Instead of building a strong permanent army, Henry devoted his attention to the more important, but less expensive, task of creating a royal navy.

Henry's son, Edward VI, ruled for six years and died in 1553. Before Protestantism was finally established in England, there occurred a brief Catholic interlude. It may be that when Edward's half-sister Mary Tudor, daughter of Henry VIII and Catherine of Aragon, came to the throne in 1553, the majority of the English people were still either Catholic or sufficiently indifferent to the nuances of theological conflict to accept either church. The proof is that Mary, herself a devout Catholic, was able with the aid of Parliament to restore Catholicism as the official religion and to reunite the English Church to the Roman. There was no rebellion, and the Catholic restoration might have been successful but for two factors. In 1554, Mary married Philip II of Spain and undertook a close alliance that reduced England to the position of a Spanish satellite. She also persecuted Protestants with a harshness that won for her the name Bloody Mary. The Spanish alliance, coupled with the persecution and the restoration of papal authority, aroused national resentment and hatred of Spain and the Papacy. When Mary died, most Englishmen were formally Catholic, but Catholicism had become unpopular. The religious issue was still to be decided, however.

The crucial decision was made by a young woman of twenty-five, Elizabeth I (1558-1603), daughter of Henry's second wife, Anne Boleyn, and the last of the Tudors. She had been raised a Protestant but was no fanatic. What she wanted was a national church, free from Rome and subject only to the royal authority,

Mary Tudor, daughter of Henry VIII and wife of Philip II. This work is by Antonio Moro, a Flemish painter praised for his lifelike portraits.

Protestant in character but liberal enough so that all but the most stubborn extremists would conform. She procured it by act of Parliament in 1559. In the matter of church government, Elizabeth followed the example set by her father. An Act of Supremacy re-established the Anglican Church under the supreme authority of the crown, with the old episcopal system otherwise unchanged. This was followed by an Act of Uniformity, which prescribed the use of a Book of Common Prayer as the only legal form of worship.

Having secured the outward uniformity that was essential for political reasons, Elizabeth was prepared to leave a good deal of leeway in matters of doctrine. The creed as stated in the Prayer Book and the later Thirty-Nine Articles was predominantly Protestant, but the phrasing at crucial points was vague enough to allow moderate Catholics, who did not adhere rigidly to the pope, to attend the national church without experiencing too great a shock to their consciences, while almost all Protestants, whether they had taken their opinions from Wittenberg or Geneva, could interpret it to suit their own convictions. The Elizabethan settlement of the church was a characteristically English compromise and was amazingly permanent. Elizabeth reigned long enough to see it firmly established, and its main outlines have prevailed to our own time. Divergent parties soon arose, and many dissenters later seceded but, in Elizabeth's time at least, the great majority of English people remained within the Anglican Church. Only the more radical Protestant sects and the secret Catholics remained stubbornly aloof. They were punished and harassed by fines, but were not usually persecuted so severely as to arouse public sympathy. Saint Edmund Campion (executed in 1581) and other Jesuit martyrs were exceptions to this policy.

Scotland was still a very backward country, almost medieval in its social

Elizabeth I, daughter of Henry VIII and half-sister of Mary Tudor and, for a time, courted by Philip II. Probably painted from life around 1575, this portrait gives a striking impression of the firm character of the English queen.

and political structure. Its church, dominated by lawless nobles, was disproportionately wealthy for a poverty-stricken country and was probably the most corrupt in Europe. It was an easy target for the attacks of the Protestant reformers. Moreover, the latter had patriotic national sentiment on their side. The Scottish people were growing restless under the rule of the French regent, Mary of Guise, while their queen, her daughter Mary Stuart, was living at the French court and in 1558 married Francis II, heir to the throne of France. They resented the treatment of Scotland as a dependency of France, and as the Guises were ultra-Catholic, Catholicism came to be associated in the popular mind with French domination. The materials for a conflagration were present.

All that was needed to set the land ablaze was the fiery preaching of John Knox, who had imbibed Calvinism at its source during a period of exile in Geneva. In 1557, a congregation of Scottish nobles signed the first covenant for the defense of the Protestant faith. Two years later, Scotland was in armed rebellion against the French Catholic regent, and in 1560 Elizabeth sent aid to the rebels to help them drive out the French troops.

When Mary Stuart came to rule her Scottish kingdom in 1561, she found the Calvinist Presbyterian Church already firmly established. The fact that the Reformation had come to Scotland in the form of Calvinism and in opposition to the government made the religious situation in Scotland different from that in England. The Presbyterian Church was founded as the result of a revolution that swept away the old episcopal system. As was characteristic of Calvinist churches everywhere, its organization was essentially democratic, with the final authority vested in the congregations and their elders and ministers. Such a church could not be controlled by the state, but could bring powerful pressure to bear on the government. This Mary Stuart soon learned to her cost. Through seven years of folly and romantic adventure she fought the power of the church, only to be beaten by it. At last she fled the country to take refuge in England, leaving her infant son, James VI, to be brought up by Presbyterian divines.

Given this religious turmoil, it is surprising that Philip II of Spain did not attack England; he would have had a chance of success. But there were a number of good reasons for his delay. At first he had hopes of restoring ascendancy over England, which he had lost on the death of his wife Mary Tudor, by marrying Elizabeth or by playing upon her fear that France would support the claims of Mary Stuart. Elizabeth's astute diplomacy maintained the delusion as long as possible. Then the Netherlands revolted and Philip put off war with England in order to regain control of his northern possessions. He lacked the sea power to land an army in England, as long as the English could count on the aid of Dutch and Huguenot privateers, and with every passing year the English themselves became more formidable opponents on the sea. Philip accordingly turned to conspiracy with English Catholics to rid himself of Elizabeth and to restore Catholicism in England by replacing the Protestant ruler with the Catholic Mary Stuart.

The weak points in Elizabeth's position were that she was the last of the direct line of Tudors; that her legitimacy was disputed by all good Catholics, who had never recognized the validity of Henry's divorce from Catherine and marriage to Anne Boleyn; and that Mary Stuart, great-granddaughter of Henry VII, was the next claimant to the throne. For years Elizabeth's life was in constant danger from Spanish-Catholic plots—which aroused in patriotic Englishmen an undying hatred of Catholic Spain. So long as Mary Stuart lived, neither English independence nor Protestantism was safe. Elizabeth protected the unhappy queen of Scots as long as she could, but at last in 1587 she submitted to the popular demand and ordered her execution for treason. There was then nothing to delay Philip any longer. He immediately declared war, which lasted until after the end of Elizabeth's reign. Though the war dragged on for years, its outcome was settled at the very beginning by the dramatic defeat of Philip's great Armada in 1588. The destruction of the Armada marked a definite stage in the decline of Spain's power, while for England it was the start of a great era of ascendancy on the sea.

Suggestions for Further Reading

S. T. Bindoff, *Tudor England** (1950). A concise, readable introduction, part of the Penguin History of England series. All volumes in the series are good starting points for the interested undergraduate.

K. Brandi, *The Emperor Charles V,** trans. by C. V. Wedgwood (1968). Many people consider this to be the definitive biography of Charles V. It is a portrait of the age as much as of the emperor.

J. H. Elliott, *Imperial Spain, 1469-1716* (1964). A major contemporary work on Spain during the years of its illusory greatness and depressing decline.

G. R. Elton, *England Under the Tudors* (1955). Geoffrey Elton has made major contributions to our understanding of the "new monarchy" in England under the Tudors.

G. R. Elton, *The Tudor Revolution in Government** (1953).

P. Geyl, *The Revolt of the Netherlands,** rev. ed. (1962). A balanced, detailed study, it has superseded the nineteenth-century classic by John Lothrop Motley.

H. Holborn, *A History of Modern Germany,* vol. 1 (1959). First volume of a history of Germany from the late Middle Ages to the fall of the Third Reich, covering constitutional, political, religious, intellectual, social, and economic developments [AHA, 551, in part].

J. R. Major, *Representative Institutions in Renaissance France* (1960). Important studies of the French monarchy and its institutions in the fifteenth and sixteenth centuries.

G. Mattingly, *The Armada** (1959). A masterpiece showing that one can write good history and exciting drama at the same time—or at least that Mattingly could.

G. Mattingly, *Renaissance Diplomacy** (1955, reprinted 1971). By now a standard work. Mattingly knew the Italian archives as have few other scholars. He also knew how to write sparkling historical prose.

J. E. Neale, *The Age of Catherine de Medici** (1943). A brief, interesting introduction to the age.

J. E. Neale, *Queen Elizabeth** (1934). A fine biography.

A. L. Rowse, *The Elizabethan Age,* 2 vols. (1951-1955). A wide range of topics—social, intellectual, and political [AHA, 432].

J. J. Scarisbrick, *Henry VIII** (1968). Both the Scarisbrick and Smith biographies are up-to-date, scholarly, and readable.

L. B. Smith, *Henry VIII** (1971).

C. V. Wedgwood, *William the Silent** (1944).

*Available in a paperback edition.

Early Modern Europe

FIVE

The Age of Exploration and Colonization

23

> If the Strait is found . . . the king of Spain . . . might call himself the lord of the whole world.
>
> HERNANDO CORTEZ TO EMPEROR CHARLES V

Expansion of the European Horizon

The dynamism of European civilization, a product of a combination of factors—growing technological superiority, the Christian impulse, a lust for domination and adventure—may be termed the Faustian element in Western civilization. The Faust of poetry was a man tormented by a desire for continual satisfaction, which he never seemed to obtain. To some historians he became the symbol of Western civilization, always in motion, always reaching out, whether for the Indies or for the moon.

What knowledge medieval Europe possessed of the world outside its narrow borders it had inherited mostly from ancient Greek geographers. The Greeks had been aware that the earth is a sphere, and Eratosthenes (c. 200 B.C.) had calculated its circumference with remarkable accuracy at about twenty-five thousand miles. Most of the ancient fund of knowledge was transmitted to medieval Europe through the encyclopedic *Geography* of Claudius Ptolemy (c. A.D. 150), who believed the circumference of the earth to be much smaller—about eighteen thousand miles—and so inspired explorers with undue optimism. More precise information about the outlines of the known world was provided by medieval Moslem and Christian navigators and map-makers. On the best medieval maps, Europe, northern Africa, western Asia, and the lands bordering the Indian Ocean were shown fairly accurately.

Much as the medieval navigators did for the science of geography, however, the first great addition to Western knowledge of the world during the Middle Ages was made by travelers who pressed overland until they reached the rich and populous countries of the distant East. Of these the most important were three members of an enterprising Venetian merchant family. In 1271, Niccolò and Matteo Polo, who had already traded in the western portion of the great Tartar Empire that covered central Asia and eastern Europe, set out on a second expedition to the East. This time they took with them Niccolò's young son Marco. They pressed on through central Asia until they arrived at the court of the Tartar emperor, Kublai Khan, in the Chinese city of Pekin. They were kindly received and were given positions of honor in the Tartar government.

After his return, Marco Polo published his memoirs. His account of what he had seen is amazingly accurate, though to his contemporaries it seemed the wildest exaggeration. Still, if only part of what "Marco of the Millions" recounted was true, there was in the East wealth such as Europe had never dreamed of—held, moreover, by a people who loved the arts of peace more than war. To Europeans, poor and warlike, Cathay (China) became the promised land of unbelievable wealth, an easy prey if only it could be reached, or at any rate the source of a fabulously rich trade.

Aside from Marco Polo's story, the West already had ample evidence of the rich possibilities of trade with the Far East. The trade in pepper, cinnamon, and other spices highly valued in an age when artificial means of preserving food were rare, as well as in silk, precious stones, and other luxury goods, had helped to found the fortunes of Venice, Genoa, and Pisa. But the Italians could not trade directly with the producers of these commodities. Moslem middlemen who commanded the land and water routes between India and the Mediterranean took the lion's share of the profits. The long overland route through central Asia was impractical for regular trade. Was there not some other way of reaching India and China, a direct route by water that would enable Western merchants to sail directly to the source of Eastern wealth?

The Church had an interest in a new route to the East, for the desire to convert the Mongols and outflank Islam was very strong in Christian Europe during the late Middle Ages. The hope of finding such a route, by sailing either south around Africa or west to Asia—believed to be much closer to Europe than it actually is—inspired daring Portuguese, Spanish, French, and English seamen of the fifteenth century and earlier to set out on perilous voyages of exploration into the unknown Atlantic. Fear of the Atlantic was ingrained in the minds of European sailors, accustomed as they were only to coastal voyages, though the use of the magnetic compass as a guide in the open sea had long been known, and the caravels developed by the Portuguese in the fifteenth century were seaworthy little ships, capable of long ocean voyages.

Had it not been for the authority of the great state governments, backed by the capital and demands of the merchant class, the age of discovery might have been postponed indefinitely. It is doubtful that it could have been achieved by the medieval system of guild and city economy. It was no coincidence that discovery followed the rise of centralized states and the beginnings of capitalism, nor was it coincidence that the explorations were nearly all sponsored by the states along the Atlantic seaboard. The people who faced the Atlantic felt the need of a new route to the East more keenly than did the Italians, who were content with their monopoly of the Eastern trade.

The little kingdom of Portugal, situated at the southwest tip of Europe, took the lead in fifteenth-century exploration of the east coast of Africa and the neighboring islands of the Atlantic. The Portuguese were not the first to set out, but they were the most persistent, thanks in large part to the intelligent direction and unflagging enthusiasm of a prince of the royal family, Henry "the Navigator," who for more than forty years prior to his death in 1460 devoted himself to the encouragement of exploration. Henry's motives were a strange mixture of scientific curiosity, crusading zeal, and national ambition. Some of his ideas—such as his hope of reaching the upper Nile from the western coast by way of the Senegal River and thus outflanking the Moslems in North Africa—proved erroneous. Nevertheless, his explorers achieved important results. Before his death they had founded permanent settlements on the islands of Madeira and the

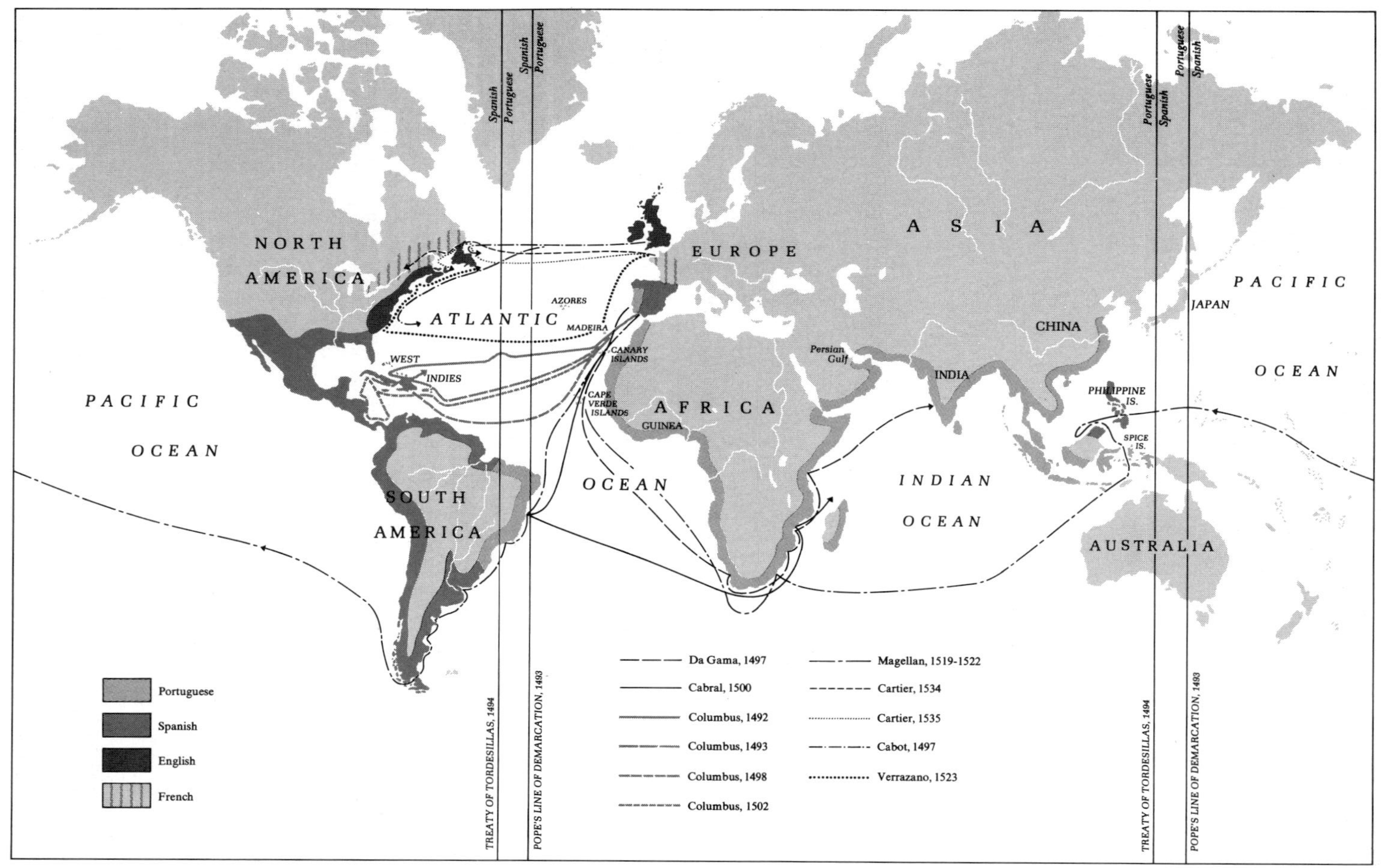

PRINCIPAL VOYAGES AND EXPLORATIONS OF THE FIFTEENTH AND EARLY SIXTEENTH CENTURIES

Azores and had set up a regular trade, partly in slaves, with the Guinea coast of western Africa and were already pushing farther south. The sure profits of the Guinea trade, however, tended to keep explorers from going farther, and twenty-six years passed before the first Portuguese ship, commanded by Bartolomeo Diaz, rounded the southern extremity of Africa in 1486, opening up the way to India and the Spice Islands (Indonesia). In 1498 a Portuguese fleet under Vasco da Gama sailed into the Indian harbor of Calicut and established the first direct commercial contact between Europe and the Far East, thereby giving the Portuguese a monopoly on the rich Eastern trade, which they held for nearly a hundred years.

In the meantime, while the Portuguese were making their way down the African coast, other explorers were following the lure of the East out across the open Atlantic. Since they knew nothing of the two continents of North and South America that barred the way, the explorers who sailed due west had every reason to believe that they were taking the shortest and most convenient route to China or India. In the plans of the Genoese captain Christopher Columbus, who sailed westward with a charter from the Spanish government in 1492, there was nothing novel except his determination to sail on until he encountered land, instead of turning back, as his predecessors had done, to look for the mythical islands of the Atlantic. Columbus' determination was founded upon faith in his mission and unquenchable optimism. Selecting from the estimates by ancient and medieval geographers those which were most favorable to his purpose, he assumed the distance from the Canary Islands to the east coast of Asia to be less than a third of what it actually is. On his first voyage into the unknown, wind and weather favored his little fleet all the way, and after thirty-three days Columbus sighted land just about where he expected to find it. Having touched the Caribbean islands of the Greater Antilles, he returned convinced that he had found India. Three later explorations, in 1493, 1498, and 1502, brought disillusionment. In the next few years, Spanish explorers coasted the mainland from Florida to Brazil and found it to be an impassable barrier.

Despite their disappointment at not reaching the East, the Spanish adventurers applied themselves to the conquest and exploitation of the lands they had found. This process was accompanied by the most frightful cruelty to the natives. For all their brutal exploitation, the Spaniards discovered in the islands where they first settled no great or sudden wealth, though the colonies they founded proved permanently valuable. Not until they reached Mexico was their dream of finding El Dorado realized. The conquest of the Aztecs of Mexico by Hernando Cortez and a small Spanish force in 1519 brought to light a store of gold and silver such as no European had ever seen. A few years later, a handful of Spaniards under Francisco Pizarro began the conquest of Peru. They took from the peaceful Incas quantities of gold and silver that surpassed even the riches of Mexico.

The Spanish government, meanwhile, had not given up all hope of establishing direct contact with the East and cutting in on Portugal's trade with the Spice Islands. Spanish-Portuguese rivalry dates back to the beginning of the discoveries. As early as 1493, Pope Alexander VI had divided the newly found lands into two hemispheres, assigning to Spain all territory lying west of a line drawn three hundred seventy leagues to the west of the Azores and to Portugal those east of that line. In the following year Portugal and Spain formalized their agreement over this demarcation in the Treaty of Tordesillas. The pope's decision seemed to be a sign of the power of the medieval Papacy; however, the two countries actually relied upon their own treaty, which was a realistic expression of the rise of the national monarchies and the decline of the Roman Papacy in the late Middle Ages.

One of the first results of the demarcation was that Portugal claimed that Brazil—which was touched on by the Portuguese captain Cabral on his way to India in 1500—extended to the east of the line. The division also caused a dispute about whether the East Indies were in the Eastern or Western Hemisphere. To settle this dispute and to find a western route to the East, the Spanish government in 1519 sent out an expedition of five ships to sail around South America. The expedition was commanded by a Portuguese noble, Ferdinand Magellan, who had sailed with his countrymen to the East but had since entered the service of Spain. The voyage was long and hazardous, one of the most daring and important of all the explorations.

After following the eastern coast of South America to its southern tip, Magellan passed through the dangerous straits that are still called by his name and struck out into the southern Pacific. Three terrible months passed before he sighted inhabited islands. Magellan himself was killed a little later in a fight with natives of the Philippines, but what was left of his crew went on with their one remaining ship. In September 1522, their number reduced to eighteen, they arrived home, the first men to have sailed completely around the world. They had proved that, despite the immense size of the Pacific Ocean, it was possible to sail westward to Asia, but also that it was an impractical route under sixteenth-century conditions. And they had discovered the Philippine Islands and claimed them for Spain.

The Commercial Revolution

The expansion of European commerce overseas greatly accelerated the growth of capitalism. What were the cumulative effects of the commercial revolution? It increased the volume of production and exchange, which had been growing steadily since the middle of the fifteenth century. Overseas trade extended over far longer routes than any known to the late medieval Italians. Large sums of money were required to finance voyages to India and to the New World, and the returns were often long delayed. The immense profits which might accrue from worldwide trade were thus available only to individuals or corporate groups who could afford to invest large sums of capital and leave them tied up over a considerable period of time. Though the early explorations were financed and directed by state governments, which claimed a share of the profits, capital made the new trade possible and capitalists, in the final analysis, profited most.

The discovery of North and South America had an incalculably stimulating effect upon the European economic system entirely aside from the general expansion of the market which it brought about. The growth and smooth functioning of capitalist business demanded an adequate supply of coinage, even though much business was conducted on credit and the techniques by which monetary exchange was carried out on paper were constantly improving. The flood of gold and silver which for more than a century poured into Europe from Mexico, Peru, and other parts of the New World met this demand to an unprecedented degree. It made possible larger accumulations of money, lubricated the wheels of business, and caused a steady rise in prices to the advantage of the entrepreneur. Some two hundred tons of gold and eighteen thousand tons of silver, by official count, entered Spain between 1520 and 1660 and thence spread throughout Europe, since much of Spain's new wealth was used to maintain armies abroad and to purchase goods from countries with advanced industries.

The Portuguese discovery of an all-water route to India struck a fatal blow to Italian commerce. Italy's industries and trade with the lands bordering the Mediterranean continued, but in a diminishing degree, for both suffered from growing French, Dutch, and English competition. Inherited wealth and skill also enabled the Italians to retain for a long time an important though no longer dominant position in international finance. But Italian capitalism was no longer a dynamic force.

South German cities such as Augsburg and Nuremberg also suffered a decline in the late sixteenth century. The importance of the great European trade routes—going from the old Hanseatic cities to the Mediterranean by way of Alpine passes and Italian ports such as Pisa, Genoa, and Venice—was surpassed by that of Atlantic ports in the west. These German cities became sleepy backwaters until the nineteenth century.

For a time in the sixteenth century, Antwerp, before being ruined by the revolt of the Netherlands against Spanish rule, took the place of the Italian cities as the center of European commercial and financial capitalism. From 1485, the Antwerp Bourse, or Exchange, was open daily and was used by merchants of all nations for the exchange of goods. It was also the scene of frantic speculation. Antwerp was the first great money market and its Bourse the first great exchange of the modern world.

Capitalism and the State: Mercantilism

With some notable exceptions, the horizon of the medieval merchant was bounded by local trade fairs and the rules of his guild and the city council. With the expansion of trade in the late Middle Ages the concerns of wealthy merchants, particularly in western Europe, came to include the economic policies of the monarchies in which they lived. The early modern monarchical state, in turn, took a profound interest in the economic activities of its merchants.

For transoceanic trade—in which it was necessary to equip fleets for long voyages, deal on distant shores with native potentates, build forts, fight for trade against pirates or competitors, and sink capital for long periods in planting colonies—regulated companies in which each merchant traded on his own capital proved inadequate. In Spain and Portugal, the monarchy took over the supervision of trade and colonization. Elsewhere the need for large and continuous operations was met by the formation of joint-stock companies. Though these companies resembled the state-regulated companies in having been granted a monopoly and semi-official status by the national government, they were formed by the sale of shares to a large number of investors. The investors made a profit or suffered losses in proportion to the size of their investment. The shares, once the company was formed, could be bought and sold on the open market; they represented a new kind of transferable property.

Such a national economic policy is generally known as mercantilism. Mercantilism consists essentially of the regulation of industry and commerce by the state government, with a view to making the state more prosperous and hence more powerful in relation to neighboring states. An important aim of mercantilist policy was the accumulation in the state of a large supply of money—gold and silver. The government regulated trade whenever possible, to encourage exports and limit imports—that is, to maintain a favorable balance of trade. If a country sold more than it bought, more money would come into the state than would leave it. Another aim, closely allied to the first, was to increase the wealth of the state by founding colonies—as Spain and Portugal did in the sixteenth century and England, France, and Holland did in the seventeenth—and to exploit them in the interest of the mother country.

The mercantilist state always tried to maintain an exclusive monopoly on trade with its colonies, exchanging manufactured goods for raw materials of greater potential value. Since war was an ever-present possibility, the preparation for war was a regular aspect of every government's economic policy. This explains why some states, like France, frequently forbade the export of grain, so that the country would not be dependent on its neighbors for food in case of war.

WORLDWIDE COLONIAL HOLDINGS, C. 1689

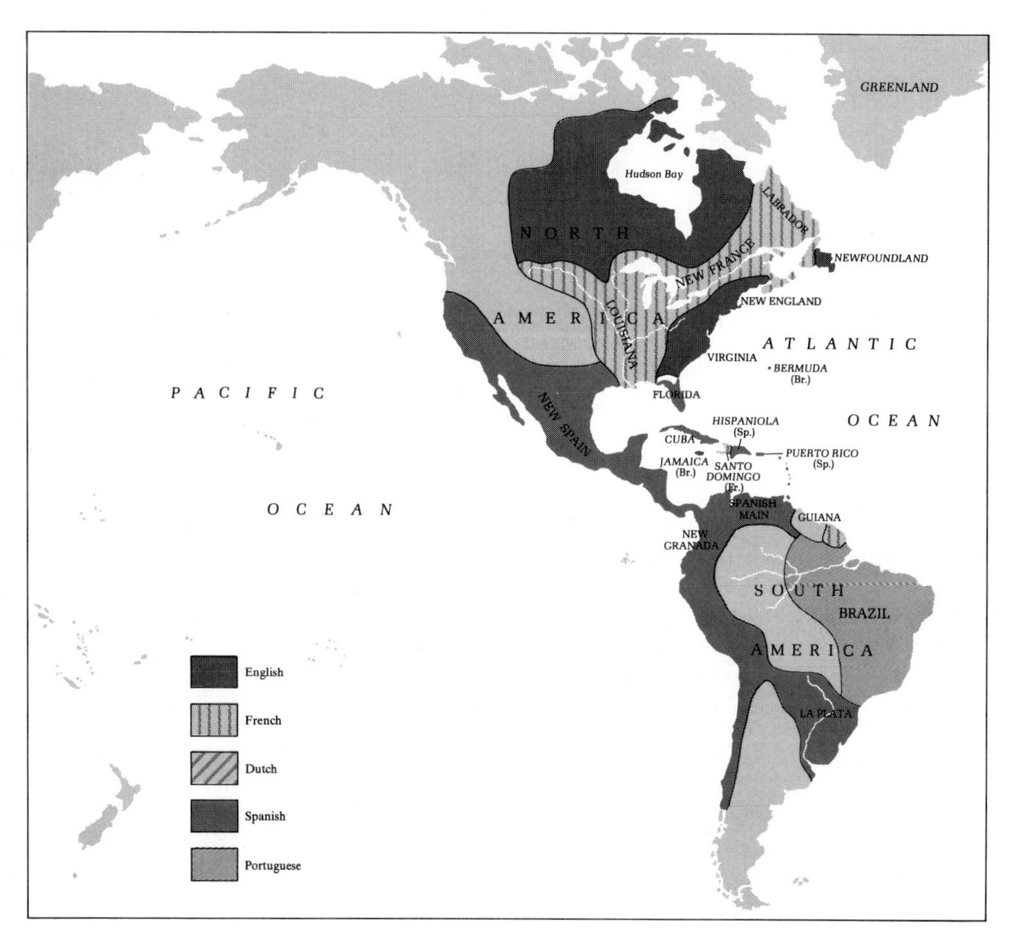

It was also one of the reasons why maritime states like England promoted the shipbuilding and fishing industries and issued navigation acts to encourage native shipping, thus building a merchant marine manned by trained seamen which could serve as a naval reserve.

In regulating industry, the mercantilist governments adhered to the same principles that motivated their commercial legislation. In the late sixteenth century the silk industry was introduced into France with government aid, and the glass industry was founded with royal monopolies in both France (1551) and England (1567). Government regulation and aid, however, did not always serve their intended purpose, and not infrequently industries were more hampered than helped by the well-meaning efforts of a paternalistic state.

When the state took upon itself the task of controlling the economic life of its citizens, it was forced also to assume responsibility for adjusting the social problems that arose from economic conditions. The Elizabethan Poor Laws and the famous Statute of Apprentices (1563) are examples of numerous state laws intended, in part at least, to care for the poor and protect laborers.

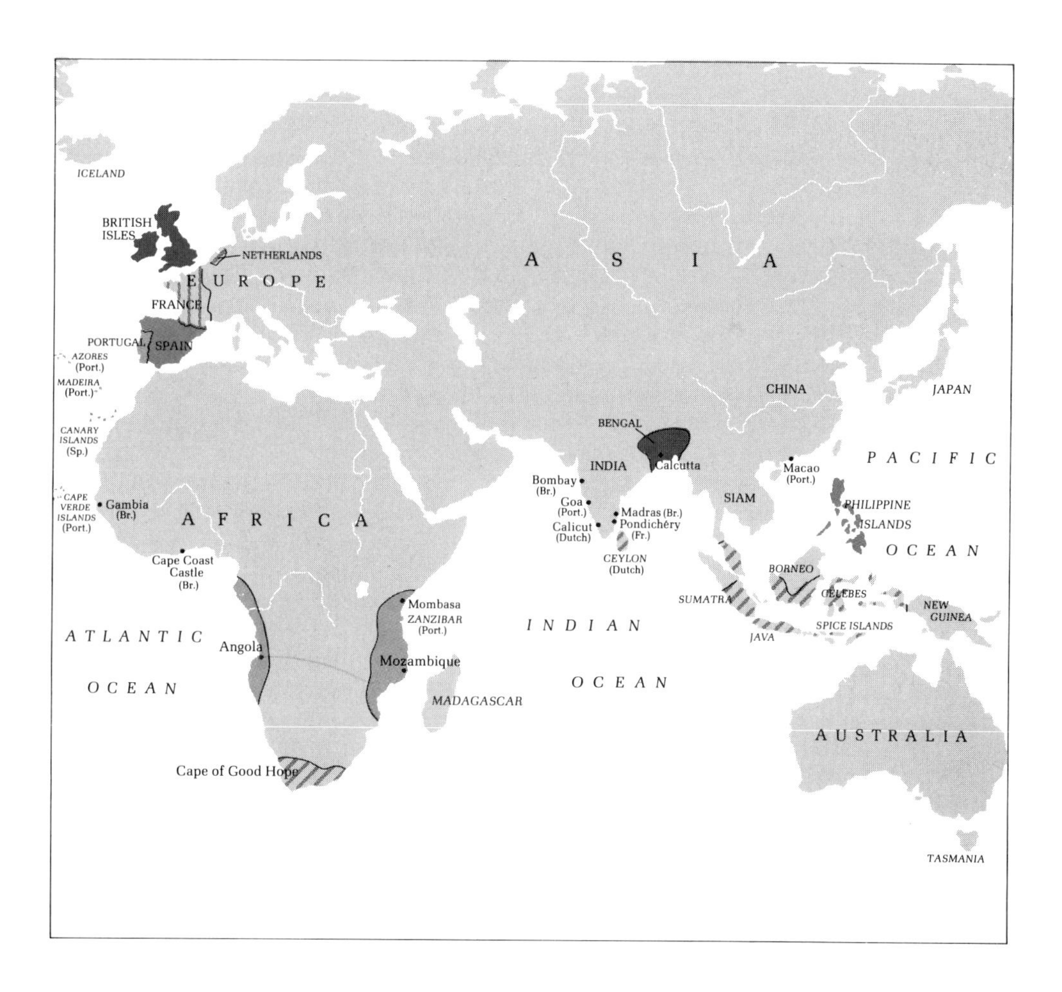

Portugal and Spain Overseas

The western or Malabar coast of India, where Vasco da Gama landed near Calicut in 1498, was peculiarly well suited to serve as a base of operations for Portuguese expansion in the East. Taking advantage of the mutual jealousy of the local princes, the Portuguese gained allies and secured the right to establish fortified posts at strategic points along the coast. From these bases they maintained a permanent fleet and waged a war of extermination on the Moslem merchants who traded westward. The flimsy Arab craft, built only to sail before the periodic monsoon winds, crumbled under the fire of Portuguese cannon, and after a large Egyptian fleet had been destroyed in 1509 without the loss of a single Portuguese ship, the Moslem traders withdrew from the Indian Ocean. In the same year the great Portuguese viceroy Afonso de Albuquerque seized Ormuz, the port which commanded entrance to the Persian Gulf, and in 1510 he gained possession of the city of Goa on the Malabar coast, a magnificent harbor which for centuries remained the capital of the Portuguese empire in the East.

Complete domination of the trade west from Malabar was only the first step in the fulfillment of Albuquerque's dream of conquest. The next step was to move eastward and plant strategic naval bases in the Malay archipelago and the Spice Islands, thus extending control of the spice trade to its source. The Portuguese were fortunate in finding populations ruled by petty princes, none of whom was strong enough to resist them. From these Far Eastern bases, the Portuguese were able to establish more or less direct trade with China and even to open contact with the distant island kingdom of Japan. In the islands, as on the Indian mainland, the Portuguese made no attempt to conquer or colonize on a large scale. What they sought was a trade monopoly, and for that they needed only bases from which to control the commerce of the eastern seas. Trade in the most valuable commodities, such as pepper, cloves, nutmeg, mace, Chinese silk, and lacquer, were reserved as a royal monopoly to be handled exclusively by authorized Portuguese ships. Native merchants were permitted to trade in other types of goods, but only under Portuguese license, and any ship sailing without an official pass was liable to be seized.

The purely commercial and maritime character of the Portuguese empire in the East accounts in part for its rapid rise and almost equally rapid decline. It struck no deep roots. The Eastern trade was regulated primarily for the profit of the royal government. It brought wealth to the monarchy and to the capitalist firms to which the government farmed out portions of its monopoly. It also enriched numerous noble officials who used their positions to line their pockets in more or less legitimate ways. But for the few who found wealth, there were countless more who found in the East Indies nothing but disease and death. The Portuguese government in the East was an autocratic bureaucracy, which in time became hopelessly corrupt. The authority of the viceroy in Goa, appointed for a three-year term by the home government, was in theory absolute but in practice was limited by the difficulty of keeping in touch with scattered posts separated by hundreds of miles of water.

The arrival of Dutch and English interlopers in the East at the end of the sixteenth century struck a death-blow to the Portuguese monopoly there. Appalling mortality on shipboard and in tropical harbors was depriving overseas Portugal of manpower, and the quality of the emigrants was deteriorating. In one respect only did the Portuguese settlements retain their original character.

Thanks to the activity of the clergy and the favor shown the Church by the royal government, the Portuguese in the East remained strongly Catholic, and most of the native inhabitants of their settlements were converted to Christianity. Missionary activity also gained numerous converts throughout the East, though they could not have comprised more than a small minority of the vast population.

Absorbed in its Eastern venture, the Portuguese government for a long time ignored the land in the Western Hemisphere claimed by Cabral in 1500. More than thirty years passed before any attempts were made to colonize Brazil, and at first the colony grew slowly. Eventually, however, profits from mining, sugar plantations, and lumber attracted more immigrants, and Brazil became a prosperous colony. After the sixteenth century it was by far the most important Portuguese possession overseas, and it has remained a center of Portuguese culture in Latin America to the present day.

The colonial empire which Spain was building in the New World grew slowly from an unpromising start. No profitable trade could be carried on with the primitive tribes of the Caribbean islands. Even the Aztecs and the Incas on the mainland had nothing much to offer but their accumulated stores of gold and silver, and these the *conquistadores* cleaned out in one colossal act of armed robbery and mass murder. Thereafter, Spanish trade with the newly discovered lands depended on the founding of colonies to exploit the natural resources of the land—mineral wealth and people. Force of circumstance determined that, whereas the Portuguese empire in the East was purely commercial and maritime, the Spanish empire in the West was necessarily colonial and required territorial conquest and the enslavement of the native population. The Spanish empire overseas did, however, resemble the Portuguese in two respects. It was the work of adventurers seeking easy wealth rather than of immigrants looking for land to cultivate by their own labor, and it was throughout its career subject to the autocratic royal government of the mother country.

Much of the vast Spanish territory was only sparsely occupied by Spanish immigrants. Mexico City, Lima, and three or four of the principal ports became large cities and centers of transplanted Spanish culture. But elsewhere the Spaniards were a thinly spread ruling class, who lived by exploiting the native population. The Spaniards who came seeking easy wealth showed no inclination to work as long as they could force natives or imported African slaves to do it for them. Most tropical lands produce a few marketable crops—sugar, cotton, tobacco, indigo—that can be grown profitably on large plantations with cheap labor, and thus offer little inducement to small independent farmers. Mining, which produced most of the wealth of the New World in the sixteenth century, lent itself to exploitation by large firms working with forced native labor. Royal policy furthered this tendency by conferring land in large blocks, together with the native populations, on noble adventurers and royal favorites. The normal pattern of society in Spanish America became, and has largely remained, one of concentrated wealth in the midst of extreme poverty, of the arrogant exercise of economic and political power on the one hand and servile subjection on the other—with few gradations in between.

Genuine as the missionary zeal of the Spanish monarchs undoubtedly was, it did not preclude a lively interest in the profit that might accrue to the crown from possessions in the New World. In accordance with prevailing mercantilist theory, the royal government was primarily interested in the importation of gold and silver bullion—on which it claimed a royalty of 20 per cent. Mercantilist theory also prescribed close governmental regulation of trade and the exclusion of all foreigners. The colonies were to serve the double purpose of supplying the mother country with raw materials and furnishing a market for the products of Spanish industry. The work of directing the colonial economy to achieve these ends was carried out by the Casa de Contratación (House of Trade) in Seville, under the supervision of the Council of the Indies. The time required to communicate with the colonial authorities made its task extraordinarily difficult, and many of its regulations, however well intentioned, did more harm than good. In the second half of the sixteenth century, Dutch and English privateers, who found the bullion carried by the Spanish fleets irresistibly attractive, created further difficulties, as did the tendency of the colonists to carry on illegal but untaxed trade with foreign interlopers. After 1562 an attempt was made to meet these hazards by limiting all trade with the colonies to one great fleet a year.

The Conquest of North America

The kings of England and France were as eager as their southern neighbors to find a route to the lands of spices and gold, but they had less immediate success. As early as 1497, Henry VII sent out a Genoese captain, called by the English John Cabot, who touched the borders of the New World at Cape Breton and Labrador. Francis I also sent out explorers to search for a route to China. Under his orders the Florentine navigator Giovanni da Verrazano in 1523 probed the coastline of North America from the Chesapeake Bay to Maine, and in two voyages in 1534 and 1535 Jacques Cartier explored the St. Lawrence River as far as the site of Montreal, where he was checked by the impassable Lachine Rapids. In 1541, Francis sent Cartier out once more, this time with instructions to found a colony. The expedition was a failure, and the king lost interest in land that promised little wealth and served only to block the road to the East.

The vain search for a northwest passage to China continued throughout the sixteenth century by English, French, and Dutch explorers, who were frustrated again and again by the impassable Arctic ice. The hope of finding the passage finally died with Henry Hudson in 1610, but even before then it had become apparent that Portugal and Spain controlled the only trade routes or colonies that offered large and easy profits. Not until later in the seventeenth century did France and England begin to utilize the North American land by establishing the colonies that were to form the basis of their great colonial empires.

Philip II could never be reconciled to the loss of England for the Catholic Church and the Spanish sphere of influence, and the hostility between Spain and England was further aggravated by the growth of commercial rivalry. English commerce and industry expanded rapidly in Elizabeth's reign, as English merchants began to carry on a profitable trade with the Spanish colonists in the New World, despite the efforts of the Spanish government to exclude them. The fact that open trade with the Spanish colonies was officially denied to them forced English merchants to become smugglers and pirates and made England a militant sea power. Merchant-privateers like Sir Francis Drake and Sir John Hawkins plundered the Spanish Main, captured treasure ships, and perfected new techniques of naval warfare. Religion added bitterness to the commercial rivalry. The English merchants were mostly Protestant, and they took a double satisfaction in every blow struck against the commercial monopoly of Catholic Spain. This was known as "singeing the beard of the king of Spain."

Nor were the English the only Protestant seamen who combined profit with religious satisfaction in daring assaults on Spanish commerce. The sea power of both the Netherlands and France was almost entirely in the hands of Protestants—the rebellious Dutch and Huguenots respectively—who held the best Atlantic ports and issued forth to prey on the shipping of Spain. From the North Sea to the Caribbean, militant Protestantism rode the waves and harassed the great Catholic state, whose land armies were still regarded as invincible. English privateers, Huguenots, and the "Sea Beggars" of Holland, by strangling Spanish trade and cutting Spain off from the Netherlands, made possible the success of the Dutch revolt. The aid, official and otherwise, sent from England to the Protestant rebels in the Netherlands may also be considered a decisive factor. Small wonder that Philip II finally determined to crush the island kingdom which had become the chief menace to his cherished plans for the aggrandizement of Spain and the restoration of Catholicism to Europe. In 1587 he declared war on England, but in 1588 his Armada was defeated by the English.

Around the turn of the seventeenth century the Dutch and the English, both at war with Spain and therefore with Portugal, which had fallen to Philip II in 1580, determined to break the Portuguese monopoly and invade Portugal's Eastern preserves by the southern route. In the following years, the English, Dutch, and French governments at last sent out colonists to make what they could of the unpromising lands in North America not claimed by Spain.

The newly founded Dutch republic was peculiarly well equipped to challenge Portuguese and Spanish maritime power. Since the fifteenth century, when the Dutch had begun to exploit the herring fisheries of the North Sea, their sea-borne trade had grown tremendously. They had also developed a great shipbuilding industry. Ships that were the most efficient and economical in the world to operate, hardy sailors and vigorous merchants, international finance concentrated in Amsterdam, and a government wholly devoted to promoting commerce combined to make the new republic a commercial power capable of challenging any European rival.

In 1621 the Dutch West India Company was founded with a monopoly similar to that of its Eastern predecessor. Under its direction a Dutch colony was established in the Hudson Valley of what would become New York, which had been discovered and claimed for the Dutch by Henry Hudson in 1609. The Dutch settlements, however, were scarcely more than fur-trading posts, and in 1664 the colony fell into the hands of the English. The real interests of the company lay farther south, where it fought, raided, and smuggled among the Spanish and Portuguese colonies. It captured Curaçao and some other islands and gained a foothold in Guiana on the South American mainland. These possessions served as bases for trade but were otherwise of no great importance.

English sea-borne commerce, though growing rapidly, lagged behind that of the Dutch at the beginning of the seventeenth century. English merchants were the first to make extensive use of joint-stock companies, backed by royal charter, as a means of opening up new and distant trade areas. The most important of the English joint-stocks was the East India Company, founded in 1600 for much the same reasons that inspired the contemporary venture of their fellow Protestants in Holland. Open war with Spain had broken out in 1587, and as a result the English merchants had been excluded from their profitable trade with Lisbon. The new company was founded to trade directly with the East. It was not in the beginning a permanent joint-stock enterprise, and it had at first nothing like the financial backing of its Dutch rival. After some years of conflict it was forced to abandon trade with the Spice Islands, which remained a Dutch preserve, and to concentrate its attention on the Indian mainland. There the company gained a firm foothold and in the period after 1660 fought successfully against Dutch and French competitors, subdued native states, and laid the foundations for the British Empire in India.

The first sixty years of the seventeenth century were years of promise rather than achievement for England in the West as well as in the East. Beginning with the Virginia colony planted at Jamestown in 1607, joint-stock companies and noble proprietors who had been granted charters by the crown founded a series of colonies on the inhospitable eastern coast of North America from New England to the Carolinas. Other, and for the moment more profitable, colonies were also established on the West Indian islands, Bermuda, and the Bahamas. The English colonies on the mainland were very different from the tropical settlements of the Spaniards. They were not under the direct control of the mother country as was New Spain. The English found no gold or silver. The native population was sparse and warlike and could not be enslaved. The land produced no profitable export crop until the Virginia colony began to cultivate tobacco successfully, and there was little hope of profitable trade until the colonists themselves became sufficiently numerous to furnish a market for the products of the mother country. The one potentially great advantage the English colonies possessed was that they attracted immigrants in large numbers.

The French colony founded in Canada at about the same time as the earliest English settlements in America, on the other hand, was from the beginning inspired and directed by the royal government in accordance with mercantilist principles. During most of the sixteenth century, the French kings were too deeply absorbed in foreign and civil wars to pay much attention to colonization. In 1660 the French population in Canada numbered only about twenty-five hundred, most of which were traders, soldiers, or missionaries. After that date, the colony received a new stimulus from the vigorous mercantilist policy of Colbert, the great finance minister of King Louis XIV. An autocratic government like that of the home country was established, and a circle of forts was constructed to contain the growing English colonies and to fight them for control of the vast inland area which French immigration was inadequate to colonize.

Suggestions for Further Reading

A. W. Bettex, *The Discovery of the World: The Great Explorers and the World They Found* (1960).

C. R. Boxer, *Four Centuries of Portuguese Expansion, 1415–1825** (1961).

C. R. Boxer, *The Dutch Sea-borne Empire, 1600–1800* (1965).

F. Braudel, *The Mediterranean and the Mediterranean World at the Time of Philip II*, English ed. (1972). A highly original work, based on intensive archival

*Available in a paperback edition.

investigation on the physical and human geography, internal conditions, and the Italian, African, and Turkish involvements of Philippine Spain within the framework of sixteenth-century Mediterranean history as a whole [AHA, 510].

B. W. Diffie, *Latin-American Civilization: Colonial Period* (1966).

L. H. Gipson, *The British Empire Before the American Revolution,* 13 vols. (1936–1967). The colossal life's work of a famed historian.

C. H. Haring, *The Spanish Empire in America** (1963).

S. E. Morison, *Admiral of the Ocean Sea: A Life of Christopher Columbus,* 2 vols. (1942). The best biography of Columbus. Morison, a distinguished American historian, puts Columbus into the context of navigational aids, past traditions of exploration, and the political climate of his time. An abridged version is available.

W. Notestein, *The English People on the Eve of Colonization, 1603–1630** (1954). Excellent survey of English institutions and social life at the opening of the seventeenth century [AHA, 432].

J. H. Parry, *Europe and a Wider World, 1415–1715* (1949). A useful introduction to the colonial and mercantile eras by a great authority.

J. H. Parry and P. M. Sherlock, *A Short History of the West Indies,** 3rd ed. (1971).

E. Sanceau, *Henry the Navigator* (1947, reprinted 1969).

The Scientific Revolution

24

> The men of experiment are like the ant; they only collect and use: the reasoners resemble spiders, who make cobwebs out of their own substance.
>
> SIR FRANCIS BACON

> If I have seen farther than Descartes, it is by standing on the shoulders of giants.
>
> SIR ISAAC NEWTON

The New World of the Baroque

In the sixteenth and seventeenth centuries a revolution occurred in Western civilization. This was a revolution of ideas, involving a new concept of man and his place in the universe. In medieval cosmogony, man and the earthly drama of his fall and redemption were at the center of the universe, and the sun was thought to revolve around the earth. Against the background of the loss of monolithic Christian unity in the West, the lessened prestige of the Roman Church, and the development of new scientific concepts (some borrowed from the ancient Greeks), men like Copernicus and Galileo developed an entirely new view of man's place in the universe. Man was now better able to understand how things worked, if not why they worked. Natural philosophers such as Galileo and Bacon no longer assumed, as had Thomas Aquinas and Dante, that everything Aristotle said about nature was necessarily correct. They no longer assumed that the Old Testament's story of Joshua miraculously making the sun stand still proved that the earth did not revolve around the sun. Early modern culture, call it what we will—late Renaissance, High Renaissance, Mannerist, Baroque, the Age of Reason—reflected a new sense of man's destiny, the new concept of an open rather than a closed universe.

In the open universe all things were in constant motion and flux. The idea of a dynamic universe was reflected in both the daring ambitions of Vasco da Gama and Columbus and in the ecstatic tensions of Baroque art. This new age (roughly 1492-1700) of an expanded world was characterized by a sense of discovery and exultation. The closed universe had been one in which the Christian drama was miraculously revealed to man. Now man discovered a universe in which the drama of existence was logically and comprehensibly implicit in every aspect of nature. Above all, everything could become knowledge and knowledge could become power. Although man was no longer at the center of nature, he had gained greater control over nature. Western man, in this great, tragic abandonment of the medieval world-view, established the foundations of modern thought.

Around the year 1600, new styles in art and music opened an era in cultural history generally termed Baroque, a period which lasted for about a century and a half. Within that period there were many conflicting tendencies, making it difficult to define exactly what is meant by Baroque style, although anyone who has paced the endless corridors of the Louvre or entered the churches built in that period from Rome to Montreal will recognize it. The Counter Reformation had lost both the enthusiasm and the morbid piety that had characterized its first half-century, but the feeling for the authority, might, and power of the Church Eternal, which the Jesuits and the Council of Trent inspired, remained and found expression in the construction of churches of unparalleled magnificence.

Almost everywhere in continental Europe this was an age of absolute monarchy, and the cultural tone was set by royal or princely courts, which existed solely to enhance the prestige of the sovereign. It was an age that revered power and authority, and art both served and expressed what the age admired. Grandiloquent design, complex ornamentation filling every inch of space, a general effect of opulence, and great virtuosity in execution were all characteristic of Baroque architecture, sculpture, and painting and, in somewhat different terms, of Baroque music as well. But though this age loved authority, religious and intellectual cross-currents robbed it of complete assurance, and the impression one receives from the excessively ornamented buildings and the swirling draperies and violent movement that characterize much of Baroque painting is one of restlessness and turbulence. This excitement expressed an exultant sense of discovery of the powers and knowledge of modern man. It gave spirit to the fast movements of a Vivaldi concerto, the whirling figures and translucently blue skies of the late Baroque painter Tiepolo, and the open universe of Isaac Newton. The discovery of an open universe did not liberate and delight everyone, however. The French philosopher Pascal said that the eternal silence of infinite space terrified him.

Italy was still the schoolmaster of Europe in the Baroque age, and the painters who seem most typical of the period show strong evidence of Italian influence. This is notably true of Peter Paul Rubens (1577–1640), the Flemish artist whose opulent and voluptuous paintings express the quintessence of the Baroque spirit. Choosing dramatic themes for his pictures, Rubens filled them with massive figures in violent motion, not clearly outlined but consisting of color and light.

The incomparable Rembrandt van Rijn (1606–1669) created his own style. A genius who was too individualistic for his own age, Rembrandt was to be appreciated for his full worth only by later generations. In a Rembrandt painting a light burns within the very soul of the subject, and this too was an aspect of the new Baroque culture. Internal, mystical illumination complemented the ecstasy—and sometimes the lonely sadness—felt in the discovery of an open universe.

The Origins of the Scientific Revolution

Viewed from our own scientifically oriented period, the pre-eminent characteristic of the Baroque age may seem to be the revolution in scientific thought which laid the foundation for the modern conception of the natural sciences. To this age we owe the discovery of a great many of the basic principles which, when further developed and applied, have enabled modern man to master the forces of nature and to use them, for good and ill, in ways that have transformed civilization. The rise of modern science was a late fruit of the transition from medieval to modern times, but like so many other Baroque developments, it had its roots in the past. Many of these roots extended back to antiquity and drew nourishment from the speculations of Greek mathematicians, physicists, and astronomers. The legacy of the inquiring Greek mind was partially recovered by the scholastic philosophers in the twelfth and thirteenth centuries, aided by Arabic intermediaries. In the early fourteenth century, under the influence of the nominalist school of philosophy, promising beginnings were made at the universities of Paris and Oxford in the direction of experiment and observation of individual phenomena. At Padua in Italy, late medieval natural philosophers, following the teachings of

Peter Paul Rubens' painting Abduction of the Daughters of Leucippus *(c. 1619). The grandiose design and lush figures in swirling motion are typically Baroque.*

Averroës, paved the way for Galileo's discoveries at the end of the sixteenth century.

Another source of the new science, albeit an ambiguous one, was Renaissance humanism. The humanists, primarily men of letters, had no great interest in science but were interested in anything written in the age of classical antiquity. They corrected and published all the works of the ancient scientists they could find, giving new inspiration to scientific thought. Inspiration of a very different kind came from the Renaissance artists, engineers, technicians, and inventors, who conducted practical experiments in an effort to solve their professional problems. The invention of printing from movable type deserves much of the credit for the scientific advances of the following centuries, for it enabled scientists to communicate their ideas widely and rapidly and to profit almost immediately from work done by other scientists. Many books on science were illustrated with copper engravings, the accuracy of which owed much to the realistic technique developed by the Renaissance artists.

The spread of education among laymen broke the monopoly on learning held by the clergy in the Middle Ages and enhanced the secular content of culture. The men of the sixteenth century were not irreligious, but their thought was less exclusively confined to the sphere of theology and metaphysics than was that of the churchmen who dominated the culture of the Middle Ages. Michelet's and Burckhardt's characterization of the Renaissance as the discovery of the world and of man is something of an exaggeration, but the Renaissance did witness a shift in emphasis from the spiritual to the physical world, from the infinite future to the finite present.

Aristotle ascribed the behavior of physical things to their inherent "qualities." Thus, the concept of motion was difficult to come to grips with because it was due either to the tendency of an object to seek its natural place of rest or to violent force imposed upon the object from the outside. Aristotelian physics was highly subjective, depending upon a combination of empirical observations (which could be misleading) and teleological assumptions. The term "teleological" in this context refers to the concept that every object has a natural place or goal in the universal order. In early modern post-Aristotelian physics, motion was no longer assumed to be unnatural, nor could it be explained by tendencies inherent in the object. Aristotle had explained the why of things; early modern physicists and natural philosophers more modestly tried to explain the how. Medieval Aristotelian physicists, for example, could not describe acceleration except as "uniform diform" motion (an awkward, limited concept), because it involved dynamic forces largely foreign to the Aristotelian way of thought—gravity, mass, velocity, distance. These concepts are crucial to modern physics, however.

Mathematics, experiment, and measurement were the intellectual tools of the new science. The most important of these was mathematics, for by means of it men manipulated the data and formulated the results drawn from the other two. As scientists began to think of the relations of things in terms of mathematical order—numbers, ratios, geometrical figures—their interest led to great advances in every branch of the mathematical sciences. Without such advances the scientific revolution could not have progressed as it did. Analytical geometry, the process by which any algebraic equation can be plotted as a geometrical figure and any geometrical figure can be expressed in an algebraic equation, was invented by the French philosopher-scientist René Descartes and published in

1637 as a sequel to his great philosophical *Discourse on Method.* Descartes (1596–1650) was one of the most revolutionary thinkers of the seventeenth century. His influence gave new impetus to the tendency of scientists to reduce all science to mathematical abstraction. In the long run, however, his method, which depended largely on deductive logic, proved less fruitful than the more purely experimental science championed by his English forerunner Francis Bacon (1561–1626).

"Sun Stand Thou Still": Copernicus to Galileo

The greatest scientific statement of the sixteenth century was the Copernican hypothesis, which revolutionized astronomy. It bears out the thesis that the essential aspect of the first part of the scientific revolution was a new way of looking at nature, instead of more accurate observation. To appreciate the immense mental leap that Copernicus must have made to reach his hypothesis, one must bear in mind the conception of the universe accepted in western Europe since the introduction of Greek science in the High Middle Ages. It was based on Aristotle's description of the cosmos, revised and made more consistent with the observed movements of the planets by the Alexandrian astronomer Ptolemy in the second century A.D., and later given a Christian coloring by the medieval schoolmen. For the modern student the most vivid medieval description of the Ptolemaic system is to be found in Dante's *Divine Comedy.* According to this theory, the earth is a stationary sphere at the center of the universe, and about it the planets—the moon, Mercury, Venus, the sun, Mars, Jupiter, and Saturn—and beyond them the fixed stars move in a series of concentric circles. Aristotle assumed that each planet was carried at a uniform speed in a perfect circle by a crystalline sphere, which fitted into the sphere outside it. The spheres were moved about the earth by Intelligences, which the Christian philosophers translated into angelic spirits, and the whole apparatus received its initial movement from an invisible outer sphere called the Primum Mobile or first mover, beyond which Christian thought placed the motionless heaven which is the abode of God.

Even before Ptolemy's time, it became evident that this beautifully simple system did not conform to all the observed movements of the planets. Ptolemy found it necessary to add epicycles to the spheres—that is, to assume that the planets moved in a small cycle around a point fixed upon the moving sphere—and later observers were forced to add further epicycles and even epicycles on the epicycles. By the sixteenth century the system required eighty cycles in all. Apparently the conviction that there must be a simpler way of accounting for the movements of the planets led Copernicus to his epoch-making discovery. His sense of classical beauty and desire for simplicity owed much of its inspiration to the concepts of the humanists, who saw in classical art the simple lines of the purest, most ethereal structures.

Nicolaus Copernicus (1473–1543) was a Polish scholar of wide intellectual interests. During a ten-year stay in Italy, he studied medicine, mathematics, astronomy, and canon law and then retired to a life of peaceful speculation in his native country as a canon in the cathedral at Frauenburg. Precisely when he hit upon the solution to the problem presented by the bewildering complexity of Ptolemaic epicycles is not certain. The results were published in a book entitled *Concerning the Revolutions of the Heavenly Bodies,* which appeared just before his death in 1543. Copernicus dedicated his book to Pope Paul III. He did not see any necessary conflict between his heliocentric thesis and the teachings of the Church, and such a conflict did not arise until the full force of the Catholic Reformation dominated the Church toward the end of the sixteenth century: Giordano Bruno, with his theory of multiple worlds, would pay for his ideas with his life in 1600, and Galileo would suffer greatly at the hands of the Inquisition some years later.

Copernicus' approach was that of a mathematician. He made few independent observations and depended almost entirely on data already known, merely shuffling them into new combinations. Although he may have profited by hints contained in the recently published works of ancient astronomers, his hypothesis was in fact an original creation, the first heliocentric or sun-centered system worked out in mathematical detail. Once having made the assumptions that the sun is the center of the universe, about which all the planets including the earth revolve, and that the apparent revolution of the whole system about the earth is actually caused by the daily rotation of the earth on its own axis, he found that all the pieces of the gigantic puzzle fell into place. Or almost all, for, after rejecting so much of Aristotle, Copernicus still clung to the Aristotelian notion that planetary motions must be circular; thus his theory was not in fact consistent with all the observed phenomena.

It was not his errors, however, that were chiefly responsible for delaying the general acceptance of Copernicus' hypothesis. Other objections, quite reasonable in light of the knowledge available at the time, prevented most scientists from accepting it until well into the seventeenth century as anything more than a technique for facilitating calculation. Meanwhile, theologians rejected it as contrary to the teaching of the Bible, and ordinary folk as contrary to simple observation and common sense. However, new evidence acquired by more accurate observation and new discoveries which tended to discredit the Aristotelian system in other sciences worked in its favor, and in the long run the appeal of the Copernican system to the mathematically minded proved irresistible.

Copernicus' cosmos was much simpler than that of Ptolemy. Could it not be made simpler still? Could not the whole system of planetary motion be reduced to a mathematical formula? This dream inspired the German astronomer Johann Kepler (1571–1630) through years of arduous calculation. Kepler was aided by the improved instruments and systematic observations that had earlier been provided by the Dane Tycho Brahe and also by advances in mathematics made after the death of Copernicus. Equally important was his conviction that the movements of the heavenly bodies must conform to mathematical order. His search for mathematical harmony in the universe led Kepler down many blind alleys before he discovered the three laws that have ever since been connected with his name. The first is that the orbit of planets moving about the sun is an ellipse, of which the sun is one focus. The second is that each planet moves more rapidly as it approaches the sun, its relative speed being such that a line drawn from the sun to the planet would sweep equal areas in equal times. Ten years of further calculation led Kepler to his third law, published in 1619. Copernicus had noted that the planets near the sun revolve in a shorter time than do those farther away. Kepler now discovered that the squares of the periods of revolution of the planets are proportional to the cubes of their mean distance from the sun.

While Kepler thus corrected and supported the Copernican hypothesis with discoveries in the realm of abstract mathematics, the brilliant Florentine scientist Galileo Galilei (1564-1642) was bringing to the attention of the reading public new and more concrete evidence in its favor. Having in 1609 constructed a telescope that would magnify by thirty diameters, Galileo discovered many things in the heavens that could not be seen with the naked eye, and all were in accord with the Copernican system. His findings, communicated to the world in a readable book entitled *The Messenger of the Stars* (1610), did more to convince people than could any amount of abstruse mathematics. Theologians became alarmed. No longer able to ignore the possible truth of the Copernican hypothesis, they launched a campaign against it. Galileo was warned by the Inquisition in 1616 and again in 1633, after he had published a second work defending the Copernican system. Once, when Galileo was being led away from the Inquisition tribunal after having publicly recanted his view, he is supposed to have muttered the heretical but sarcastic words, "And still it moves," referring to the earth.

The New Sciences of Physics and Mathematics

Though less shocking in their implications to the general public, discoveries in physics during this period were equally revolutionary and more numerous. Medieval physics, adopting the methodology of Aristotle, had tended to be deductive. That is, a natural philosopher might observe a phenomenon and without experimentation draw certain conclusions. Of course, the observation itself might omit factors that could not be seen or sensed without refined instruments of measurement. Seeing that a stone falls to the ground more rapidly than a feather, medieval philosophers concluded that the different rates of fall resulted from properties inherent in each object, not because of such factors as mass, gravity, and friction. Early modern physics replaced inappropriate or crude empiricism with mathematics, precise measurement, and induction. In brief, induction involves proceeding from the particular to the general; deduction is the opposite.

The new experimental method was a habit of thought and procedure developed to bridge the gap between theory and practice. No statement, however often repeated by ancient and venerable sages or long assumed by the mass of mankind to be too obvious for argument, was to be accepted if it contradicted established facts. The Englishman Francis Bacon (1561-1626) first reduced to systematic form the process of working from experimentally determined data toward general laws and principles.

To an unusual degree Galileo combined the ability to construct mechanical experiments with the mental power to induce from them valid generalizations. The discoveries he made concerning the motion of falling bodies, the oscillation of the pendulum, the principles governing mechanical action, and the cohesive power of solids were so numerous and of such fundamental importance that he may be said to have laid the foundation of modern physics. He was, however, only one, though the most brilliant, of the scientists who enhanced knowledge in what has been called the century of genius.

Compared with physics, chemistry advanced relatively little during this period. Robert Boyle (1627-1691), best known for his discovery that the volume of air varies inversely with the pressure imposed upon it, made important contributions to chemistry, but he was a somewhat isolated figure in the seventeenth century.

In the biological sciences, the new interest in accurate observation and measurement produced few advances in theory but much in description and classification. During the sixteenth and seventeenth centuries, a number of encyclopedic books were published, illustrated by competent artists, describing and classifying thousands of species of plants and animals. This work had to be done before there could be any further advance in either botany or zoology.

The combination of the scientist's observation and the artist's skill in portrayal also served the science of descriptive anatomy. In this field the most important contribution in the sixteenth century was made by Andreas Vesalius of Brussels (1514-1564), whose book *On the Construction of the Human Body* (1543) was based on surgical dissection and illustrated with remarkably accurate drawings. Vesalius was willing to believe the evidence of his eyes, even when it contradicted the opinion of the Greek anatomist Galen, although reverence for Galen was fervent enough in the sixteenth century to be a real obstacle to further advances. Progress was also made almost impossible by anatomists' lack of understanding of the function of the heart and the circulation of the blood. This basic problem was finally solved by William Harvey (1578-1657), who explained in a book published in 1628 that the blood is pumped out of the heart through the arteries and returns through the veins in a constant circular motion. The laws of life and the laws of the planets seemed to parallel each other.

In breaking with tradition, the new thinkers came to prize independence of judgment over mere book learning and reason over dogma. Thomas Hobbes (1588-1679), who sometimes acted as secretary to Bacon and later wrote works on political philosophy, was wont to boast that if he had read as much as most

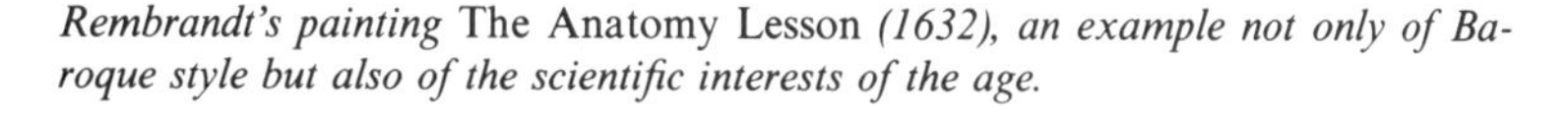

Rembrandt's painting The Anatomy Lesson *(1632), an example not only of Baroque style but also of the scientific interests of the age.*

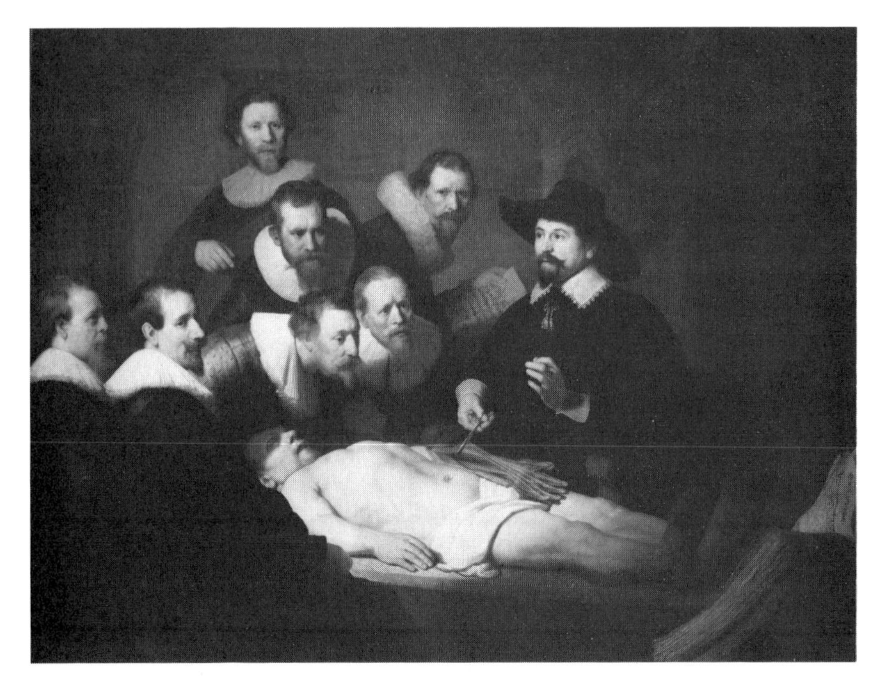

men he would probably know as little. "Reasoning from the Authority of Books," he declared in his caustic fashion, ". . . is not Knowledge, but Faith." And Descartes found so many errors in the works on anatomy he consulted that he turned to nature for the truth. "These are my books," he told a visitor, pointing to the bodies of animals which he was dissecting.

The experimental method seemed to promise man infinite possibilities to learn the laws of the natural world and, through this knowledge, to achieve control over his environment. The ultimate cost of this control may not yet be apparent. The destruction of the environment and of nature's balance have created problems which are pressing, if not overwhelming, in the last half of the twentieth century.

European scientists of the seventeenth century were the first to recognize clearly that "mathematics is the skeleton of God's plan of the universe." The most brilliant conclusions of the astronomers, from Kepler's discovery of what he well termed "the harmony of the heavens" to Newton's formula for gravitation, were all expressed mathematically. Natural philosophers were delighted to think that they had at last stumbled upon the language in which nature wrote its secrets. "True philosophy," proclaimed Galileo, "expounds nature to us; but she can be understood only by him who has learned the speech and symbols in which she speaks to us. This speech is mathematics, and its symbols are mathematical figures." To Descartes the physical universe appeared to be a vast machine created by a supreme mathematician. "The laws of nature are identical with the laws of mechanics," he declared. "You can substitute 'the mathematical order of the universe' for 'God' whenever I use the latter term."

A peculiar charm invested the language of numbers, for it was flexible, accurate, and international. It proved equally helpful to scientists who sought to formulate abstract generalizations and to engineers and navigators who coped with practical problems. Mariners used astronomical tables (which forecast the phases of the moon and the movements of the planets for years ahead) to determine the position of their ships when far from land. Gunners found that formulas furnished by the mathematicians were an invaluable aid in calculating the distance to the target and the trajectory their shot must describe in order to reach it. War was a great spur to invention among natural philosophers in the early modern period, though so distinguished a modern historian of science and technology as John U. Nef would contest this thesis. Even an artist such as Leonardo da Vinci left behind notebooks filled with numerous sketches of warlike devices.

It remained for Isaac Newton (1642-1727), the greatest mathematician of the age, to explain the movements of all bodies, earthly and celestial, as expressions of one general principle. He reached his epoch-making conclusion in 1665 at the age of twenty-three, in what he called "the prime of my age for invention," but he did not publish it until 1687. Then, in his immortal *Principia,* he offered mathematical proofs for his hypothesis that the force of attraction between two bodies varies directly as the product of their masses and inversely as the square of the distance between them. To test this principle he applied it to the movements of the moon about the earth. When he found his figures working out correctly, he was so deeply stirred by his discovery that he had to ask a friend to finish the calculations for him. As a further verification he extended his computations to the planets, the tides, and even the apparent vagaries of visiting comets, and all confirmed the universality of the law his genius had discerned.

Newton never attempted to explain the ultimate cause of the phenomenon of gravity, remarking only, "I don't create hypotheses." The story of Newton's inspiration by an apple that fell on his head may be apocryphal, but it is instructive, because Newton reached his great conclusions by describing in mathematical terms what actually happens, not by speculating in the metaphysical, medieval manner about why something happens. Newton did not define gravity; he explained its predictable effects.

The Social Setting of the New Science

The new, practical humility was related to another great source of the new science—the marriage of theory and practice. "Science is the captain, practice the soldiers," Leonardo da Vinci observed early in the sixteenth century. A hundred years later Galileo declared that those who liked to theorize about nature ought to visit shops and shipyards to watch artisans and mechanics at work. Francis Bacon, in a Latin work he called *Novum Organum* (New Instrument), warned that "neither the hand without instruments, nor the unassisted understanding, can do much." But he insisted that great progress would result from a combination of theory and practice or, as he phrased it, "from the close and strict union of the experimental and rational faculties, which have not hitherto been united." Indeed, this union of theory and practice, of abstract speculation and material greed, has been the hallmark of Western civilization since early modern times. It ultimately conquered the world.

A remarkable aspect of the scientific revolution was its reflection of the European commonwealth of intellect. Copernicus was a Pole, Brahe a Dane, Kepler a German, Galileo an Italian, Newton an Englishman. Because of its international nature, the new learning required a fitting institution for its communications. Such an institution was the scientific society. In 1660, thirty-four years after Francis Bacon's death, some of his fellow countrymen organized the Royal Society for Improving Natural Knowledge by Experiment. Frankly acknowledging their debt to him, they declared their aim to be "the multiplying and beautifying of the mechanick arts," and they "exacted from their members a close, naked, natural way of speaking . . . preferring the language of artisans, countrymen, and merchants before that of wits and scholars." These natural philosophers realized that they could learn from common craftsmen, from machinists and miners and mariners. The union of theory and practice which they advocated proved to be a factor of profound importance in fostering the growth of modern science.

Although the scientists of the seventeenth century sometimes scorned the learning of earlier centuries, they understood the value of sharing their discoveries with each other. "If I have seen farther than Descartes," admitted Newton, who lived half a century later, "it is by standing on the shoulders of giants." The easiest way to share ideas is through personal contact, and societies organized for discussion and experiment were among the first proofs that the scientific revolution had begun. An Academy of the Lynx-Eyed was formed at Rome in 1601, and an Academy for Experiment made its appearance at Florence in 1657.

After 1660, when war ceased for a time to absorb the attention of princes, several new societies were established under royal patronage. The most distinguished were the Royal Society for Improving Natural Knowledge, organized in 1660 and incorporated at London in 1662, and the French Académie des Sciences, chartered by Louis XIV in 1666. Charles II granted the members of the Royal Society permission "to enjoy mutual intelligence and knowledge with all and all manner of strangers and foreigners, whether private or collegiate, corporate or politic, without any molestation, interruption, or disturbance whatsoever." To record their deliberations and experiments these academies published scientific journals, and to encourage research they collected funds to build libraries and observatories and to purchase retorts and furnaces, telescopes and microscopes, chronometers, barometers, air pumps, and all the other paraphernalia that laboratory workers had discovered they needed in their pursuit of natural philosophy.

In the century and a half following the death of Copernicus, scientists stripped most of the mystery from the heavens. Inexorable laws were found to govern the movements of all sidereal bodies, so that the smallest comet hurtling through the darkness of outer space could not vary a hair's breadth from the path prescribed for it by mathematical calculations. Edmund Halley, a friend and disciple of Newton, was able to compute the orbit of a comet which appeared in 1682 and predict its reappearance in seventy-seven years. Halley's comet not only justified this computation by reappearing in 1759; it returned in 1835 and 1910, and may be expected again about 1986. The medieval belief that comets were sent to announce an impending disaster or the death of a king was thus forced, like many another superstition, to yield to the matter-of-fact explanation of the scientists.

By the eighteenth century, scientists were no longer persecuted; they were honored and rewarded. Galileo had been reproved by the Inquisition in 1633 for his novel opinions, but when Sir Isaac Newton died in 1727, less than a century later, he was buried with honors befitting a king. Science had begun to capture the popular imagination. Even people who did not understand much about it were persuaded that it was a new and marvelous method for unveiling nature's

Louis XIV visiting the Académie des Sciences, which he chartered in 1666.

secrets. Cultured ladies and gentlemen attended lectures on astronomy and read books explaining Newton's laws. Voltaire himself wrote such a volume. Some wealthy men equipped laboratories and conducted experiments of their own in the hope of adding to the sum of human knowledge. Many people hoped that the new science and rationalism of the seventeenth century would prevent the recurrence of the horrors of war. Theorists such as the Dutchman Grotius hoped to prevent future wars through the wise application of rational thought. Yet the seventeenth century was disfigured by the brutal Thirty Years' War, and rationalism and peace have still not triumphed.

Suggestions for Further Reading

E. N. da C. Andrade, *Sir Isaac Newton: His Life and Work** (1958).

J. D. Bernal, *Science in History,** 4 vols. 3rd ed. (1965). A Marxist study.

H. Butterfield, *The Origins of Modern Science,* rev. ed. (1965). An arresting, sweeping survey, the merit of which lies in considering the hurdles that had to be overcome before science could be placed on a solid foundation [AHA, 12].

G. N. Clark, *The Seventeenth Century,** 2nd ed. (1947). An excellent overview.

A. C. Crombie, *Medieval and Early Modern Science* (1961). Covers the subject from Augustine to Galileo. Crombie has written a readable, scholarly survey, one that has interest for the general reader as well as for the specialist.

L. Geymonat, *Galileo Galilei** (1965).

A. R. Hall, *The Scientific Revolution, 1500-1800** (1954). The best introduction to the scientific revolution of this period. Excellent introductory chapter on background [AHA, 12].

P. Hazard, *The European Mind: The Critical Years, 1680-1715* (1953). A classic of intellectual history.

T. S. Kuhn, *The Copernican Revolution** (1957). The best book on the subject.

F. Manuel, *A Portrait of Isaac Newton* (1968). A Freudian approach.

F. L. Nussbaum, *The Triumph of Science and Reason, 1660-1685** (1953). Part of the Rise of Modern Europe series edited by William L. Langer. Despite its title, this book is really an excellent survey of all major aspects of European history in the late seventeenth century. It has detailed bibliographies.

C. Singer, *A Short History of Scientific Ideas to 1900** (1959). The work of one of the major figures in the study of the history of science.

V. L. Tapié, *The Age of Grandeur: Baroque Art and Architecture* (1960). An instructive, usefully illustrated study of the Baroque, particularly in architecture.

S. Toulmin and G. J. Goodfield, *The Fabric of the Heavens** (1963). Cosmological and astronomical theories from their origins to the seventeenth century.

B. Willey, *The Seventeenth Century Background** (1953). A brilliant study of seventeenth-century literature and philosophy; highly original and stimulating.

A. Wolf, *A History of Science, Technology, and Philosophy in the 16th and 17th Centuries* (1951).

*Available in a paperback edition.

The Last Religious Holocaust: The Age of the Thirty Years' War

25

I would not have believed a land could have been so despoiled had I not seen it with my own eyes.
GENERAL MORTAIGNE DURING THE THIRTY YEARS' WAR

This is the Generation of that great Leviathan, or rather (to speake more reverently) of that *Mortall God,* to which we owe under the *Immortall God,* our peace and defence.
THOMAS HOBBES ON THE STATE

Background of the War

The first half of the seventeenth century witnessed the last and greatest of the religious wars, which for thirty years (1618–1648) devastated Germany. Before the war was over, Germany lay prostrate; the Holy Roman Empire had been reduced to an empty shell; and out of the final settlement emerged the early modern state system. In 1660, after nearly a century of civil and international warfare, the people of Europe once more enjoyed the almost forgotten blessings of a general peace. The era thus ended—the century of tumult between 1550 and 1660—is often termed the Period of the Religious Wars. What were the origins of the Thirty Years' War?

By 1600 the militant efforts of a reformed Catholic Church, spurred on by the Jesuits, had led to the reconversion to Catholicism of large areas of central Europe. Sections of southern Germany, including Bavaria, the Austrian Hapsburg lands, and the ecclesiastical states of the Rhineland, were purged of their large Protestant populations and became almost unanimously Catholic. By the beginning of the seventeenth century, German Catholicism had developed a decidedly militant spirit and had found two powerful and devoted champions in the young Maximilian, duke of Bavaria, and his contemporary, Ferdinand of Styria, cousin and heir of the Hapsburg emperor.

In contrast to this Catholic revival, Lutheranism seemed to be sinking into passivity and apathy. All that was positive and aggressive in the Protestant faith was now concentrated in Calvinism, which had established itself in several of the upper Rhineland states and in Bohemia and had won over the elector Palatine and the elector of Brandenburg. The stern faith of Calvin provided the moral force needed to compete with the revised energy of Catholicism, but the growth of Calvinism in Germany weakened rather than strengthened the Protestant cause, for Lutheran and Calvinist were divided by an antagonism almost as deep as that which separated Protestant and Catholic.

The growth of Calvinism was one of the principal factors that tended to nullify the settlement of the Religious Peace of Augsburg. In 1555, Calvinism had not yet become a power to be reckoned with in Germany, and the Calvinists had been excluded from the terms of the peace. Thus, unlike their Lutheran neighbors, they had no legal status.

But even the Lutherans were no longer fully protected by the religious peace. It had recognized the right of the Lutheran princes to hold the Church lands they had confiscated prior to 1552. A good deal of Church land, however, was secularized (that is, taken over by the Lutheran lay governments) after that date. So long as Protestantism was in the ascendancy, no effective protest could be made, but as the Catholic forces gained new strength, they asserted that these lands still belonged to the Church. A similar problem arose from the interpretation of the part of the peace known as the Ecclesiastical Reservation. According to this clause, ecclesiastical princes (bishops or abbots ruling territorial states) who became Protestant were required to give up their land, which was to be retained by the Church. This provision, however, had been violated on numerous occasions, and most of the bishoprics in northern Germany, as well as many smaller ecclesiastical principalities, had become secular Protestant lands.

The growing feeling of insecurity among the Protestant princes led in 1608 to the formation of an armed league, the Evangelical Union, under the leadership of the Calvinist elector of the Palatinate. The league was composed largely of Calvinists, for they were in the most serious danger. Some Lutherans joined, but the sequel was to show how little they were prepared to sacrifice for their Calvinist allies. The following year, the challenge of the union was met by the formation of a Catholic League led by Maximilian of Bavaria. Protestant and Catholic forces in Germany were now organized into hostile armed camps. Peace was maintained only by the even balance of power. Should any circumstance upset the balance, war would be inevitable.

This intricate situation in Germany was further complicated by the anomalous position of the Hapsburg emperors. Though they were all orthodox Catholics, the emperors who reigned between the abdication of Charles V in 1555–1558 and the outbreak of the Thirty Years' War were not aggressive champions of Catholicism. Their interests were confined in large measure to the aggrandizement of their hereditary lands, which included, besides Austria and the other Hapsburg territories in southern Germany, the kingdoms of Bohemia and Hungary. Always intensely conscious of their dynastic solidarity, the Austrian and Spanish branches of the house of Hapsburg, though divided since the abdication of Charles V, had maintained a very close relationship, reinforced by frequent intermarriages. A German war involving the Austrian Hapsburgs, therefore, would also certainly involve Spain, which, though greatly weakened by internal decay, was still to all outward appearances the greatest power in Europe.

The spark that ignited the conflagration was the revolt of the Bohemian Calvinists against their Hapsburg ruler. This rebellion was motivated by a mixture of national and religious aspirations. Nowhere in Europe was national consciousness more highly developed than in this Slavic land, where a Czech population had for centuries been ruled by German kings. Heresy was a strong force among the people, many of whose ancestors two centuries before had defied the might of Catholic Christendom in memory of the martyred John Huss. Under the feeble rule of Holy Roman Emperors Rudolf II (1576–1612) and Matthias (1612–1619), Bohemian Protestants, the most aggressive of whom were Calvinists, had gained a measure of religious freedom. Their rights were guaranteed by a royal charter, and they counted on the weakness and tolerance of the emperor. This dependence explains the consternation of the Bohemians when, in 1617, the childless Matthias designated as his heir his cousin Ferdinand of Styria, notoriously the most fanatical opponent of Protestantism in Germany. To make matters more alarming, Matthias forced the Bohemian Diet to accept Ferdinand as a hereditary king, in violation of the ancient tradition that the Bohemian crown was elective. Seeing both their religious and their national freedom endangered, the Czech nobles determined to strike without delay, before Ferdinand could consolidate his power.

The Thirty Years' War

The Bohemian revolt began with a dramatic gesture of defiance. Determined to commit their fellow countrymen irrevocably to rebellion, in 1618 a group of Czech noblemen entered the royal palace at Prague and heaved two of Ferdinand's representatives out of a window into the moat below. No one was fatally injured because of the enormous amount of dung which had accumulated in the moat. After this humiliating event, usually referred to as the defenestration of Prague, there was no turning back. The Bohemians deposed Ferdinand and

Pike and musket, typical infantry weapons during the Thirty Years' War. In the hands of well-drilled troops they were effective against a cavalry attack.

chose the Protestant prince Frederick of the Palatinate as their king. They organized an army, though with characteristic irresponsibility the nobles refused to contribute the money necessary to make it really effective. On the other side, Ferdinand began to mobilize his forces. He received some support from Spain, the pope, and the Catholic League, and early in 1619 the opportune death of the aged Matthias gave him the additional prestige of the imperial title as Ferdinand II (1619-1637). The campaign in Bohemia was brief and decisive. The combined army of the emperor and the League, commanded by General Tilly, routed the undisciplined Bohemians outside of Prague in the fall of 1620, and the unfortunate Frederick fled the country. This Battle of the White Mountain marked the end of the first phase of the war and the widespread destruction of the Czech nobility, who had been the bearers of the Czech patriotic idea for many centuries. Their lands were confiscated and given to Catholic Hapsburg loyalists. The notion of a Czech nation would not revive until the middle of the nineteenth century.

The Catholic League had forgotten neither the confiscated Church lands nor the secularized bishoprics and abbacies. If the lost ecclesiastical states could be won back for the Church, the principle of *cuius regio eius religio,* which empowered a prince to dictate the religion of his people, would enable Catholic bishops and abbots to stamp out Protestantism in some of the richest cities and territories in northern Germany. An Edict of Restitution prepared the way for this Catholic effort, for under it many Protestant areas would revert to Catholic rule. The enforcement of the edict depended on Ferdinand's brilliant general Wallenstein and his personal army, for it could be put into effect only by brute force. But Wallenstein, who disapproved of the edict, was fast drifting into open antagonism to the League. Ferdinand thus had to choose between the two. In 1630 he submitted to the demands of the League and dismissed his general.

When Ferdinand thus gave up the only armed force strong enough to enforce his rash policy, a new champion of the Protestant cause had already landed in Germany. The decision of Gustavus Adolphus, king of Sweden (1611-1632), to take up the cause of his fellow Lutherans in Germany opened another period of the war, that of the Swedish intervention. Gustavus' motives, like those of most of the participants in the war to this point, were a mixture of religious partisanship and territorial greed. Religion was a sincere motive with this hero-king, "the Lion of the North," but his territorial ambitions were part of a long campaign to make his country secure and a power in the north.

Ever since his accession at the age of seventeen to the throne of a beleaguered, impoverished, and divided kingdom, Gustavus had fought to consolidate his state and to win for it the supremacy in the Baltic upon which its economic and political life depended. His reign was from the beginning a perpetual war—war with Denmark, 1611-1613, with Russia, 1614-1617, and with Poland, 1617-1629. As a result of each conflict, Gustavus had won territory on the Baltic coast and more control of the Baltic trade. All that he needed to make the Baltic a "Swedish lake" was a foothold in northern Germany. For years he had been watching the course of the war in Germany, biding his time. In 1630, he decided that the moment for intervention had arrived. Gustavus Adolphus at that point saved the Protestant cause in Germany and won notable victories, but he was killed in the great Battle of Lützen in 1632. Despite their king's death, the momentum of victory carried the Swedes on to further conquest under the guidance of Chancellor Oxenstierna, who acted for the young Queen Christina.

But they were weakened by heavy losses and by the defection of the elector of Saxony, who refused to cooperate any longer, though he continued to fight as an independent party.

Meanwhile, Wallenstein was leisurely refitting his army in Bohemia and refusing to take decisive action. Perhaps he was plotting treason. Ferdinand at any rate decided, now that the great Swedish peril was past, to rid himself of his dangerous general. In 1634, Wallenstein was assassinated by some of his own soldiers. In the same year the Swedes were defeated at Nördlingen by an imperial army. The tide was turning against them, and they soon lost a large part of their conquered territory. The emperor was quick to take advantage of this favorable turn to make peace with Saxony and the other German Protestant states, for both sides were tired of the war and the emperor's resources were nearly exhausted. According to the terms of the Peace of Prague (1635), all disputed ecclesiastical lands were to be restored to those who had held them in 1627. This amounted to a revocation of the Edict of Restitution. With the signing of the Peace of Prague, the religious phase of the war ended. The war itself might have ended too, had France been willing to permit it.

The religious significance of the war had always been a matter of secondary importance to Cardinal Richelieu, maker of French foreign policy. The cardinal's aims were clear and simple, however complex the methods he saw fit to use. Richelieu could never forget that France was surrounded by Hapsburg territory. To make his country secure and powerful, the Hapsburg states had to be reduced to impotence, and France had to win defensible frontiers on the Rhine and the Pyrenees. As long as other powers—German princes, Denmark, and Sweden—were wearing down the resistance of Spain and Austria, Richelieu was content to wait, offering no more than diplomatic and financial aid to the enemies of the Hapsburg dynasty. After the Peace of Prague, however, the war seemed about to end with the Hapsburg power still not completely crushed. The Swedes were not included in the treaty, but they could not continue fighting long alone. It was time for France to act.

With the intervention of France in 1635, the conflict took on Europe-wide dimensions. Before declaring war on Spain and Austria, Richelieu had formed an alliance with the Swedes, the Dutch (who were to attack the Spanish Netherlands), and Savoy (which was the gate to northern Italy). German princes were again involved in the war on both sides. The fighting seemed to drag on interminably, but at last, in 1648, peace terms were agreed upon. The stalemated Thirty Years' War ended with the Peace of Westphalia.

The Peace of Westphalia and the Peace of the Pyrenees

The Peace of Westphalia (1648) was the work of the first great European peace conference. It marks the end of the age of religious strife and the beginning of the new era of dynastic and national wars for economic or territorial aggrandizement. In its adjustment of territorial boundaries and its recognition of the sovereignty of states hitherto considered subject to the Holy Roman Empire, it laid the foundations for the early modern state system of Europe.

The victors in the long struggle demanded and received grants of territory as compensation for their efforts. France, the laborer come late to the vineyard, profited most, finally receiving title to the strategically important bishoprics of

Metz, Toul, and Verdun (effectively seized almost a century earlier), and the "sovereignty" of Alsace except for the free city of Strassburg. France thus made a notable advance toward the Rhine. Sweden obtained western Pomerania and some neighboring territory on the Baltic, as well as the bishopric of Bremen on the North Sea. Brandenburg, in return for the surrender of western Pomerania, received three secularized bishoprics and the succession to the archbishopric of Magdeburg and was confirmed in the possession of eastern Pomerania.

The treaty also recognized certain important changes in the political status of the powers involved. The Holy Roman Empire, though continuing to exist as a formal entity, was practically dissolved. Each prince in Germany was recognized as a sovereign power, free to make peace or war and to govern his own state independently. As a result, the authority of the imperial Hapsburgs was limited more than ever to their own hereditary lands, and their policy increasingly became strictly Austrian. France and Sweden acquired, in addition to lands in the Empire, the right to vote in the imperial Diet. The accomplished fact of the independence of the Netherlands and Switzerland was formally confirmed, and they entered the state system of Europe as free and independent powers.

The religious issues of the war, almost forgotten, were settled in the simplest way by recognizing the facts of the existing situation. Secularized Church

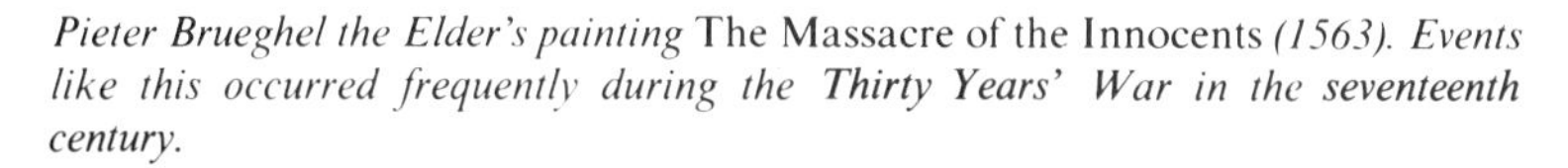

Pieter Brueghel the Elder's painting The Massacre of the Innocents *(1563). Events like this occurred frequently during the Thirty Years' War in the seventeenth century.*

lands were to remain in the possession of those holding them in 1624. The Calvinists were admitted to the privileges of the Religious Peace of Augsburg with the right, accorded to Lutheran and Catholic princes, to determine the religion of their states.

The most important results of the war for Germany were not of a kind that could be summarized in the terms of a peace treaty. For three decades the Four Horsemen of the Apocalypse had ridden throughout the rich land of Germany, leaving death, disease, and destruction behind them. Pitched battles were few and unimportant compared to the loss of life from famine, disease, and the brutality of marauding soldiers. The armies on both sides plundered, burned, tortured, raped and killed, without regard to the supposed friendship or enmity of the helpless people. Such statistics as can be procured reveal that the total population of Germany and Bohemia was reduced by about one-third. The relative loss of property may have been still greater. The German people long remembered the terrible devastations of this and later conflicts of the seventeenth century. One of the few happy results of the Thirty Years' War was a growing sense of religious tolerance, particularly among intellectuals. A new respect for the political and religious status quo animated most German princes and their counsellors long after 1648.

For Spain too the war was disastrous. The country had been drained of its vitality and was to suffer still more. Spain was not included in the Peace of Westphalia. Portugal had taken advantage of the war to assert its independence, and Spain had lost Roussillon in southern France to the French. Nevertheless, King Philip IV hoped to recoup some of his losses. France was loath to make peace until Spain was completely ruined. The war between them, therefore, continued.

At first it seemed certain that nothing could save Spain from crushing defeat and the loss of its most valued possessions. However, Spain was saved by the outbreak of the Fronde in France, a futile rebellion of the French nobles. When this revolt was over, France was too weak to carry on the war alone. In 1657, France made an incongruous alliance with the English Protestant dictator Cromwell and, thus reinforced, again had the advantage over its feeble enemy. In 1659, Philip IV had to accept a peace which was humiliating but not so bad as it might have been if France had been able to push home its first successes. The Peace of the Pyrenees ended the long struggle between the rival dynasties of France and Spain. It ended also the last vestige of Spain's claim to ascendancy in Europe, transferring that claim to France.

The Decline of Spain

The misguided policy of the government may be held responsible for many of the ills afflicting Spain. Trade was hampered by the debasement of the coinage and the enforcement of various monopolies. In 1609 His Most Catholic Majesty Philip III (1598-1621) had ordered the Moriscos (descendants of Christianized Moors) expelled from the country, a measure which strengthened the religious solidarity of the realm but deprived many trades and handicrafts of skilled workmen. By the reign of Charles II (1665-1700), all manufacture save that of a few necessities had come to an end. Beggars multiplied and privation increased, until many, even among Spain's half-million nobles, were reduced to a degree of poverty all the more pitiable because their pride forbade them to confess it.

Charles II, called Charles the Sufferer because of his numerous physical and mental ailments—the heritage of Hapsburg inbreeding—was the tragic symbol of a monarchy and a nation which appeared to have reached the nadir of exhaustion. Charles' sad life was a long death-watch. He was so feeble that an heir was out of the question. Charles was impotent and a royal marriage would have been doubly unpleasant for the bride, since the king's doctors refused to let Charles bathe for fear of exacerbating his many illnesses. Rapacious neighbors waited impatiently for Charles' death as a signal to partition imperial Spain and confiscate its possessions, while within the kingdom misery increased, trade and population continued to decline, and the credit of the state foundered in a sea of bankruptcy.

The decline in agriculture was no less serious. Too much property was owned by absentee landlords whose agents neglected it. Large areas that might have been rendered productive were used as pasture for sheep-raising, an occupation which attracted the indolent and by promising easy profits discouraged the industry, thrift, and foresight required for successful farming. The agricultural districts were gradually deserted and the fields abandoned. The population of Spain declined steadily throughout the seventeenth century, for the overseas colonies lured the most venturesome spirits in each generation, while the ten thousand convents and monasteries withdrew the most devout from the pursuit of power and worldly gain.

The Spaniards clung tenaciously to their peculiar customs and revealed slight susceptibility to foreign influences. Little affected by the new humanism of the Renaissance, and still less by the Protestant Reformation, they had a distinctive culture which in the sixteenth and early seventeenth centuries was imitated by other nations because of Spain's commanding position as a colonial and military power. This golden age of Spanish civilization was the prelude to a swift decline. Art degenerated, literature grew pompous and empty, the universities became strongholds of medieval theology, and the Spanish Inquisition discouraged free speculation and scientific inquiry. "*Novedad, no verdad,*" Spaniards said, summarizing in this play on words their conviction that "what is new is untrue." They had another saying too, "*Mudar costumbre a par de muerte*"—"To change a custom is as bad as death."

The System of Centralized Territorial States

The treaties of Westphalia and the Pyrenees restored peace to most of Europe. But in the north war clouds still hung over the Baltic, where Frederick William of Brandenburg was exploiting the old enmity between Sweden and Poland with the aim of securing a free title to East Prussia. Even the warlike Baltic powers, however, were weary of war, and in 1660 the intervention of England, the Netherlands, and other great states was sufficient to bring the northern struggle to an end. Brandenburg, Sweden, and Poland signed the Treaty of Oliva, recognizing Frederick William's free sovereignty in East Prussia, and all Europe was at peace for the first time in more than a generation.

A new Europe was thus hammered out upon the anvil of war. A map of Europe in 1660 is remarkably modern in appearance. All the wars and revolutions from that year to this have changed the boundaries of the states surprisingly little. By 1660 most of western and central Europe was divided into territorial areas which correspond to the European states of today. No such centralized territorial states existed in the Roman Empire or during the Middle Ages. They emerged slowly as the Middle Ages waned and just as slowly organized themselves. Not until the seventeenth century did the concept of Christendom as a united whole yield definitely to that of a state system composed of autonomous, self-governing territorial units, and for this reason modern history is often said to begin in the seventeenth century.

To the political philosopher Thomas Hobbes (1588–1679), the sovereign state appeared so portentous a social organism that he called it a Leviathan, a "mortall God." In his opinion subjects submitted to the authority of the state because they realized that such despotism was their only sure protection against anarchy and that in a condition of anarchy life would be "solitary, poore, nasty,

EUROPE IN 1660

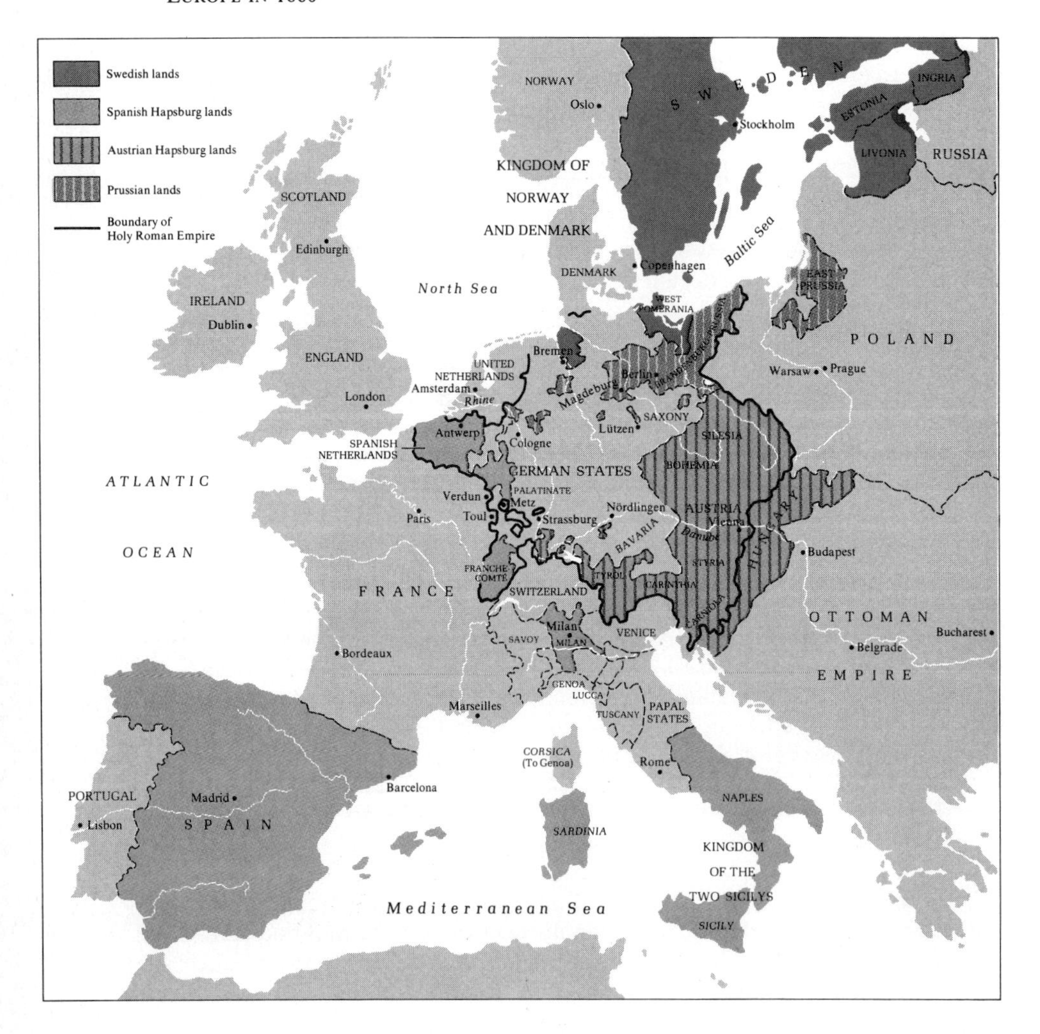

brutish and short." Like most of his contemporaries Hobbes considered monarchy the best form of government, and held that the sovereign expressed in his august person the concentrated will, authority, and majesty of the state.

In 1660 monarchy was the most widely accepted form of government throughout Europe. It was not always absolute: the English, for example, imposed limits on the power of their kings. Nor was it always hereditary: the kings of Poland, like the emperors of the Holy Roman Empire, were elected. Switzerland, the United Netherlands, and some of the Italian states were republics. Despite these exceptions, however, monarchy seemed the normal and logical form of government to most Europeans in the later seventeenth century.

The danger that as the states developed the wars between them would grow more frequent and more destructive alarmed far-seeing statesmen and philosophers even before 1660. The Duke of Sully, able minister of Henry IV of France, formulated in his master's name a "grand design" for uniting all the European states in a permanent alliance. Most statesmen, however, ignored such dreams. The result was the formation of alliances for purposes of offense and defense, a process which often went forward until the states of Europe were aligned in two hostile groups. If the groups were evenly balanced, the outcome of a war between them was difficult to predict, a circumstance which the diplomats extolled as the best possible guarantee of peace.

Suggestions for Further Reading

J. H. Elliott, *Imperial Spain, 1469-1716* (1964). A recent and highly regarded narrative.

C. J. Friedrich, *The Age of the Baroque, 1610-1660** (1952). A scholarly survey with excellent bibliographies. Part of the Rise of Modern Europe series edited by William L. Langer.

J. H. Parry, *The Spanish Seaborne Empire* (1966). Readable account by an outstanding scholar.

M. Roberts, *Gustavus Adolphus* (1953).

S. H. Steinberg, *The Thirty Years' War and the Conflict for European Hegemony** (1966). A useful introductory account.

R. H. Tawney, *Religion and the Rise of Capitalism** (1926). A controversial book following the main premises of Max Weber's study.

C. V. Wedgwood, *The Thirty Years' War** (1939). An excellent, detailed account of the war and its diplomacy.

*Available in a paperback edition.

Art Credits

Maps drawn by Dick Sanderson

3 Palette of King Narmer, Metropolitan Museum of Art, Dodge Fund
8 Trustees of the British Museum
9 Ewing Galloway
10 Art Reference Bureau
21 Marburg/Art Reference Bureau
23 Rapho Guillumette
29 *Top*: Alinari/Art Reference Bureau *Bottom*: Vatican
41 Louvre, Paris
43 Marburg/Art Reference Bureau
57 Landesmuseum für Vorgeschichte, Halle
60 University of Uppsala, Sweden
67 Statue of Charlemagne, Caisse Nationale des Monuments Historiques
69 Stadtisches Museum, Weisbaden
76 Anderson/Art Reference Bureau
85 Alinari/Art Reference Bureau
87 Fototeca Unione, Rome/Art Reference Bureau
89 *Top*: H. H. Kreider, Black Star *Bottom*: Erich Lessing, Magnum
91 Bibliothèque Nationale, Paris
104 Stadtbibliothek Trier/Art Reference Bureau
110 Bibliothèque Nationale, Paris
111 Bibliothèque Nationale, Paris
119 Trustees of the British Museum
120 Bodleian Library, Oxford
131 Bibliothèque Nationale, Paris
133 The Bettmann Archive
146 Alinari/Art Reference Bureau
151 Trustees of the British Museum
161 Polde Limburg, *Month of February,* Giraudon
163 Ewing Galloway
164 Bernard Silberstein, Rapho Guillumette
166 Bibliothèque Royale de Belgique, Brussels
167 Bibliothèque Nationale, Paris
178 Universitätsbibliothek, Heidelberg
181 Staatliche Museen, Berlin
185 Marburg/Art Reference Bureau
186 Marburg/Art Reference Bureau
187 Singer Features
199 Trustees of the British Museum
206 Giraudon
207 Giraudon
211 Trustees of the British Museum
227 Österreichisches Staatsarchiv
236 The Metropolitan Museum of Art, The Cloisters Collection
238 Alinari/Art Reference Bureau
242 Herzog Anton Ulrich-Museum, Braunschweig
247 Verrochio, *Lorenzo de Medici,* National Gallery of Art, Washington, D.C.
252 Scala
262 Alinari/Art Reference Bureau
264 Alinari/Art Reference Bureau
265 Biblioteca Ambrosiana, Milan
271 Rosgartenmuseums, Konstanz
273 Trustees of the British Museum
274 Courtesy of Museum of Fine Arts, Boston, Gift of Miss Ellen Bullard
282 The Toledo Museum of Art
285 Bibliothèque Publique et Universitaire, Geneva
290 Anderson/Art Reference Bureau
302 Alte Pinakothek, Munich
306 Museo del Prado, Madrid
313 Alinari/Art Reference Bureau
314 Museo del Prado, Madrid
315 National Portrait Gallery, London
319 From *Leviathan* by Thomas Hobbes, 1651
336 Alte Pinakothek, Munich
341 Rijksmuseum, Amsterdam
344 Trustees of the British Museum
348 From Wallhausen's *Krychs-Konst te voet,* 1617
351 Kunsthistorisches Museum, Vienna

Index

BCDEFGHIJ–M–798765